CHRISTIANITY IN CULTURE

CHARLES H. KRAFT is Professor of Anthropology and African Studies, School of World Mission, Fuller Theological Seminary. He received his B.D. from Ashland Theological Seminary and his Ph.D in Anthropological Linguistics from the Hartford Seminary Foundation. He has served as a missionary in Northern Nigeria and done field linguistic and ethnological research on Chadic languages, with a focus on Hausa. His publications include *A Study of Hausa Syntax, Teach Yourself Hausa*, and dozens of periodical articles. Chuck Kraft and his wife, Marguerite, have four children and make their home in South Pasadena, Calif.

CHRISTIANITY IN CULTURE

*A Study in Dynamic Biblical Theologizing
in Cross-Cultural Perspective*

Charles H. Kraft

ORBIS BOOKS
Maryknoll, New York 10545

Acknowledgment is gratefully extended to E. J. Brill, Leiden, for permission to reproduce the lists in Figures 13.1, 13.2, and 13.3, which originally appeared in *The Theory and Practice of Translation*, by E. A. Nida and C. R. Taber.

The Catholic Foreign Mission Society of America (Maryknoll) recruits and trains people for overseas missionary service. Through Orbis Books Maryknoll aims to foster the international dialogue essential to mission. The books published, however, reflect the opinions of their authors and are not meant to represent the official position of the Society.

Library of Congress Cataloging in Publication Data

Kraft, Charles H.
  Christianity in culture.

  Bibliography: p.
  1. Christianity and culture. I. Title.
BR115.C8K64   261   78-13736
ISBN 0-88344-075-X pbk.

Orbis Books, Maryknoll, NY 10545

To Meg

Contents

Foreword

I write this foreword from the perspective of one who, though a theologian, pioneered perhaps the first course in an evangelical Protestant school to teach anthropological science to missionary candidates. I join the author in believing that one of the most significant contemporary issues that Christians have to deal with is the concept of culture as it is understood by people in the behavioral sciences. Anthropologists and other behavioral scientists tell us that to be human is to be immersed in some specific culture. All human beings "live and move and have their being" within a culture. Culture touches all people at every point. It is both internal to us and the immediate environment in which we live.

If the behavioral scientists are right about the nature and extent of the impact of culture on people, Christians must face the problem squarely. To begin with, there are a number of cultures reflected in the biblical writings. Furthermore, as the early church spread out from Palestine into the Roman world it encountered other cultures. As the missionary program advanced through the centuries the same process of church and culture confrontation continued. The problems raised by the encounter between Christianity and culture are especially acute today where missionaries and mission societies labor. In the light of our modern knowledge of culture, how does the Christian church realistically come to terms with unfamiliar cultures in its evangelistic and missionary work? And once a church is established in a new culture how does such a church interpret the Christian message in the language and concepts of that culture?

In this volume, Charles H. Kraft of the School of World Mission, Fuller Theological Seminary, addresses himself to these questions from the point of view of an evangelical Protestant committed to biblically defined Christianity. For this task he brings the right qualifications. He is a linguist, an anthropologist, a missionary, and now a professor. In guiding those for whom the problems of culture—both biblical and contemporary—are a pressing concern, he lives with such problems at both academic and practical levels. He hereby presents to the rest of us the theory and practice that has emerged from his formal education in anthropology and linguistics, his missionary work in Nigeria, and his years of teaching missionaries and guiding their research into these problems. He has concerned himself particularly with the application to biblical interpretation of insights afforded us by recent breakthroughs in the areas of Bible translation and communication theory.

One of the very pressing problems for "biblical Christians" today is the manner in which they must answer the question: "If the writers of Holy Scripture were conditioned by their cultures, how can their message be the Word of God for us today?" The same question can be asked another way: "Knowing that language and culture are intimately intertwined, how can we effectively translate the Scriptures and communicate the message embedded in the cultures and languages of the distant biblical past into the language and concepts of contemporary cultures?"

Such questions raise the issue of the transcultural in Scripture. Many feel that any admission of cultural conditioning within God's Word totally relativizes Scripture and negates its applicability today. And yet serious biblical scholarship finds it impossible to ignore the pervasive influence of the cultures of the authors and receptors of Scripture on the presentation of their messages. In what sense, then, is the Word of God transcultural and in what sense cultural? One of the remarkable things that Dr. Kraft has done in this book is to show how we can come to meaningful terms with the cultural yet transcultural character of Holy Scripture. No easy task but well done.

Furthermore, the church is confronted with the same problem when it comes to theology. Theologians in Europe and America are in the main highway of what has been dubbed "western culture." Our theology has been written in this context and from this cultural perspective. If Christians come out of an African or Asian or Latin American Indian culture, we presume too much (according to Christian anthropologists) if we think they can meaningfully express their Christian theology by simply translating our theological terms and concepts from our language into theirs. For Christian theology to be meaningful to these peoples it must be developed and expressed within their language and cultural context, just as for us it has been meaningfully expressed within our language and cultural context. Dr. Kraft also addresses himself helpfully to this issue, frequently referred to as "the contextualization of theology."

I would like to suggest caution at two points. I agree with the growing community of Christian anthropologists and linguists that this sort of task must be done. Unfortunately, not very many conservative Christians really know the issues here. They could, therefore, jump to wrong conclusions. Dr. Kraft is to be commended for taking on a subject with such high potential risk of misunderstanding. This is a pioneering effort to synthesize anthropological understanding with theological convictions that are true to the Bible. We have waited too long for such a work.

Secondly, the book will pose difficulties for Christians who have no understanding or contemporary knowledge of anthropology, culture, and linguistics. It will be a problem to them to grasp Kraft's unique effort to develop a perspective on Christian theology within the context of our modern anthropological and linguistic knowledge. To such readers I appeal for their patience and that they make the effort to learn something of anthropology and linguistics before they judge the book adversely.

Bernard Ramm

Modesto, California
October 1978

Preface

In 1971 I introduced a course entitled "Christianity and Culture" into the curriculum of the School of World Mission, Fuller Seminary. This was to be an advanced course, presupposing at least an elementary exposure to both theology and anthropology. The intent was to lead our career missionaries into a solid grappling with the multiplicity of cultural and theological problems that become burning issues for those who seek to communicate Christianity to the members of another culture. The first two times we offered the course we made do with a hodgepodge of readings, including Niebuhr's *Christ and Culture* (1951), Taylor's *The Primal Vision* (1963), Mbiti's *New Testament Eschatology in an African Background* (1971), and various articles from *Practical Anthropology*, *International Review of Mission*, and similar sources. Our students had already been through such available sources as Nida, *Customs and Cultures* (1954) and *Message and Mission* (1960); Smalley (ed.), *Readings in Missionary Anthropology* (1963); and Luzbetak, *The Church and Cultures* (1963). Feeling the need for a textbook specifically designed to serve as the basis for that class, I chose to devote a one-term sabbatical (Fall 1973) to developing one. A first draft was produced at that time and a collection of reactions to it begun. The present book has benefited from use in eleven offerings of that course issuing in three major revisions of the original manuscript.

The effort has been an exicting learning experience for all of us. I have been heartened by the fact that the response of even the most conservative of our missionary students has been largely positive. In the classroom setting, we seem to have been able to establish the absolutely crucial trust and mutual respect that Mayers, in *Christianity Confronts Culture* (1974:32–33), points to as foundational to all cross-cultural communication. The issues we deal with and the way we attempt to deal with them are such that the bond of trust between us as sincere Christians committed to practicing and communicating biblical Christianity could easily be broken. But this has seldom happened in the classroom, the only occasions being with those who have had no cross-cultural experience and for whom, therefore, the classes were purely academic exercises. In the classroom, though, the professor can monitor what is happening to the students' trust and inject trust-building statements to reassure those who find their trust being undermined.

Such "mid-course corrections" cannot be made in a book, however. Printed media are "one-way conversations" that don't allow for feedback and consequent adjustment of the communication. So I cannot predict whether or not you, the reader, will grant me the trust that will enable you to get from this book what most of my students have received from the classes in which it has been used. Toward this end, however, I have attempted to include quite a bit of my own personal experience and a number of statements that will, I hope, reassure you, if at times you should doubt my commitment to biblical Christianity (interpreted, in my case, from the point of view of evangelical Protestantism).

Two other areas that might militate against your trusting me and/or your feeling the relevance of this presentation are (1) a lack of cross-cultural experience and (2) a lack of background in both theology and anthropology. I am powerless to do much about either except to recommend that you read books such as those cited above. You will find those by Nida, Mayers, Luzbetak, and Smalley especially helpful.

A suggestion concerning how to read this book: it has been found better to assign students first to skim the whole book rapidly from start to finish before beginning to read it carefully. Each part of the book depends rather heavily on every other part. The necessity to write in a linear or sequential fashion demands, however, that certain things be presented before other things. This causes problems. Let me recommend, therefore, that you first skim through the whole book, then read the overview of the models presented in the appendix before settling down to study the detailed presentation.

This book is part of a process that is not complete even though the book is published. As part of a process, even a search, it is printed with the realization that it is very imperfect and will, one hopes, soon be superseded by something better. I, too, am in process but, unlike a printed book, I can learn and grow. I invite your contributions to that learning and growing. I also ask what some of our young people used to ask via lapel buttons: PBPGINFWMY (Please be patient, God is not finished with me yet).

I owe much to many for their assistance in getting this book (and me) to the present point. I am particularly grateful to Drs. Jack Rogers, Donald Larson, Eugene Nida, Charles Taber, David Hubbard, Chalmer Faw, and Pat Townsend for going carefully through previous versions of the manuscript and making detailed comments at many points. The students who have done likewise are too numerous to mention but among them I owe most to Darrell Whiteman, Ken Ross, Phil Elkins, Wayne Dye, and Bob Gordon. A series of secretaries have over the years expended on the successive stages of the manuscript energy and concern worth much more than I was able to pay them. I am, therefore, greatly indebted to Kristen Burckhart, Carol Heise, Joyce Showalter, Ruth Whitt, Linda Ferguson, Laurie Whiteman, and Carolyn Alexander. Additional thanks go to Carol and Kristen for preparing the index. The greatest debt of all, however, is the one I owe my wife, Marguerite (Meg), my sons Chuck and Rick, and my daughters Cheryl and Karen. Thanks so much to you all.

List of Figures

Outline of the Models and Their Components

Bible Versions

ASV   The American Standard Version. New York: Thomas Nelson and Sons, 1901.

KJV   The King James Version, 1611.

LB   The Living Bible. Wheaton, Ill.: Tyndale House, 1971.

NASV   The New American Standard Version. La Habra, Calif.: The Lockman Foundation, 1973.

NEB   The New English Bible. London: Oxford and Cambridge, 1961.

NIV   The New International Version. Grand Rapids: Zondervan, 1978.

JBP   The New Testament in Modern English. London: Geoffrey Bles, 1958. (J. B. Phillips, translator)

TEV   Good News Bible: The Bible in Today's English Version. New York: American Bible Society, 1976.

PART I
THE PERSPECTIVE

1. Cases of Need

Who needs this approach? With the following two case studies I attempt to establish the need of missionaries for a broader approach, such as this, to doing Christian theology. The scriptural data that we seek to understand may be likened to a great mountain filled with gold ore. To mine that ore a number of mine shafts need to be drilled into the mountain. To date, the theological mineshafts into the mountain of revealed truth have nearly all been drilled in a strictly limited area. This area is defined by western culture. There are several shafts, representing several varieties of western cultural perspectives. But most of those shafts have either combined with one another to make a single large tunnel of western Christian theologizing or they have been abandoned with a HERESY sign posted over the entrances to them. Meanwhile, throughout the world, the members of the other six thousand or more cultures have largely been given the impression that mining in God's mountain can be done only by entering where western theologians have drilled, as long as there is no HERESY sign over the entrance. The rest of the mountain remains largely untouched.

Career missionaries have been most responsible for communicating this approach to biblical mining to the rest of the world. Missionary training has been such as to make it very difficult for them/us to do anything else. But the Christians of the other six thousand cultural worlds are getting less and less patient with such an approach in the name of a movement that claims to have cross-cultural validity. There is, however, a broader perspective available to us.

CASE ONE: THE CAREER MISSIONARY

"If I had only understood things this way my whole ministry would have been greatly different and considerably more effective." The speaker was a career missionary with fifteen years of experience as a professional communicator of the Gospel in another language and culture. He had been brought up in the United States and, in order to meet the requirements of the missionary sending organization under which he served, had studied three years in one of America's better theological seminaries before he went to the field.

The things that he learned in college and seminary seemed to make sense to him while he was learning them. Most of the questions and concerns of his instructors and textbooks he either already shared or easily learned to share.

And most of what he did not come to share immediately he was willing to accept as valid on the basis of his faith that his teachers, having had so much more experience than he, knew better than he what he needed to learn. Since he was headed for cross-cultural missionary work he took the elective offered by his seminary entitled "The History of Missions." This was taught by the church history professor, who had once been a missionary and taught in a seminary overseas.

The professor criticized the long dominance of missionary organizations over the churches they have founded. He also criticized the strong tendency of the national leaders of those churches to perpetuate the same policies once they gain control, but not to be very efficient about the way they carry them out. The church leadership, he maintained, also showed tendencies toward a lack of proper concern for maintaining strict doctrinal orthodoxy. The perpetuation of a high concern for denominational distinctives and their historical rootings, for example, has suffered noticeably wherever nationals have replaced missionaries. Nor do the nationals seem to be properly concerned with evangelism. The majority of the seminary graduates either take administrative positions within the church organization or are wooed away by some other organization. Comparatively few become pastors and none become evangelists or missionaries.

The professor treated the whole subject academically. He was willing to discuss the issues and face the problems at an academic level, but it was clear that his real interests lay elsewhere. The professor in his teaching sometimes used illustrations from the language and thought patterns of the people in the area in which he had served. But he never gave any indication that he had learned their language well or that he regarded their ways of thinking with anything more than idle curiosity.

During the next fifteen years this missionary did a number of things in the field. He spent his first term teaching (in English) at a seminary. When, due to indigenization, that job was filled by a national, he was asked to go to another part of the country to work with national pastors. There he had to face a whole new set of problems, including those raised by being forced to learn a new language and culture. He eventually became reasonably proficient in the language but could never quite conquer the frustration he felt every time discussion of an important issue would degenerate into what seemed to be some irreconcilable difference in thought patterns between missionaries and nationals.

When the missionary went to the field and during most of his time there he did not realize that there might be deficiencies in the way he understood the events in which he participated. He noticed, of course, that there were many problems for which he had no answers. But he assumed that no one had answers to those problems. He also recognized a rather high degree of ineffectiveness in many of the operations of the mission in which he served.

Like his missions professor and most of his colleagues, however, he felt that the reasons for that ineffectiveness lay in the fact that the nationals hadn't learned to do things properly. Perhaps one reason for this was that he and the other missionaries were not getting their points across as well as they might. So he had plodded on doggedly, more or less convinced that the answer to each dilemma lay basically in doing essentially the same things that they were already doing, but doing them better. Undoubtedly there were deficiencies in the approach of the mission. Undoubtedly they had made and continued to make mistakes. But surely God would overrule in all such cases. And surely, sooner or later, God would bring about a breakthrough in the understanding of the people as well—leading them to turn away from their pre-Christian ways to Christian ways.

As the missionary's language ability grew and he became more and more closely involved with the local-level communication of the Gospel, however, certain nagging doubts that he harbored concerning the rightness of the way the work of Christ was being conducted grew very large. He often felt guilty about his doubts. But he also felt guilty about what he was now coming to see as the extreme limitedness of his ability to help these people. Perhaps supporting him to do the job he had been assigned to do at no better level than he was able to do it was in reality but a waste of the Lord's money. Was anything in his ministry going right? Could anything go right? Was the problem a lack of knowledge? A lack of training? A lack of dedication? He began to realize that he could neither answer these questions nor imagine where to begin to seek answers to them.

These frustrations led the missionary to spend his next furlough in a study program that taught him to look in a different way at all in which he was involved. He was exposed to what often amounted to a radically different perspective on the problems that he had been facing (often unsuccessfully) day in and day out for the past fifteen years. And now, fifteen years later, the missionary could look back with new eyes on both the training he had received and the experience in cross-cultural ministry in which he had participated. What made the difference? And why did he feel that his ministry would have been greatly changed for the better if he had been exposed to this approach to Christianity earlier in his experience?

The answer lies in the fact that he had come to look at all of those events with a new perspective. He had experienced what philosophers of science call a "paradigm shift" (Kuhn 1970), or a change of worldview. Conversion to Christ is one such paradigm shift, involving as it does a radically new way of interpreting and responding to reality. In the missionary's case, however, this shift of perspective was not conversion to Christ (that shift had long ago taken place) but conversion to a new perception of the nature of the work of Christ to which he was already committed. It is a major aim of this book to meet the need of such a missionary by leading him into just such a shift of perspective.

The foregoing is not an imaginary story. It is, rather, a "typicalized" version of the kind of story I have heard over and over again from career missionaries studying at the School of World Mission, Fuller Seminary. It is a story that I can identify with from my own experience as a missionary.

CASE TWO: THE AUTHOR'S

My experience as a field missionary has been in northern Nigeria. Much of what follows is so strongly influenced by and draws so greatly from that experience that it will be helpful for the reader to become aware of at least certain aspects of my "pilgrimage." For among the most important of the needs that this volume seeks to meet are my own.

One day, soon after I began to understand the language of the people with whom I was working, I was faced with a question that my training had not equipped me to answer. The question was, Do you believe in evil spirits? I was supposed to be the expert on theological matters but there was nothing in my college or seminary training that equipped me to answer that question except perhaps at a highly theoretical level. At the gut level, I frankly didn't know whether I believed in evil spirits or not, for my culture denies the reality of evil spirits. What does one do when he feels he has been well trained for his task and suddenly realizes that those to whom he goes are asking quite different questions from the ones he has been trained to answer?

On another occasion I was presenting the Gospel message in the best way I knew how and came to the point where I asserted that the supreme proof that the message of God is true rests in the fact that God raised Jesus Christ from the dead. "Very interesting," one of my hearers replied. "My son rose from the dead just last week, and my uncle last month. My uncle was climbing a tree and he fell out of the tree, died, and, after half an hour, rose from the dead." What does one say to people for whom death and unconsciousness are in the same category?

A third major problem area for me was the question, Will God accept believing polygamists? The answer of my missionary colleagues revolved around the American assumption that having sexual relations with someone other than one's first wife falls into the category of adultery. Obviously, these people did not believe that having a second wife was adulterous. They, like every other culture in the world, had a law against committing adultery. But to them a plurality of wives comes under the "marriage" category, not under the "adultery" category. What was I to do, especially since they could read the Old Testament and discover that among the Hebrews God accepted polygamists?

As we studied the Bible together, then, I frequently was jolted by the perspectives of my Nigerian brethren. On one occasion we were studying the book of Romans. We had previously studied a Gospel and the book of Acts and now in sequence proceeded to Romans. After a few sessions one of the Nigerian church leaders said to me something like, "What's all this stuff anyway? Can't we study something interesting? Can't we go back to the Gospels or, better yet, back to the Old Testament?" I was shocked. For my theological training had taught me that the book of Romans is probably the most important book in the Bible.

My theological training had not equipped me to handle problems such as these. But I had another kind of training in my background—anthropological and linguistic training. My temptation, however, was to separate these kinds of training from my theological-biblical training and to rank-order the two perspectives in such a way that I looked for answers to theological problems from my theological training and to what I considered purely cultural problems from my anthropological training. The possibility of combining anthropological perspectives with theological perspectives was not always in the forefront of my mind. Yet my anthropological training told me that I must take my hearers seriously if I ever expected to be taken seriously by them.

I observed in one of my colleagues a disturbing type of behavior that I wanted at all costs to avoid. He took a great interest in the culture of the people he worked among but, when he discovered their secrets, he consistently used this information against them. His attempts to communicate the Gospel constantly compared their customs with what he called "the Christian custom." When he described "the Christian custom," however, it always bore a striking resemblance to an idealized version of an American custom. My anthropological training had led me to be suspicious of such ethnocentrism; my theological training made me feel that theological answers were sacred and were simply to be delivered to my hearers as God's truth.

And yet, as my experience with these Nigerians increased and I was able to enter more fully into their understandings of life, I came to realize more and more how limited and narrow my preparation had been for service in this Nigerian culture. At times I was tempted to turn my back on the theological training that I had received. I began to feel that I had been betrayed by being required to spend so much time learning answers to questions that nobody in this Nigerian context was asking. But if I abandoned my theological undergirding, to what would I turn? To relativistic anthropology? Surely that was a worse option, for anthropology made no claim to deal with ultimate truth.

Somewhere in my pilgrimage it began to dawn on me that continuing to compartmentalize the theological side of my thinking from the anthropological side was a source of great frustration to me. I found myself constantly having to decide which compartment any given question should be assigned to. Then, too frequently I would come up with two different answers to the same question—one answer on the basis of anthropological principles and the other on the basis of what I had learned to call theological principles. And not infrequently the answers that I arrived at on the basis of theological principles seemed to approximate more the answers that the Pharisees gave to the questions of their day than those that Jesus gave his inquirers. I began to wonder if there were not some tools in my anthropological toolbox that would help me to be more theologically correct, as well as more relevant, in my approach to the problems I was facing. This started me toward the attempt to integrate anthropological with theological insight. I decided that, since theological thinking is always done by applying the perspectives (or biases) of the theologian to scriptural data, I might attempt to do theology from a cross-cultural, anthropological perspective.

I began to realize that, if I were to face the problems of the Nigerian situation squarely, I would have to become more *open* than I had been. I, like the majority of my generation of evangelical Protestants, had been taught to fear heresy above almost anything else in the world. I had been taught to respect the nearly two thousand years of western theological study and to assume that such dedicated theologians had answered just about every problem worth answering. I had also got the impression that we in the West, in view of our extensive experience with Christianity, need not take very seriously insights into Christianity attained by recently Christianized peoples in the rest of the world. How could they know anywhere near what our students of Scripture had come to understand and had passed on to us? But I began to see the need to be more open than these attitudes allowed me to be.

Only much later did I understand what I was going through at that period in my life. I had been taught to preserve my orthodoxy by closing my mind to other options. Other options were ordinarily labeled "liberal theology." As best I could tell, however, I was not becoming liberal in my theology. I was merely modifying my methodology to some extent by opening myself to ways of doing things that nobody in my home churches or seminary, due to the limitations of their experience, had even imagined. I was becoming an "open" conservative (see model 2c, chapter 2)—open to learning things from people of a different culture concerning what biblical Christianity should look like in their culture. I had learned only what it could look like in a part of my culture. There was nothing in my church background or theological training that would enable me even to counsel those who were interacting with God in terms of a different culture. Fortunately, at this time in my life I was able to avail myself of the stimulus and insights of such perceptive anthropologically oriented Christians as E. A. Nida, W. A. Smalley, and W. D. Reyburn, largely through their writings in the journal *Practical Anthropology*. With their stimulus and input, plus a series of encouraging demonstrations of the value of such a perspective, I began to chart a new course.

This attempt to integrate my anthropological understandings with my theological understandings was opening my mind to the probability that God wanted to lead the Nigerians in their attempts to be faithful to Christ in a way different from the way he wanted to lead me and my people. So I began to *suggest* rather than to dictate. I began to ask questions concerning their problems rather than simply to state solutions to them. I began to recognize that I did not know all that I thought I knew. I began to respect and encourage their attempts to define problems, to search the Scriptures for answers that would be satisfying to them, and to claim the leading of the Holy Spirit in seeking satisfying answers to those problems.

This new approach came as a surprise to these Nigerian leaders. They had been used to more authoritarian missionaries. One day in a Bible study class, when we had finished reading the passage, they looked at me and asked: "What does this mean?" I replied, "I don't know." Their amazed reaction was to wonder if I had never studied the passage in seminary. I assured them that I had indeed studied this passage many times. They suggested that it was the missionary's job to tell them what each passage meant, for this is the way they had been taught to relate to the missionary. Finally, after I felt they had got enough out of that particular line of reasoning, I said to them, "I know what the passage means *to me* and to people in my culture. I just don't know what the Spirit of God wants to teach *you* from it." They wondered what that had to do with it and tried again to get me to interpret the passage for them.

At that point I suggested that we make a deal. I promised that if they would tell me what it meant to them, I would then share with them what the passage meant to me. This they reluctantly agreed to, even though they were quite sure that none of their opinions would amount to anything. After listening to them share their impressions for awhile, I expressed to them my amazement that anyone could possibly get from the passage what they were getting from it. And yet, I pointed out to them how thrilling it was to me to see how the Spirit was working with them to make the passage meaningful to them in terms of their own particular problems. Then I shared with them what the passage meant to me. It was their turn to be amazed. For they had difficulty seeing how anyone in his right mind could interpret the passage the way I had!

To illustrate one such difference in perception, Dr. Jacob Loewen (unpublished lecture) once asked a group made up of Africans and missionaries to tell him the main point of the story of Joseph in the Old Testament. The European missionaries all pointed to Joseph as a man who *remained faithful to God* no matter what happened to him. The Africans, on the other hand, pointed to Joseph as a man who, no matter how far he traveled, *never forgot his family*. Both of these meanings are legitimate understandings of the passage. But differing cultural backgrounds led one group to one interpretation and the other group to the other interpretation. Evidently, God speaks to the different groups through that same passage in ways that are appropriate to the different focuses of their cultures.

As my eyes opened to this perspective on understanding the Scriptures, I began to develop some insight into the problems that I have raised above. The Bible is a multicultural book, much of it directed to Hebrew audiences, while some of the latter portions were directed to audiences whose primary language was Greek. Since European culture has been greatly influenced by Greek-type thinking, we Euro-Americans are naturally attracted to those portions of the Scriptures that are directed to Greek-speaking peoples. Thus the book of Romans, which presents the Gospel in a cultural style that we warm up to, is very important to us. We westerners see God most clearly when he is presented in this way. But we tend to ignore or even, like Martin Luther, to disdain those portions of Scripture that are presented in more typically Hebrew ways (Reuss 1891:322). Well and good for Europeans, but what if one's cultural perspective is more like that of the Hebrews than that of the Greeks? This, in fact, is the case in Nigeria.

It is, then, for *cultural* (not theological) reasons that Nigerians prefer those parts of the Bible directed to Hebrew audiences. When I came to realize the significance of this cultural dimension, the preference of these Nigerians was no longer surprising to me. It took me longer to overcome my surprise at how clearly they were able to see God and the Gospel message through the Old Testament. This recognition has led me to a much greater appreciation of the Old Testament and a deeper conviction of its inspiration than I had learned in all my previous church and seminary experience. I also learned a new approach to dealing with problems such as those cited above.

With respect to the problem of the lessened impact of the resurrection of Christ, I began to ask myself if there was anything in the Scriptures that would in their Nigerian context convey the same kind of impact that the resurrection accounts convey in my culture. So I asked some Nigerian church leaders what they felt to be their biggest problem. They pointed to the constant difficulties that they have with evil spirits. At that point I began to look at the Scriptures for answers to a set of problems that I had not really taken seriously before. The New Testament has much to say about evil spirits (e.g., Rom. 8:38; Eph. 1:21, 6:12; Col. 2:10). From my cultural perspective I had virtually ignored these passages, since they scratched me where I didn't itch. My Nigerian friends, however, felt their greatest need to be spoken to by these very passages that I had ignored. The truth that Jesus could conquer the evil spirits carried in their experience an impact that I judged to be even greater than the impact of the resurrection in my experience.

As for polygamy, my background had led me to feel that, though God once allowed customs such as this, he no longer allows them. This impression was, of course, conveyed to me by people who never really had to face this issue. Suddenly, though, I was being faced daily by people who were apparently sincere in their faith in Christ but who would not be allowed to join the church because they had, in keeping with the ideals of their culture, committed themselves in marriage to more than one wife. I began to wonder if perhaps the God who was patient with Abraham and David would not be patient today with Nigerians who, though chronologically A.D., were B.C. in their understandings of God and his works. Perhaps the guidelines concerning what God seeks to do today should come from those parts of the Scriptures that record what he did in similar cultures in times past, rather than from those portions of the Scriptures that we believe show his ideals. Perhaps there is a range of behavior within which God is willing to work, even though it is less than ideal. Perhaps God wants us to seek to *understand* and, in love, to accept people *within* their cultural context rather than simply to *impose upon them* what we have come to understand from within our cultural context to be the proper rules.

These kinds of experiences plus many others have led me to devote myself to trying to understand God's truth from a cross-cultural perspective. In training cross-cultural witnesses we in the School of World Mission deal daily with problems that western theological perspectives have never had to deal with. Those whose experience has not taken them beyond the western cultural matrix (and this includes most traditional theologians) have usually not even considered a multitude of problems arising within the other six thousand cultures of the world. But we who specialize in the problems encountered in taking the Gospel to the peoples of the rest of the world must struggle with such problems. We must appreciate as valid the perspectives and biblical insights of peoples of other cultures. Though we must be faithful to the Scriptures, we dare not condemn the perspectives and insights of others who see the same Scriptures through different eyes. We who espouse the Golden Rule—we who seek to treat others as we would like them to treat us—must certainly apply this scriptural principle in our dealings with the peoples of nonwestern cultures.

Not infrequently, considerations such as these raise the specter of "creeping liberalism" in the minds of even open conservatives. There is a fear that, if we once admit that God's revelations are conditioned by culture, we will not be logically able to stop short of the totally naturalistic perspective that has led many liberals to question the very existence of God (see Schaeffer 1976). Monica Wilson, a noted anthropologist who is also a committed Christian, writes helpfully concerning this issue. She points to the "curious inclination to suppose that religious, but not scientific, ideas are invalidated by being related to society" (1971:5). Western Christians recognize that ideas concerning scientific matters (though not the reality being observed) can change, one hopes in the direction of greater preciseness and helpfulness. Should we be upset if the same kind of change occurs with respect to our understandings of Christianity within the cultural matrix?

Ideas are not necessarily untrue because they have been shaped by the society in which they emerge. What is false is to suppose they can escape reformulation as societies change (Wilson 1971:5).

Wilson sees development in our understandings of Christianity as part of what Jesus promised.

Christ specifically taught that his revelation was not complete: "I have yet many things to say unto you, but ye cannot bear them now. Howbeit when he, the Spirit of truth, is come, he will guide you into all truth" (Jn. 16:12–13). To me this implies two things: first that creeds are as tentative as scientific hypotheses. The difficulty is to recognize that the reality does not depend upon the formulation: God exists though men quarrel over his attributes. An honest Christian may struggle all his life with doubts (Mk. 9:24); we are past the dogmatic certainty of medieval or Victorian times and back to the position of John's disciples who, when sent to ask Jesus who he was, were told to look at the evidence for themselves. . . .

The second implication is that the awe-inspiring discoveries of science are part of the leading of the Spirit. They are indeed a fruit of men looking at the evidence (Wilson 1971:5).

Perhaps among Wilson's "awe-inspiring discoveries of science" she would agree to include the application of anthropological and communicational models to the analysis of the relationships between Christianity and culture.

THE AIMS OF THE BOOK

One of my primary aims is to attempt to develop biblically grounded theological models that will enable us to be more effective than we have ever been before in communicating the Christian message in a multicultural world. As missiologists we must grapple with the realities of cultural diversity in ways that those working within western culture may not even perceive to be necessary. We dare not add to the absolutes of God principles and judgments that, though valid within western culture, are not to be absolutized for every culture. The cross-cultural approach to theologizing that I am attempting to develop here helps to protect us and our hearers against the unconscious ethnocentrism in theological matters of which we have so often been guilty.

Today's missionary communicator of the Gospel cannot be content simply to learn the culture of the people to whom he or she goes in order better to force on them the theological understandings developed by other people in other times to answer other questions. This is what my insensitive colleague did when he spied out the cultural secrets of one group of Nigerians in order to use what he learned to argue against their customs. Owing to the cultural distance between European cultures and Hebrew culture, it is likely that American understandings of Scriptures written from a Hebrew cultural background will be further from the intent of the original authors than African and Asian understandings. For even at this distance, the latter are often culturally closer to ancient Hebrews than are Euro-Americans.

As we grapple with how best to convey the Christian message to those of the other six thousand cultures of the world, we discover a pressing need for a more broadly based, multiculturally applicable theological perspective than the ones that have been traditionally taught in Euro-America. To attempt to meet this need, I have written what follows. This book is an effort to develop (or at least to stimulate the development of) a broader, cross-culturally valid theological perspective. Not all such theology is going to be different, of course, since this cross-cultural Christian theology, like monocultural western biblical theology, is based on the same Scriptures and deals with the same topics. But the conceptualization of each doctrine has to be tested in a wide variety of different cultural contexts to discover whether the result is understanding of *God's* message or of some other message. For God, in the data we study for theological purposes, always reveals himself *to* people—never away from them or simply into thin air (see chapter 9). Likewise, doing theology must have the receivers of the theology always in mind—never just thin air (see chapter 15).

In developing this perspective I seek to bring to bear certain of the models, perspectives, and understandings of cross-cultural studies such as anthropology, linguistics, translation theory, and communication science on areas of life and thought that have ordinarily been regarded as theological. It is expected that such understandings may sooner or later be systematized into a theological discipline based upon the application of cross-culturally valid perspectives to biblical data. This cross-cultural Christian theology is tentatively labeled "Christian Ethnotheology" (see chapter 15 and Kraft 1973f). Whether my presentation is simply idiosyncratic "Kraft theology" or a genuine step in that direction is left for the reader to decide.

The method here employed is to present and discuss a series of understandings of reality (labeled "models") that differ significantly from those to which missionaries are ordinarily exposed. The hope is that either (1) through adopting the new models or at least (2) through the kind of learning that can come from the discussion of alternative approaches to the same problems, those who work through this material will be better equipped than previously to communicate the Christian Gospel effectively.

The primary audience envisaged is that group of cross-cultural witnesses for Christ who, like myself and the missionary described earlier, have found their effectiveness severely hampered by factors beyond their control. It is assumed that at least some of the more important of these hindering factors are not "out there" but deep within us. By encouraging a shift in perspective, this book will attempt to enable missionaries better to perceive and deal with such factors.

In using previous drafts of this book it has become clear that there are at least two other audiences as well: (1) many who are not engaged in cross-cultural work (as ordinarily defined) have found that most of the principles here applied to *inter*cultural missionary work are also applicable to *intra*cultural Christian witness (i.e., within the same culture); (2) in addition, those whose primary interest is in theological methodology have found much here to speak to the issues with which they are concerned.

NEEDS IN VIEW: A SUMMARY AND AN ELABORATION

When things around us don't seem to make sense we need new mirrors, new models, new perspectives on reality. This volume is written out of the kind of deep frustration created by a multitude of situations similar to these where the familiar perspectives didn't work in the cross-cultural context.

1. One of the major areas of frustration felt by the author and expressed by generations of western missionaries stems from the discovery, mentioned above, that much of the theology taught to us in our home churches, Bible schools, Christian colleges, and seminaries turns out to be extremely difficult to use in cross-cultural contexts *in the form in which we learned it*.

Missionaries (and, not infrequently, pastors and others who are engaged in communicating the Gospel across socio-cultural boundaries) have found it necessary to ignore many of the issues about which our professors were exercised. Often such matters as the critical details of biblical text and authorship on which so much of our training focuses and even such topics as proofs of the existence of God or of the occurrence of miracles are simply irrelevant to the people of other cultures and subcultures. In many cultures they, like the Hebrews, never question either the Bible or the existence of God. And they perceive miracles as happening every day. Many other issues on which our training focused are, of course, relevant to the people of other cultures. But they often need "conceptual translation" if they are to carry the proper meaning and impact. Yet we were never taught what to do if we discover that the use of concepts basic to scriptural imagery results in serious misperception of the Gospel message.

What should a cross-cultural witness do when he discovers that presenting Satan as a dragon (Rev. 12) to Chinese results in their regarding him positively? Or presenting Jesus as the Good Shepherd (Ps. 23; Jn. 10) in parts of Africa results in their understanding him to be mentally incompetent? Or telling the story of Jesus' betrayal results in Judas being regarded as the hero (Richardson 1974)? Or presenting Jesus as the Lamb of God (Jn. 1:29, 36) in parts of Indonesia, does not, for that audience, convey John's intent nearly so well as analogies concerning his sacrificial work springing from their use of pigs? What should we do if people are more attracted to the Old Testament than to the New? If they show no perceptible guilt over sin from which to be saved? Or if they find other parts of the Christian message more attractive than those on which we have learned to focus?

There are large numbers of committed people who have left missionary work completely as a result of the frustrations brought on by the inability to deal with such questions. There are also, unfortunately, many who have found it possible to stay on as missionaries only by agreeing with themselves, as it were, not to think about such issues. And yet for many cross-cultural witnesses the problems cannot be dismissed. Would a new perspective, a new mirror on reality provide any better solution to these problems?

2. A closely related set of problems that many Christian witnesses have experienced, both overseas and at home, stems from what appears to be the great distance between the way traditional "conservative" theology is spoken and written and the way ordinary Americans are thinking. Many of us who go as missionaries have, as a part of our involvement in Euro-American education, been taught to think critically about virtually everything. In dealing with "basic" Christian doctrine, however, whether in church or in Christian schools, our teachers have often virtually forbidden us to employ those same critical faculties. We were carefully warned against questioning certain approved formulations of the cardinal doctrines of Christianity. We were simply to give our uncritical assent to these. In other areas of life we learn to examine

and understand other approaches, to weigh them in comparison to older approaches, and to decide which to adopt. Boundaries of "orthodoxy" may be (and often are) set in the humanities and natural and social sciences, but there is a basic assumption that all truth is not yet known in these areas. We are therefore, to quest continually after new truth even at the expense of previously held understandings. Fear of change is to be abandoned, risk is to be encouraged. The search for new truth requires freedom to search.

The conservative mentality of much of Christianity, however, has ordinarily taken a more closed approach to Christian truth (see model 2c). Revealed truth interpreted according to the "naïve realism" model described in chapter 2 (and in Barbour 1974) allows for little or no search for new understandings, since it tends to equate "orthodox" understandings with truth itself.[1] The more one studies theology, the more one becomes aware, as theologians are aware, of the existence of diverse understandings at nearly every point. But often even sincere conservative theologians fall into the habit of studying and leading their students to study other points of view simply to criticize them and, by contrasting them with "orthodoxy," to support the status quo.

Because we were taught that Christian orthodoxy was possible only within a culturally conservative package, many of my contemporaries, when they felt it necessary to modify or abandon their conservative lifestyle, felt constrained to seriously modify or even abandon Christianity as well. Others seem to have copped out on life completely by retaining the conservative package intact. These tend to build their own walls higher and thicker to keep out any threatening stimuli. And to make sure that their children are preserved for conservatism they often seek out and find the kind of schools and churches where they will be carefully protected from other lifestyles and from having to face problems that conservative Christianity refuses to deal with.

But such an approach to life is extremely brittle. It is very much like an earthenware vase or a china plate that functions quite well as long as nothing strikes it sharply. It must, however, be very carefully packed when shipped and very carefully handled when one is setting the table or washing it. And if it is struck sharply or dropped it is likely to smash to pieces and become good for nothing.

Such is the fate of the conservatism of many Christians. When the bombardment from outside becomes too great; when the evidence shows that what they have been taught concerning this or that doctrine is no longer tenable for thinking persons; when they begin to realize just how irrelevant to real life much of what the church stands for seems to be; when they feel they can no longer simply dismiss the criticisms leveled by outsiders against the missionary endeavors of their church—the whole brittle system smashes to pieces, at least for those who take these criticisms seriously.

1. See R. Kraft (1975) for a discussion of the cultural bases for distinguishing between "orthodox" and "heretical."

Could it be that for those who remain within the fold such conservatism has at points stifled the Holy Spirit as he seeks to lead us "into all truth" (Jn. 16:13)? I assume that biblical Christianity ought to take seriously scriptural injunctions to avoid heresy (e.g., Gal. 3; 1 Jn. 4), but does an avoidance of heresy also require a closedness to new approaches to or applications of Christian truth? Could it be that (mixed in with genuine heresies) at least certain of the diverse theological understandings labeled "heresy" either historically or contemporarily are in fact often not heretical? Perhaps, rather, they are valid interpretations of scriptural truth from other perspectives (according to alternative, equally valid models). Jesus in his day, Paul in his, Augustine, Luther, Calvin, Wesley, and others in their days reinterpreted theological data in ways that have come to be seen as improvements over previous understandings, even though they often opposed the orthodoxy of their times.

Could it be that the cross-cultural witness especially is called to discover and *imitate the process of theological innovation* in which people like these engaged, in order to effectively influence contemporary peoples in new cultural and subcultural contexts the way they did? Yet missionaries are often those most conservative and protective of the products of the orthodox thinking of the past. They are often among those most prone to become rigid and inflexible in their theology. Would a new perspective, a new understanding of what theological faithfulness to God means, provide a better solution?

3. Into this situation comes the widespread influence of the "behavioral sciences"[2] on both the academic world and the populace as a whole. These disciplines, like most academic disciplines, are dominated by those who operate from non-, or even anti-Christian biases. But behavioral scientists often work in terms of these biases to develop new understandings (models) of and approaches to many of the same problems that have exercised Christians through the years. Since they often develop answers that seem diametrically opposed to Christian answers, conservative Christians (including missionaries) often tend to regard the behavioral sciences and the perspectives that they have developed with a good bit of suspicion at best and antagonism at worst (see Kraft 1977).

Creationists often take a dim view of those who assume biological evolution. Those who believe that ultimate truth comes from divine revelation are disposed to deny the validity of positions that see no truth beyond that discovered by humans. People who have come to understand Christianity as absolute and timeless have little use for perspectives that see their religion and its teachings as relative and limited to a single cultural tradition. Those who

2. The "behavioral sciences" are anthropology (including anthropological linguistics), sociology, psychology, and those disciplines (e.g., communication science) and parts of disciplines (e.g., cultural geography, ethnohistory) that have been influenced by these disciplines. The term should not be equated with the deterministic psychology labeled "behaviorism" and associated with B. F. Skinner.

seek to be supernaturalistic and God-centered feel they cannot endorse insights generated on the basis of a naturalistic, human-centered worldview. Traditional Christian understandings of the sinfulness of human beings are felt to be incompatible with perspectives that assume that human beings are essentially good. And so on (see Kraft 1977).

The fact that many laypersons and liberal theologians often seem to evangelicals to have been negatively influenced by positions developed by the behavioral sciences makes it very difficult for evangelicals to regard these disciplines positively. Certain behavioral-science understandings (or frequently, misinterpretations of them) are identified as basic to concepts like cultural and ethical relativism, situation ethics, the "new morality," biological evolution, demythologizing and other attacks on the authority of the Bible, and the like. As conservative Christians we are so often put into positions where we are forced to defend biblical Christianity with reference to such concepts that it is very easy to see the behavioral sciences as the enemy. As David Hubbard, president of Fuller Theological Seminary, has said, "The greatest challenges to evangelical Christianity are coming from the behavioral sciences." And many conservative Christians who are not as open as he is to the use of new models in the attempts to understand Christianity are even more fearful than he of the behavioral sciences (e.g., Schaeffer 1968 and 1976; Lindsell 1976).

Some conservative Christians seem to have made their peace to an extent with psychology and sociology. Perhaps they have come to feel that many of the techniques and understandings of psychology and sociology can be utilized by those whose biases are Christian, even though they may have been developed by anti-Christian scholars. Could it be that we will make the same discovery with respect to anthropology? Could it be that Christians can learn to avail themselves of anthropological insights into culture and its workings without being forced to adopt the anti-Christian biases of the anthropologists who developed them, just as we have learned to do with respect to certain psychological and sociological insights? There would seem to be good reason for antagonism between committed Christians and anti-Christian anthropologists at the level of basic presuppositions. But if this kind of antagonism is to be legitimately applied to the insights and models developed by anthropologists, it needs to be demonstrated that those understandings *cannot* be built on Christian presuppositions. It is not enough to assume the total unusability of anthropological insight on the basis of the observation that most (not all) anthropologists are not Christians, and therefore apply their understandings in ways that are not usually supportive of Christian positions.

Bible translators working around the world have for years found the insights, methodology, and general perspective of anthropological linguistics invaluable in their work. But, in spite of the widespread support of these translators by conservative Christians, one sees surprisingly little of that perspective fed back into their supporting churches, becoming a part of seminary curricula (see Nida 1971) or adopted by other missionaries. In fact, many conservative Christians support anthropologically sound "dynamic equivalence" translation procedures (see chapter 13) overseas but argue in favor of literal translations at home. And missionaries talk much about indigenous churches but still tend to produce and favor church structures that are more similar to the missionary's home denomination than to the socio-cultural matrix of the converts (see Smalley 1958 and below, chapter 16).

Traditional problems such as the following, arising from the relationships between Christianity and culture, will not go away: What is absolute and what relative? What are the relationships between God, Christianity, and culture (Niebuhr 1951; Tillich 1959)? What is the relationship between biblical content and the linguistic symbols in terms of which it is presented? How clearly can we see revealed truth? What is that core of Christian truth that we must communicate to all peoples and what is peripheral? Just what is conversion? What happens within people and within their cultures when people turn to Christ? Might it be that a new attitude toward anthropological (including linguistic) insights into cultural phenomena (including language) could lead to better solutions to such culture-related problems?

4. To attempt to do something about these problems from within a biblical Christian frame of reference is a very risky business. To date, the models available have seemed to demand that a person choose between the authority of the Bible as interpreted by conservative theologians and a liberal theological option that denies biblical authority. I will seek to develop a perspective that holds strongly to biblical authority and inspiration but not at the expense of being forced to deny much valuable insight that happens to have been discovered by those who do/did not hold a "high" view of Scripture.

There will be those who feel that any attempt to re-examine theological insights arrived at through centuries of dedicated scholarly endeavor is ill-advised, especially if the re-examination is in terms of insights developed by anthropology. They may feel threatened (see McGavran 1974:3–5) by the fact that many anthropologists have (at least intellectually) so firmly embraced a relativistic approach to life that they have virtually absolutized relativity. Whether or not such an endeavor as this book will be regarded as legitimate by such skeptics will have to await their judgment of the result. The feedback from students (some very skeptical at first) exposed to trial runs of this approach to theology has been encouraging. Such feedback, plus my own experience in approaching theology in this way, compels me to risk whatever must be risked. For it is important to me at least to attempt to assist students and others to gain what I feel I have gained by opening myself up to a culturally informed perspective on Christianity and Christian theology.

But the risk is very real, since an important part of the theological indoctrination to which many of us as conservatives have been subjected teaches us to fear heresy greatly.[3] But does God want us to be so fearful that we refuse to

---

3. See Allen 1956:55–76 for a disturbing but fair appraisal of the disastrous effects of this fear

reflect upon him and his revelation? All growth demands risk. It is risky to follow the leading of another—even if that leader is the Holy Spirit. If God is the God our theology tells us he is and if, as Jesus promised, the leading of the Holy Spirit is a present reality for the Christian, is he not in favor of our risking our previous understandings to come to understand him better? Could God favor the turning off of our mental capacities with respect to theology? Hadn't Peter, writing under the guidance of the Holy Spirit, enjoined us all to "be ready at all times to . . . explain the hope" we have in us (1 Pet. 3:15 TEV)? And hadn't Paul written that "God has not given us a spirit of fear" (2 Tim. 1:17)? And wasn't the reason for the condemnation of the servant who buried his master's money (Mt. 25:14–30) the fact that in fear *he refused* to risk what his master had entrusted to him?

J. B. Phillips, through his concept of "the God who is too small" (1952 and 1954), had much to do with my own change in this regard. Encouraged by Phillips' writings, I began to re-examine with my adult mind the theology I had been taught in my youth. I began prayerfully to examine my understandings of God and his Word in the same way that I had learned to examine the ideas I had been taught in every other area of life. And when I opened myself up in this way to the individualized leading of the Holy Spirit in this most important area of my life, I found that the God who had once been too small began to get very big! I found that the small understandings I had once feared to risk began to be swallowed up by and expanded into much larger and more meaningful understandings. I began to grow.

I have become convinced that it is my (and every Christian's) obligation to risk whatever theological frame of reference we have been trained into for the sake of such growth. Only by risking prior, less mature understandings can we gain more mature understandings that we can embrace with our adult minds. And such a quest should involve us in facing squarely the implications for the understanding of our faith of the issues raised by such problems as cultural/subcultural diversity. In addition to the obvious need for such thinking-through by missionaries, it is, I believe, also necessary for those living and seeking to witness in American contexts. For even Americans who have not traveled are daily faced with both the diversity of cultures and the increasing impact of behavioral-sciences perspectives on life. To relate Christianity to Americans (including ourselves), therefore, we need to take the risk of attempting to translate traditional formulations of theological truth out of the language and concepts of traditional theology into those of the behavioral sciences. If we refuse such a risk we should not be surprised if both non-Christians and those who unenthusiastically stay within the churches assume that (a) God is behind the times, (b) he is not concerned with being relevant to contemporary life and thought, or (c) he cannot cope with this latest change in thought patterns.

in missionary work. He concludes, "when we are dealing with the Gospel fear is a very bad master" (p. 76).

5. Risk of tradition is prerequisite to contemporary relevance in every culture. Large numbers of our contemporaries (both in Euro-America and elsewhere) have come to feel strongly God's irrelevance because of the refusal of churches to take the risks necessary to becoming contemporary. As long ago as World War II, J. B. Phillips demonstrated this fact by asking a group of British young people to respond quickly (i.e., without reflection) to a single question. The question concerned what was in that day the latest scientific advance—radar. Phillips' question was, "Do you think God understands radar?" He then writes:

They all said "No," and then, of course, roared with laughter as they realized how ridiculous the answer was! But the "snap answer" showed me what I suspected—*that at the back of their minds* there was an idea of God as an old gentleman who lived in the past and was rather bewildered by modern progress (1954:65).

This impression of God as an old gentleman who cannot cope with the modern world is communicated by the church in hundreds of ways. Many churches continue to insist on literal Bible translations that simply are not in a kind of English anyone speaks. We continue to be attached to antiquated forms of preaching, worship, theology, and organizational structure. We of the Christian in-group frequently manifest a condemnatory or "holier-than-thou" attitude toward the non-Christian out-group. These characteristics combine to communicate irrelevance in the strongest possible way. Leslie Dewart (1966) rightly asks, "Have We Loved the Past Too Long?"

Overseas, where occasionally we have broken out of such ruts, the situation is often not much better. "If Christianity had been presented to me in these terms, I'd still be a Christian," remarked a highly schooled Liberian on one occasion in response to the approach advocated in this book. He had been brought up in missionary schools but, as he became better acquainted with western culture, had come to regard the Christianity he had been taught as utterly irrelevant. An approach to Christian theology that viewed both his culture and western culture as alternative, equally valid vehicles for expressing Christianity would have made it possible for this man to remain a Christian. As it was he, like millions of others in mission lands, had been led to believe that Christianity is but the tribal religion of the Euro-American tribe. Thus, acceptance of Christianity was perceived by him as only a part of the cultural package to which he was being asked to convert. But he was led into this heresy—which, by the way, is nearly identical to that of the Judaizers who required just such conversion to Jewish culture as a prerequisite to Christianity (see Acts 15)—by sincere missionaries whose theology made no distinction between Christianity and Euro-American culture. He had fallen victim to what has been called "the greatest secularizing force in the world"—mission schools.

"What I would like these young men to know before they embark for

Nigeria is that it is *God* who is taking *them* to Nigeria *not* they who are taking God," said a Nigerian concerning a group of prospective missionaries. He continued:

> When missionaries first came to my country, they spoke of the God who created the world as if he were a different God from the one we already knew about. We listened and compared what we heard and read in the Bible about this God and discovered that he is the very same God we had always known about. We received many new insights from the missionaries and especially we heard that we could come to know God personally through Jesus Christ. But everyone except the missionaries realized that your God is the same as our God.
>
> In other words, *our* God had brought the missionaries to add to our understanding and commitment. The missionaries had not brought a new God with them. And this is what I would like these young people to realize before they go so that they don't waste so much effort trying to change our ways but devote themselves to building something worthwhile on the foundations that are already there (Kraft 1969).

As missionaries we have steadfastly maintained that God is more than simply "the White Man's God." Yet, because our understanding of him and of Christian theology is so culture-bound, we often find ourselves unable to give any other impression to members of other cultures. The theological questions we raise are those that occur to Euro-Americans (and, often, only the philosophically oriented subculture within Euro-America). And, of course, the answers we give, couched in the interpretations of the Scriptures that occur to us as applicable, are thoroughly Euro-American. So the Africans, cringing in their fear of evil spirits, puzzled by the relationship between the Christian God and their living (though physically deceased) ancestors, and uncomprehending over the discrepancy between the attitude of the missionaries and that of the Bible toward polygamous marriage, hear from western Christianity no serious attempt to deal with their pressing problems. What they hear, rather, is frequently but another, to them irrelevant, discussion of alternative (western) theories of the atonement or of biblical inspiration or some apologetic for the existence of God or of miracles (in which they already strongly believe without the need for apologetic). As John V. Taylor has put it:

> Christ has been presented as the answer to the questions a white man would ask, the solution to the needs that Western man would feel, the Saviour of the world of the European world-view, the object of the adoration and prayer of historic Christendom. But if Christ were to appear as the answer to the questions that Africans are asking what would he look like? If he came into the world of African cosmology to redeem Man as Africans understand him, would he be recognizable to the rest of the Church Universal (1963:24)?

Theology should, however, be culturally relevant—whether that culture be African or American. Theology should be, as Bengt Sundkler has well put it, an ever-renewed re-interpretation to the new generations and peoples of the given Gospel, a re-presentation of the will and the way of the one Christ in a dialogue with new thought-forms and culture patterns. . . . Theology . . . is to understand the fact of Christ . . . (1960:211).

This study is an attempt to take seriously our responsibility to re-present the given Gospel in "dialogue with new thought-forms and culture patterns," whether these be American, African, Asian, or other. We dare not cop out; the stakes are too high. Rather, we take the risk of rethinking in the conviction that the possible gain for Americans in general, for missionaries, and for the disillusioned products of both American and missionary churches is so great that whatever fears we might have had concerning the risk must be overcome.

2. Mirrored Reality

In this chapter we lay the foundations for developing the answers we seek. "Toward an Answer" introduces the problem a bit more and then shows some hope from the experience of a missionary who claims to have gone through a second "conversion." Next we discuss the distinction between reality "out there" and the way we structure our perceptions of that reality inside our heads. The concept of models is then dealt with in some detail and a biblical Christian model presented.

TOWARD AN ANSWER

Centuries ago the apostle Paul wrote, "What we see now is like the dim image in a [poor] mirror. . . . What I know is only partial . . ." (1 Cor. 13:12 TEV). It has taken western science generations of trial and error to come to the same recognition. Perhaps the newness of the insights that scientists kept coming up with misled them into assuming that they were finally seeing reality directly. Or perhaps such an apparent overestimation of the accuracy of what scientists were discovering was due to a kind of (unconscious) arrogant desire to displace God and revelation with empirical scientific discovery as the ultimate source of truth. Whatever the basic reasons may have been, both the scientific community and millions of those within western societies (including Christians) whose schooling exposed them to the results of scientific discovery came to believe that the knowledge we were gaining was bringing us ever closer to an ultimate understanding of reality. People within western culture developed a faith in science and the scientific process that approached credulity. For many, a statement such as "scientists have proved" is enough to settle any argument.

An interpretation of history that sees western culture as having "progressed" or evolved ever upward, plus an inordinate pride in the accomplishments of western culture, kept most of us from questioning such assumptions. Since we believe our culture to be at the top, the reason must be that we are superior. In addition, most of the rest of the world seems to be anxious to borrow gadgets, insights, and techniques from us. This must mean that they too recognize our superiority—a superiority that rests solidly upon our superior knowledge. Or so we assume.

Western Christians, though they have often had their difficulties with the scientific establishment, have more often shared than questioned its basic premises. They might argue over whether ultimate knowledge is totally attainable through scientific experimentation, but seldom over whether ultimate knowledge of many things is ever attainable. They might discuss whether the reason they do things in a superior way is because of their Christianness, but seldom question *that* they do things in a superior way. They might vehemently deny biological evolution but seldom question the concept of cultural evolution or "progress" that provided the model on the basis of which the biological evolutionists developed their theory.

The point is that as westerners and Christians we may be claiming too great a correspondence between reality, on the one hand, and what we think we know and how we understand what we do on the other. If we are only able to see that reality as a "dim image in a poor mirror," however, is such a claim justified?

I believe that the understandings advanced by modern philosophers of science concerning the relationship between reality and our view of it are more in line with that of the apostle Paul than with contemporary popular understandings, based as they are on previous scientific theory. For scientists (like the missionary in chapter 1) have recently gone through one or more "paradigm shifts" (see below), worldview changes, or even "scientific revolutions" (Kuhn 1970), with the result that they now think and talk differently about reality and their relationship to it.

A "paradigm" is defined by Webster's *Dictionary* as an example or pattern (1967:610). The concept is treated in more detail below. The diagrams in Fig. 2.1 provide convenient, though elementary, illustrations of a visual pattern or paradigm that has the built-in capacity for seeming to shift when the observer looks at it differently. Actually the lines on the page do not shift—they, like reality, remain constant. There is, however, a "shift" in the perception of the observer (the picture of reality that the observer constructs in his or her mind) that is similar on a small scale to a paradigm shift or worldview change. As you go through the fairly simple procedure necessary to see these realities differently, try to imagine the complexity of a paradigm shift that leads to a radically different understanding of all reality.

Missionary-professor Marvin Mayers indicates that not only scientists go through paradigm shifts. He writes:

At a time when studies in history, literature, theology, and other disciplines deriving from the humanities and the humanities-oriented social sciences were considered adequate for missionary preparation, I was enlisted in a mission enterprise with my wife, and entered Central America. During my first term of service in Guatemala, numerous problems arose that were impossible of solution with the tools I had available to me. From time to time consultants would shed light on a problem or two but by the end of that tour, I was convinced that most of these problems simply had to be left in the "hands of the Lord" to resolve. I did have an uneasy feeling about that since I had the distinct impression, at times, that my wife and I had been adding to the problems rather than providing answers to them.

During our furlough, we were privileged to attend the University of Chicago to

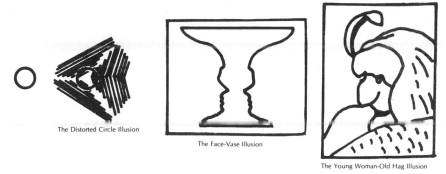

The Distorted Circle Illusion

The Face-Vase Illusion

The Young Woman-Old Hag Illusion

Fig. 2.1. Patterns that shift when the observer shifts perspective.

pursue advanced studies in linguistics. My wife chose to study in the humanities division, and I chose the social sciences division and entered the department of anthropology. It was there that I came into contact, for the first time, with social anthropologists and the teachings of the British school of social anthropology. Resolutions to the various problems I had left behind in the field began to fill my mind. I experienced what I now call my "behavioral sciences conversion." I had gone to Central America as a change agent under the direction of the Spirit of God, but I had not been trained as a change agent, nor had I been given the tools that should have been given to one who was committed to changing another. Therefore the changes introduced into the total setting by my introduction of the Gospel were partial, inconsistent, resisted, or modified in ways over which I had no control.

I do not suggest that my training in social anthropology was a cure-all for every problem, but I realized that many problems we had faced in our mission program were problems amenable to solution with the proper tools. Our second term on the field proved this in a large percentage of cases (Mayers 1974:7-8).

Mayers' retooling for more effective service as a cross-cultural communicator came through a paradigm shift (his "behavioral sciences conversion"). Through this experience he came to look at the reality around him differently and, as a result, was able to function more constructively in it. What is the nature of this perception problem that can cripple a person in another context? And where does one look for answers?

REALITY "OUT THERE" VERSUS THE CONCEPTUAL MODELS OF THAT REALITY IN PEOPLE'S HEADS

The view that made little or no distinction between the reality "out there" and the scientific understanding of that reality (in the minds of scientists) prevailed among western scientists until around the turn of the century. Barbour calls this theory "naive realism," saying of it:

With few exceptions, most scientists until the present century assumed that scientific theories were accurate descriptions of "the world as it is in itself." The entities postulated in theories were believed to exist, even if they were not directly observable. Theoretical terms were said to denote real things of the same kind as physical objects in the perceived world. Theoretical statements were understood as true or false propositions about actual entities (atoms, molecules, genes, etc.) (1974:34).

This position assumed a real, ordered world outside the observer. Subsequent scientific theories have largely continued to operate on this assumption. There has, however, been a growing recognition of the part that the observer plays in the interpretation and description of that ordered reality. For, it has become clear, the ordered reality "out there" is never described by a human being except in terms of an internal psychological ordering (a "picture" of that reality in the observer's head) that involves various kinds of individual bias. Individuals perceive the data of reality in terms of such things as preferences, biases, focuses, and other types of group and individual predispositions toward that data. These are constructed by observers on the basis of their psychological and socio-cultural experiences. Individuals and groups, for example, organize their perceptions of reality so as to ignore, distort, or exaggerate its features in ways that differ to a greater or lesser extent from the organized perceptions of that reality described by other individuals and groups. We understand in terms of the pictures of reality inside our heads, via the lenses of our cultural and psychological cameras (or glasses). If those lenses are, for some reason or other (such as sickness, limitedness of experience, perversity, etc.) dirty or distorting (as with a camera out of focus), the way we perceive reality is greatly affected (see, e.g., Gearing 1970 and Kluckhohn and Leighton 1962 for illustrations of strikingly different perceptions of reality).

The assumption that scientific observers should or even can work without bias—without in some way imposing the ordering inside their heads on the ordering of reality "out there"—has, therefore, been largely abandoned by the scientific community (though not by large segments of the populace as a whole). One way of describing the role of the observer in the scientific process is to suggest that,

In the first place, the observer can work only with his experiences, and these are limited by his senses and the instruments he uses to extend his senses. . . . Consequently, our picture of the real world is always incomplete.

Secondly, the observer is highly selective in choosing his data. Life is a narrative of ever new and often unpredictable events. . . . But he is really interested or concerned with only a few of these. Other experiences are consciously or unconsciously screened out. . . . What a scientist discovers depends, to a great extent, on what he is looking for—on the questions he is asking (Hiebert 1976:5,6).

People with different interests, different academic disciplines, and different cultures and subcultures diverge from each other in their perceptions of reality, not because the reality differs but because their experience of and reflection upon that reality differ. They ask different questions concerning reality—questions that they have been conditioned or stimulated to ask by their experience with themselves, with others, and with traditions in which they participate. The answers and the organization of those answers into individual, disciplinary, subcultural, and cultural perspectives are increasingly being labeled conceptual "models" or "mental maps" of reality.

Such conceptual models are

imaginative mental constructs invented to account for observed phenomena. Such a model is usually an imagined mechanism or process, which is postulated by analogy with familiar mechanisms or processes. . . . Its chief use is to help one understand the world. . . . It is not a literal picture of the world. . . It is used to develop a theory which in some sense explains the phenomena. And its origination seems to require a special kind of reactive imagination (Barbour 1974:30).

Hiebert pictures this understanding (or model) of the relationship between external reality ("the external world") and the perception of that reality inside our heads ("mental organization") in the diagram that follows. Note the decrease in the amount of data that human beings handle from the rather large number of "potential experiences" to the more limited number of those potential experiences that one actually undergoes to the even more limited number that one reflects on either consciously or subconsciously. Only the latter play a major role in the mental organization that one develops.

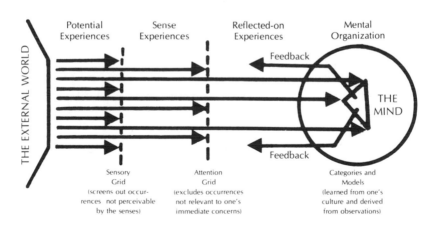

Fig. 2.2. A conceptual model of certain relationships between reality "out there" and the mental organization of the perception of that reality in the mind (adapted from Hiebert 1976:6).

Note (1) that "reflected-on" experiences include those at the important sub-conscious level and (2) that there are powerful "feedback" influences of one's mental organization of reality on the selection one makes of those experiences upon which to reflect. The model "tells one," as it were, which of the things that happen to oneself to believe, which not to believe (or even notice), and how to interpret both. We will refer later, as an example of this phenomenon, to the fact that many Euro-Americans who do not believe in the existence and activity of supernatural spirits in human affairs may actually be experiencing such activity though interpreting it as something else.

One who accepts this "critical realism" approach to the understanding of the relationship between external reality and human perception of it

recognizes the importance of human imagination in the formation of theories. He acknowledges the incomplete and selective character of scientific theories. Theories . . . are abstract symbol systems which inadequately represent particular aspects of the world for specific purposes. The critical realist thus tries to acknowledge both the creativity of man's mind and the existence of patterns in events not created by man's mind. Descriptions of nature are human constructions but nature is such as to bear description in some ways and not in others. No theory is an exact account of the world, but some theories agree with observations better than others because the world has an objective form of its own (Barbour 1974:37).

The assumption is that whether we are dealing with the reality of the physical environment, the reality of human nature and psychology, or the reality of divine revelation, the process of coming to know always involves the process of theory and model building on the part of the observer. We perceive data in terms of some combination of the theories that we have been taught and the theories that we construct. We never see that data except through such grids or filters as "dim images" (1 Cor. 13:12). We cannot now see as God sees—objectively, as things really are.

All humans participate in all-encompassing overall perspectives held by and pledged allegiance to by the communities of which they are a part. In terms of these perspectives they generate sets "of recurrent and quasi-standard illustra-tions of various theories in their conceptual, observational, and instrumental applications" (Kuhn 1970:43). These recurrent pictures or models of reality are sometimes termed "paradigms" (Kuhn 1970, Barbour 1974, Black 1962). Paradigms are

models from which spring particular coherent traditions of scientific research. These are the traditions which the historian describes under such rubrics as "Ptolemaic astronomy" (or "Copernican"), "Aristotelian dynamics" (or "Newtonian"), "corpuscu-lar optics" (or "wave optics"), and so on. The study of paradigms . . . is what mainly prepares the student for membership in the particular scientific community with which he will later practice. . . . Men whose research is based on shared paradigms are committed to the same rules and standards for scientific practice (Kuhn 1970:10-11).

Another term that may be employed with reference to a similar, though more complex, organization of reality is "worldview" (Kuhn 1970:111). Worldviews are more total views of reality than paradigms and models and employ many paradigms and models (see chapter 3 for a detailed introduction to the concept of worldview). Differing worldviews, paradigms, and models are characterized by their distinctive views of reality. These distinctive views of reality, though created and modified by previous members of the community, are passed on fully formed to the current members of the community by those who have gone before. This is true whether the community is a culture, a subculture, an academic community, a church community, a voluntary organization of some kind, or a family.

Worldviews and paradigms can be seen, on the one hand, as organizations of the theories in terms of which their proponents perceive reality and, on the other, as those conceptualizations that lead people to generate those theories. The theories, in turn, may be seen as organizations of conceptual models that

attempt to represent symbolically, for restricted purposes, aspects of a world whose structure is not accessible to us (Barbour 1974:37–8).

The fact that as human beings we see reality *not as it is but always from inside our heads* in terms of such models means that "no direct comparison of model and world is possible" (ibid.:38). We cannot, therefore, take our models (or our paradigms and worldview) literally or absolutely. We must, however, take them seriously. They are, to be sure, "limited and inadequate ways of imagining what is not observable" (ibid.:38), but they are, apparently, the only ways we have. Furthermore, they seem to be productive. As Leonard Nash states:

To the hypothetical entities [models] sketched by our theories we must venture at least provisional grants of ontologic status. Major discoveries are made when invisible atoms, electrons, nuclei, viruses, vitamins, hormones, and genes are regarded as *existing* (1963:257).

There are, however, dangers to be avoided in using models. Rogers warns:

A model is not the same as the real thing. But it helps us to understand reality. A model takes the essential pieces of the real thing and scales them down so that we can understand them. That is to say, we speak of God by analogies, models from life. We say God is our Father. We mean that we see in his acts some of the best characteristics of certain fathers we know. When we forget that we are making models and speaking by analogies we run the risk of idolatry. Idolatry consists in worshiping the created model rather than pointing to the creator it represents. We must not get too attached to our thought forms, our fine distinctions of language, our cultural packaging (Rogers 1974:59).

Models, theories, and whole worldviews may be changed—or, perhaps better, *exchanged* for new ones. A new model offers a new way of looking at a

given phenomenon or set of phenomena. It can, indeed, suggest a new approach to the exploration of given aspects of reality (e.g., the experience of
Mayers or the author). If taken far enough, then, the application of new models
can lead to radical shifts in theories, paradigms, and whole worldviews. When
a group changes models, "the world itself changes with them, and they begin
to see reality differently" (Kuhn 1970:111). In science this creates what Kuhn
calls a "scientific revolution." Applying this concept to Christianity we may
speak of Christian conversion as a paradigm shift, a worldview change, or even
a spiritual revolution (see chapter 17). Christian conversion is at least as
worldview-changing as the shift from Ptolemaic earth-centered astronomy to
Copernican sun-centered astronomy or from a flat-earth model to a round-
earth model. When "the eyes of one's understanding" are opened (Eph. 1:18;
Lk. 24:45), it is because (at the human level) one has changed the model of
reality, the perspective, the interpretive principle in terms of which one is
viewing the events under analysis.

Jesus continually worked toward model and paradigm shifts on the part of
his hearers. His parables were regularly introduced with some phrase such as
"The kingdom of heaven is like . . . " The whole concept of a kingdom that is
to function *within* earthly kingdoms, rather than to compete with them, was a
radically different model of reality. Its differentness from the models already
in his hearers' minds is attested to by the extreme difficulty they had in
understanding and converting to it. Then, in presenting the kingdom, Jesus
continually employed model-type analogies such as mustard seed, the sower,
leaven, a treasure, a pearl, etc. He presented God as "Father" and himself as
"Son." This is a powerful and pervasive model based on the importance in the
minds of his Hebrew hearers of the first son in the Hebrew family. Jesus'
presentation of himself as a peasant who identified with the common people
was very difficult for many to accept because it was such a different model
from what they had learned to expect of their Messiah. Indeed, the whole
model of the almighty God become human in the Incarnation is a concept that
Jesus' followers from his time to this have had difficulty understanding. For
Jesus became a human, flesh-and-blood model of God (Jn. 14:9). When God is
spoken of throughout the Scriptures as having eyes, ears, hands, etc., it is on
the basis of a concept (model) of God that analogizes from human beingness.
The church understood as a body or as the bride of Christ is likewise a model.

God thus employs models as "form pictures" designed to teach something
about the way he functions. Models are teaching devices used to enable people
to conceive of some aspect of reality as a whole. When the model is substituted
for the reality of God rather than used simply to assist humans in conceiving of
it, the result is idolatry (Rogers 1974:59, quoted above). The problem is
illustrated in the Scriptures from the lives of the Pharisees, the disciples, those
to whom the prophets spoke, Jonah, Job and his "friends," Paul, etc. The
history of doctrinal controversy in the church also illustrates both the use of
models and the difficulty of changing models. Each discussion of the nature of
God, the relationship of Jesus to God the Father, the nature of the church,

etc., involves the comparing and contrasting of various models in terms of which these ideas are conceptualized.

Major advances in scientific endeavor happen, according to Kuhn, when scientists shift from one way of viewing their data to another way of viewing it. For "our vision is more obstructed by what we think we know than by our lack of knowledge" (Stendahl 1976:7). Such paradigm or model shifts are continually happening in all areas of life, from trivial levels such as that illustrated above with the use of pictures to the most profound level of Christian conversion. Between these levels is the level at which this book is intended to bring about a paradigm shift in you, the reader. For this volume seeks to introduce the reader to a series of alternative models in terms of which to view theological phenomena of relevance to cross-cultural communicators. The hope is that you will experience the kind of paradigm shift that the author and countless other cross-cultural Christian witnesses have experienced.

CHARACTERISTICS OF CONCEPTUAL MODELS

The terms "model," "theory," "paradigm," and "worldview" have been introduced above. Though to some degree we may regard these terms as signifying four levels of conceptual complexity, we see no need to continue to use all four of them. In what follows, therefore, the terms "theory" and "paradigm" largely disappear, while the terms "model" and "worldview" are used extensively to label the more specific (model) and more general (worldview) perspectives with which we must deal. We will label attempts to understand reality differently as shifts in or substitutions for previously held models or worldviews. Our detailed treatment of worldview begins in chapter 3. That of models begins here. Some of the characteristics of models (as here employed) are the following.

1. Conceptual models differ in complexity and, therefore, in the comparative ease with which they can be explained and understood. Some models are fairly simple and easily pictured in a two-dimensional format such as a road map or an architect's sketch. Three-dimensional models such as scale models of physical objects like airplanes and buildings are only slightly more complex. Often, however, even fairly simple concepts defy all attempts to picture or construct two- or three-dimensional visual aids of them. Words and word pictures help and are often the best we can do. But the rather severe limitations under which we work become readily apparent when one considers the impreciseness and inadequacy of such attempts to understand certain aspects of human thought processes as likening the mind to a computer, or the attempt to understand human communities (such as Christian churches) by likening them to human bodies, or the attempt to understand God by employing models such as father, slavemaster (Lord), king, person, and shepherd. Such words, metaphors, analogies, and pictures reveal important dimensions of what they are applied to, but they also may distract or even distort.

Nevertheless, with all their limitations, God has chosen to employ such conceptual devices to communicate his truth. Analogies, such as parables and other kinds of models, are devices by means of which

something in one universe of discourse is employed to explain, illustrate, or prove something in another universe of discourse. . . . In special revelation God chooses that element in *our* universe of discourse which can serve to convey the truth in *his* universe of discourse (Ramm 1961:41; see also Wright 1952:48–49).

2. Conceptual models may be static or dynamic. A static model (e.g., a road map) simply shows relationships between elements. It shows the items of which a given concept is made up and their arrangements vis-à-vis each other. A dynamic model, on the other hand, focuses on the processes in which the items are involved. Often, though, the "staticness" or "dynamicness" of a given model lies not in the model itself but in the interpretation of that model. Seeing the church as a body, for example, results in a static concept if one focuses merely on the organizational arrangement of the group into "head," "hands," "feet," etc. It is possible (and sometimes necessary) for one to look at such a "body" in this static way, just as it is both possible and profitable for a medical student to dissect a cadaver. But the body model of the church was used, I believe, with a more dynamic intent. Passages such as 1 Corinthians 12 focus on the fact that the body parts are to *function* (a dynamic word) as a unity, not simply to exist in a bodylike *arrangement* (a static word).

Our language and culture give us problems at this point by constantly focusing our attention on *pattern* rather than on *process*, on *entity* rather than on *function*. Note the difference in impact of statements like "The church *is* a body" versus "The church *functions like* a body," or "God *is* our Father" versus "God *behaves* toward us as a Father," or "We *are* brothers in Christ" versus "We *treat each other* as brothers." Many languages (e.g., Navaho, Hebrew) force those who speak them to focus more on the latter (dynamic) process and function type of statement than English does. English and many if not most of its linguistic relatives (including Greek) pressure their speakers into making more of the former (static) type of statement. The purpose of the Scriptures is, however, not to tell us about God's essence (though, because of our cultural interest, we deduce much on this subject) but to show us how he relates to us (Berkouwer 1975). God's focus appears to be more on function and process, less on entity and form.

3. A third important characteristic of models is the tendency of a given kind of model to occur with others of a similar nature. Models often occur in interrelated strings, probably because the use of one suggests the possibility of following it with others of the same type. Reference to God as Father, for example, suggests the use of a son model not only for Jesus but also for all those who call God "Father." If, though, we all call God "Father," why not see our relationship to each other in terms of a brother model? Such strings can be carried too far, as, for example, in the tendency of some to add a deified Mary to the Godhead that was already understood in terms of "father" and "son"

models. What could be more natural than to develop a total family model that includes a mother as well?

4. A further characteristic of special relevance to the subject matter of this volume is that models cannot be automatically assumed to be cross-culturally valid. Models are developed within specific cultural contexts for particular purposes and must, therefore, be interpreted first within that context and then evaluated for their cross-cultural potential. The Bible employs a great many models. These were invariably developed in specific situations with the needs and limitations of specific audiences in view. The value of each such model in its original setting is beyond doubt. The value of those same models in settings as distant from those contexts in culture, time, and space as contemporary settings are must be re-evaluated. The father-son model, for example, was interpreted by the original hearers as a claim by Jesus of equality with God (Jn. 5:18). Is this a good model to use in cultures (like Euro-American cultures) that regard the father-son relationship as a hierarchical one? Likewise, is the God as shepherd model, so vivid and truth-conveying for rural Hebrews, a good model for those who have no acquaintance with sheep?

In this volume I will attempt to gravitate toward less complex rather than more complex models that are, on the one hand, cross-culturally valid and, on the other, dynamic rather than static.

A BIBLICAL CHRISTIAN MODEL (Model 2)

In what follows I endeavor to be biblically Christian in keeping with the Protestant "evangelical" tradition (see Coleman 1972:76ff). I do not intend to be bound by traditional models of theologizing, however—especially those that I have experienced as either static or applying only to some segment of Euro-American culture. I accept the Bible as both inspired by God and an accurate record of the Spirit-guided perceptions of human beings who were committed to God.

1. *I attempt to distinguish between the biblical data that is the primary subject-matter for theological analysis and the theological perspectives (models, theories, paradigms) in terms of which that data is interpreted.* I contend that, though the scriptural data is inspired, *inspiration does not extend to any extra-scriptural interpretive perspective.* It is therefore valid, as well as instructive, to examine that data from new perspectives—even those of academic disciplines such as anthropology, which some suspect of being incapable of Christian application. The intent is to select from such disciplines understandings and perspectives that can be employed by those committed to the basic tenets of evangelical Protestantism. I specifically do not intend either to accept or to recommend the anti-theistic assumptions on the basis of which many (not all) anthropologists operate.

When employing any perspective (new or old) it is necessary to distinguish insofar as possible between features that characterize the data being studied (the reality) and the characteristics of the interpretive concepts (models) in terms of which that data is being studied. Though it seems to be true that there is "no bare uninterpreted data" (Barbour 1974:95), it is important to recognize the basic biblical data (including the interpretations of the original authors) as a thing apart from extra-biblical interpretations of that data. Otherwise it is difficult to keep from identifying the conceptual model with the reality that it is designed to explain in part. Nonspecialists who handle theological interpretations of inspired scriptural data seem particularly prone to regard both the scriptural data and their pet interpretations of it as sacred. Not infrequently such "folk theologians" seem to believe that the particular interpretation they subscribe to is *demanded* by the text (the data).

"Closed" conservatives (see Fig. 2.5) often fall into this trap rather readily. But many who are fairly knowledgeable concerning the existence of theological variants within western culture also find it difficult to accept variations based upon the perspectives of nonwestern cultures or of academic disciplines such as the behavioral sciences. Such difficulty may be seen as resistance to "paradigm shifting" based upon a too ready identification of their understandings with the demands of the data. It is likely that they have not had the kind of experience with people whom they respect who possess radically different worldviews that would push them to recognize the validity of models other than their own. Unfortunately, this kind of theological ethnocentrism often characterizes conservative Christians such as missionaries in their attitudes toward (1) the perspectives of other cultures and (2) those of disciplines such as the behavioral sciences. The acceptance of the validity of this volume may require a paradigm shift on their part.

The position taken here is that *valid* theologizing may be done on the basis of a variety of cultural, subcultural, and disciplinary models. Not everything said or done in the theological realm is valid, since not everything is allowed by the data. But different understandings of reality generate different questions with respect to biblically revealed data, just as they do with respect to the natural world. And the answers obtained, when systematized, result in different "indigenous" theologies. This process is often referred to as the "contextualization" of theology (see Fig. 2.3. Note that, unlike some liberal concepts of contextualization, *these theologies are all based on biblical data.*

2. *I attempt here to develop insights concerning scriptural data via the application to that data of anthropological understandings and perspectives.* A large number of such understandings and perspectives will be introduced throughout this volume. There are, however, four basic components of an anthropological approach that need to be mentioned here as distinguishing characteristics.

First, an anthropological perspective is *wholistic* (or "holistic"). "Anthropology sets as its goal the study of mankind as a whole" (Hoebel 1972:6). It does not simply select a single aspect of (western) human experience to focus on, as do traditional studies of music, literature, philosophy, economics, and even history and geography. Instead,

anthropologists take a comprehensive approach to the study of humanity. They assume that no understanding of human beings is complete without study of the full range of

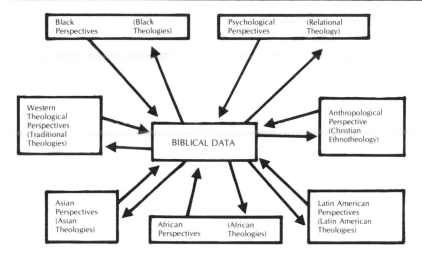

Fig. 2.3. Visual aid portraying this conceptual model of theological contextualization (model 2a). Read: Black perspectives on scriptural data yield "black theologies." Psychological perspectives yield such theologies as "relational theology," etc.

the human phenomenon. As individuals, anthropologists may concentrate their studies on a specific society or aspect of the human being, but they put their findings into a broad theoretical perspective that seeks to include all of human experience. This "holistic" approach is reflected both in an interest in the broad *variety* of human beings and in a *comprehensive approach* to the study of human beings (Hiebert 1976:20).

Anthropological "wholism" will be evident throughout this book.

Second, an anthropological perspective depends on and develops *the culture concept.*

Anthropology has demonstrated that the distinctive behavior of different human populations . . . is overwhelmingly the product of cultural experience rather than the consequence of genetic inheritance (Hoebel 1972:7).

Chapters 3 through 5 are devoted to the elaboration of the culture concept and its application to the problems at hand.

A third focus of the anthropological perspective is called *cross-cultural comparison.* This component both springs from and feeds the wholistic and cultural emphases. It is of great importance in the study of cultural diversity. It is also of great importance in the study of human commonality (chapter 5).

The anthropologist refuses to accept any generalization about human nature that emerges from his experience with his own society alone, or even with two or three other societies, especially if these are a part of the same cultural tradition in which he has been brought up (Hoebel 1972:7).

The crucial importance of this principle to the following presentation can hardly be overestimated. *We seek here a cross-culturally valid understanding of Christianity.* It cannot be based simply on experience within one society or within two or three societies that participate in "the same cultural tradition." Theologizing based on such limited cultural experience is like the single mineshaft drilled into the mountain of gold mentioned above. Furthermore, it risks the danger of regarding God's single message in different cultural clothing (e.g., in Old Testament and New Testament) as if it were different messages.

The fourth basic component of an anthropological perspective is its dependence on *field work* in other cultures for obtaining data and testing hypotheses. Studying human beings cannot be done effectively via laboratory experimentation—though anthropologists are not averse to employing laboratory methods in the limited areas where they seem to be appropriate. For the total range of human behavior, anthropologists obtain their data and test their theories via field study, using what has come to be called the "participant-observation" approach. This method, of high relevance to Christian communicators, involves investigators in living with the people they are observing. They seek, thus, to get a bit of the feel of the people's life and to learn to appreciate that approach to life. Such investigators realize that in seeking to understand people they need to study the insider's perspective (the *emic* perspective, or model) as well as the outsider's perspective (the *etic* perspective). If they seek to be objective only, they are likely to be ethnocentric as well. If, however, they only become involved in the life of the people they are studying, they lose their ability to observe and analyze effectively. The effective cross-cultural communicator of Christianity needs both to participate in and to analyze the cultural context in which he or she witnesses.

These four basic components of an anthropological approach underlie all that is said in the following pages. These principles are not to be our masters—as Christians we serve another Master—but they can be very helpful servants in our attempts to be more effective cross-culturally.

3. The resulting "cross-cultural" or "ethno-" theology thus seeks to formulate at least certain scriptural truths in ways that evangelicals have not become accustomed to. To the extent that such understandings and perspectives necessitate the development of new categories of thought and terminology we will be forced to innovate them. By and large, however, it will be found that *such new categories and models as are developed will broaden and elucidate, rather than completely displace, traditional theological concepts.* I am, I believe, just as committed to biblical theology (see Vos 1948:14–18 for a concise definition) as any evangelical. I find myself readily agreeing with the essentials of the evangelical Protestant position outlined by Coleman (1972:76ff). I do, however, find that my position also allows the incorporation of some important characteristics of

certain liberal positions (ibid.:80ff) that have been attractive to evangelical Protestants but could not heretofore be readily handled on the basis of an evangelical commitment. If, though, as Quebedeaux states, evangelicalism is best described (contra Lindsell 1976) as "a 'spirit' rather than a well-defined theology" (1974:40), there is room for another set of models such as those here set forth.

Not all the unfamiliar terminology is new. At times I will employ terminology and concepts that others use in other ways. Bultmann and his followers, for example, seem to recognize that it is highly important for our contemporaries to understand and embrace the deeper meanings of the Scriptures even at the expense of replacing the cultural forms in terms of which that content was originally expressed. I will say something similar to this concerning the priority of content (meanings) over symbols (cultural forms). But I will seek, in so doing, to affirm solidly both the historicity of the original events and the importance of that historicity to the purpose of God.

I do not intend to say that the cultural forms (i.e., words, sentences, grammatical patterns, metaphors, etc.) in which the biblical content (meaning) is expressed are unimportant merely because they are culturally and historically specific. I hold that the message, in addition to its historico-cultural specificity, has a cross-cultural relevance that the original cultural forms do not have. But I believe that that content must be expressed in the linguistic and cultural forms of the receivers of the message. The cultural forms in which that content is expressed are therefore *extremely* important.

The major difference between the content and the forms in which it is expressed is not one of importance, but one of constancy. The message is to remain constant (see model 10b in chapter 11), while the cultural forms in which it is expressed are to be appropriate to the language and culture in which the expression is being made. I would liken the forms of culture (such as words, customs, ceremonies, and the like) to the piping through which water flows or the wiring over which electricity flows. The content or meanings are like the water that is channeled by the pipes or the electricity that is guided by the wires to produce constructive rather than destructive ends.

4. *A "Biblical Christian Model," contrary to the opinions of many, is not a static model.* It has long been in vogue to label "conservative" any theological stance that takes the Bible seriously. For such positions are seen as dedicated to the conservation and perpetuation of static, "orthodox" doctrinal formulations, organizations, and lifestyles. And it must be admitted that many conservative people, employing static models of Christianity and of life in general, have sought to venerate and preserve the past, to look back for guidelines, and to resist change at any cost. But those who seek to "conserve" biblical Christianity ought not simply to preserve, as if in formaldehyde, past approaches to Christian life and doctrine—approaches that succeeded in their day because they met felt needs, but in our day are static, conveying an air of antiquity and even death.

Biblical Christianity should *imitate* in our day what Jesus, Paul, Augustine,

Aquinas, Luther, Calvin, and Wesley *did* in theirs, not simply *preserve* the theological and organizational products that they produced. Biblical Christianity must not be understood in terms of static, conservative models. When the early church realized that there was a problem with respect to the Greek-speaking widows they did not look to the past but, claiming the leading of the Holy Spirit, faced the problem and worked out a solution (Acts 6:1–6). Though the early church ordinarily required Gentiles first to convert to Jewish culture (symbolized by circumcision) in order to become Christians (Acts 15:1), Paul, Barnabas, and Peter advocated a change in the rules. Then, in a meeting of the church leaders in Jerusalem, they convinced the rest of the leaders to adapt their approach to the realities of the new situation (Acts 15:19–29).

The Christianity that we see in the pages of the New Testament is *not conservative but dynamic, adaptive, unafraid to risk* the old understandings in its desire to face realistically the present and the future in the power of the Holy Spirit. There was about the early churches (as there is today among charismatic Christians) a spirit of adventure and experimentation that characterizes Christians who do not believe that all truth has been discovered but who claim Christ's promise of the leading of the Holy Spirit "into all the truth" (Jn. 16:13). The early Christians were not unconcerned with truth or with the scriptural bases for their action. In fact, it is noteworthy that Acts 15:15–18 records that the apostles sought (Old Testament) scriptural justification for the adaptation that they made.

But concern for truth, coupled with their belief in the continuing leading of the Holy Spirit, led the early Christians to be *devoted to truth in a sense different from the way in which evangelicals ordinarily think of it.* They were not content with the comfortably abstracted formulation of truth that often seems to be the primary concern of contemporary conservatism. The truth for which the early followers of Christ gave themselves had come to them with the kind of impact that comes only through life involvement with those (Jesus and the apostles) who had sold out to that truth. It was *dynamic, impactful truth.* And it was manifested in transformed behavior, not merely in intellectual credence to accurate but static statements concerning that truth. They sought to live out the life of the Christ who called himself the truth (Jn. 14:6; Phil. 1:21). They ventured with Christ, the truth.

This inquiry attempts to be faithful to that truth by recalling us to the dynamism of New Testament Christianity. *I attempt to be orthodox with respect to the truth but venturesome in its application.* For I believe that a part of my responsibility as a Christian is to take that which God has entrusted to me (i.e., the "talent" of my particular training, experience, insight, etc.) and to use it as the master in the parable (Mt. 25:14–30) expected his servants to use (risk) what he had entrusted to them—for the sake of the master's greater gain. Thus, if I am to be truly Christian, *I dare not be simply conservative*, especially in a day when people are turning from and misunderstanding Christianity because they fail to see the dynamic of this truth that once "turned the world upside down" (Acts 17:6).

5. Implicit in all of this is the belief that *truly biblical Christians are not closed-minded.* The venturesomeness and risk of the early Christians (cited above) was not characteristic of their closed-minded contemporaries, the Pharisees and the Judaizers. Nor does it characterize certain of our contemporaries who, in their "naive realism," feel that they (and often they alone) can see God's truth absolutely.

Biblical Christianity is realistic about differences in understanding—though it allows no differences of ultimate allegiance (1 Kings 18; 1 Cor. 12:3). Jews, by and large, continued to practice Jewish Christianity and Greeks, Greek Christianity, with concomitant differences in theological understandings at many points, but with a single allegiance to God (Eph. 4:4–6; Jude 3).

The tendency, especially among American Christians, is to evaluate people and groups according to where they fit doctrinally along a single conservative-liberal scale. Under the influence of the American value system (see Arensberg and Niehoff 1971:207–31 for one valuable description) Americans tend (1) to evaluate cognitive things such as doctrine more highly than behavioral things such as allegiance and (2) to evaluate alternative positions in a polarizing manner as either good or bad, black or white.

The rise of evangelicalism has made it more difficult to categorize people in such a simple unidimensional fashion. For evangelical Christianity is a movement centered in a common allegiance to God through Christ, rather than in allegiance to a single doctrinal statement (Winter 1976). Though Bible-centered, it allows for a variety of denominational and personal interpretations of the Bible. It seeks to be open, rather than closed, to intellectual investigation with its concomitant diversity of understanding concerning biblical Christianity.

To those (e.g., old-line fundamentalists) who evaluate all Christian positions along a single conservative-liberal axis, evangelicals who understand key doctrinal issues differently from their norm can only be classified as "more liberal," or "more toward the liberal end of the spectrum." Their evaluational line might look like this:

Fig. 2.4. Single conservative-liberal axis for understanding theological positions.

A more accurate representation demands a model that includes another dimension: the "closed to innovation and diversity—open to innovation and diversity" dimension.[1] By adding this dimension we arrive at a chart such as the following with typical positions inserted in their appropriate spots:

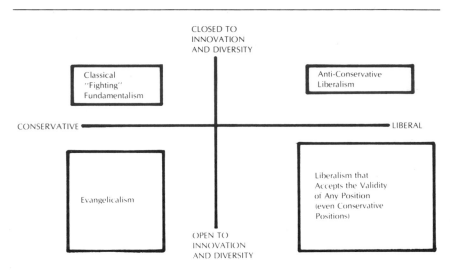

Fig. 2.5. A two-dimensional understanding of theological positions (model 2c).

One important fact that this understanding makes clear is that there is a distinction between closed-mindedness and theological "conservatism." It has often puzzled people in both theological camps to discover open-minded conservatives and closed-minded liberals. If closed-minded conservatives evaluate along a single conservative-liberal axis, they are likely to regard as liberals all those who are open-minded enough to read, discuss without condemning, and occasionally accept ideas from liberals and non-Christians. This is the position of classic fundamentalism. There are, however, rigid, closed-minded persons who are theologically liberal. A single conservative-liberal axis does not allow one to distinguish between them and the theological liberal who is open-minded enough to allow for the validity of more conservative positions.[2]

A second important fact clarified by this understanding is the distinction between the classic fundamentalism of certain groups of theological conserva-

1. I am indebted for this concept to my colleague Dr. Paul Hiebert of the School of World Mission, Fuller Seminary.
2. See Quebedeaux (1974) for an analysis supportive of this position.

tives and the open evangelicalism of other groups that agree theologically with the fundamentalists on almost every major doctrinal issue. Those who call themselves evangelicals tend to range from more closed-minded to more open-minded at the conservative end of the chart.

I see, therefore, a biblical Christian paradigm as characterized by (1) a central allegiance to God through Christ as revealed in the Christian Scriptures, (2) a recognition of the differences between the inspired data of the Scriptures and the fallible interpretations of theologizing human beings, (3) the primacy of the timeless content of the Scriptures over the historico-cultural forms through which that content is communicated to human beings, (4) the dynamic nature of both essential Christianity and the theologizing process, (5) the primacy of the behavioral practice of faith-allegiance to God over the intellectual conceptualizing of Christian doctrine, and (6) the need for openness to innovation and diversity in the development of helpful understandings of God and his workings. On this basis I seek to be true both to my allegiance to God and to the mood of evangelical Protestantism by being open and venturesome.

One further characteristic of this (or any other) paradigm or set of models needs to be specially underlined. This is the fact that *these models will suffer from the inadequacies and impreciseness from which all models suffer.* We seek here to build an understanding of Christianity that is cross-culturally valid and useful. Because there is never a one-to-one fit between model and reality and because this scheme is of necessity but one faltering step in the direction in which we seek to go, I expect that further study and experimentation will lead to modifications and shifts in this perspective. We must not only see Christianity as dynamic, we must also see our understandings of Christianity as dynamic and growing. This perspective is not intended to be a static, final, inspired answer to even the selection of problems here in view. *You, the reader, are therefore free to disagree and to pick and choose those things that you find most valuable from this presentation.* You are furthermore encouraged to join me in the quest for greater insight into these matters.

ALTERNATIVE MIRRORS

If the traditional mirrors of reality are found to be inadequate, it is incumbent upon us to provide alternative mirrors. Quite a number of such mirrors or conceptual models will be employed in the following pages in an attempt to lead the reader to new understandings of certain relationships between Christianity and human culture. Most of these models derive from one or more of the author's fields of specialization: anthropology (including linguistics), communication science (including Bible translation theory), and cross-cultural theology. Though there are many models employed, I have attempted to work them into an overall coherence that will be constructive in the reader's attempt to rethink and to communicate Christian truth more effectively.

In recognition of the fact that the number and novelty of the conceptual models employed could lead to confusion on the part of the reader, I provide a brief overview of them in the appendix. Though each model will be dealt with in detail as we proceed through the book, the reader may find it useful to read that overview at this point. There is a good bit of interdependence among the models that shows up more vividly in such an overview than in the detailed treatment in the body of this volume. For the necessity to arrange the detailed treatment in a particular sequence often requires us to assume a model that has not yet been introduced in order to fully present the model in focus.

The models relate to four basic areas of the subject at hand. The relationship between these areas may be pictured in the following "process" diagram:

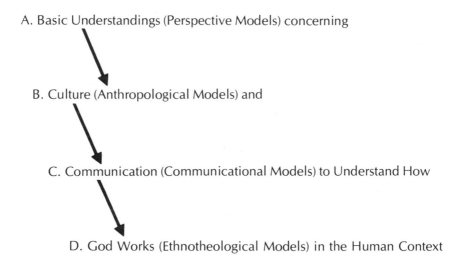

A. Basic Understandings (Perspective Models) concerning

B. Culture (Anthropological Models) and

C. Communication (Communicational Models) to Understand How

D. God Works (Ethnotheological Models) in the Human Context

Fig. 2.6. Process diagram of the areas within which the models employed in this volume cluster.

The development of the book and the overview in the appendix proceed according to this progression.

PART II
THE CULTURAL MATRIX

3. Human Beings in Culture

We have now completed laying the groundwork for the treatment that follows. The first aspect to be dealt with (in chapters 3, 4, and 5) is the cultural matrix within which human beings exist and in terms of which we interact with each other and God. In this chapter we discuss anthropological insight and its application (model 3) including the crucial culture concept (model 3a), the concept of cultural validity (model 3b), and the concept of worldview (model 3c). From a consideration of worldview we proceed to a discussion of the relationship between different cultural conclusions and the different assumptions from which various peoples start. We conclude the chapter by dealing with the question of cultural (and theological) determinism.

THE CULTURE CONCEPT (Model 3a)

Thoughtful people have long discussed and debated the nonbiological component(s) of humanness. Such debates within western culture have often centered around whether a human being is properly regarded as consisting of two parts (body and soul) or of three (body, soul, and spirit). Theologians, in addition, have given attention to the relationship between the non-corporeal part(s) of human beings and the "image of God" in which we were created (Gen. 1:26). That a human consists of more than merely a physical body and that it is this "moreness" that distinguishes the human from the animals has seldom been disputed.

Many have tended to define this "moreness" in terms of the human ability to reason. Some have pointed more to artistic and musical creations as the supreme demonstration of human superiority over animals and, not infrequently, of our closeness to God. A person knowledgeable about such things as art, music, and philosophy came to be called "cultured." The use of the term "culture" in this way was borrowed from French. Many English-speakers still think of the term "culture" as referring primarily to artistic or philosophical expertise or even to good manners and other accoutrements of the "upper" social classes.

There is, however, a more technical sense in which the word "culture" (Ger. *Kultur*) has been employed in Germany from at least as early as the beginning of the nineteenth century. This was the usage that the pioneer anthropologist E. B. Tylor borrowed into English in 1871 to designate *the total nonbiologically transmitted heritage of man.* [1] This usage has become customary in the behavioral sciences and, increasingly, in informed popular thought.

A major reason for the development of this understanding of the concept is the fact that a whole academic discipline has devoted itself largely to the study of culture. It would seem to be beyond dispute that anthropology's "most significant accomplishment . . . has been the extension and clarification of the concept of culture" (Kroeber 1950:87). Certainly "the concept of culture is . . . the anthropologist's most significant contribution to the missionary endeavor" (Luzbetak 1963:59). It is, to my way of thinking, an equally significant contribution to further development in theological understanding.

In this respect, we can seek enhancement in understanding through the application of the culture model to at least three areas of concern. The first (and most difficult) of these areas is the influence of culture on ourselves. If, as here contended, we are all thoroughly immersed in and totally influenced (though not totally determined) by our culture, it behooves us to look for and to analyze the ways in which such immersion affects us. Second, we need to understand how the culture in which our hearers live and move affects them. And third, we need to discover how God in his interactions with human beings relates to the cultures in which they (though not he) are immersed.

Culture is seen by anthropologists as

the integrated system of learned behavior patterns which are characteristic of the members of a society and which are not the result of biological inheritance (Hoebel 1972:6).

Kroeber and Kluckhohn have summarized the culture concept as follows:

Culture consists of patterns, explicit and implicit, of and for behavior acquired and transmitted by symbols, constituting the distinctive achievement of human groups, including their embodiments in artifacts; the essential core of culture consists of traditional (i.e. historically derived and selected) ideas and especially their attached values; culture systems may, on the one hand, be considered as products of action, on the other as conditioning elements of further action (1952:357).

It is this understanding of culture that will be employed throughout the present volume. Perceiving of reality in this way has become fundamental and germinal to the behavioral-science perspective in which this book participates. This perspective sees the relationship between culture and human beings as in many respects similar to that between water and fish. Humans are understood to be totally, inextricably immersed in culture. Each human individual is born into a particular socio-cultural context. From that point on persons are conditioned by the members of their society in countless, largely unconscious,

---

1. See Kroeber and Kluckhohn 1952 for an exhaustive discussion of the history and contemporary usage of the term.

ways to accept as natural and to follow rather uncritically the cultural patterns of that society.

Each of us is thus shaped in the nonbiological portion of our being by the culture into which we are born. We are shaped by a culture transmitted to us by the adults in our life. Humans thus may be regarded as culture-shaped and culture-transmitting beings. But we not only are shaped by and participate in the transmission of our culture; we also influence it and contribute to its reshaping. Indeed, as far as the behavioral sciences can tell, humans originally created culture. This ability to produce, bear, and transmit culture provides the sharpest distinction observable by naturalistic behavioral scientists between humans and animals.

Our culture is that in terms of which our life is organized. It may be looked at as the rules guiding our lives (Spradley 1972:18–34)—rules developed from millions of agreements between the members of our society. We remain largely unconscious of the vast majority of these rules or patterns. With respect to others, such as certain of those governing our language, courtesy, eating, defecating, and the like, our elders have chosen to invest a considerable amount of energy in making us aware of the rules by which we are expected to conduct these aspects of our lives.

It is comparatively irrelevant whether or not we are conscious of the rules and patterns that govern our lives. The influence of these patterns upon our lives is all pervasive. We are not as free as we may imagine ourselves to be. Keesing and Keesing instructively discuss the "rules" or cultural agreements governing one aspect of American courtship behavior as follows:

Consider the problem that a single American girl continually encounters of where to place herself on the roughly forty inches of front seat of an American car when a male is driving. Does she sit in the middle? Close up? Against the door? Clearly there is a code here, and clearly it is based on communications and shared understandings about the girl's relationship to the driver. In long-standing American courtship ritual, she is supposed to begin somewhere in the middle; and as the relationship becomes more intimate, she acknowledges this by moving closer and closer to him. If she is angry, she moves against the door, expressing coolness and distantness. If the driver is ineligible for courtship, she sits in a neutral position; to move against the door would communicate the wrong thing. How soon the girl moves over, and how far, clearly expresses something about what kind of girl she is as well as what her relationship to the driver is. Such codes are learned but not written; and constantly tested and compared but seldom talked about. They are premises and rules and meanings we draw on to communicate and to understand one another, yet we are rarely conscious of them (1971:21–22).

A large number of similar examples fill the pages of such books as *The Silent Language* and *The Hidden Dimension* by E. T. Hall and *Body Language* by J. Fast.

Not only is our physical behavior governed by such cultural patterns. Our mental behavior is likewise pervasively influenced by our culture. Our culture shapes both our acting and our thinking. Those of us who have been brought up within a variety of Euro-American culture think, reason, and perceive of the world around us in ways that are more similar to the ways of other members of Euro-American culture than to the ways of any member of a culture of New Guinea or Africa.

It is as though we—or the people of any other society—grow up perceiving the world through glasses with distorting lenses. The things, events, and relationships we assume to be "out there" are in fact filtered through this perceptual screen (Keesing and Keesing 1971:21).

Culture, therefore, provides the model(s) of reality that govern our perception, although we are likely to be unaware of the influence of our culture upon us. For the way we understand things seems to us to be "just natural" or "human nature." It's just natural to eat three meals a day, isn't it? It's only human nature for teenagers to rebel against their elders, isn't it? The answer to both questions is, of course, No.

But we wouldn't know this unless we had been exposed to information concerning a multitude of other cultures where it is considered "just natural" to eat only one or two meals a day or where there is no pattern of teenage rebellion similar to that which we carefully teach our youth (see Mead 1928). There are a variety of culturally governed logics or conceptual frameworks. There are, therefore, a variety of culturally governed logical behaviors. And many of these perceptions, conceptualizations, and logical behaviors will differ markedly from what our culture has conditioned us to perceive or to regard as the logical thing to think or do under similar circumstances.

Unless we have been exposed to such information from other cultures and have learned to appreciate the fact that they view reality through very different cultural glasses than our own, we tend (unconsciously) to look down our noses at their behavior. That behavior seems strange to us, irrational or even wrong. Our customs seem to us to be the right ones because they are (to us) the "natural" ones.

To view other people's ways of life in terms of our own cultural glasses is called ethnocentrism. Becoming conscious of, and analytical about, our own cultural glasses is a painful business. We do it best by learning about other people's glasses. Although we can never take our glasses off to find out what the world is "really like," or try looking through anyone else's without ours on as well, we can at least learn a good deal about our own prescription (Keesing and Keesing 1971:21).

The nearest we can come, then, to arriving at an antidote to an ethnocentric "monocultural" perception of reality is to develop what may be termed a "cross-cultural perspective." This is a perspective that always takes into account the fact that there are a variety of culturally governed perceptions of any given segment of reality. It is the intent of the author to apply such a cross-cultural perspective to the topics dealt with throughout this volume.

CULTURAL VALIDITY (Model 3b)

"Cultural validity" is a doctrine developed by anthropology (ordinarily referred to as "cultural relativism") that maintains that an observer should be careful to evaluate a culture first in terms of its own values, goals, and focuses before venturing to compare it (either positively or negatively) with any other culture. This doctrine was developed to combat the prevailing ethnocentric tendency to evaluate other cultures to their disadvantage by always focusing on areas of life in which the evaluator's culture has specialized. Westerners thus tend to evaluate as "primitive" all cultures that do not show a degree of technological development comparable to that of western cultures. The cultural-validity model is based on the recognition that certain cultures have specialized (often "warped" themselves) in one area of life while others have specialized in other areas of life (e.g., technology for certain cultures, solid family structures for others). Comparisons between cultures tend, therefore, to be made unfairly on the basis of whatever criteria the one who does the comparing deems most important.

Anthropologists have found that "it is objectively impossible to distinguish world-wide levels of cultural progress" (Beals and Hoijer 1959:720). They have concluded that cultures are to be regarded not as assignable to some level of overall superiority or inferiority with respect to other cultures but, rather, as more or less equal to each other in their overall ability to meet the needs felt by their members. In this sense it is felt that any given culture shapes a way of life that must be seen as valid for those immersed in it. Cultures are therefore both as good as each other and as bad as each other in shaping that way of life. None is anywhere near perfect, since all are shaped and operated by sinful human beings. But none in its healthy state is to be considered invalid, inadequate, or unusable by God and humankind (see Turnbull 1972 for a description of an unhealthy culture).

Cultural validity (relativism), says Melville Herskovits, one of its most active advocates,

is a philosophy which, in recognizing the values set up by every society to guide its own life, lays stress on the dignity inherent in every body of custom, and on the need for tolerance of conventions though they may differ from one's own. Instead of underscoring differences from absolute norms . . . the relativistic point of view brings into relief the validity of every set of norms for the people whose lives are guided by them, and the values these represent (1948:77).

"The very core of cultural relativism," he continues, "is the discipline that comes of respect for differences—of mutual respect" (ibid.).

This doctrine is, on the cultural level, what personal acceptance (the Golden Rule) is on the individual level (Mayers 1974). It recommends that, rather than moralizing about the good or bad in the given culture (or in the given individual), one should *accept the validity* of that culture (or individual), whether or not one's own set of values predisposes one to *approve* of the behavior of that culture (or individual). A belief in the validity of other cultures does not obligate one to approve of such customs as cannibalism, widow burning, infanticide, premarital sex, polygamy, and the like. But it does insist that *one take such customs seriously within the cultural context in which they occur* and attempt to appreciate the importance of their function within that context.

Nor does acceptance of cultural validity commit one to change one's behavior in the direction of the values or practices of another culture. On the contrary, a commitment to accept the validity of any culture on its own terms carries with it the obligation for persons to take their own culture just as seriously as they take others. It is an unfortunate fact that many uninformed people, in the name of cultural relativism, have turned to a moral or ethical relativism. They reason that since a given custom (e.g., premarital sexual license) seems to function quite well in some other culture, it is permissible in theirs. The doctrine of cultural validity (relativism) does not imply such a view (see Mayers 1974).[2]

The previously prevalent attitude, both within and outside anthropology, was that of cultural evolutionism. The evolutionists, strongly influenced by the traditional ethnocentrism of western culture, "saw individual cultures mainly as illustrative of particular stages in a world-wide evolutionary sequence" (Beals and Hoijer 1959:720). They, of course, placed our so-called civilized (i.e., European) cultures at the top of their pyramid and arranged the technologically less developed cultures in descending order down to the technologically most "primitive" societies at the bottom. This ethnocentrism was developed in the crucible of a society that tends "to arrange objects on a single scale of value, from best to worst, biggest to smallest, cheapest to most expensive, etc." (Mead 1964:113)—a society that insists on evaluating all other perspectives toward life as either black or white, good or bad, superior or inferior. Since "judgments are based on experience, and experience is interpreted by each individual in terms of his enculturation" (Herskovits 1948:78), cultural difference is interpreted by Euro-Americans as cultural inferiority.

In a culture where absolute values are stressed, the relativism of a world that encompasses many ways of living [is] difficult to comprehend. Rather, it [offers] a field-day for value-judgments based on the degree to which a given body of customs resembles or differs from those of Euro-American culture (Herskovits 1948:78).

However, while much of the thinking public in the western world converted

2. A popular misunderstanding of cultural relativism is presented and rightly condemned by McGavran (1974:2–6) without taking seriously either contemporary anthropological understandings or the great potential for Christian use of the doctrine.

(at least nominally) to the relativistic viewpoint, the western church (reinforced by ethnocentric theological thinking that is often insensitive to the validity of other cultures), along with a large percentage of the rest of the population, has for the most part retained the evolutionary position. Much of the Christian populace, for example, has simply continued to assume that such features of our society as monogamy, democracy, our type of educational system, individualism, capitalism, the "freedoms," literacy, technological development, military supremacy, etc. are all products of our association with God and therefore can be pointed to as indications of the superiority of our culture over all other cultures. A balanced comparison of our culture with other cultures, however, shows us to be strong only at certain points, while very weak at others. We are strong in technological areas and, as a concomitant of this, militarily. Our system of government, borrowed from the pre-Christian Greek city-states, seems to us to be superior to other forms of government but is showing increasingly an inability to cope effectively with a multitude of the problems facing it. Monogamy, too, came to us from our pre-Christian cultural forebears. It is very difficult to support the contention that such cultural strengths as these (if they be strengths) are the result of the influence of Christianity in our culture. It is easier, and perhaps more accurate, to suggest that when individuals and groups within our culture commit themselves to Christ they frequently (not always) use these and other features of our culture in a more Christian way than those who do not have such a Christian commitment.

When one turns to the weaknesses of our culture, the myth of our cultural superiority falls to pieces. For example, we have poured so much of our resources into technological development that we have created social disorientation and disruption at every level of our society. Many families fall apart because they are unable to compete with our so-called educational system. The latter, for the sake of some imaginary "better" future (defined in technological and materialistic terms) indoctrinates our youth against the past in general and their parents in particular (including any religious commitment they may have). Our quest for freedom and individualism mitigates against the development of close friendships, neighborliness, and stable marriages. Our extreme competitiveness, expressed interpersonally, intergenerationally, economically, vocationally, politically, and even between churches, is ripping our society apart. The naturalistic worldview at the center of our culture, the depersonalization of our people, the uncontrolled competitiveness between the various segments of our society, the choice usually to value the unknown and untried above the known but imperfect—these and so many other features of our society point not to its superiority but to its sickness.[3]

3. See Kluckhohn 1949, chapter 9, "An Anthropologist Looks at the United States," for a fine discussion of both the weaknesses and the strengths of our culture.

Anthropologists can point to any number of other cultures that, though weak where we are strong, are strong where we are weak. None of these has achieved nearly what ours has technologically or medically. But we have not achieved what they have in social organization. Many of them have achieved a balanced approach to life that is seriously lacking in our own culture. And the cultural equilibrium and its concomitant increase of individual security produced by such a balance make such cultures look strikingly superior to ours overall. They seem to meet the psychological and personal needs of their members more effectively than Euro-American culture does. Though they have their own problems, one wonders if they are as serious as ours in fundamental areas of life.

The point is not simply to castigate our culture or to produce in us an envy of cultures that seem to have achieved a better balance than ours has. The point is to suggest that our feelings of cultural superiority are completely unwarranted and utterly untenable in the face of the mass of anthropological data coming to us concerning the six thousand or more other cultures of the world. True, these cultures often show serious difficulty in areas where ours shows strength. But this fact merely supports a major point that the doctrine of cultural validity is attempting to make: *that no culture, especially not ours, can be regarded as superior in every way to every other culture.* That is, there has not been an evolutionary development of cultures from a state of overall inferiority to a state of overall superiority. Our culture is thus no better overall than any other culture, though in the areas of our expertise we may claim superiority. In comparing Euro-American cultures with other cultures, we must give at least equal attention to areas where other cultures show strength, not simply to those areas where our culture is strong. For in the areas of their primary concern, others may show us the utter inappropriateness (not to mention the unchristian arrogance) of our ethnocentric tendency to evaluate them in terms of their achievement or lack of it in areas of our strength.

A cross-cultural perspective on our culture and the influence of Christianity in it gives no support to the assumption that through the influence of Christianity ours has become the most ideal culture in the world. Christianity has indeed had an important impact on our culture but so has human sinfulness —and the latter appears to be winning out, culturally as well as individually. For this reason and because the Christian knows that God is continually at work in every culture (not just ours) at all times (Acts 14:17), it behooves us to accept a good bit of the doctrine of cultural validity. We need to recognize that cultures are essentially equal (rather than superior or inferior to each other) with respect to at least three things: (1) their adequacy for those immersed in them, (2) the pervasiveness of the expression of human sinfulness manifested in and through them, and (3) their potential usefulness as vehicles of God's interaction with humanity. In fact, the Christian goes beyond the atheist at least in recognizing that cultures are not only relative to each other but are also relative (although in this case inferior) to the supracultural (Smalley 1955:60).

WORLDVIEW (Model 3c)

Cultures[4] pattern perceptions of reality into conceptualizations of what reality can or should be, what is to be regarded as actual, probable, possible, and impossible. These conceptualizations form what is termed the "worldview" of the culture. The worldview is the central systematization of conceptions of reality to which the members of the culture assent (largely unconsciously) and from which stems their value system. The worldview lies at the very heart of culture, touching, interacting with, and strongly influencing every other aspect of the culture.

The worldview of any given culture presumably originated in a series of agreements by the members of the original group concerning their perception of reality and how they should regard and react toward that reality. This, like all other aspects of culture, has undergone constant change so that it now differs to a greater or lesser extent from the original worldview and from other extant worldviews that have developed (in related cultures) from that common-ancestor worldview.

A worldview is imposed upon the young of a society by means of familiar processes of teaching and learning. In this way each youngster reared in a given culture is conditioned to interpret reality in terms of the conceptual system of that culture. If a person's culture conceives of the relationship between the universe and humanity as a dominance-submission relationship in which persons simply submit uncomplainingly to circumstances without seeking to gain dominance over them, those persons will ordinarily learn to perceive their relationship to the universe in these terms. If a person's culture conceives of disease as the result of the activities of personal malevolent spirits, that person will ordinarily learn to perceive any disease in his or her experience to be so caused. However one's culture conceives of the division of time or space, one will ordinarily come to perceive of them in these terms.

The position (model) here espoused sees the worldview of a culture or subculture as the "central control box" of that culture.[5] With respect to the organization or patterning of the culture, the worldview may be seen as the organizer of the conceptual system taught to and employed by the members of that culture/subculture. With respect to the behavior or performance of the participants in the culture/subculture, the worldview may be thought of as that which governs the application of the culture's conceptualizations of their relationships to reality. These facts and some of their implications may be represented in the visualization of this model in Fig. 3.1 on p. 54.

---

4. It is technically incorrect to personalize culture in this way. It is not culture that does such and such a thing; it is the people who operate culture who do whatever is done. For brevity, however, and because it is traditional, we engage in a convenient fiction and speak of cultures as if they did things on their own.

5. See Redfield 1953, chapter 4, for a more detailed discussion of worldview.

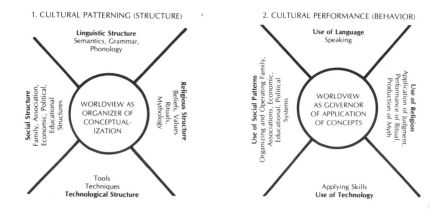

Fig. 3.1. Worldview in relation to cultural patterning and cultural performance.

Everything in the patterning and the performance of culture ties into this central conceptualization. The centrality and consequent importance of the worldview become very clear when one considers the centrality to life of the functions served by the worldview of a culture.[6] A people's worldview is their basic model of reality.

Five major functions may be described:

1. The first function is the *explanation* of how and why things got to be as they are and how and why they continue or change. The worldview embodies for a people, whether explicitly or implicitly, the basic assumptions concerning ultimate things on which they base their lives. If the worldview of a people conditions them to believe that the universe is operated by a number of invisible personal forces largely beyond their control, this will affect both their understanding of and their response to "reality." If, however, a people's worldview explains that the universe operates by means of a large number of impersonal, cause-and-effect operations which, if learned by people, can be employed by them to control the universe, the attitude of these people toward "reality" will be much different.

These ideas are customarily articulated in the mythology[7] of a people. This

6. See Malinowski 1925 and Keesing 1958 for a similar discussion of *religion*. They use the term "religion" to designate that part of culture that I (and, increasingly, contemporary anthropological orthodoxy) label "worldview."

7. The term "myth" is here used in its technical sense to denote any story (whether historically factual or not) that is employed to unfold, support, or explain a part of the worldview or practice of a people. Under this usage the Bible may be technically classed as mythology. Evangelical Christians contend, however, that the Bible is historically factual whether or not the term "myth" is applied to it.

mythology takes a variety of forms from culture to culture. In a large number of cultures one would look to fables, proverbs, riddles, songs, and other forms of folklore for overt and covert indications of the worldview. In more complex societies one finds, in addition to the folklore, printed literature which often overtly philosophizes the mythology of, for example, science, religion, politics, etc. The portion of the worldview and mythology of which people are conscious is thus often more easily observable in the various subcultures within western (i.e., Euro-American) culture than it is in preliterate societies.

2. The worldview of a people serves an *evaluational*—a judging and validating—function. The basic institutions, values, and goals of a society are ethnocentrically evaluated as best and, therefore, sanctioned by the worldview of their culture or subculture. Other people's customs are judged to be inferior or at least inappropriate. And for most of the cultures of the world the ultimate ground for these sanctions is supernatural. It is by their God or gods that most people understand their worldview and their culture as a whole to be validated. He/they are seen to value these customs more than those of any other peoples. And even when no external supernatural is postulated (as in communism and naturalistic American ideology) a sort of "internal supernatural" is generally present in the virtual deifying of such concepts as communism or "the American way of life." Thus, in the American conceptual system we find sanctions (supernatural or pseudo-supernatural) for such institutions as democratic government, a capitalistic economy, and monogamous marriage, for such values as scientism (with or without God), individual rights and freedoms, and private property, and for such goals as world peace (on our terms), personal and national prosperity, and a college education for everyone who wants one. As with its explanatory function, the evaluational function of a people's worldview is integral to every aspect of the life of the social group. All important and valued behavior, whether of the in-group or of other groups, whether classified as economic, political, "scientific," social, educational, or whatever, is judged in terms of a culture's worldview assumptions, beliefs, values, meanings, and sanctions.

3. The worldview of a group also provides *psychological reinforcement* for that group. At points of anxiety or crisis in life it is to one's conceptual system that one turns for the encouragement to continue or the stimulus to take other action. Crisis times such as death, birth, and illness; transition times such as puberty, marriage, planting and harvest; times of uncertainty; times of elation—all tend to heighten anxiety or in some other way require adjustment between behavior and belief. And each tends to be dealt with in a reinforcing way by the worldview of a society. Often this reinforcement takes the form of ritual or ceremony in which many people participate (e.g., funerals, harvest celebrations, initiation or graduation ceremonies). Frequently there are also individual worldview-required reinforcement observances such as prayer, trance, scientific experimentation, or "thinking the matter through" for the purpose of squaring a prospective decision with one's conceptual underpinning. In such ways the worldview of a group provides security and support for

the behavior of the group in a world that appears to be filled with capricious uncontrollable forces.

4. The worldview of a culture or subculture serves an *integrating* function. It systematizes and orders for them their perceptions of reality into an overall design. In terms of this integrated and integrating perspective, then, a people conceptualizes what reality should be like and understands and interprets the multifarious events to which they are exposed. A people's worldview "establishes and validates basic premises about the world and man's place in it; and it relates the strivings and emotions of men to them" (Keesing and Keesing 1971:303).

Thus in its explanatory, evaluational, reinforcing, and integrating functions, worldview lies at the heart of a culture, providing the basic model(s) for bridging the gap between the "objective" reality outside people's heads and the culturally agreed upon perception of that reality inside their heads. The worldview formulates for the members of a social group the conceptualizations in terms of which they perceive reality. It filters out for them most glimpses of reality that do not conform to the beliefs concerning the way that reality should be. It provides for its adherents

a system of symbols which acts to establish powerful, pervasive, and long-lasting moods and motivations in men by formulating conceptions of a general order of existence and clothing these with such an aura of factuality that the moods and motivations seem uniquely realistic (Geertz 1966:4).

5. A group's worldview does not completely determine the perception of all its members at all times. Though there is characteristically a very high degree of conservatism to such conceptualization, there is change in this as well as in all other areas of culture. People do on occasion shift in their perceptions of reality. They come to see things in ways slightly or drastically different from the ways that their worldview has conditioned them to perceive of them. They change one or more of their conceptual models and reinterpret their perceptions. And such shifts in perception, especially if engaged in and reported by socially influential persons, may be accepted by other members of the social group. This results in groups altering their conceptual structuring, their models of reality.

Thus over a period of time groups such as the ancient Hebrews moved from belief in many gods to a strong concept of monotheism (Kautzsch 1904). Likewise, large segments of western culture have moved through Renaissance, Industrial Revolution, and American Frontierism from a belief in the supremacy of the Judeo-Christian God to a belief in the actual or potential all-sufficiency of the technological human.

Ordinarily such conceptual transformation takes place slowly. Sometimes, though, the pressure for rapid change is great. Particularly in the face of such pressure we observe a fifth function of a people's worldview, which relates directly to the more disintegrative aspects of culture change. That function may be labeled *adaptational*. Wallace suggests that inherent in worldviews is the ability to reduce "internal structural contradictions" that occur in the process of culture change (1966:27). People, by adjusting their worldviews, devise means for resolving conflict and reducing cultural dissonance. That is, in circumstances of cultural distortion or disequilibrium there is a resilient quality to worldviews by means of which people reconcile hitherto apparently irreconcilable differences between old understandings and new ones. If a society gets into ideological difficulty "it may be far easier to reinterpret values than to reorganize society" (Wallace 1966:29).

Where mutually contradictory cognitions (including perceptions, knowledge, motives, values, and hopes) are entertained, the individual must act to reduce the dissonance. While, theoretically, he can do this by changing the real world in some respect, so as to modify the data coming in, he may also achieve the same effect by modifying his perceptions of self and of the real world in such a way that one horn of the dilemma is no longer recognized (Wallace 1966:29).

In extreme cases this adaptation to changing perception calls for major replacement and what Wallace calls "revitalization." But short of such drastic "cultural surgery" the adaptational quality of worldviews is constantly in evidence in all sorts of culture-change situations, whether these be mild or intensive.

DIFFERENT WORLDVIEW ASSUMPTIONS
LEAD TO DIFFERENT CONCLUSIONS

As we shall point out in chapter 5, there is a good bit of similarity to human behavior in spite of cultural differences. There is even a considerable body of evidence to suggest that human reasoning processes are essentially the same no matter what one's culture is. For this reason it has been stated that humans differ not so much in the processes by means of which they reach their conclusions as in their starting points.[8] That is, the members of different cultures arrive at different conclusions concerning reality because they have started from different assumptions.

Note, for example, the conflict between underlying assumptions in the events recorded in Acts 14:8–18. Paul and Barnabas had healed a lame man in the town of Lystra. A considerable commotion arose over the event because the Lystrans assumed that only the gods could effect such a healing. When they saw what happened they concluded that Paul and Barnabas were gods and began to worship and offer sacrifices to them. The assumption in the

8. Nida 1960:90–91 says: "The fundamental processes of reasoning of all peoples are essentially the same, but the premises on which such reasoning rests and the basic categories that influence the judgment of different peoples are somewhat different. . . . Men differ . . . not so much in their reasoning powers as in their starting points."

apostles' minds, of course, was that by healing the lame man they would enhance their witness in that place. Typical (non-Christian) Americans observing such an event would be likely to conclude that Paul was simply a good psychologist, since they would assume a naturalistic (not a supernaturalistic) explanation for such events.

In Acts 28:1–6 we see the people of Melita arriving at a conclusion similar to that of the Lystrans. They, too, assumed that only gods could survive the bite of a poisonous snake. Americans observing such an event would again come to a different conclusion because their assumptions would be different.

We assume that the natural universe is predictable, understandable, and scientifically describable. We therefore attempt to understand and describe the causes, or at least the factors involved in such phenomena as storms (and weather in general), sickness and health, misfortune and success. If something happens we are determined to at least find out how it happened, whether or not we can explain why. And this determination to probe, to analyze, to explain just "comes naturally" to us because our culture assumes that it can and should be done.

But the people of other cultures start from other assumptions concerning the universe and, of course, come out with very different conclusions. Their logic may be just as good (or bad) as ours and the way they reason from assumption to conclusion may be similar to the way we would do it, but their basic (worldview) assumptions may be very different. Their assumptions, too, may be just as valid as ours, but focused in on a part of the data that we ignore. For example, there is a great deal about the universe that defies neat description even when the most precise western scientific techniques are applied. But we, in our faith in the ability of human science to master any and every problem, ordinarily choose to ignore the capricious, unpredictable aspects of the natural universe. In fact, we are often so focused in on the *how* or *immediate why* of happenings (e.g., earthquakes and other natural disasters, the geological record of prehistory, the march of human history), that we seldom concern ourselves with the *ultimate why* of such happenings.

Many cultures, however, teach those immersed in them to show much more concern for the ultimate causes of things and less concern for the details of how they come about. To these societies the universe seems a good bit less predictable and understandable. They cannot be content simply to describe *why* a person contracted a certain disease; they want to know *how* it was that that person got ill and not another. And their concern leads them to regard the universe as basically capricious (rather, in the hands of capricious personal beings) and unpredictable.

If there is a tragedy, it is due to the whim or displeasure of a personal spirit. Radios, automobiles, airplanes, etc. likewise may be understood to have come about due primarily to the whim of a supernatural being who chose to give to certain people the knowledge and skill to produce them. For, they must assume, only God could give people the ability to perform such wonders. The fact that the members of such cultures start with a different set of assumptions from ours determines that they will arrive at conclusions different from ours.

As members of an individualistic western culture, Americans are increasingly concerned that up to the present women have not been regarded as "equal" to men. We define "equality" in terms of the right of a person to move freely both geographically and socially, to compete freely for employment or leadership, to speak out freely, to be free from tasks that we regard as drudgery, etc. That is, *we link equality with freedom*, we judge that men have heretofore been allowed greater freedom than women, and we conclude, therefore, that the position of women is unequal to that of men, since it is not the same with respect to the possession of individual freedom. In order to solve the problem, we seek to equalize the position of the sexes vis-à-vis this single criterion of equality. And given our basic assumptions, this is the direction in which we must move.

But suppose we, like a large number of the world's cultures, assumed that the most valuable thing a culture can give to its women is not freedom but *security*. Whereas we might say, "A woman is so valuable as an individual that she should be just as free as possible," such a society might reason, "A woman is such a valuable member of society that she should be made just as secure as possible." Starting from this latter assumption, these cultures frequently conclude that women must be provided with (1) secure marriage and home (secured often by such customs as brideprice, polygamy, and the levirate), and (2) a relatively routine and restricted set of expected achievements in order that (3) she may in turn provide a maximum of security for the newest and most vulnerable members of the society, the children. In such societies "equality" between the sexes means the provision of different things for men and women—security for women, freedom for men. There seems to be no feeling of compulsion on the part of these societies to give both men and women the same kind of thing, since they regard male and female roles as complementary (i.e., nonoverlapping). They therefore seek as much as possible to do away with all competition between the sexes. Furthermore, ideally the cultural assignment of greater freedom to men is to enable them to use that freedom to assure greater security for the women.

Certainly in terms of their assumptions (and probably even in terms of our own) high security for women is just as valuable as (more valuable than?) greater freedom for men. Likewise the right of women to wield almost total power over young boys and all girls may be ultimately just as valuable as the right of men to wield political power. Thus the status of men and women in such a society may be "equal," though their roles are utterly different from the roles that we in our society feel betoken equality. For equality to them can mean "equal but thoroughly different," whereas for us it is coming more and more to mean sameness.

In this same vein the moulding influence of culture may be indicated by charting several typical examples of different assumptions leading to different conclusions. (The tribe or area in which the custom is found is given in parentheses.)

Cultural Feature	Assumption	Conclusion
Clothing	1. Immodest to go naked (U.S.A.).	1. Must wear clothes even to bed.
	2. One covers one's body only if hiding something (Gava people Nigeria).	2. Go naked to prove yourself.
	3. For ornamentation only (Higi people Nigeria).	3. Wear on "occasion" only. Rearrange or change in public.
Buying	1. Impersonal, economic transaction (U.S.A.).	1. Fixed prices. No interest in seller as a person. Get it over quickly.
	2. Social. Person-to-person (Africa, Asia, Latin America).	2. Dicker over price. Establish personal relationship. Take time.
Youthfulness	1. Desirable (U.S.A.).	1. Look young, act young. Cosmetics.
	2. Tolerated. To be overcome (Africa).	2. Prove yourself mature. Don't act young.
Age	1. Undesirable (U.S.A.).	1. Dreaded. Old people unwanted.
	2. Desirable (Africa).	2. Old people revered.
Education	1. Primarily formal, outside home, teacher-centered (U.S.A.).	1. Formal schools. Hired specialists.
	2. Primarily informal, in the home, learner-centered, traditional (Africa).	2. Learn by doing. Discipleship. Proverbs and folktales.
Family	1. Centered around spouses (U.S.A.).	1. Compatibility of spouses all-important.
	2. For the children (Africa).	2. Mother-child relationship paramount.
Rapid Change	1. Good. Change="Progress" (U.S.A.).	1. Encourage rapid change and innovation.
	2. Threat to security (Africa).	2. Conservatism valued. Aim at stability.

Fig. 3.2. Chart of the relationship between cultural assumptions and conclusions.

In these and every other aspect of life we are moulded by our cultures to make assumptions concerning reality and to act on the basis of those assumptions to work out the details of life.

ARE WE DETERMINED BY CULTURE?

For some time now an impression of determinism has been given by much anthropological and psychological literature. It appears that an ever increasing number of the attitudes and actions that we have previously attributed to free will are actually rather strictly determined by the cultural, social, and psychological forces to which we are subject. Certain behavioral scientists have been so impressed with the influence of these factors on our lives that they believe everything about human life is well-nigh absolutely determined (e.g., Skinner 1971, White 1949). Such a belief is, however, a matter of faith based on the fact that the more we learn about culture (including society and psychology) the less scope seems to remain for free will.

Leslie White, for example, in dealing with the individual in relation to culture, simply states that

the individual . . . is merely an organization of cultural forces and elements that have impinged upon him from the outside and which find their overt expression through him. . . . the individual is but the expression of a supra-biological cultural tradition in somatic form (1949:167).

B. F. Skinner states that "autonomous man" (that is, humankind with some freedom of self-determination) "is a device used to explain what we cannot explain in any other way" (1971:191). This kind of explanation of human activity he labels "pre-scientific" and pleads for the abolishment of such thinking. For, he says, in a statement of faith that at one point he admits seems inconsistent (p. 21), "a scientific analysis of behavior dispossesses autonomous man and turns the control he has been said to exert over to the environment" (p. 96).

The positions of White and Skinner within the behavioral sciences are not entirely dissimilar from the theological determinism advanced by those who hold to extreme views of predestination. Indeed, Skinner in support of his position broadly states that "theologians have accepted the fact that man must be predestined to do what an omniscient God knows he will do" (1971:17). Theological determinism, of course, sees God rather than culture as the determining agent (a considerable improvement over a blind, unreasoning force like culture). Furthermore, theological determinism is more difficult to argue against, since it is based less on empirical descriptions of real-life data than cultural determinism purports to be.

The advocates of both positions share a faith in an external force (whether God or culture) that absolutely determines the destinies of human beings. The starting point for this faith seems to differ. In the case of theological determinism the starting assumption seems to be: since God is all-powerful and *can* determine anything, he *does* determine everything. With cultural determinism, on the other hand, the reasoning seems to proceed from the shock of being continually forced to recognize that more and more of the behavior we once attributed to free will is largely (they would say totally) explainable in terms of the social conditioning to which a person has been subjected. Even murder and rape, for example, are now often interpreted in such a way that the individual's accountability for such acts is out of focus.

Whether or not such extreme determinism is warranted is a matter of considerable debate both within theology and within the behavioral sciences. And those who openly label their views "deterministic" become very controversial. But, to return to the behavioral sciences alone, even many anthropologists, sociologists, and psychologists who do not go to such an extreme position make statements concerning the pervasiveness of cultural conditioning that lead others to assume that they are adopting a deterministic position. In fact, some of my readers may feel that I have moved too far in that direction. *The model here presented is not a deterministic model* even though it may appear so to those who are accustomed to thinking of human beings as largely self-determining.

Rather, though the case made by the behavioral sciences that human behavior is *largely* conditioned is convincing, I don't feel that the facts warrant the kind of faith pledged by White and Skinner in the eventual proof of absolute determinism. That is, though the assumption may have once been that human behavior was perhaps 85 percent free and only 15 percent determined, it appears to me that the insights of the behavioral sciences require us to suggest that all (100 percent) of human behavior is *conditioned* or *influenced* by cultural and psychological factors, but that this conditioning, though pervasive, falls somewhat short of total determination.

Likewise, in the theological realm I attempt to distinguish between what God in his omnipotence *can* do and what in his dealings with human beings he *chooses* to do. To me, a multitude of scriptural examples convincingly indicate that in major ways God (who has the power to do otherwise) for some reason chooses to allow human beings a fair degree of autonomy. He then holds us responsible for the use of it. I am convinced by the teaching of passages such as the parable of the Talents, David's sin with Bathsheba, Peter's denial, God's judgment of Sodom, Gomorrah and Nineveh, God's appeal to Cain, Jesus' appeal to Nicodemus, to the rich young ruler, and to the adulteress. God appeals and eventually judges but refrains from coercion. He must be allowing a measure of freedom.

This freedom is not total. Nor could it ever be. We are limited by God's sovereignty to those areas within which he restrains his omnipotence and allows us freedom. We are further constrained by our involvement with humanity. For human beings have produced and imposed upon us an incredibly complex culture from which, to the end of our days, we cannot escape.

Before we were old enough to know what was going on, we had already been carefully taught and had responded by developing the habits appropriate to perhaps 90 percent of the total cultural heritage in terms of which we would live all of life. We were conditioned linguistically, socially, attitudinally, and in every other way to such an extent that we can never function without reference to that early conditioning. That is, we have acquired the very necessary frame of reference, the rules of the game, the design for living without which, apparently, no human being can exist. And it is the pervasiveness and totality of this conditioning, especially as it contrasts with the impression of greater freedom that we once understood to be the case, that has induced some to subscribe to a doctrine of cultural determinism.

This understanding of the relationship of people to culture is elaborated in the following chapter.

4. Cultural Forms, Patterns, and Processes

Among the most important concepts arising from anthropological and linguistic study are the distinctions between cultural forms and their functions, meanings, and usages (model 3d) and that between cultural patterning and cultural performance (model 3e). The discussion of these features of culture lays the groundwork for the treatment of culture change (model 3f).

FORMS, FUNCTIONS, MEANINGS, AND USAGE (Model 3d)

A very important submodel of the culture concept is one that enables us to distinguish between the component entities of culture and the purposes they serve. To introduce this submodel it will be helpful to define each of the four aspects of culture with which it deals. Note that implicit in this submodel is a basic two-way distinction between cultural forms and their functions, meanings, and uses. Many analysts simply refer to forms and functions (see Downs 1975:111–20 for an excellent presentation) or forms and meanings (as I shall regularly do in the following chapters). The nonform category of this distinction is complex. It is thus useful (following Linton 1936:402–4) to deal with three distinguishable aspects of that nonform component (points 2, 3, 4, below).

1. The *forms* of a culture are the observable parts of which it is made up.[1] These are the customs arranged in patterns or the products of those customs. Many cultural forms are conceptualizations of material items; most are conceptualizations of nonmaterial items. Axes, hoes, houses, clothing, automobiles, dogs, people, etc. are concepts represented by material forms. Marriage customs, family structures, words, grammatical patterns, singing, dancing, speaking, sleeping, etc. are concepts of nonmaterial cultural forms. A description of the shape, size, type, structuring, or other observable parts of a custom is a description of some portion of that custom's form. Cultural forms in and of themselves are static.

The early anthropologists were much concerned with the forms of the cultures they sought to observe and describe. They often went into greater detail in describing the items of culture (or of language) and the way these items were arranged than in dealing with any other part of culture. Many such

---

1. This usage is not to be confused with the way certain schools of philosophy use the word "form."

descriptions tended to dissect and classify kinship systems, religious rituals, grammatical systems, economic patterns, and the like much as a medical student dissects a dead body. We can learn much about the inventory of a culture from such descriptions but not much about its dynamics.

2. Each of the forms of a culture is used (see below) by the people of that culture to serve particular *functions*. Certain of these functions are general, universal functions, relating to basic human needs that every culture must meet. Others are more specifically related to nonuniversal, individual, and group concerns. At the general level, it can be said that the (or a) function (or purpose) of marriage is to legitimize procreation or that the (or a) function of eating is to maintain biological existence. At a more specific level, marriage may function to enable young people to escape from their parents, and eating to solve one's feelings of insecurity or apprehension. Cultural forms frequently serve several functions at once—some general, some specific.

The contributions a cultural form makes to the overall structuring of the culture or to the individual usage of that culture are its functions. As each form is used to play its part in relation to the other elements (forms) of the culture, it is seen as serving its functions. The participants in a culture may or may not be aware of the functions served by any given cultural form. Or they may be aware of certain functions and unaware of others. Some people may be aware of the fact that they eat to keep alive, but not that they eat also to reduce their fear of unknown situations.

3. One of the most important functions served by every cultural form is to convey *meaning* to the participants of a culture. The meaning of a cultural form consists of "the totality of subjective associations attached to the form" (Luzbetak 1963:139). In many ways "culture is communication" (Hall 1959). Each cultural form, therefore, is the bearer of impressions, values, attitudes, and connotations from person to person and group to group. The meanings that cultural forms conjure up in the minds of those who employ them are a crucial aspect of the way those forms function in a culture. The use (see below) that the participants in a culture make of their customs is also critically related to the meanings attached to these forms within the cultural system. Indeed, what a given custom means is determinable only from an observation of its functions and uses within its specific cultural context. There are apparently no cultural forms that convey exactly the same meanings in any two different cultures (see Nida 1960:89–90).

Just as cultural forms may serve several functions at once, so they typically convey more than one meaning at the same time. Certain of the meanings conveyed are at the conscious level for most or all participants, but many are below the threshold of consciousness for a majority of those who use the forms. Furthermore, many (if not all) of the forms of a culture will signify (mean) at least some different things to different individuals and groups within the culture. A wedding ceremony within American culture, for example, probably signifies to all Americans the legitimization of the right of the couple to live together and to produce and raise children together. There will, however, be certain additional different (and often unconscious) meanings symbolized by that same ceremony in the minds of the couple, the parents of the bride, the parents of the groom, the organist, the preacher, the guests, the janitor, etc. What for nearly everyone may symbolize total happiness may also symbolize apprehension to the couple, debt to the parents, extra work to the janitor, surprise that these two ever got together to some of the audience, fear lest he or she make a mistake to the organist, and routine to the preacher.

4. Closely interrelated to function and meaning is the matter of how a cultural form is *used*. This consideration, more than others, makes explicit the active part that human beings take in the operation of culture. The forms of culture are relatively passive in and of themselves. How they function and what they mean are dependent upon the way active human agents employ them. Most of the ways in which forms are used are routinized through the processes of culture learning. Thus, most people within a culture employ most forms of that culture within a relatively fixed range of variation allowed by the traditions of the culture. Within this range there is room for individual and subgroup variation in most customs. We may speak, then, of both culturally patterned usage and individual variation in usage.

The culturally patterned use of the wedding ceremony to legitimize the setting up of a new family may be intersected by a number of other culturally approved (or, at least, allowed) individual usages, and also by certain culturally disapproved usages. It is approved, for example, for the organist and the preacher to use such a ceremony to earn money. It is culturally allowed (and sometimes approved) for certain of the participants to drink to excess in many American wedding celebrations. It is not unknown, though never culturally approved, for certain persons or groups to use a wedding celebration as an occasion for revenge or stealing.

It will be helpful to illustrate further how this very important model applies by designating additional cultural forms and applying the model to them.

TABLE. An American table is a cultural artifact, a *material form* produced as a part of the operation of American culture. It exists within American culture in a variety of sizes, shapes, colors, and materials. It is usually (not always) fairly easy to distinguish from other items in the category "furniture," such as chairs, cabinets, couches, and footstools. There are, however, several different kinds of tables, such as dining tables, end tables, coffee tables, and picnic tables. Several closely related items such as desks and certain cabinets may alternatively be referred to as tables. Tables *function* as articles of furniture in places such as homes, schools, churches, and even parks. They serve as things to set other things on, such as lamps, books, dishes, etc. Dining tables function as places at which Americans sit to eat.

A table *means* such things as property, a place to sit at for eating, working, etc., an object to dust, an object to keep an attractive tablecloth on, a lamp holder, and the like. Ordinarily people *use* tables according to their culturally assigned functions. Dining tables are sat at for eating, end tables are used to hold lamps, coffee tables are used to hold books, magazines, newspapers, and (sometimes) coffee, etc. Ordinarily a distinction is made between a table as something one sits at and a chair as something someone sits on. On occasion, however, an individual will use a table to sit on. This usage is sometimes within the culturally allowable range though often outside of it (depending on the circumstances). It is seldom an approved usage.

AND. This is a *linguistic form* that occurs in the English language. It consists of three phonemes and exists in a variety of pronunciations differing from dialect to dialect. Prominent among these pronunciations /ænd/ in the "standard" American dialect and / and/ in "standard" British and certain non-standard American dialects. The word also exists in written form (e.g., and; in Braille; symbols such as + and &), can be spelled out in code (e.g., Morse, semaphore), can be represented by gestures (e.g., "signing" for the deaf), etc. It *functions* within the language "to indicate connection or addition especially of items within the same class or type" (Webster's *Dictionary* 1967:33). Since *and* is "a function word" rather than "a content word" its *meaning* is largely determined by how it functions and how it is used within the language rather than by any referent outside of the language. In contrast, a "content word" such as *dog* or *table* each functions as a noun within the language and refers to an object that exists outside the language. Those objects exist whether or not anyone talks or writes about them. The word *and*, however, derives its meaning almost entirely from its functioning and usage when people talk and write.

It is, then, *used* within the language largely for the purpose of joining "sentence elements of the same grammatical rank or function" (ibid.). A person using the word in this way within a sentence is regarded by all as operating within the range assigned by the language. Some would question whether it is "proper" (i.e., assigned) to use the word as the first word in a written sentence, as I often do in this volume. I would maintain that it is certainly allowable and also within the assigned range of acceptable usage. In conversation, the word is often used to signal something like "Wait for me to formulate my next thought before you interrupt me." To use it for this purpose the speaker finishes one sentence and starts the next with a drawn out "Aaaaand . . ." followed by a pause while attempting to formulate how to say the next thought. At other points in a conversation, a person who is not speaking may use *and* as the lead word in an attempt to butt into the conversation. In this usage it may mean something like "Here's an important additional point that you ought to mention."

The ritual of water BAPTISM. This is a ceremonial, *nonmaterial form* or custom that involves, for most Christian groups, the use of water. In performing this ritual an official of a given Christian group either immerses an initiate in water or sprinkles or pours water on the initiate's head. A complete description of the form of this custom would involve the detailing of such factors as the place, time, personnel, method, clothing, words, and all other aspects of the ritual. Baptism *functions* for most Christian groups as a rite of initiation and incorporation of new members into the group. For the group its primary function is as the doorway through which new recruits pass. For the individual it functions to confirm one's passage from outside the group to inside it.

Baptism may have a variety of *meanings* to both the group and the initiate. Not all of these are intended or even approved by either individual Christian bodies or by corporate Christianity. The biblical intention would seem to be that the rite be accompanied by enthusiasm, love, joy, and Christian concern on the part of the initiate and of the group the initiate joins. It should mean these things plus the open commitment of the initiate to allegiance both to God through Christ and to that specific group of Christians. Water baptism frequently does signify just such meanings. Other meanings are often present as well, either in addition to or in replacement of these more ideal meanings. The fact that the ritual is a foreign one, borrowed from another culture, unknown in American culture outside the church, and labeled by a Greek word that has never been translated (*baptizo* = baptize), affects its meaning at both general and individual levels. It very easily comes to mean a sacred, even magical, ritual that one goes through only because it is required by God and an antique church organization. When such a meaning becomes prominent it results in a great contrast between the way in which baptism is perceived today and the way it was perceived in New Testament times. For in the first century water initiation rites were used to induct people into a number of different groups. Among these were Judaism (for proselytes) and the Greek mystery religions as well as the church. The function and purpose of baptism were well known to those outside as well as to those inside these groups. Perceptions of baptism influenced by understandings of historical conflict over the mode, the theological teaching concerning the practice, the attitude of the participants toward the church organization and personnel, etc. can also result in significant differences between how the form is seen today and how it was seen in the early church. Such factors greatly influence the meanings attached to a given cultural form.

Interacting with all this, and contributing markedly to the meanings of water baptism, is the way the form is *used* by the groups and individuals employing it. Many groups use and impose the form as if it were handed down by God and, therefore, is sacred and even magical *in itself*, whether or not the perceived meanings correspond with scriptural meanings. Other groups (e.g., Society of Friends, Salvation Army) have become so upset with the constant arguing over water baptism that they have abandoned the use of the form (though not necessarily the intended meanings) altogether. Other groups fall somewhere between these extremes.

We will return later to this model. The usage component of this model is incorporated into the next submodel (3e) as the "performance" component of that model.

CULTURAL PATTERNING AND CULTURAL PERFORMANCE
(Model 3e)

"Orthodox" (or majority) anthropology, sociology, and psychology do not go all the way with the determinists. However narrowly one may be channeled by one's culture in any given area of life there is usually some "room to wiggle." That is, even though it might not occur to a given individual or group within a given society that a particular custom could be altered, they have the freedom to do so if they choose. If for some reason external or internal to their culture they feel the need to alter that custom, they may choose to alter it and actually go about altering it.

That culture "shapes" us and rather strictly channels our behavior must, I think, be granted. But to prove that it *determines* our behavior one would have to demonstrate that culture in any (or every) situation allows no alternative. It would have to be proved that culture so tightly channels behavior that cultural causation is the only appropriate explanation. On the contrary, what we observe is that, with respect to at least most (if not all) aspects of culture, human beings are presented with more than a single possible choice of behavior. One's culture, rather than forcing only a single response to given stimuli, ordinarily presents one with a culturally allowable selection of alternatives, one of which a person selects, usually as a matter of habit. Though we ordinarily operate nearly every aspect of our culture in an unthinking, habitual way, we may choose to operate any given aspect according to another culturally acceptable (though perhaps not preferred) alternative.

The fact that cultural behavior is strictly channeled and ordinarily operated habitually has impressed the determinists. What they minimize or ignore is the fact that there are allowed alternatives which may be selected (and habituated) differently by the different human beings within the same group who are subject to the same cultural conditioning but respond to it differently. Even

folk societies, though relatively homogeneous, show that the individual is never completely submerged. In every society individuals vary in temperament, aptitudes, and intelligence. A few can be counted upon to thrust themselves vigorously, or even violently, into unconventional roles, to disturb the patterned rounds of life, to innovate or even desecrate. Most individuals at least occasionally toy with such impulses; some act on them now and then, a few distinguish themselves by the frequency or the extremity of their unpatterned thrusts (Goodman 1967:194).

The model of culture here advocated attempts to take account of both the patterning of culture and the performance or use of culture made by individuals and groups. The *cultural patterning* is that enormously complex cultural grid into which we are indoctrinated before we realize what is happening to us. This aspect of culture is sometimes referred to as the "press" of culture (Gillin 1948).

What this patterning, or press, provides for the members of a culture is an extremely large number of rules, or boundaries, with reference to which they must operate.

But boundaries are not directives. Within the life space defined by his boundaries our man is at liberty. It is within this space that he exercises those faculties . . . to which self-determination can be attributed. Moreover, the boundaries are potentially alterable. Fortuitous circumstances (e.g., meeting Jane Jones who has grown up in a very different society and culture) or a conscious choice (e.g., to spend his savings on travel) may significantly expand his life space. Man's potential for mastery of his conditions is, of course, limited, yet it is the less limited the more he becomes aware, thoughtful, and confident of his own powers (Goodman 1967:57).

This use that a person makes of his culturally allowed "life space" will be here referred to as *cultural performance*. Performance is what we do with (how we use) the "room to wiggle" allowed us by our culture. This part of socio-cultural experience is not passed down to us by a previous generation. We supply it as we make use of inherited cultural patterns. In our use of the cultural patterning (our performance), we both follow and alter the culture that we receive. The cultural patterning that we pass on to the next generation, though it retains an extremely high degree of similarity to the patterning that we receive, is never exactly the same.

The stage is set for such change by the fact that the culture we receive consists of patterns adapted to the life experience of generations previous to ours. To the extent that the life experience of our generation approximates that of previous generations, the patterns that served them well will serve us well. To the extent that the experience of our generation differs, the patterns developed to serve their needs will be unsuitable to serve our needs maximally. With respect to language, Nida speaks (contra Sapir-Whorf) of grammatical patterning as "arbitrary" and "fossilized." Present structures "may have represented alternative choices some thousands of years ago," but they come to today's generation as "arbitrary and conventional" (1971:83–84). The lack of fit between such conventional patterning and contemporary problems stimulates desire for change most urgently in those parts of culture where lack of fit "hurts" most. Language structuring, though clearly exemplifying the problem, is generally not perceived of as "pinching" people badly. It can thus often go for many generations without generating intense pressure for structural change. Dysfunctional patterns for obtaining food, however, are often the subject of rather strong pressure for change.

Whether under duress or not, each person and group constantly alters the cultural patterns they have received, usually in fairly minor ways, and passes on to those of the next generation a slightly differing set of patterns than those received. In this way every culture is constantly having its patterning altered. Thus the cultural patterning altered by generation I becomes the received patterning of generation II, that altered by generation II becomes the received patterning of generation III, etc.

We do not, therefore, merely relate to our cultural patterning passively. We respond by interacting with this patterning. And, since a certain amount of leeway is built into every aspect of cultural patterning, we do not all choose to respond to the same aspect of the patterning in the same way. Frequently, once we have made a choice between the culturally allowed alternative responses, we install our chosen response as our new habit. Thus our cultural performance is habitual on at least two levels: (1) on the level of the overall cultural patterning that we have inherited and (2) on the level of the alternative response to each pattern that we choose.

My culture says that I may shave or grow a beard—though it weights the choice for my peer group in favor of the former by assigning certain meanings to the growing of a beard that my peer group considers undesirable. Among these are nonconformity, insecurity, attempting to identify oneself with another age group, and the like. In acquiescence to the cultural pattern (including its meaning) I once chose to shave regularly and made shaving a habit. I have for years continued to choose both that habit and several other contingent habits (each reflecting other choices between alternatives made earlier in my life). Among these are the use of a safety razor rather than an electric razor, the order in which I deal with the various parts of my face, the frequency with which I shave, the time when I shave, etc.

On occasion I review and revise my performance of these cultural patterns. And sometimes I choose to change such things as the kind of razor I use, or the time and place of shaving, or the type of shaving cream I use. I even chose once (and may again) to grow a mustache. That is, I have chosen at various times to alter my use of this aspect of my culture. And certain of these usages have won my approval to the extent that I have installed them in my life in addition to or in place of my previous habit. They have in this way become a part of my habitual usage.

Thus, though the major part of our culture, including both broad and more specific patterns, is merely accepted and followed (chosen) habitually by us, there is at every point a considerable amount of leeway for alternative individual and group choice. And our activity in selecting between alternate (i.e., socially allowable) courses of action is a highly significant aspect of our involvement in it. For, in making the choices we do, we from time to time alter our use of one or another cultural pattern and effect changes of habit within our cultural performance.

Hiebert pictures certain aspects of this model, focusing on the press and pull of culture (Goodman 1967) within the channeling of behavior dictated by mental (outer channel), biological (middle channel), cultural (inner channel), and individual structuring. The last mentioned (indicated below by the inner box) includes the individual's ego strategies within the limits of his or her "personally possible" in response to (but not determined by) the pressures and enticements (pull) of his or her culture. The model presents a view of the channeling and pressuring of human beings by forces largely beyond their control without neglecting the very important fact that the individual produces a unique, nondetermined performance within the "life space" provided by those boundaries.

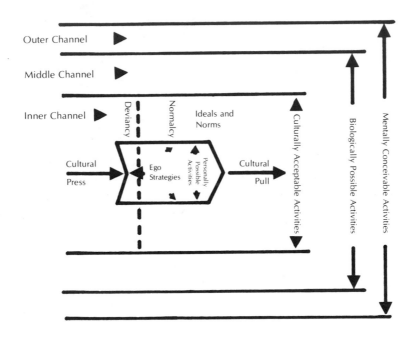

Fig. 4.1. Relationships between culture and the individual (after Hiebert 1976:432).

THE PROCESS OF CULTURE CHANGE (Model 3f)

Alterations of habitual behavior, especially those engaged in by influential persons, not infrequently "catch on" with others in the society, resulting in new socially accepted habitual behavior. Thus, rather trivial customs like lengthened sideburns for men, the wearing of pants by women, and the acceptability of green with blue in clothing and decorating have recently become widespread in American life. But thus, too (over a longer period of time), much more earth-shaking changes have taken hold. One such change has been the shift in the understanding of the universe within western culture from God-centered and God-controlled to a very mechanistic understanding with humans either actually or potentially in control at every point. In each case the process of choice between allowed alternatives, followed by the development of new habits, has been the primary process accounting for the change.

Most often the option chosen in such cultural performance is one already at least potentially allowed (though often not approved) by the existing cultural patterning. Frequently, though, especially in rapidly changing cultures like our own, where innovation is highly valued, individuals and groups decide to go beyond the culturally allowed alternatives. They then either adopt a substitute pattern or deliberately expand the scope of allowed alternatives within the existing patterning. Not long ago, for example, the possibility of a woman choosing to wear pants (once called "slacks") on dress-up occasions did not exist in American society. In recent years, however, the range of culturally allowed alternatives for female attire on such occasions has been widened. Now certain types of pants outfits are frequently allowed (especially in urban areas) in addition to traditionally acceptable possibilities.

Likewise, with regard to the commercial use of evenings and Sundays. Not long ago the idea that business establishments such as grocery and department stores would be open in the evening or on Sunday was not only unacceptable to but unimagined by the majority of Americans. Now, however, through the widening of the range of allowed alternatives in this sector of our culture we not only have evening and Sunday shopping but, in certain cases, twenty-four-hour shopping as well. Banks and certain other consumer establishments have not yet gone this route (though some now have Saturday hours), but the widening of the range of allowed alternatives by other businesses makes it now at least imaginable that they might someday.

With respect to marriage customs we observe both the widening of the range of possibilities and the replacement of previous customs with innovative practices. The range of allowable (i.e., socially acceptable) places to be married and persons performing wedding ceremonies has recently undergone widening in America. With regard to who acceptably lives with whom, further, certain "respectable" segments of our society have begun to innovate by approving of couples who simply arrange to live together in place of formalized marriage of any kind. This kind of replacement or partial replacement of one custom by another custom is a more drastic type of change than the simple widening of a range of acceptability. It is presently forcing our society to reconsider a wide variety of definitions and practices with regard to marriage, adultery, legitimacy of children, the relationships of sex and marriage, etc.

Each aspect of this process is extremely relevant to the discussion of cultural transformation by Christianity (model 13). Christians are anxious that culture change be affected by the infusion of Christian concepts into the cultural context. Note that the key factor paving the way for any change is the development of some alteration in a person's or group's perception (model) of reality. This may be a change either in the perception of reality itself or of the understanding of what reality could be. Ordinarily we perceive reality in terms of our culturally governed conceptions (worldview) of what that reality ought to be. If some factor such as a new discovery or an awareness of information coming from outside our culture affects either our perception of reality or our imagination of possible reality, this is fed back into our worldview and brings about a change there (see above concerning the adaptability of worldviews). Thus the discovery (in proof of a previous theory) that the world is round altered the worldview of western culture. Likewise, the information (coming to many cultures from western culture) that cultivation may be done by means of an animal pulling a plow rather than by hand hoe is in our time affecting the conceptualization of millions of tribal peoples the world over.

The nature of the feedback from perception to worldview is all-important. Usually, no matter what the reality may be, the feedback is interpreted in such a way that it confirms, or at least does not disconfirm, the worldview. People who believe that God has a hand in every event of life are continually confirmed in this concept because they understand and interpret every event in terms of the participation of God in that event. Those who conceive of every event as the result of purely naturalistic forces, on the other hand, interpret the same events in such a way that their naturalistic worldview is confirmed.

If persons whose worldview is naturalistic are faced with one or a series of perceptions that they find themselves unable to interpret satisfactorily on the basis of their naturalistic conceptualizations, they may choose to alter their worldview. Or they may choose to disregard their perceptions. We find the pages of the New Testament full of differential responses to the same set of phenomena (though the worldviews in focus there are not naturalistic but supernaturalistic). Most Pharisees would not alter their conceptualizations concerning how the Messiah would come and how he would act, in spite of Jesus' miracles. Many common people, as well as Nicodemus, the Pharisee, however, changed their minds. They had been carefully taught those same concepts, but they allowed the feedback from their perceptions to alter their conceptualization.

The stimulus to change one's cultural pattern or one's use of it (1) may be generated from within the culture (as with women's use of pants or Nicodemus' acceptance of Jesus), (2) may be at least partially the result of exposure to another culture (as with "beat" music and, probably, at least certain aspects of the "trial marriage" forms), or (3) may come (as the Christian message does) from a supracultural source (see model 4c). The selection of a culturally allowed alternative or of a replacive practice is always up to those within the society. And this is true even when the suggestion for change comes from outside one's society (see Barnett 1953). In Barnett's terminology, though an outsider may "advocate" a change, only the members of a society may "innovate" for (i.e., actually bring about changes of patterning within) that society. That is, how the cultural patterning is to be used—whether for the perpetuation, alteration, or replacement of the present practice—is totally up to the members of the culture or group in question. An outsider, though he may appeal for change, is limited to his ability to win over some insider who will then effect the change(s) from within. (See chapter 19 for further elaboration of this concept.)

The performance part of culture is very complex—probably much more complex than the patterning part. Cultural patterning is complex, but static. The complexity of performance is *a dynamic complexity of process.* Though we cannot prove exactly what goes on in this process, it may be helpful (and, we hope, not too inaccurate) to think of it in terms of the following model (pictured as Fig. 4.2). This process seems to involve a person in the dynamics of (1a) selection from the cultural inventory of available patterned, structured cultural forms. Or, the person may choose (1b) to innovate a cultural form not previously in the available inventory. The person then (2) behaves according to the pattern within guidelines such as those set forth in Figure 4.1, above, to achieve goals that one has consciously or unconsciously adopted.

The person (3) monitors his or her behavior with the aim of evaluating its relationship to those goals. This evaluation may be seen as related to and coordinated by one's self-image, a part of one's individualized worldview. As one reflects and evaluates one's performance, one takes account of feedback both from self and from the community of which one is a part concerning one's performance. On the basis of this information, the person generates feelings of (4a) satisfaction with the performance, leading him or her to (5a) continue and habituate the behavior, or dissatisfaction (4b). In the latter case, the person re-enters the circle by either (5b) reselecting from the cultural inventory or (5c) innovating a new pattern. Or under certain circumstances, such as if one's self-image is low, one may simply continue the present behavior even though dissatisfied with it.

The vast majority of the behaviors we have habituated are chosen, performed, evaluated, and even changed without our being conscious of what is going on. We seem to choose and evaluate habitually. And, with respect to most of our behaviors, we seem at some point to stop considering alternative patterns. The way we walk, the facial expressions and other gestures we employ, the myriad of characteristically American attitudes, and most parts of our language, for example, are so unconsciously employed by most of us that it never occurs to us to re-evaluate or to change them. We "selected" these behaviors before we were old enough to question them and soon became so used (habituated) to selecting them that they seem to be "just natural" to us.

The possibility of re-evaluation, reselection, and (with difficulty) the development of new habits is always with us, however. As the result of some

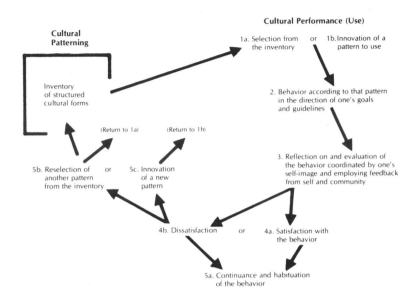

Fig. 4.2. The process involved in cultural performance.

stimulus we may decide that we are dissatisfied with some behavior. We therefore conclude that it will need to be altered, modified, or replaced. Perhaps we have habituated smoking, or a hypercritical attitude toward someone, or an ethnocentric attitude toward other people's customs. On evaluation of that habit we may choose to return to the selection or innovation stage and reselect a culturally allowed alternative such as nonsmoking, noncriticism, or the doctrine of cultural validity.

Continuous dynamic interaction between the patterning of culture and the individual and group usage (performance) of it is the process that results in every culture continually changing (whether rapidly or slowly). As Beals and Hoijer state:

Cultures are never static and unchanging. This fact . . . is obvious to the most inexperienced observer. Our grandparents, for example, follow somewhat different ("old-fashioned") modes of behavior, evident in their dress, their speech, and their manners. Old books, newspapers, and photographs yield similar evidence. . . . In short, just as contemporaneous cultures may differ more or less in rough proportion to their separation in space, so do single cultures differ slightly as between adjacent generations, more widely from one century to the next, and so on increasingly as the time periods compared are more and more distant from each other (1959:705–6).

This contemporary understanding of the universality of the change process within culture (see Keesing and Keesing 1971:346–72) contrasts sharply with popular stereotypes that see preliterate cultures as essentially unchanging for thousands of years. Anthropologists, however, though strongly impressed with the stability of cultures, have been continually forced to recognize that even in the most conservative societies widespread changes have taken place during the course of their histories. Though some cultures change less rapidly than others, none avoids change—the only questions concern the pace and nature of the changes that take place. Certain cultures change very rapidly (e.g., American). Other cultures change much more slowly. In addition, certain aspects of a given culture are designated by that culture as legitimate areas for great innovation and creativity (e.g., music and clothing styles in American culture), while others are designated as areas of conservatism (e.g., politics, religion, athletics in American culture).

Change may take place in an apparently unguided manner or as the result of the effective agency of some member(s) of the culture. Certain persons in every society are looked to for innovation and are therefore more likely to be followed when they innovate. But all persons innovate to a greater or lesser extent during their lifetimes, with greater or lesser acceptance of their innovations by others.

FELT NEEDS AND REFERENCE POINTS
FOR CULTURE CHANGE

Innovations are most likely to be accepted by others when they combine a felt need (i.e., a need that people feel they have) with a novel solution. The felt need always comes from within the culture. The identification of the need as a need (rather than as an inevitable "fact of life") and the realization that it is possible to solve it may, however, be the result of suggestions originating outside the culture (or subculture). Furthermore, there are three possible types of reference point in terms of which a solution to the felt need may be developed: (1) an in-culture reference point, (2) an other-culture reference point, and (3) a supracultural (i.e., outside any culture) reference point.

The vast majority of solutions to felt needs are generated in terms of reference points within the culture itself. The basic worldview and value system embodied in a culture provide primary in-culture reference points. Thus the development of mass production was the result of the application of a solution, generated in terms of an in-culture reference point, to the felt need for a cheaper, more efficient way to produce such products as textiles and automobiles. Among the important American values that easily become in-culture reference points for change are such concepts as the desire for efficiency and inexpensiveness, conservatism or liberalism, the feeling of need to compete with and win out over others, individual self-reliance, antisupernaturalism, materialism, and the like.

Not infrequently, though, the reference point for change lies in another culture (or subculture) known to at least some of the members of the original group. Thus the members of a nonwestern culture often seek to solve one or another of their needs related to identity, power, prestige, freedom, etc., by looking to western culture. When, to meet these needs, they align themselves with western schools, medicine, religion, or politics, they are employing an other-cultural reference point for the generating of change within their culture. The culture-change process in this case is essentially the same as that involving an in-culture reference point, but the solution sought for the felt need is borrowed from a foreign source rather than generated internally.

Not infrequently this practice of looking to an outside culture for answers becomes habitual and incorporated into their worldview. What comes from this foreign culture is evaluated as "better" than previous answers to problems or newly generated answers with in-culture points of reference. This attachment of change to other-culture points of reference is often done quite consciously at first; but, as the practice becomes more habitual, the consciousness of the foreignness of the solutions adopted typically recedes. In American culture, for example, the point of reference in terms of which medical scientists construct names for new medicines is the Latin language. Many Americans are more or less aware of this fact, but are so used to it that they feel this way of doing things to be just "natural." Many, though, are unaware of the process, since it is so firmly entrenched, even though they frequently have difficulty in pronouncing the names of the medicines they use.

The reference point for change may, however, be *supra*cultural. In this case the reference point lies outside any culture—in God or in Satan. The solution to the felt need is generated by the desire on the part of those seeking the solution to do (consciously or unconsciously) what they feel will be pleasing to their supracultural reference point. When people shift (convert) from a cultural to a supracultural reference point this concern becomes a part of their worldview. It then partially or fully replaces the previous reference point in terms of which such decisions were made.

Change of cultural usage in response to a supracultural point of reference is liable to become a hit-or-miss thing unless there is some kind of in-culture guide to which people look to come to understand the desire of their supracultural point of reference. This purpose is served by a variety of written and experienced revelations perceived as coming partially or totally from the realm of the supracultural. In Christianity this purpose is served by the Bible and its interpreters. These, under the continuing leading of the Holy Spirit, are responsible to witness to others concerning the existence and implications of a supracultural reference point in God. The Bible provides contemporary witnesses with both a casebook (see model 9d) of previous experience and a yardstick (see model 9a) in terms of which to measure contemporary experience with the supracultural God. For it reports the experiences of previous witnesses—notably that of the God-become-man and of those who had direct experience with him.

With respect to in-culture and other-culture points of reference, the ends in view may be well- or ill-defined and the empowerment for the change simply that of the human beings who operate the culture. In the third case, however, though the definition of the end in view may still be either well or poorly understood by the human participants, the empowerment for the change comes at least partially from a supernatural source (e.g., the Holy Spirit or Satan) of which the human participants may or may not be aware. It is my understanding that this empowerment for change is ordinarily a cooperative matter between the human and the supracultural participants such as that referred to in Christianity as "following the leading of God."

When the third type of reference point for change is properly employed by Christians *it uses the natural culture change processes with the supernatural empowerment of the Holy Spirit to effect ends defined by, illustrated in, or at least pointed to by the Scriptures.* This process is here labeled "Christian transformational change" (see model 13). We may diagram this process as follows:

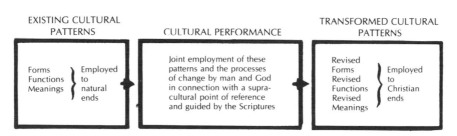

Fig. 4.3. Christian transformational change.

In this way Christians, working in terms of already existent cultural patterns and processes but with God's will as their reference point and his Spirit to empower them, may have an important influence on the direction in which the culture changes. And one important result of such directed change will be the transformation of certain of the cultural patterns and processes to serve Christian ends more adequately. However, this transformation, though often impressive (e.g., elimination of slavery and polygamy), has never in history approached complete "Christianization," and one despairs of the possibility of such cultural transformation ever proceeding far enough in any culture that one might accurately describe that culture as thoroughly Christian (contra McGavran 1974:8–9).

As impressive and important as the diversity of human cultures is, it is of great importance that we be constantly aware of the great amount of human commonality shared by all peoples. We now turn to this aspect of the human condition.

5. Human Commonality

Anthropologists often pay relatively little attention to those things that all humankind shares. Yet the assumption of basic human similarity has always been an important factor in anthropological research, for the search has been for "a theory of man," not "theories of men." The tendency of monocultural disciplines has been to generalize about all humankind on the basis of experience within western culture alone. Anthropologists have sought to get beyond such myopia to discover what peoples have in common who live in radically different cultures. What they have discovered is impressive.

In this chapter we deal first with cultural diversity and human commonality. We then relate the discussion of forms and meaning to human commonality, follow that with a section on evaluating cultural forms, and conclude by dealing with the fitting of nonrelative meanings to cultural forms.

CULTURAL DIVERSITY AND HUMAN COMMONALITY
(Model 3g)

Beneath the vast array of differences between human cultures lies an equally impressive substratum of basic human similarity. The Scriptures as well as the behavioral sciences assume this similarity. The study of humanity within western culture, however, has tended to identify many specifically western cultural traits as basic human characteristics. Western logic was considered to be proper logic and those who do not think in our way were said to be "prelogical," "prescientific," or possessed of a "primitive mentality" (Levy-Bruhl 1923). Western Christians often saw such divergence from "normality" as the result of unchecked sin in these other cultures. If such peoples were to be won to Christ, they would first need to be "civilized" in order to be evangelized (Anderson 1838 in Beaver 1967:147–67).

On the basis of such assumptions western Christians felt not only that the consciences of all people should convict them of sin (Rom. 2:15), but that they should convict them of the same sins in the same way. It was felt that those who practice polygamy or tell what westerners consider to be lies, or who (in terms of western values) mistreat their women, or who practice other "strange," "heathen" customs either know down deep in their hearts that these things are wrong or are so completely deluded by Satan that they no longer know right from wrong. The result of such misunderstanding of human commonality on the part of western Christians tended to be intolerance, condemnation, and an intense desire to convert the "heathen" to western cultural practices as well as to Christianity. Intense effort was (and is) put into westernizing customs relating to clothing, housing, cleanliness, medicine, education, economic practices, political structures, religious structures, etc. on the assumption that divergence from our ways was sub-Christian and counter to God's desire.

In reaction to such ethnocentric absolutizing of western concepts of human commonality, anthropologists developed the doctrine of cultural relativism (see model 3b). Since western interpretations of Christianity tended to strongly support this ethnocentric understanding, anthropologists became strongly opposed to Christianity and denied the validity of Christian missionary work. They also tended to overstate cultural relativism, often, in fact, absolutizing cultural relativity and so stressing cultural diversity that the basic underlying human commonality was ignored. Yet anthropology, like theology, must either assume such basic commonality or abandon the attempt to forge generalizations concerning human beings that are valid cross-culturally.

In view of the extremity to which anthropologists have gone in their reaction against western ethnocentric absolutism it is of great interest to read the more balanced approach of Walter Goldschmidt (1966) of the University of California (Los Angeles), one of today's leaders in American anthropology. His perspective calls anthropologists to task and paves the way for the more effective use of anthropological models for Christian purposes. In describing the contribution of anthropology to the development of a broader understanding of human diversity, he suggests that because of the input of anthropological perspectives we have been enabled to move away from biological thinking and toward appreciation of the force of culture; it has made us aware

of our own customs and beliefs as one of the many and apparently arbitrary modes of thought. In doing this it has promoted a cultural relativism, and this has placed anthropology itself in the mainstream of an old scientific tradition. For as astronomy moved the earth away from the center of the universe and biology moved man out of his unique position in the living world, so, too, anthropology has removed Western man from the pinnacle and quintessence of human perfectibility and placed him with the Australian aborigine and the Hottentot as one of so many diverse cultural beings (Goldschmidt 1966:ix).

Such a paradigm shift must be regarded positively, even though it has often proved confusing to Christians strongly influenced by the preceding evolutionary tradition that saw western culture as the end product of a long development toward "the perfect culture." Seeing the aborigines and the Hottentots as possessors of traditions just as long as our own, rather than as examples of "stunted growth" in a process that was intended to make them like us, enables us better to appreciate God's concern for and fairness to all people, not simply westerners. Such a view, further, helps us to recognize that Christianity is considerably more than merely the "tribal religion" of western culture—as many of our critics contend.

However, as Goldschmidt goes on to point out, getting people to accept the fact that ours is but one of many essentially equal cultures is basically a negative achievement. It has torn down an invalid ethnocentrism but it has not erected a satisfactory replacement. For, says Goldschmidt,

the positive accomplishment of a theory of man has not been developed, and there seems to be little evidence on the horizon that it is developing as we worry over the kinship system of obscure tribes or the minutiae of native taxonomies (1966:x).

We must get beyond these interesting but actually trivial details of human diversity, says Goldschmidt, in order to get down to the real business at hand. That business is to determine the theoretical relevance of what anthropologists are doing to the development of a "theory of man," as they call it. A primary step in moving in this direction is to divest ourselves of at least certain of the implications of cultural relativism, including the tendency of some to absolutize relativism. Goldschmidt feels that

it was necessary for anthropology to go through a relativistic phase in order to relieve social philosophers of the habit of evaluating cultures in terms of our own culturally determined predilections. Yet by now we can certainly appreciate the contextual value of infanticide without advocating it, or can see the merits and demerits of polygamy without concern over our own convictions or regulations. . . . There are enough instances on record of primitive peoples not being happy in their own customs but (like many a married couple) not knowing how to escape them . . . so that we, too, should begin to understand the phenomenon of dysfunction and establish relevant criteria for functional efficacy. This means, among other things, that we anthropologists must rid ourselves of the Rousseauean "good savage," must cease to use ethnographic data either as an escape or as a vehicle for expressing our personal social discontent, and begin to look at primitive societies for what they can tell us not only about the possible but about the probable, and about the consequences—to individuals and to societies—of either (1966:138).

These are extremely significant words coming from a respected anthropologist. They provide us with a strong mandate for the kind of synthesis of anthropological and theological insight that this present volume is attempting. For Goldschmidt goes on to ask

What is the nature of man? . . . What . . . are the recurrent problems of human interactions? What are the tenable solutions to these problems? What are the secondary consequences to such solutions? (1966:133).

What, in short, is "the nature of man to which culture must adapt?" (1966:135). For

while it is true that no human can ever be truly culturally innocent, it is still not true to say that human behavior is culturally determined. While it may be true that it is possible, out of cultural motives, to make *some* individuals do almost anything and many individuals do *some* things, it is not true that culture can make *all* persons do *any*thing (1966:133).

In fact, in order to get people to do certain things that may be easily assumed to be unnatural for any being (such as to remain celibate), a culture (or subculture) must often exert *extreme* pressure. And it may even then find itself frequently being forced to settle for an appearance of the ideal rather than for the real thing. For, as anthropologists have described and theorized concerning the multitude of the cultures of humankind, they have succeeded in demonstrating not only the great diversity of cultural expression but, according to Goldschmidt,

that people are more alike than cultures; that . . . the average behavior under any culture tends toward the center of the range for humans as a whole. . . . There is . . . a good deal of evidence that, for instance, the average Zuni and the average Kwakiutl man behave a good deal more like each other than the normative patterns of the two cultures are alike (1966:134).

Nida suggests that such evidence indicates that "the similarities that unite mankind as a cultural 'species' are much greater than the differences that separate" (1964:55). The relativism that applies to cultural patterning does not, therefore, apply to basic human beings at the deepest level. For, as Goldschmidt goes on to point out, cross-cultural studies of human cultures suggest a series of generalizations concerning human commonality that dare not be as lightly dismissed as has been the custom of many anthropologists. Such generalizations relate to at least four major areas of human experience: biological, psychological, spiritual, and socio-cultural.

1. Human beings are so similar *biologically* that even the attempt to classify human populations on the basis of race is being widely abandoned by knowledgeable scholars (see Montagu 1964, Livingstone 1964). The only major biological difference between populations would seem to be sexual. And this difference divides *within* populations rather than *among* them. The race concept is now regarded as "a scientific dead-end" in the explanation of culture (Herskovits 1965:10). There are so-called "racial" differences, to be sure. There are differences of color, facial features, stature, etc. These differences are less impressive, however, than the fact that "human anatomy and human physiology are, in the large, about the same the world over" (Kluckhohn 1953:515).

Human biology provides the backdrop for all that we know as human. It "sets, limits, supplies potentialities and drives, provides clues which cultures neglect or elaborate" (ibid.:513).

That man's biological makeup is *one* of the bases of human ways is self-evident. All societies without exception, for example, need food, drink, and rest; all normal human beings must urinate and defecate. . . . Sex, too, is a biological necessity for the continuation of the human species. . . . All men go through the same phases of life: infancy, childhood, puberty, youth, adulthood, and old age. . . . All mankind must cope with time, place, and quantity because all human beings are biological entities. All men, too, are subject to accidents, disease, injury, and death. . . . In short, *man's biological constitution gives rise to problems that are common to all societies; such common problems are a partial reason for the common framework of cultures* (Luzbetak 1963:322, emphasis his).

From this biological or physiological base springs one important set of needs that must be cared for by culture. Different cultures care for these needs in different ways. But that they must be cared for is a given. These may be called "primary needs" or "biological imperatives" (Luzbetak 1963:173–76; Piddington 1950:219–35). That is, they must be tended to or life cannot go on, no matter how well other, more secondary, needs are cared for.

2. *Psychologically*, the evidence at hand seems to point to what is often termed the "psychic unity of mankind." This doctrine holds that "the resemblances between institutions of different cultures are to be accounted for by the similar capacities of all men" (Herskovits 1948:233). This psychic unity results both in cultural similarities and in rather impressive similarities in the thought processes of the peoples of various cultures. "In a certain deep sense the . . . modes of interpreting relationships between phenomena . . . of all members of the human species are the same" (Kluckhohn 1959:279). The reason for the differences between cultures does not seem to lie in differences in people's fundamental reasoning processes but in differences in "the premises on which such reasoning rests and the basic categories that influence the judgment of different peoples" (Nida 1960:90–91; see above, chapter 3).

Anthropologists have often had occasion to dispute the claims of psychologists and others concerning certain types of psychological similarity between peoples of different cultures. One of the motiviations for Mead's study of adolescence in Samoa (Mead 1928) was to check the cross-cultural validity of the view that sees teenage discontent and rebellion as rooted in human psychological commonality. Her study, of course, pointed to the fact that, though such discontent is very real in certain cultures, the reasons for it lie in cultural conditioning, not in psychological commonality. Anthropologists have often dismissed the findings of Freud and others because their findings seemed to be so culture-specific. Further investigations by anthropologists, however, have led at least some of them to take a second look at the possible universality of some of the findings of psychology. Kluckhohn states in this regard that

the facts uncovered in my own field work and that of my collaborators have forced me to the conclusion that Freud and other psychoanalysts have depicted with astonishing correctness many central themes in motivational life which are universal. The styles of expression of these themes and much of the manifest content are culturally determined, but the underlying psychologic drama transcends cultural difference (Kluckhohn and Morgan 1951:120).

There appears to be, behind the differing cultural approaches to reasoning and thinking, a series of basic psychological needs. Among these are (1) the need for meaning in life and (2) the need for people to maintain their individual psyches. People seek understanding of life and freedom from the threat of psychological crippling. The psychologist Maslow (1954 and 1970) attempts to distinguish various levels of psychological needs that are basic to humankind. He sees these needs as biologically based or "instinctoid" (1971:379–90) and built on top of the most basic "physiological needs." Those psychological needs that appear to me to be human universals are:

Safety Needs—the need people have for "security; stability; dependency; protection; freedom from fear, from anxiety and chaos; need for structure, order, law, limits; strength in the protector; and so on" (Maslow 1970:39). Aronoff suggests that "if the safety needs have been deprived, the individual will feel insecure and mistrustful . . . , will seek those areas of life which offer the most stability and protection . . . , will attempt to organize his world to provide the greatest degree of safety and predictability possible" (1967:7).

Love and Belongingness Needs—people need to feel wanted and loved by other people. We need to belong to a group. We "hunger for contact, for intimacy, for belonging." We "need to overcome . . . feelings of alienation, aloneness, strangeness, and loneliness" (Maslow 1970:44).

Esteem Needs—this, according to Maslow, involves "first, the desire for strength, for achievement, for adequacy, for mastery and competence, for confidence in the face of the world, and for independence and freedom. Second, . . . the desire for reputation or prestige (defining it as respect or esteem from other people), status, fame and glory, dominance, recognition, attention, importance, dignity or appreciation" (1970:45).

3. Human beings share common *spiritual* characteristics. At the cultural level this aspect of commonality is evidenced by such facts as the universality of religion and the universality of sin. In this regard, Goldschmidt points to human universals such as the search for "some kind of symbolic eternity," and "the essential self-interest of the human individual" (1966:136). These correspond, of course, with heaven and sin in Christian belief.

"Man and woman were made for God," the Christian contends, and they will not find the true meaning of life until they get into a relationship with God. Such a contention is an attempt to state a spiritual universal that we know not from observation of the cultural scene, but because God has revealed it to us. The fact that faith in God is the basis for this relationship with God is another revealed spiritual universal, as are the love with which God relates to us, the forgiveness of our sinfulness that he gives when we believe, and the like. The essence of the Gospel and its appeal to human beings of every culture are rooted in the spiritual commonality of humanity.

4. *Socio-culturally*, the high degree of human commonality in biological, psychological, and spiritual realms is expressed in the development and maintenance of human society and culture. This results in widespread and striking similarities in the basics of the sociocultural systems in terms of which

human beings operate. At the most basic level, the biological, psychological, and spiritual needs give rise to a series of universal cultural functions— functions performed by every culture. Biologically, the need for such necessities as food, shelter, air, etc., requires that each culture provide for the continuous obtaining of these biological necessities. Likewise at the psychological level, culture must provide for a measure of meaning in life, personal security, psychological integration, some degree of freedom, and whatever other basic psychological needs human beings have. Spiritually, all cultures provide explanations of and responses to beings and/or powers beyond the biological and psychological.

The organization of sociocultural structures to meet biological, psychological, and spiritual needs appears either to uncover or to create a series of additional needs that we may label separately as socio-cultural needs. Culture responds to these needs by providing such things as the organization of social activity, communication, social control, and the indoctrination of succeeding generations in the cultural system.

In a famous attempt to list a representative number of items "which occur, so far as the author's knowledge goes, in every culture known to history or ethnography," G. P. Murdock (1945:124) presents the following seventy-three categories, "arranged in alphabetical order to emphasize their variety":

age-grading, athletic sports, bodily adornment, calendar, cleanliness training, community organization, cooking, cooperative labor, cosmology, courtship, dancing, decorative art, divination, division of labor, dream interpretation, education, eschatology, ethics, ethnobotany, etiquette, faith healing, family, feasting, fire making, folklore, food taboos, funeral rites, games, gestures, gift giving, government, greetings, hair styles, hospitality, housing, hygiene, incest taboos, inheritance rules, joking, kin-groups, kinship nomenclature, language, law, luck superstitions, magic, marriage, mealtimes, medicine, modesty concerning natural functions, mournings, music, mythology, numerals, obstetrics, penal sanctions, personal names, population policy, postnatal care, pregnancy usages, property rights, propitiation of supernatural beings, puberty customs, religious ritual, residence rules, sexual restrictions, soul concepts, status differentiation, surgery, tool making, trade, visiting, weaning, and weather control (1945:124).

The number and nature of such universals are impressive. For they demonstrate that human beings, though participants in radically different cultural systems, have a great deal in common. And it is this great similarity among human beings that provides the basis on which cross-cultural human understanding and the potential for intercultural communication rest. If the diversity among human populations immersed in different cultures were such that there was nothing similar about different peoples, there would be no basis for intercultural communication. There would be no way that persons from one culture could legitimately suggest that the kind of experiences they had within their culture could have any relevance to anyone from another culture.

But such is not the case. "Even though specific behavior within any one area of life may differ, the range of common human experience is sufficiently similar to provide a basis for mutual understanding" (Nida 1964:55) and, therefore, for intercultural communication. "The inescapable fact of cultural relativism does not justify the conclusion that cultures are in all respects utterly disparate monads and hence strictly noncomparablities" (Kluckhohn 1953:520).

Differences between cultures do require adjustment on the part of those who would communicate cross-culturally. But this ability seems also to be a universal characteristic of human beings.

It would seem that we possess a kind of grid which we can employ to reinterpret experience in terms of some other conceptual framework, provided, of course, that there is a measure of willingness to do so and a degree of good will inherent in the activity (Nida 1964:55).

These recognitions concerning human commonality and its relationship to cultural (including worldview) diversity may be helpfully diagramed as follows:

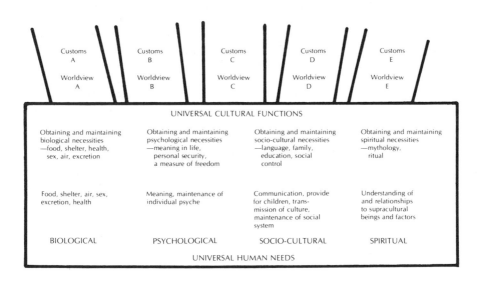

Fig. 5.1 Human commonality and cultural diversity.

In the diagram above, note the fact that those categories closest to the bottom of the chart show human commonality, whereas greater divergence is shown at the top of the chart. There seems to be less diversity between worldviews than between the creative ways in which the members of various human societies express themselves via their customs. Another way of saying essentially the same thing is to suggest that the surface-level forms of cultures differ more from each other than do the deep-level meanings (worldviews) and functions they express.

FORMS, FUNCTIONS, MEANINGS, AND HUMAN COMMONALITY

It is noteworthy that in order to get beyond relativism Goldschmidt felt it necessary to focus his attention on something other than the specific customs, the forms of culture. He, in fact, scores his fellow anthropologists for their over-concern for cultural forms such as "the kinship system of obscure tribes or the minutiae of native taxonomies" (1966:x). Into the same category he would put the specific cultural forms of family, marriage, social organization, political organization, religion, and the like. What he seems to be asking is, What are the basic human needs that necessitate the presence in every human culture of *some* form or set of forms to meet them? What, then, are the basic nonrelative human functions and meanings that this vast array of relative cultural forms are employed to serve?

Goldschmidt sees two broad categories or "general classes" of such functions and meanings:

(1) . . . those relating directly to human needs: obtaining food, providing shelter, procreating and the nurture of the dependent infants, protection against external threats, and the transmission of requisite knowledge. Essentially these are the animalistic requirements of man . . . and must be performed by any living creature with similar physical characteristics, but in human communities some or all of them are regularly performed by supra-familial groups and

(2) . . . the provision of the institutional machinery to maintain the social system as a system, in order to prevent the society from being rent by the centrifugal tendencies of individual self-interest. That is, the society must institutionalize behavior, form collaborative groups and maintain their internal harmony, and harness the individual to community action (1966:58–59).

It is, therefore,

useful to think of human society as that system of organization which mediates between the psychobiological drives of the individual on the one hand and the resources out of which life is sustained and protected on the other, utilizing the techniques that the community is heir to . . . . At the same time human society must also be seen as the means by which the ego-centered psychobiological needs of the individual are both given satisfaction and held in check, for these ego-oriented needs—whether they be food and protection, sexual gratification, or personal self-satisfaction—can only be attained by man in a social interaction system (Goldschmidt 1966:59).

A person's culture, then, is designed to serve the basic functions that all humanity needs to have provided for. It supplies people with forms (including structures and patterns) via which these functions will be met and the necessary meanings expressed. But it is these *functions*, with their accompanying *meanings*, that are universal and nonrelative, not the specific cultural forms in terms of which they are met in any given society.

It will be helpful to chart (see Fig. 5.2) the relationship between the six nonrelative basic human functions listed (above) by Goldschmidt and a representative selection of relative culture-specific forms developed to serve these functions. But as Christians we need to add to that list a vertical dimension that the naturalistic anthropologist often either fails to see, or perceives but dimly. When Kluckhohn states that "a system of beliefs, profoundly felt, is unquestionably necessary to the survival of any society" (1949:190), we may suggest that he has glimpsed this vertical universal of human life. Many anthropologists, in fact, have noted that, for most people, concern for their relationship to supernatural beings is at or near the core of their culture. These anthropologists are, however, generally loath to see the centrality of such supernaturalism as demonstrating one's need to have a vertical relationship with a God who stands outside of culture. Christians would claim that, in addition to the very important horizontal functions that supernaturalism serves (see the listing of the functions of a worldview in chapter 3, above), it betokens a universally human need for a relationship with the supracultural God. We thus add point 7 to Fig. 5.2.

What we are saying is that there are, in addition to the forms of culture, a number—actually a much larger number than the seven pointed out here—of nonrelative basic human functions or needs that cultures attempt to fulfill by means of specific cultural forms. If these needs are to be met adequately there must be a proper "fit" between the cultural form and the function it is attempting to serve.

EVALUATING CULTURAL FORMS

As pointed out above, the members of a culture not only do things, they evaluate them. And when such evaluations are made, certain criteria are employed. How a given cultural feature is evaluated is dependent on the criteria used in the evaluation.

If the area of cultural experience is hunting, for example, and the criterion of evaluation is *efficiency*, we may say that a gun is "better" than a rock. If, instead of efficiency, our criterion were *ready availability* on a steep slope where a gun would be too heavy to carry and too dangerous to use, the rock might be evaluated as "better." Similarly, if our criterion of evaluation is *extent of light shed*, an electric light is "better" than a flashlight. If our criterion is *ease of portability*, the flashlight is "better." If, with respect to housing, our criterion is *permanence*, standard American housing is "better" than a tent. If *portability* is the criterion, the evaluation is reversed.

Nonrelative, Basic Human Functions/Needs	Relative, Culture-Specific Forms Developed to Serve These Functions
1. Obtaining Food	a. Hunting b. Gathering c. Agriculture d. Exchange/Purchase
2. Providing Shelter	a. Cave b. Lean-to c. House
3. Producing and Providing for Children	a. Nuclear Family b. Extended Family c. Parents plus Nursery
4. Protection against External Threats	a. Individual Weapons b. Community Protection Groups c. Armies
5. Transmission of Knowledge	a. Imitation b. Informal Instruction c. Formal Instruction
6. Maintenance of the Social System	a. Taboos b. Laws c. Police Force d. Communal Groupings e. Ethnocentrism f. Patriotism
7. A Relationship with the Supracultural God	a. Belief Systems b. Ritual c. Prayer d. Worship

Fig. 5.2. Universal, nonrelative functions and relative forms.

Certain criteria of evaluation seem to be more appropriate when applied to certain aspects of cultural experience than when applied to other aspects. *Efficiency* seems to be a useful criterion for evaluating a large number of technological processes. It is important, for example, for an expensive machine to produce as many products as possible in a given amount of time. And most of our manufacturing plants operate on the basis of this evaluational criterion in that area of our culture. A problem arises, however, when human beings are expected to run such machines efficiently. Frequently in such situations human beings find themselves experiencing feelings of diminished personal worth, frustration, boredom, and the like. For, as they operate the machines, their work, like that of the machine, is evaluated in terms of the efficiency criterion. And efficiency is not an appropriate criterion in terms of which to evaluate people—unless, of course, a person is regarded as no more than a kind of machine. Much psychological harm results from such "machinizing" of human beings in a culture like ours. If, however, a *personal fulfillment* criterion were applied to manufacturing (as it once was), we would likely find both psychological dysfunction and efficiency in production decreasing.

Americans apply the efficiency criterion to people over a wide range of cultural activity. They substitute efficiency for *personalness* (an alternative criterion) in buying and selling, in mass-media communication (one too many), in transportation (isolated in cars or herded in mass-transit vehicles), and in many other aspects of American life. In judging personal worth, therefore, Americans tend to evaluate themselves as they would a machine—in terms of how much they get done most efficiently in the shortest amount of time. In many (most?) cultures the criteria for evaluating people in such situations are criteria of personalness—criteria more appropriate to people than to machines.

The worldview of a culture defines its own criteria for evaluating the way the forms and the people of that culture function. Americans have learned to live more or less well with "machinizing" evaluational criteria. They have also learned to live with criteria that evaluate individual freedom as "good" no matter how damaging this might be to the good of the group. They consider mobility, privacy, personal wealth, independence, and a host of similar things "good." They consider personal restrictions of various kinds, for example, family responsibility, poverty, illness, lack of privacy, dependence, autocratic government, etc., to be "bad." Whether these things are considered to be good or bad, however, depends on the worldview criteria of evaluation.

With respect to the inventory of cultural forms and the functions they serve, the basic appropriate evaluational criterion would seem to be the concept of "fit" or "fulfillment." The question to ask is, How well does this cultural form fit or fulfill such and such a function? In the case of the foregoing examples of the "use" of human beings in American culture, my bias is to suggest that the need of people for personal fulfillment is not well met by the occupational (and other) forms in which they participate. There is not, therefore, a good "fit" between the cultural forms and their intended function (assuming, of course, that personal fulfillment is a proper function of such occupations). If, however, the primary function of an occupation is to get the work done efficiently without regard to the emotional expense to the person, then the "fit" seems good.

Taking the foregoing listing of basic human functions, how can we adequately evaluate the cultural forms employed to express them? What should our criteria be? I suggest that criteria such as efficiency—criteria that relate well to material phenomena—would be appropriate to the first two categories (food and shelter). When it comes to the "people categories" (3–6), some such criterion as "adequacy to meet and balance personal and cultural needs" might be appropriate. The forms for category 7 may also be judged in terms of their adequacy for meeting human needs, but with an added dimension. That is the matter of their adequacy in properly relating human beings to God. The complexity of the cultural forms, the multiplicity of functions served, and the likelihood that our judgments will be tainted by ethnocentrism make such evaluating a very tricky business.

So why even discuss evaluating cultural forms? Because there seems to be no question about whether or not we will evaluate. All people seem to make such evaluations. The only question is, On what bases do we make our evaluations? It is hoped that by raising these issues we will be enabled to (1) discover some of our unconsciously employed evaluational criteria, (2) learn to employ more appropriate criteria (such as "fit" and "adequacy"), (3) learn to evaluate components of culture rather than whole cultures, (4) recognize the complexity of the task, (5) recognize the likelihood that we will be culturally biased in our evaluations, and (6) develop a cautious and humble attitude in our evaluating.

In cross-cultural ministry we will want to give considerable attention to the evaluation of many aspects of the cultural life of our receptors. We will be particularly concerned to assess the functions and meanings of their religious forms. "Is this practice usable within Christianity or does it express an allegiance that is incompatible with faith-allegiance to God through Christ?" Perhaps the following five principles will be both helpful and in accord with the insights generated so far:

1. As a first step toward evaluation, every cultural system should be sized up in terms of its own ideals, not those of some similar system in another culture (see model 10e and the case study on sin in chapter 12). What problems does this sytem set for itself and how well do its forms fit the functions/needs of which the people and their culture as a whole are aware? The folklore, especially the mythology, of a people will often be very helpful in defining these needs.

2. In evaluating any aspect of any culture (including our own) it is important to be constantly aware of the fact that the pervasiveness of sin is a universal. One implication of this fact is that every aspect of culture is less than totally adequate, even in terms of providing for the fulfillment of the ideals it sets for its members. That is, every cultural system falls short of providing adequately even for the needs that it defines for itself.

3. Even with the benefit of the biblical revelation, Paul felt constrained to state that "what we see now is like the dim image in a mirror. . . . What I know now is only partial . . ." (1 Cor. 13:12 TEV). It is therefore highly unlikely that we understand as much about the specifics of how God seeks to work in culture (even our own) as we often think we do.

4. We should recognize, as anthropologists point out, that a people's religious system does serve several extremely important horizontal functions whether or not it adequately fulfills the necessary vertical functions. Traditional religions, furthermore, "reveal fragments of truth—much more than many missionaries have supposed" (Wilson 1971:24). It is therefore likely that the majority of the forms of the religious system and many of its meanings can profitably be retained even after conversion to Chris-

tianity. They will thus be better able to serve their intended functions.

5. We should recognize the universal need for the fulfilling of the function of relating human beings to God. All people need this relationship with God through Christ. They need to experience it, however, without the necessity of converting from their particular set of cultural forms to, for example, our cultural forms (see Acts 15). For our forms are not prerequisite (or even necessarily the best) for adequately expressing the fulfillment of this vertical function in their culture.

Jesus seems to illustrate the application of such principles as these at numerous times in his ministry. One such time was in his dealing with the rich man who asked what he could do to receive eternal life (Mk. 10:17–22). Jesus first pointed the man to his own ideals (the commandments) and even accepted the man's own evaluation of his having lived up to them. This was at least a start on the horizontal level. But, by the man's own admission (i.e., his question as to how he could receive eternal life), the vertical dimension was missing. And Jesus' way of meeting that need (fulfilling that function) was in terms of a recommended new allegiance (to Jesus rather than to money), not in terms even of a change in religious forms.

Thus cultural forms and systems of forms can to some extent be validly evaluated. But this must always be (1) in terms of their adequacy in providing for the fulfillment of universal, nonrelative functions and (2) always within the system of which they are a part.

FITTING NONRELATIVE MEANINGS
TO RELATIVE CULTURAL FORMS

We now see that the acceptance of a certain degree of cultural relativism is no real departure from what orthodox Christianity has always contended: God is so desirous of reaching humans that he adapts his approach to human understanding. The major new things set forth here are (1) the more specific understandings of the cultural concomitants of such adaptation, and (2) a greater understanding of the relationships between the supracultural meanings (see chapter 7) to be conveyed and the cultural (including linguistic) forms by means of which they must be expressed if they are to be intelligible to human beings.

It is these latter—the cultural forms—that must be specific to the human receptors and therefore must vary from receptor to receptor and from culture to culture. The choice of forms is crucial to the impact of the message, but which forms are chosen is relative to the psychological, cultural, temporal, situational, and perhaps other factors in which the recipient is involved. The message to be conveyed, however, is a "constant."[1] It exists for all humans everywhere, for as long as humans inhabit the earth.

---

1. A constant is something that does not change within human experience. A constant, since it relates to finite, time-bound human beings, is presumed to be neither eternal nor absolute.

There are several such constants that originate outside of culture (with God) and are communicated via the relative forms of human cultures to human beings who are totally immersed in relative cultural contexts. One category of constants consists of the meanings that God seeks to communicate to all peoples at all times. We shall deal with these in chapter 11 when we discuss God's revelation to humans.

But there are categories of constants that originate within culture as well. Among these are things that are common to all human experience, such as culture itself (including its various subsystems identified above as universals). The fact of culture is not relative in the human context, since all persons everywhere are immersed in one culture or another. Apparently the overall functions that culture and its subsystems fulfill for human beings are constant. They appear to be demanded by human nature. Likewise, the fact of human sinfulness is constant (though the particular cultural perceptions and expressions of sin are relative), since all persons everywhere participate in sin. Sinfulness is, therefore, a universal or constant "function" (though not a need) expressed through relative cultural forms.

Cultural forms are seen here as essentially neutral vehicles employed by personal agents to express functions and meanings (such as sinfulness, familiness, or the message of God's salvation) many of which are universal to all human beings at all times and in all places. A large number of these functions and meanings (expressed via cultural forms) are (as far as we know) totally a matter of human expression. But God and Satan, usually (though not obligatorily) in partnership with human beings, also operate via cultural channels (forms) to serve constant human functions by expressing thereby supracultural meanings.

We may instructively illustrate these points by discussing the relationship between the constant function "sinfulness" and the relative cultural manifestations of the universal principle that sin infects all of life. For how sin is perceived by people differs markedly from culture to culture. In a very general way we may express this fact by means of a chart such as the following:

UNIVERSAL PRINCIPLE: All sin and experience alienation from God (Rom. 3:23)

REPRESENTATIVE CULTURAL MANIFESTATIONS (RESULTS) OF THIS PRINCIPLE:	Hebrew	Greek	American	African
	1. Idolatry	1. Going astray	1. Meaningless-ness	1. Fear of evil spirits
	2. Breaking the covenant	2. Falling short of perfection	2. Self-centeredness	2. Breaking one's relationship to one's kinship group
	3. Missing the mark	3. Unrighteous-ness	3. Loneliness	
	4. Transgression of the law	4. Lawlessness		
	5. Rebelling			

Fig. 5.3. Relative cultural manifestations of sinfulness.

The fact of sinfulness is beyond relativity. The perception of it, however, is in terms of specific cultural forms that are relative in that they may differ from culture to culture (they don't always). The chart above is not intended to suggest that the perception of sin in each culture is limited to the factors here identified with each culture. It does, however, attempt to highlight the fact that the same nonrelative element in human experience is perceived in a variety of forms each of which is relative and appropriate to the specific culture in question. See Dye 1976 (and below, chapter 12) for a useful discussion of this matter.

Another instructive approach to illustrating the relationships between the constant and the relative is to focus on a particular cultural form and to point to the variety of meanings that may be perceived through that form. Note that in this case we must deal in a primary way with the motivations of those who make use of the form. Furthermore, we must recognize that these motivations change from time to time and from situation to situation, even within a single culture. So do the perceptions of those who observe and attempt to understand what those who use the form intend. Though we all recognize that "nothing [i.e., no cultural form] is impure in itself" (Rom. 14:14), we also know that all sorts of forms frequently used to good ends may at other times be used to bad ends.

The cultural form *refusal to work on the Sabbath,* for example, conveyed a particular meaning to each of several groups with whom Christ dealt. Some of these meanings may be depicted thus:

Cultural Form	Possible Meanings
OBSERVANCE OF THE SABBATH	1. Devotion to God
	2. Formal obedience to God's law
	3. Formal obedience to Hebrew religion
	4. Fear that disobedience might bring misfortune
	5. The oppressiveness of the religious leaders
	6. Pride in living up to the letter of the law

Fig. 5.4. Various meanings of Sabbath observance in Jesus' day.

The Pharisees, to whom Sabbath observance probably had meanings 1, 2, 6 (and possibly 4), had worked out an elaborate array of rules and regulations (additional cultural forms) concerning just how one was to go about observing the Sabbath. These rules and regulations may have been fine as long as they functioned to enhance the Pharisees' understanding and expression of meaning number 1. But Jesus raised some doubts that this was the function they served even for the Pharisees themselves (see Mt. 23:5). And he berated them severely because their use of these forms communicated meaning number 5 to the common people (Mt. 23:4, 13–28). It was not in the forms themselves that the trouble lay, but in the purposes (functions) for which the Pharisees employed them, and the meanings that they thereby communicated to those who cried out for divine sympathy but received only Pharisaic oppression. The devotion to God, or lack of it, lies in the way in which the forms are used. The forms themselves are essentially neutral vehicles.

Similarly we may illustrate this form-function-meaning relationship by turning to the supracultural principle *love one another*. On the assumption that an American person genuinely seeks to express love in terms of each of the forms listed below, let us contrast the meaning that is likely to be perceived first by an "average" American, then by a rural, unwesternized African when this American employs these forms of expression:

Intended Function	Forms Employed	Perceived Meanings	
		American	African (rural)
	1. Kiss	Love, sex	Horror!—only monkeys kiss
EXPRESSION	2. "I love you"	Love, sex	"I want you sexually"
OF	3. Give money	Charity	Tokenism by miserly rich people
LOVE	4. Build a hospital	Compassion	Puzzlement—to Africans medicine is personal, not institutional
	5. Invite to church	Join another club	Play a European game
	6. Sit by a sickbed	Love and concern	Love and concern

Fig. 5.5. Forms and perceived meanings of attempts to express love.

There are, then, such things as principles, functions, and meanings that are constant. The expression of these, however, takes place through relative cultural forms. As we shall see below, we suffer from the tendency to absolutize the forms in terms of which important meanings have come to us, and to seek, as the Pharisees did, to impose these forms on others for our benefit rather than theirs. Though there are absolutes, universals, and constants, it is extremely important to distinguish them from the relative forms in which they must be packaged.

Many Christians have for so long associated Christianity with western culture that they have come to view the conversion of peoples of nonwestern cultures as synonymous with their adopting western culture. Church people to whom I speak concerning missions frequently make such statements as the following: "Of course when they become Christians they will realize that they should wear clothes, have only one wife, give up their drinking and dancing, go to church instead of to market on Sundays, have their weddings and funerals in church, stop going to the medicine man, etc." Such people are often startled when I reply, "No, not necessarily," since they have become so accustomed to missionary presentations that have focused on the changes in cultural forms resulting from response to the Gospel message. For missionaries have regularly given the impression that measuring the Christianization of a people is merely a matter of measuring the distance they have moved away from the cultural forms they practiced when first approached toward the adoption of western cultural forms.

With this understanding of what Christianization involves firm in their minds, those Christians and non-Christians alike who have swung over to a relativistic point of view are frequently heard to question the validity of Christian missions. "What right have we to assume that our ways are better than theirs and to try to make them adopt our culture?" they ask. Or they confidently assert, "They are happy the way they are," as if persons in other cultures have *no* problems simply because they may not have the same problems that we do.

Though it is easy to make this assumption on the basis of ignorance of other people's cultures, it is not possible to retain such an attitude once one has got beneath the surface of another culture. For, as Goldschmidt points out and Christian theology has long contended, humanity is not basically loving and good but, rather, selfish, sinful, and in need of cultural restraint (according to Goldschmidt) and of a redeeming relationship with God (according to Christian theology). Both recognitions of need focus not on cultural forms but on necessary (universal) functions.

Both cultural patterning and the Christian message deal primarily with serving universal functions. The only requirements with regard to forms are (1) that there be cultural forms—for, just as water cannot be transported except in containers, so universal functions cannot be performed except through cultural forms—and (2) that the forms employed be appropriate, within the total cultural system, to the functions that the members perceive and seek to express through them. For example, attempting to express God's love by oppressing people as the Pharisees did does not work, since there is a lack of "fit" between the intended message and the cultural forms employed.

Seeing beyond relativism to constants and universals (such as the sinfulness of all people) enables us to see the validity of cross-cultural witness to the Gospel message. But if response to that message is not to be evaluated in terms of subsequent change in the forms of a people's culture, how is it to be evaluated?

The principle here seems to be that *Christianness lies primarily in the functions served and the meanings conveyed by the cultural forms employed,* rather than in the forms themselves. Indeed, at this very point we can most clearly see beyond mere relativism. If it is true, as we contend, that God seeks to work in terms of cultural forms (which are relative), it is for the purpose of leading people into a relationship with himself. For that message, while appropriately expressed in terms of those forms, transcends both the forms themselves and the meanings previously attached to those forms. That is, God seeks to use and to cooperate with human beings in the continued use of relative cultural forms to express absolute supracultural meanings. *The forms of culture are important not for their own sake but for the sake of that which they convey.* And an appropriate fit between form and content is all-important.

With this background concerning the cultural matrix, we are prepared to investigate the relationship of God to culture.

PART III
GOD THROUGH CULTURE

6. God's Attitude Toward Culture

In Part III we probe the relationship between God, who is not bound by human culture, and human beings who are. We advance the theory that God's basic attitude toward culture is that which the apostle Paul articulates in 1 Corinthians 9:19–22. That is, he views human culture primarily as a vehicle to be used by him and his people for Christian purposes, rather than as an enemy to be combatted or shunned. To do this we introduce a series of models and submodels (models 4 and 5) relating to theological topics.

This basic position is developed in the present chapter against the backdrop of various theories that have been advanced concerning God's relationship to culture. First we treat the question of the origination of culture. Then we deal with the theory that God is antagonistic toward human culture. This is followed by discussions of two "God-in-culture" positions and five "God-above-culture" positions. The last of these (model 4a) sees God as "above" or outside of culture, but choosing to work through and in terms of the cultural matrix in which human beings are immersed.

The remaining two chapters in Part III deal (1) with the relationships between God's meanings and the cultural forms that they are to be fitted into and (2) with the principles of communication that exist in human contexts that God chooses to employ to communicate his messages to humans.

GOD THE ORIGINATOR OF CULTURE?

It is crucial in treating a topic such as this to give attention to just what God's position is with regard to culture. We may safely contend that in some way he is responsible for the presence of culture, for he created human beings in such a way that they are culture-producing beings. As far as anthropology can tell there is not now, nor ever has been, a human being who is not totally immersed in and pervasively affected by some culture. Neither anthropology nor theology can speak conclusively about when culture began. But from what we are able to observe about contemporary people we must assume either that the first humans began to produce the first culture the moment they became conscious of the world around them, or that God gave them a culture at or very soon after that time.

Some might contend that the production of culture did not start until after humans fell into sin and were banished from Eden. But whatever one decides with regard to the beginning point for the development or reception of culture, the more significant fact would seem to be that the existence of cultures is extremely ancient. As far as we can now determine, culture has been an inescapable part of human existence from very near the start of that existence. Furthermore, since culture for some time now has pervasively conditioned all people, we may assume that God created humanity with at least the capacity for culture. Indeed, our present evidence leads to the conclusion that there is within humans the *necessity* for culture. Human beings do not seem to function well in the absence of clearly defined and consistent guidelines for behavior. Much psychological stress and dysfunction is the result of one or another kind of breakdown in such social support systems. Friction between groups is another result of a lack of or inconsistency in behavioral guidelines. Indeed, as Goldschmidt suggests, the need for ordering interpersonal and intergroup relationships to minimize conflict may be the most important reason for culture, humanly speaking (1966:59, 136). From a Christian point of view one might suggest that cultural structuring of human behavior, or at least the human capacity for producing culture, is *another of the provisions of a loving God for human well-being*.

We have dealt a bit with the implications of human involvement in culture. The question before us in this chapter is: What is the attitude toward human culture of this all-knowing God who created human beings with a capacity to produce and modify cultural systems in which they are totally, inextricably immersed? Is God negative toward human culture? Is he positive? Is he neutral? Does he have a single "sacred" cultural ideal in mind, such as Hebrew culture? And is he grieved because we have departed so far from this ideal? Is he in the process of leading the church to produce an ideal "Christian culture"? Or doesn't he care?

In a now classic statement of the relationships that western theologians have seemed to understand between Christ and culture, H. Richard Niebuhr (1951) treats three basic positions: Christ *against* culture, Christ *in* culture, and Christ *above* culture. The following treatment, while indebted to Niebuhr and similar to his in many respects, charts a slightly different course at many points.

THE GOD-*AGAINST*-CULTURE POSITION

For those who take the position that God is opposed to culture, the choice for commitment to God is by definition a decision to oppose culture. This is a radical position, which identifies culture with "the world" as used in passages such as 1 John 2:15–16 and 5:19, where Christians are enjoined against loving "the world," since the world "is in the power of the evil one." They take such passages as indicating that God is dead set against human culture, since the latter is wholly under the power of Satan. To those who hold this view the essence of "culture" is the evil that they see around them, and the way to holiness is to escape from and to condemn "the world."

This is a widespread and ancient position found in the very beginnings of Christianity in the antagonism of early Christians toward Jewish culture and then, in response to Roman persecution, toward Greco-Roman culture. At a later date monastic orders were developed in the belief that true holiness can be attained or maintained only by coming "out from among them" into physical separation from the evil world (i.e., culture) around them.

In contemporary experience a variety of fundamentalistic groups have strongly endorsed such an interpretation of culture and encouraged near monastic separateness in attitude if not in actual physical arrangements. Such an approach to culture (at least to other cultures) has also characterized a disproportionate number of missionaries even from more moderate churches. These have come to require of their converts (as did the first-century Judaizers) the abandonment of much or all of their own cultural systems as a concomitant of their conversion to Christianity. In a more partial form such an antagonistic attitude toward culture is manifested by those who oppose politico-economic systems like communism, socialism, or capitalism, or nationalistic or religious movements on the basis of the assumption that God *could not* work within such systems or movements.

The answer that advocates of God-against-culture positions typically recommend is for Christians to withdraw, reject, escape, isolate, and insulate themselves from the world in order to develop and maintain holiness. Their position may be pictured thus:

Fig. 6.1. The escape-from-the-world answer.

This approach, while rightly understanding that Satan makes use of human culture for his ends, makes three serious errors. First, it equates the concept "culture" with only the negative use of the Greek word *kosmos* in the New Testament. John does use this term in a negative sense but with specific reference not to the whole of culture but to a particular *use* of that culture by the forces of evil.[1] To "love the world" then is to pledge allegiance to a principle of life—a principle of cultural usage with a point of reference other than God. The Christian way is, rather, to pledge allegiance to God and to use culture for him.

1. Incidentally, *kosmos* is the word John employs in John 3:16 as well, but with a positive or neutral meaning to refer to the world as the object of God's love.

A second fallacy in this approach is to assume that culture is only an external thing. It assumes that it is possible by "running" to escape from one's culture. This is in fact not at all true to anthropological understanding. We are inalienably bound to and by our culture (of which our psychology is, to a great extent, an individualized version). Our culture is *within* us as well as around us. We cannot escape it, though it is possible (as discussed earlier) to innovate, replace, add to, transform, and in other ways alter our use of the culture that we have received.

The third fallacy of this approach is the assumption that, since Satan is able to use culture to his ends, all of culture is evil. Perhaps Paul's principle with regard to the eating of meat offered to idols applies here—"that nothing is unclean of itself" (Rom. 14:14). It is the *use* of a given cultural item that makes it something to be shunned or something to be regarded positively, not the cultural item itself, and certainly not the total culture. What should be run from is participation with Satan in his use of one's culture.

The God-against-culture groups are caught in a dilemma. They cannot escape from culture, since their culture is internal as well as external. But, because they identify the forms of that culture as inherently evil, they seek to run from it. Since they cannot escape from it, they quite unconsciously carry it with them, living by and endorsing the major part of their culture, even though they believe themselves to be free of it. They do actually make significant changes in certain of their customs. And they focus on these changes when thinking about what they have done. But the major part of the truly Christian transformation that has taken place has been in the *use* they now make of *the same culture* that they have sought to escape from, rather than in the relinquishing of that culture. And this puts them in line with what may be observed from the Scriptures with regard to God's true attitude toward culture: God seeks to cooperate with human beings in the use of their culture for his glory. *It is allegiance to the Satanic use of that same culture that he stands against, not the culture itself.* As is often the case in human experience, however, the behavior of the advocates of this position often transcends their ability to theorize their position.

TWO GOD-*IN*-CULTURE POSITIONS

Many people, either in rejection of the God-against-culture view or in a rather naive fulfillment of that view, go to an opposite extreme. They believe that, one way or another, God is contained either within culture in general or within one specific culture.

1. The first group typically sees God (or Christ) as merely a culture hero—an expression of a longing on humanity's part to deify it. "People really create God in their own image," they say, and then people bow down in reality not to someone who exists but to a concept that human beings have created. In support of such a contention its advocates (including perhaps the majority of

anthropologists) point to the widely differing culturally defined perceptions of deity abroad in the world. They maintain that these differing perceptions have each developed wholly or largely as the result of the human quest for suprahuman sanction for the kind of life that a person's culture prescribes.

Christians must reject this kind of complete relativization of God. They do, however, need to note two truths that this position recognizes (though it overemphasizes them): (1) that the members of different cultures perceive deity in quite different ways, and (2) that the differences in these perceptions are correlatable with the differences between the worldviews of these societies. When one focuses *only* on culture-bound perception it is possible to suggest that even Christians to a great extent "create God in their own image." Americans, for example, so focus on the (idealized) love of God that they have difficulty interpreting scriptural passages displaying the judgmental side of God. Likewise, participants in early Hebrew culture, focused in as they were on the majesty and righteousness of God, while finding it relatively easy to understand his judgments, often failed to understand God as loving. In such ways, *at the perceptual level only*, people "create" the conception of God to which they give credence.

2. A second group of God-in-culture advocates see God as contained within, or at least as endorsing, one particular culture. This was, and still is, the view of many Hebrews who see God as related only to their culture. It is also the position of countless tribal groups who undestand their god(s) as exclusively related to themselves.

Within Christianity a God-endorsing-my-culture perspective often stems from the God-against-culture position. It sees God as either creating, gradually developing, or endorsing a given culture or subculture, and ordaining that all people everywhere if they are to be Christian be converted thereto. This concept may take the form of an absolutization of some historical culture such as Hebrew, Greco-Roman (often referred to in these contexts as "first-century Christian culture" or "New Testament culture") or, more often in the last few centuries, some form or modification of western "civilization." Or it may refer simply to "Christian culture" (which, insofar as it is defined at all, usually looks very western) or employ a term like "biblical culture" (as if the biblical records portrayed a cultural unity).

Quite often the recommended culture is conceived of in terms of a particular denominational or transdenominational (e.g., conservative or evangelical) subculture, at least with regard to its theological, ethical, and religious beliefs and practices. And other subcultural variables are often also specified, such as democratic government, capitalistic economics, "middle-class values" (including often such trivia as hair length and clothing styles), and the like.

Such a view correctly sees that there are major cultural differences between Christians and non-Christians. It fails, however, to distinguish properly between *a Christian use* of the forms of a given culture to serve Christian functions and *a whole culture* (or subculture), the forms of which may be labeled "Christian" (whatever this would mean). Even slavery, as counter to Christianity as we feel this cultural form to be, has at times been operated by Christians with a maximum of Christian considerateness. We dare not maintain that even such a nonideal custom can never be employed in such a way that it serves Christian ends (functions). Likewise, dictatorship, warfare (as in the Old Testament), death (e.g., martyrdom), secularism, etc. If there is Christianness, though, it characterizes *the function and use, not the cultural form per se.* Similarly, cultural forms that might be designated as "more Christian" than any of these are continually operated both by non-Christians and (often unconsciously) by Christians to serve functions that are completely counter to Christianity. Even the cultural forms of "Christian" charity, church organization, evangelism, etc., as we know too well, are often operated in very unchristian ways.

The weakness of this type of understanding of God's relation to culture is that it interprets Christianness of culture primarily in terms of the *forms* of culture, rather than in terms of the *functions* to which these forms are put and the *motivations* of those who employ them. The functions and motives may or may not be Christian. "Christianness" as a measure of culture is more properly applied to functions and motives than to forms.

It was for this view of the sacredness of (rabbinic Hebrew) cultural forms that Christ continually scored the Pharisees, pointing to the primacy of motive over form. This view was likewise the view of the Judaizers, who insisted that the only valid cultural expression of Christianity was in terms of the forms of Hebrew culture. The account of Peter's being reeducated on this matter is recorded in Acts 10, while in Acts 15 we read of the decision of the Jerusalem church to no longer require that Gentiles convert to Jewish culture as a concomitant of their becoming Christian.

At one point, though, this perspective has produced a valuable insight. Certain cultural forms do, apparently, allow for a greater possibility of being employed to serve Christian functions. Therefore, when there is opportunity for the Christians within a society to bring about change from less usable cultural forms to more usable forms, such opportunity should be taken. Thus the influence of Christians to abolish slavery, define and set up democratic government, work toward racial equality and the like should be applauded and encouraged, but not because there is any hope of ultimately producing a culture which we can label "Christian."

FIVE GOD-*ABOVE*-CULTURE POSITIONS

1. Many hold that God is *above culture and unconcerned* with human beings in culture. This is the position of Deism and much popular thinking within western culture. It is also the predominant view of the peoples of many African cultures. It holds that God is above and outside culture and no longer really concerned with the affairs of people. He may be regarded as having programmed the whole thing, wound it up like a clock to run as long as the

"spring" lasts but to disintegrate when the spring runs down. Others see God as having started something that he is no longer able to control. In either event he is regarded as virtually unreachable in his unconcern or inability; it is useless for us to waste time calling to him.

Thomas Jefferson and others who had a major influence on the early formation of the United States are often characterized as Deists. A typical "Christian" version of this view, apparently held by Jefferson, is to ignore God more or less completely but to hold tightly to at least a selection of the teachings of the man Jesus. In this way much theological and nontheological humanism has found a way to hold a belief in God, on the one hand, and in a human Christ, on the other, without accepting biblical Christianity's insistence on the deity of Christ. Much of humanism has moved from unconcern with God into either denial of the existence of God, denial of our ability to know whether or not he exists, or depersonalization of God into some sort of "Eternal Principle." In any event the result of such views is to turn our attention almost completely to humanity and to focus on the necessity for us to "go it alone" without realistic expectation of external assistance. To the proponents of such a view, those who hold to a close God on whom people are continuously dependent appear to be copping out on their responsibility as human beings. They are regarded as wasting energy that should be devoted to "human betterment" by participating in meaningless institutions and rituals such as church, prayer, and the like, buttressed by meaningless, archaic language and based on disproved and socially harmful mythology.

In its African varieties this kind of God-above-culture view typically regards God as one who once was near, became alienated because of some human misdeed, and has become very distant. God is often now regarded as terribly displeased with people but not totally unfavorable toward them. Meanwhile, many African societies see themselves endlessly plagued by evil spirits that God *could* control if they could only induce him to. But he is far away and people no longer know how to make contact with him. Such a view on the part of African societies has not resulted in the same kind of individualism that it has stimulated in western society. It has, rather, contributed to a tightening of social structuring in an apparent attempt to replace the security once seen as proceeding directly from God with one seen to proceed primarily from the society—though society is often still understood to function as God's intermediary.

In any event, such God-above-and-unconcerned-with-culture views, though developing from different bases, have much in common. They do not, however, typically share a common reaction to the biblical presentation of the relationship of Christ to God. Whereas African-type points of view, if approached properly, may see Jesus as the long-sought-for missing link between themselves and God and thus readily embrace him, western cultural manifestations tend to look on Christ and Christianity as a hindrance to "progress" from which they have now been emancipated. Western humanists, therefore, are prone to reject the possibility that Christ is any solution to their life problems, since they see a pledge of allegiance to him as a step backwards rather than, as in the case of many African societies, the filling of a long-felt need in their understanding of God's relationship to them.

Except for the truth of God's transcendence, which this position has carried too far, and perhaps the longing for reconciliation that it leads some to, it is difficult to say anything positive about such a perspective. It cannot be reconciled with the biblical portrayal of a concerned, communicating, interacting God. It thus contributes little to our search for an understanding of a biblically accurate perspective on the relationship between God and culture.

Another set of understandings of God as above culture is dealt with by Niebuhr in his discussion of philosophico-theological outlooks on the relationship between Christ and culture (1951). These he designates as the views of the "Church of the Center." He describes three varieties (positions 2, 3, and 4, below) each of which has been articulated by certain important theologians and each of which seeks "to maintain the great differences between the two principles and . . . [yet] to hold them together in some unity" (1951:41). These positions have all been developed as theological positions and have been influential within important segments of Christianity. They must be taken seriously in our attempt to arrive at a more comprehensive and biblically accurate perspective.

2. The first of these positions is that of Justin Martyr, Clement of Alexandria, and Thomas Aquinas and his followers. It has had an important impact on Roman Catholic theology. Niebuhr labels it *synthetic*. Synthesists, he says, in summarizing their view, see Christ as

the fulfillment of cultural aspirations and the restorer of the institutions of true society. Yet there is in him something that neither arises out of culture nor contributes directly to it. He is discontinuous as well as continuous with social life and its culture. The latter, indeed, leads men to Christ, yet only in so preliminary a fashion that a great leap is necessary if men are to reach him or, better, true culture is not possible unless beyond all human achievement, all human search for values, all human society. Christ enters into life from above with gifts which human aspiration has not envisioned and which human effort cannot attain unless he relates men to a supernatural society and a new value-center. Christ is, indeed, a Christ of culture, but he is also a Christ above culture (1951:42).

From this point of view the Christian is accountable to follow the requirements of both Christ and culture but each in its own place. Advocates of this position point to scripture passages such as Matthew 22:21, "Render to Caesar the things that are Caesar's and to God the things that are God's" (see similar statements in Mt. 5:17–19; 23:2; Rom. 13:1,6), as indicating that we are obligated to take both Christ and culture seriously and to affirm the authority of each in its own sphere. "There are other laws besides the laws of Jesus Christ; and they are also imperative, and also from God" (1951:122). Such laws inhere in the God-created nature of people, and people are held responsible for them. They include such things as the command to procreate and the necessity to organize social relationships. History is regarded by synthesists as "a period of preparation under law, reason, gospel, and church for an ultimate communion of the soul with God" (1951:195).

This view led Thomas Aquinas eventually to reject the world as it was but to see the church as the instrument of God to bring about a true culture. In this respect this view results in the God-endorsing-a-culture perspective. It leads to the same disastrous end in which the church-produced culture "tends to be absolutized while the Infinite is reduced to mere finiteness and the true dynamic of the Christian faith is lost" (Nida 1960:209).

3. The second Church-of-the-Center theological view described by Niebuhr is that of the *dualists*. Such influential Christian leaders as Roger Williams and in many respects Luther have focused not so much on dealing with the relationship between a Christian community and a pagan world as with what they see as a basic conflict between God and human beings in general—be they non-Christian or Christian.

. . . The issue lies between the righteousness of God and the righteousness of self. On the one side are we with all of our activities, our states and our churches, our pagan and our Christian works; on the other side is God in Christ and Christ in God. The question about Christ and culture in this situation is not one which man puts to himself, but one that God asks him; it is not a question about Christians and pagans, but a question about God and man (Niebuhr 1951:150).

The dualist is very thorough in assessing the evilness of human effort, and

discerns corruption and degradation in all man's work. Before the holiness of God is disclosed in the grace of Jesus Christ there is no distinction between the wisdom of the philosopher and the folly of the simpleton, . . . between the profaning of sanctuaries by blasphemies and their hallowing by priests, between the carnal sins and the spiritual aspirations of men; . . . before the holiness of God there are no significant differences. . . . Human culture is corrupt; and it includes all human work, not simply the achievements of men outside the church but also those in it, . . . philosophy . . . [and] theology also (1951:152–53).

Thus the dualist goes to the extreme in assessing the extent and the totality of human depravity. People are all evil. God, however, is all good and has provided reconciliation and forgiveness in Jesus Christ. A person can therefore be "stopped and turned round in his tracks by another will than his own" (Niebuhr 1951:150). But everything is a paradox in the present world and the only real solution to this paradox lies in the future when the present world is replaced. The Christian is like an amphibian living in two realms,

standing on the side of man in the encounter with God, yet [seeking] to interpret the Word of God which he has heard coming from the other side. . . . Not only his speech is paradoxical . . . but his conduct also. He is under law, and yet not under law but grace; he is a sinner, and yet righteous; he believes, as a doubter; he has assurance of salvation, yet walks along the knife-edge of insecurity. In Christ all things have become new, and yet everything remains as it was from the beginning. God has revealed Himself in Christ, but hidden Himself in His revelation; the believer knows the One in whom he has believed, yet walks by faith, not sight (1951:156–57).

4. Such Christian thinkers as Augustine, Calvin, and Wesley have espoused yet another view of Christ and culture. Niebuhr labels this view *conversionist*. Though this position is close to that of the dualists in that its adherents

hold fast to the radical distinction between God's work in Christ and man's work in culture, they do not take the road of exclusive Christianity into isolation from civilization, or reject its institutions. . . . They accept their Lord, [but] do not seek to modify Christ's sharp judgment of the world and all its ways (1951:190).

Conversionists are akin to both the synthesists and the dualists in understanding Christ more as redeemer than as lawgiver. They understand sin more as the dualists do, focusing on its pervasiveness in all human activity and the consequent corruptness of all that humans do. All culture is therefore under the judgment of God. Yet they see culture as under God's sovereign rule as well, and the Christian as under obilgation to "carry on cultural work in obedience to the Lord." They are thus more positive and hopeful toward culture than the dualists, while only slightly less impressed with the sharp cleavage between God and culture.

The conversionist agrees with the dualist in asserting a doctrine of a radical fall of man. But he distinguishes the fall very sharply from creation, and from the conditions of life in the body. It is a kind of reversal of creation for him, and in no sense its continuation. It is entirely the action of man, and in no way an action of God's. . . . Man's good nature has become corrupted; it is not bad, as something that ought not to exist, but warped, twisted, and misdirected; . . . his culture is all corrupted order rather than order for corruption, as it is for the dualists. It is perverted good, not evil; or it is evil as perversion, and not as badness of being (Niebuhr 1951:194).

The problem from the conversionist perspective is thus the problem of the conversion of culture, not simply (as with the dualists) that of replacing it with something entirely new—"though the conversion is so radical that it amounts to a kind of rebirth" (1951:194). History, therefore,

is the story of God's mighty deeds and of man's responses to them. . . . Eternity . . . less the action of God before time and less the life with God after time, and more the presence of God in time. Eternal life is a quality of existence in the here and now. Hence the conversionist is less concerned with the conservation of what has been given in creation, less with preparation for what will be given in a final redemption, than with the divine possibility of a present renewal . . . . The conversionist . . . does not live so much in expectation of a final ending of the world of creation and culture as in the awareness of the power of the Lord to transform all things by lifting them up to himself (1951:195).

Culture, therefore, is seen as corrupted but convertible, usable, perhaps even redeemable by God's grace and power. Culture is perverted but not evil in essence. History is the arena in which God's works are displayed and the conversion and transformation of humanity *and* culture are both possible, issuing, of course, in the final victory of the Son of God.

Now we turn to the fifth of the God-above-culture positions.

THE GOD-*ABOVE-BUT-THROUGH*-CULTURE POSITION (Model 4a)

Such God-above-culture positions as Niebuhr describes were developed prior to the recent elaboration of the concept of culture. The developers of each tradition were forced to struggle with the very complicated area of culture without benefit of the more precise understandings available today. It is not therefore proper to belittle either their understandings or their dedication. It is, however, now possible to go beyond them in many (though not all) respects. The remainder of this book is an attempt to do just that, on the basis of a concept of a relationship between God and culture that sees God as above culture but as using culture as the vehicle for interaction with human beings.

I align myself squarely with the general God-above-culture perspective in viewing God as transcendent and absolute, completely beyond and outside of culture. I see cultural structuring, however, as basically a vehicle or milieu, neutral in essence, though warped by the pervasive influence of human sinfulness. Culture is not in and of itself either an enemy or a friend to God or humans. It is, rather, something that is there to be used by personal beings such as humans, God, and Satan. Culture is the milieu in which all encounters with or between human beings take place and in terms of which all human understanding and maturation occur. The human psyche is structured by culture, as is every expression of groupness, including family, community, and church.

As we have seen, culture consists of forms, functions, meanings, and usage. It involves both patterning and process. When we speak of something of the complexity of culture as basically a neutral vehicle, however, it is important that we make clear both the senses in which we use the term "neutral" and the limitation of the position. The basic focus of this position is on the forms and the functions of culture. Culture is seen as a kind of road map made up of various forms designed to get people where they need to go. These forms and the functions they are intended to serve are seen, with few exceptions, as neutral with respect to the interaction between God and man. Cultural patterning, organizing, and structuring of life, the functions they are intended to serve, and the processes cultures make available to human beings are not seen as inherently evil or good in themselves.

Human beings, however, are pervasively infected by sin. This means that the use humans make of the cultural forms, patterns, and processes at their disposal is always affected by sin. The meanings intended and the meanings received are likewise tainted by the ways in which humans use their cultures. Apparently no human motive is unaffected by sin. Therefore no aspect of culture is used by human beings with pure intent.

But human beings are redeemable. And redeemed human beings begin to do at least some things differently. When they do things differently, they change their usage of the cultural forms, patterns, and processes at their disposal. It is the *use* of the cultural structures that is changed (at least at first), not usually the structures themselves. Redeemed persons live pretty much according to the same patterns and processes as before they became Christians. But now they use them with a new allegiance, for the sake of a new master.

Cultural patterns and processes are constantly undergoing change due to the influence of human beings, for humans are always changing themselves and their cultures. Thus, when individual transformations take place they lead to changes both in the individual's use of culture and in the structuring itself in terms of which the person lives. When groups of people undergo such transformation, more pervasive changes may be made both in use and in structuring. When such transformation takes place as a result of a relationship with God we may speak of the influence of God on culture change. Such change, in that it often involves drastic cultural reorientations, is often labeled "transformational."

This model assumes that, though God exists totally outside of culture while humans exist totally within culture, God chooses the cultural milieu in which humans are immersed as the arena of his interaction with people. Thus, when he speaks, whether directly or indirectly, to Adam or Abraham or Moses or the disciples or us he does so by employing human, not divine, language. And this language participates fully in human culture with all its strengths and weaknesses, its heights and depths, its glories and sinfulness, its facilitating of communication and limiting of it. He uses human language with all its finiteness, its relativity, and its assured misperception of infinity.

When God sought to communicate with Hebrews, he did not first demand that they learn a language and culture that allowed them, for example, to better understand his lovingness. He employed Hebrew linguistic and cultural forms in spite of their inadequacy in this respect. He even went to the extent of endorsing (for them, though obviously not for everyone at all times) at least major portions of Hebrew culture as it was. He did this even though he knew that their culturally conditioned fear of him would constitute a serious impediment to getting his lovingness across to Hebrews. This appears to account for the fact that God chose to work with Hebrews in terms of a culturally known covenant relationship. This may have been the closest they could come to the God-human relationship that the New Testament sees as grounded in love. Hebrew culture, at least at the time of the earlier Old Testament writings, may not have been able to comprehend "love as a pure expression of psychical reality apart from legality" (Quell 1964:27)—the legality of a covenant.

Nor, when God sought to reveal himself more completely, did he reject human culture and language as either too evil or too imperfect to serve as the vehicle for his Incarnation. He, rather, employed a thoroughly human culture—imperfect and imperfectible, finite, limited—as the vehicle of his supreme revelation of himself to human beings.

Furthermore, though Jesus and his disciples operated in Aramaic culture and language, when the events of the New Testament were recorded for the sake of Greek-speaking audiences, Greek was employed—and this in spite of the well-known difficulties (including both losses and gains in information) inherent in the process of translation. God has shown himself in the biblical record as so determined to communicate himself to different segments of humanity within their own linguistic and cultural contexts that he has employed at least three completely human languages and cultures as the media of his interaction with people. We deduce, then, that the relationship between God and culture is the same as that of one who uses a vehicle to the vehicle that he uses.

But this relationship between God and culture is not a required relationship in the sense that God is bound by culture. On the contrary, God is absolute and infinite. Yet *he has freely chosen to employ human culture and at major points to limit himself to the capacities of culture in his interaction with people.* On occasion he freely chooses to transcend cultural, spatial, and temporal limitations in events that we term "miracles." But frequently even in miracles he operates largely in terms of cultural factors rather than counter to them. Any limitation of God is only that which he imposes upon himself—he *chooses* to use culture, he is not bound by it in the same way human beings are.

7. Supracultural Meanings
via Cultural Forms

Having introduced the God-through-culture concept, we next turn to the relationships between Christian meanings and the cultural forms into which they are fitted. These considerations require the development of an anthropologically informed theology to consistently distinguish between and to relate supracultural meanings and cultural forms (model 4d). Next we treat biblical cultural relativism (model 4e), followed by a consideration of human perception of supracultural truth that is found to be adequate though never absolute (model 5a). We are culture-bound in our understandings and interpretations of God's truth. Our understanding of the relationship of culture to hermeneutics is therefore crucial (models 5b–5d).

ANTHROPOLOGICALLY INFORMED THEOLOGY

In an early attempt to deal with God and culture from what I am labeling a Christian ethnotheological position, William A. Smalley and Marie Fetzer (now Reyburn) coined the terms "superculture" and "supercultural" to refer to God's transcendent relationship to culture (Smalley and Fetzer 1948). Smalley later developed this concept in the pages of the journal *Practical Anthropology* in an article entitled "Culture and Superculture" (Smalley 1955). His article was prompted by a letter published in that journal the previous year. The author of that letter betrayed a high degree of confusion as to just what roles theology and anthropology should play in our attempts to discover what is absolute and what is relative.

The author of the letter[1] contended that "one should not establish an episcopal church government simply because the society is characterized by strong kings and subordinate lords" since "the question of church government is not an anthropological but a theological one." Rather, the missionary should go into the situation convinced through a study of theology "that either the congregational or the episcopal or some other form of church government is

---

1. Since that author has now totally changed his views I think it best to refrain from referring to him by name in the text, in the references after quotations, or in the bibliography. The position he espoused is so common and so well articulated, however, that it is helpful to cite the letter directly.

the kind Jesus Christ meant for every society, all over the world and at all times." He continues,

This procedure—first the theological and then the anthropological—must be applied to a myriad of problems . . . such as theft, polygamy, premarital sexual relations, lying, lay and/or clerical marriages, etc. . . .

An anthropologist *describes* but a Christian *prescribes*. He believes that God has revealed a system which is *absolutely* right, valid for every society during every epoch. [Emphasis added.]

The writer of that letter sought to dichotomize the theological and the anthropological evaluations of the situation. He says, "it is one thing to be a Christian and another to be an anthropologist." One may look at the situation anthropologically, he contends, only in order to obtain information about the customs of the people one seeks to reach. One should have already made up one's mind on the theological issues. Thus, in applying his theological conclusions to the indigenous situation, the writer says, "I must 'play God' " and "prescribe" the system that God has revealed to me through my study of theology as "absolutely right, valid for every society during every epoch."

The writer is undoubtedly right when he says:

The anthropology minded Christian missionary . . . *must not be so enchanted by his science that he fails to pursue the consummation of his goal*: the establishment of a truly Christian but, nevertheless, indigenous Church. [Emphasis added.]

The author's desire to discover absolute models before approaching the indigenous system and his feeling that it is to theology that we should turn for understanding of these models are likewise commendable. Unfortunately, his position appears deficient at two crucial points: (1) he does not see the contradiction between the imposition from outside of an "absolutely right" system that will be the same in cultural *form* (not merely in function or meaning) "for every society during every epoch" and the necessity that a truly indigenous church spring from the employment by Christianity of indigenous cultural forms; (2) nor does he take account of the extreme limitation that the monoculturalness of most western theology imposes upon its ability to deal with these issues in a cross-culturally valid way.

What cross-cultural witnesses need is not a continuation of the current dichotomization of the theological and the anthropological perspectives but a single perspective in which the insights of each specialization are taken seriously *at the same level*. For both are human-made disciplines (in spite of the sacredness of the subject matter of the one). And both disciplines suffer from the kind of myopia that all specialization leads to. For when we specialize *into* anything we automatically specialize *out of* everything else. In attempting to understand this or any other aspect of the relationships between Christianity and culture, therefore, we cannot afford to be "enchanted" with *either* discipline. For each discipline is too limited by itself to handle the specialization of the other adequately. Our model 4b postulates that *theology (as well as anthropology) is human-made and culture-bound.* Our theology, therefore, must be informed by anthropology and our anthropology informed by theology.

From an anthropologically informed theology, then, we propose model 4c: *Christianness lies primarily in the "supracultural"* (see below) *functions and meanings* expressed in culture rather than in the mere forms of any given culture. What God desires is not a single *form* of church government "absolutely right, valid for every society and during every epoch," but the employment of the large number of diverse cultural forms of government with a single *function*—to glorify God by facilitating the smooth, well-ordered and in-culturally intelligible operation of the organizations that bear his name.

To assume that this point of view endorses an abandonment of theological absolutes (or constants) is to miss the point in the other direction. Yet this is a natural overreaction, since theological understandings (especially at the popular level) have so often focused strongly on particular cultural *forms* such as the wording of creeds, the modes (rather than the meanings) of baptism and the Lord's Supper, the supposed sacredness of monologic preaching, the merits of one or another form of church government, refraining from smoking and drinking, and the like—as if these were absolute understandings of God's absolute models. Seldom have arguments over such matters dealt with anything but the *forms* of belief or practice.

Neither the Reformation nor any subsequent church split, for example, has centered around *whether* the church should be governed (i.e., the necessity or non-necessity of the governing function). That churches *should be* governed has always been assumed, since Christian things are to be done "decently and in order" (1 Cor. 14:40). Church splits have, rather, focused on the *type* of church government—a matter of form, not of function. Nor have arguments concerning doctrine generally focused on whether or not, for example, God has provided for human redemption, inspired the Scriptures, invited human beings to respond in faith, worked in history, etc. They have nearly always dealt with the *forms* these doctrines should take. They have ordinarily centered on theories as to how they are to be understood and formulated rather than with the fact that God has provided for these very important functions.

An anthropologically informed approach, however, identifies as the constants of Christianity the functions and meanings behind such forms, rather than any given set of doctrinal or behavioral forms. It would leave the cultural forms in which these constant functions are expressed largely negotiable in terms of the cultural matrix of those with whom God is dealing at the time. In what follows, then, I will argue that it is the *meaning conveyed* by a particular doctrine (e.g., consumption of alcoholic beverages, baptism) that is of primary concern to God. There is, I believe, no absoluteness to the human formulation of the doctrine, the historical accuracy of the way in which the ritual is performed, or the rigidity with which one abides by one's behavorial rules.

This is the point at which Jesus scored the Pharisees. For they, in their strict adherence to the forms of their orthodox doctrines, rituals, and behavior, had ignored the fact that these forms had changed their meanings. The way they used the forms had come to signify oppression rather than concern, self-interest rather than divine interest, rejection rather than acceptance, God against human beings rather than God with them. That is, as the culture changed, the meanings of the forms that once adequately conveyed God's message changed, along with the rest of the culture. And those whose responsibility it was to see to it that the message of God continued to be understood became primarily concerned with perpetuating and elaborating on the cultural forms in which the message came to them. They became legalistic concerning the traditional forms. But according to Jesus, godliness lies in the motives behind the meanings conveyed by the forms of belief and behavior, not simply in adherence to the beliefs and practices as traditionally observed. The beliefs and practices are simply the cultural vehicles (the forms) through which God-motivated concern, interest, and acceptance are to be expressed. And these forms must be continually watched and altered to make sure that they are fulfilling their proper function—the transmission of the eternal message of God. As culture changes, these forms of belief and behavior must be updated in order to preserve the eternal message.

Perhaps it is this focus on function and meaning rather than on cultural form that led John to refer to Christ as the *logos*, the expression of God (Jn. 1:1, JBP). Perhaps more clearly than with other cultural forms, linguistic forms such as words are seen to be important only insofar as their function is important. In John's prologue, Christ the Word, the Expression of God, is presented functioning as creator and sustainer, as the light of the world and, latterly, as a human embodiment of God. The focus is continually on his functioning on behalf of God, on his expressing God with respect to the human context. The form that he took to communicate these functions is mentioned but never elaborated upon because it is so subsidiary to his function of expressing God.

This is not to deny the importance of cultural forms—whether they be words, rituals, behavior, beliefs, or the physical body in which the Son of God lived on earth. The forms are extremely important because only through the forms does the communication take place. Even though it may be said that the water is more important to a river than the riverbed in which it flows, it is still the riverbed that determines what the destination of the water will be (except in a flood). So it is that the forms (like the riverbed) through which the meanings of language and culture flow determine the destination of those meanings. In communication, however, as in irrigating a garden, it is of crucial importance that would-be communicators (or irrigators) choose the proper channel (set of forms). They must then direct their message (water) into that channel rather than into another one if they are to reach those whom they seek to reach. Intelligent irrigators do not choose last year's channels simply because they have become attached to them, having learned to regard them reverently because the channels served them so well last year. Rather, they decide where they want the water to go and adapt last year's channels or create new ones to reach this year's crops. Even so the effective communicator (human or God) chooses, adapts, or creates cultural forms (channels) specifically appropriate to the task of getting his or her meaning (the "water") across to the present hearers. In this way the forms he or she chooses are very important, but only as means, never as ends in themselves.

THE SUPRACULTURAL AND THE CULTURAL (Model 4d)

In the development of an ethnotheological understanding of the relationship between God and culture, Smalley's reply to the letter mentioned above was a truly significant contribution. I will here build upon that approach, though with two major and several minor modifications. The first of these is to change Smalley's term "supercultural" to "supracultural"[2] and to reject noun forms such as "superculture" or "supraculture" as unusable. That is, since I contend that there is no such thing as an absolute set of cultural forms, terms such as "superculture" or "supraculture" that would seem to imply the existence of some sort of absolute cultural structure (i.e., some set of absolute cultural forms) are so misleading that they must be abandoned.

The adjective "supracultural," however, serves a very useful purpose in signifying the transcendence of God with respect to culture. That is, God, being completely unbound by any culture (except as he chooses to operate within or in terms of culture) is "*supra*cultural" (i.e., above and outside culture). Likewise, any absolute principles or functions proceeding from God's nature, attributes, or activities may be labeled "supracultural." For they, too, transcend and are not bound by any specific culture, except when they are expressed within a culture.

The second major modification of Smalley's scheme, though noted here, will not be developed in detail in this volume. It divides the outside-of-culture realm (the supracultural) into two compartments in order to show the place of angels, demons, and Satan in relationship to God, human beings, and culture. And this leads to a distinction between "supracultural" and "absolute" that Smalley did not seem to envision. That is, though God is supracultural, standing outside culture, so are angels, demons, and Satan. The latter, however, are not absolute, as God is. Smalley dealt with only two categories—the cultural, which is relative (i.e., nonabsolute) and the supracultural, which is absolute. The present treatment, however, assumes three categories: the supracultural absolute God, the supracultural nonabsolute beings (angels,

---

2. Smalley's original term "supercultural" was developed by analogy with "supernatural." Perhaps because of such widespread terms as superman, superbowl, superstar, and the like, the prefix "super-" on a word makes it particularly prone to be employed as a noun. The use of the prefix "supra-," however, is not nearly so likely to result in a noun. I understand that Smalley himself now prefers the term "supracultural."

demons, Satan), and the relative cultural context. This understanding may be conveniently illustrated as follows:

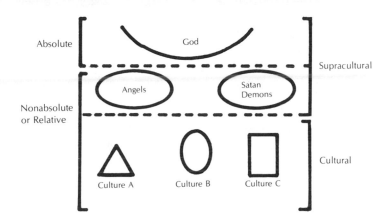

Fig. 7.1. The cultural, supracultural, absolute, and relative.

As Smalley states (in a rather Pauline sentence):

The whole question might well be phrased in the following form: Granted that there is a God above and beyond all human culture, that He has revealed Himself to man in several cultural forms (notably the Holy Scriptures and the life of His Son, lived as a man partaking fully of the life of a particular human culture), and that He has taken an active interest in parts of man's cultural behavior through time, proscribing and prescribing at various times and places; granted also that most (if not all) culture has developed through time by natural processes of development in different times and places, that particular forms in one place may have a completely different meaning in terms of function than what nearly identical forms do in another place, that God has at various historical periods proscribed certain forms of behavior which he has not proscribed at other times, that He has emphasized as highly desirable certain forms of behavior which He has not prescribed at other times, and that the heavy emotional attachment which people normally have for the familiar pattern (i.e., ethnocentrism) colors and distorts judgment; granted all this, what in human experience is God's absolute, unchanging, permanent will, and what is His will for particular times and places, and what is neutral (1955:58–59)?

In approaching an answer to this question, E. A. Nida states categorically that "the only absolute in Christianity is the triune God" (1954:282, fn. 22). If finite, limited humans are involved, Nida continues, the thing under consideration must of necessity be limited and therefore relative. Nida is clearly correct with respect to God as the only absolute *being* in the universe. Christian theology has always strongly asserted this. One might contend, in fact, that if the universe and all in it has been created, it is logically impossible to have more than one absolute related to it. Only that One who has brought the universe into being and who stands outside it can be said to be unlimited by it (as far as we know). All else that we know is somehow limited by the universe or, in the case of the angels, demons, and Satan, by God directly, and is therefore relative to either or both God and the universe. For relativity is simply "the state of being dependent for existence on or determined in nature, value or quality by relation to something else" (Webster's *Dictionary* 1967:723).

One might qualify Nida's categorical statement by suggesting that the absolute God has, in his manifold activities, manifested attributes and operated in terms of principles that are constant. These also look like absolutes from our vantage point. Smalley suggests, therefore, that the concept of the triune God as the only absolute in Christianity be interpreted as "specifically including His attributes, His nature, and His . . . ultimate, over-all will which is part of His nature and which stems from His nature" (1959:59). Other aspects of God's interaction with human beings such as "His immediate will for specific people and specific events" and any other outworking of His will in human affairs "must of necessity be relative to human finiteness, human limitations, human differences of personality, language and culture" (Smalley 1955:59–60).

The designation "supracultural and absolute," then, will be employed here for "God Himself, His nature, attributes and character, for the moral principles which stem from what He is (but not for particular acts of behavior which may attempt to fulfill those principles), for His plan and total will" (Smalley 1955:60). This designation may not by definition be applied to any cultural behavior, even if that behavior is "prescribed or proscribed by God for a given time or place, or for all time" or if the behavior is "a kind of 'relative absolute' in that a Christian is not allowed a choice in his particular situation, [for] the behavior is still cultural" (Smalley 1955:60). Christian behavior, therefore, and the specific interactions between God and humans that resulted in it are always cultural, even though God is supracultural and the principles on which the behavior is based are constants of the human condition.

But can we know these principles and can we trust our understanding of God and his will? That is, can we know supracultural truth? The answer is Yes because of God's revelation of himself. But our understanding can never be absolute or infallible, since it is only partial. Our culture-bound perspectives allow us to see even revealed truth only "like the dim image in a mirror" (1 Cor. 13:12 TEV). The Christian does, however, "know something, at least, of the nature of the [supracultural], but does not know all, and what he does know is colored by the cultural screen through which he must know anything he does know" (Smalley 1955:60).

The writer of the original letter raises another difficult question. He suggests the possibility that this view of God may portray him as extremely fickle, since he seems always to be "changing the arithmetic so that poor Jack [can] understand it." Can it be that the God whom Scripture contends is "the same yesterday, today and forever" (Heb. 13:8) has such a variety of standards that we cannot, through the study of the Scriptures, ascertain a trustworthy answer to any problem of Christian belief or behavior?

The answer to such queries lies in a redefinition of our understanding of God's consistency. I believe the Scriptures show God to be marvelously consistent, operating always in terms of the same principles (model 10a). But one of these principles (a constant) is that he adapts his approach to human beings to the cultural, sociological, and psychological limitations in which humans exist. The apostle Paul, following God's principle, endeavored to be a Hebrew to Hebrews and a Greek to Greeks (1 Cor. 9:19–23). God did not deal with Moses as if he were a Greek or with the Athenians (Acts 17) as if they were Hebrews. A culturally perceptive understanding of the Scriptures leads to the conviction that

one of the supreme characteristics of God's grace to man [is] the fact that God changed the arithmetic repeatedly so that Jack could understand it. The very fact that the Revelation came through language, a finite cultural medium, limits the Revelation, and limitation is a change. The fact that Revelation came through the life of Jesus Christ . . . living out a typical world culture modifies the Revelation, for it gives it the cast and hue of a particular finite culture at a particular period of time.

When Jesus said, "Ye have heard that it hath been said by them of old time . . . but I say unto you . . . " God was changing the arithmetic so that Jack could know more about it than Jack's grandparents knew. All church history records the changes in the cultural superstructure of Christianity. This does not mean that the [supracultural] has changed. The [supracultural] is God, His personality, His over-all will, His principles. The cultural manifestations of the [supracultural] change, and are relative to the particular situation (Smalley 1955:61–62).

We see, therefore, that what from one point of view looks like inconsistency on God's part is actually the outworking of a greater consistency. For God in his mercy has decided consistently to adapt his approach to human beings in *their* cultural contexts. Many, however (with the author of the letter cited above), will find such a view threatening. Among these will be closed conservatives who regard their particular culturally conditioned understandings of God's revelation as well-nigh absolute and their culturally moulded behavior in response to his revelation as the only behavior acceptable to God. Such persons, under the tutelage of ethnocentric theological traditions, fail to make the distinction between the inspiration of the scriptural data and the fallibility of their understanding of God and his works (see models 2a and 4b, pp. 33ff., 118, above). They therefore look on any deviation from their understandings as a deviation from orthodoxy (see Lindsell 1976; Schaeffer 1976).

The perspective presented here is not a deviation from orthodoxy. It is, rather, an attempt to modify the understanding and expression of orthodoxy in such a way that (1) it will be more useful to cross-cultural witnesses and (2) it will not have to be abandoned by anyone who recognizes that a good bit of the insight of the behavioral sciences into the relativities of human existence simply cannot be dismissed. From this point of view we are forced to recognize "that much of what [certain ethnocentric theologies have] decreed to be absolute is not, that much theological difference of view arises out of the ethnocentrism of theologians and their followers, and that God is not culture-bound" (Smalley 1955:69). For the human-made discipline known as theology has developed into "the philosophical study of almost anything identified with Christianity," including in a major way the behavior of humans and God within the cultural milieu. Theologies, therefore, concern themselves with culture—but often without the preciseness that anthropological study has developed in this area (Smalley 1955:62). Since theological study is (largely for historical reasons) often limited in its understanding of culture, its insights need to be supplemented with the insights into culture of other human-made disciplines such as anthropology. Only then can theological understandings of the relationships between supracultural truth and culture-bound expressions of that truth be (1) maximally useful to cross-cultural witnesses and (2) relevant and attractive to contemporary westerners who often know more about culture than do those trained in traditional conservative theology.

BIBLICAL CULTURAL RELATIVISM (Model 4e)

As we have seen in chapter 5, we cannot go all the way with those anthropologists (a decreasing number, by the way) who might be labeled "absolute cultural relativists." We can sympathize with the motivation to combat the evolutionary hypothesis of cultural development that, by evaluating all cultures by European technological criteria, ethnocentrically saw our culture as superior to all others. And I believe we must continue to oppose such a misinformed point of view whenever we find it (especially among Christians). But the proper alternative is not absolute relativism if by this we mean that it is never permissible to evaluate cultural behavior. For Christians (and, indeed, non-Christians) are never completely neutral toward cultural behavior, whether their own or that of others. We constantly monitor and evaluate the behavior of ourselves and of others (see the second function of worldview in chapter 3, above).

The difficulty is that too often when we evaluate the behavior of others we do not first seek to understand the behavior from the point of view of that person and of that culture (i.e., in its cultural context). We simply judge the behavior as if it were a part of our own system. Yet the meaning of that behavior is derived *entirely* from within the other's system, never from ours or from some "cosmic pool" of universal meanings (see below p. 135ff.). And when we evaluate our own behavior we frequently ignore the fact that our actions make sense *only* within the total pattern of life in which we are involved. We cannot assume that the behavior which we hold so dear and which we may feel to be so superior can simply be grafted into someone else's culture as it is and prove to be superior within that system.

We must adopt a sufficiently relativistic stance to help us toward understanding and appreciation (rather than judgmental condemnation) of another's activity within that person's cultural system (see the discussion of the cultural validity model, model 3b, in chapter 3). But we must reject emphatically the absolute relativism that simply says, "Live and let live without ever attempting to influence anyone else in the direction of one's own values since there are no absolute standards and, therefore, his system is just as good as ours" (see McGavran 1974:2–6 for illustrations of certain disturbing results of this kind of principle).

Rather, as Christians we may find helpful a model or perspective that Nida calls "relative cultural relativism" (1954:50). This model asserts the presence of absolutes (supracultural truths) but relates them all to God who stands outside of culture, rather than to any cultural expression, description, or exemplification of a God-human relationship (be it American, Greek, or Hebrew). (See above in this chapter for further explanation of the rationale for such a position.)

Nida and other Christian ethnotheologians see this "biblical cultural relativism" as "an obligatory feature of our incarnational religion," asserting that "without it we would either absolutize human institutions" (as ethnocentric positions do) or, going to the opposite extreme (as absolute relativists do), we would "relativize God" (1954:282). In his excellent discussion of this topic, Nida (1954:48–52) points out that the Bible

clearly recognizes that different cultures have different standards and that these differences are recognized by God as having different values. The relativism of the Bible is relative to three principal factors: (1) the endowment and opportunities of people, (2) the extent of revelation, and (3) the cultural patterns of the society in question (p. 50).

1. God conditions his expectations of human beings, in the first place, by making allowance for differences in the endowment and opportunities of the people with whom he is dealing. In the parable of the Talents (Mt. 25:14–30) and again in the parable of the Pounds (Lk. 19:12–27), Jesus teaches a modified relativism. For in God's interaction with people, "rewards and judgment are relative to people's endowments, for the one who receives five talents and gains five additional talents receives not only the commendation of his master but an additional talent" (ibid.)—the one taken from the servant who refused to use (and risk) that which was entrusted to him. Likewise, the one to whom two

talents were given was commended because he also had used what he had to gain more. Though the main point of the passage has to do with the importance of people using what is given them for the sake of their master, it is clear that the parable also implies *(a)* that there is relativity (i.e., difference) in what each human being starts with, *(b)* that, therefore, God expects relatively more from those who have started with relatively more, and *(c)* that his judgment of people is relative both to what they have been given and to what they do with it.

This is not an absolute relativity, since the principle in terms of which the master makes his judgments is constant and universally applicable. Note that the servant who received relatively less than the others was not condemned because he started with less, nor even because he finished with less (these are both relative), but because he refused to operate by a supracultural principle of accountability. This principle is articulated clearly in Luke 12:48: "The man to whom much is given, of him much is required; the man to whom more is given, of him much more is required" (TEV). Thus we are here dealing with a relative relativity rather than with absolute relativity, which would allow no standard of evaluation whatsoever.

2. In the second place (and partially overlapping with the first), we see in the Bible a relativism with respect to the extent of the revelational information available to given culture-bound human beings (see chapter 11). Jesus points clearly to this fact time and time again when he compares his superior revelation of God to previous (Old Testament) revelations of God. To the Hebrews of Moses' time God allowed and even endorsed their cultural principle of "an eye for an eye and a tooth for a tooth" (Lev. 24:20). But Jesus spoke differently to Moses' descendants who, several hundred years later, had an understanding of God based on the accumulation of considerably more revealed information than was available to their ancestors. To them he said:

You have heard that it was said, "An eye for an eye, and a tooth for a tooth." But now I tell you: do not take revenge on someone who does you wrong. If anyone slaps you on the right cheek, let him slap your left cheek too (Mt. 5:38, 39 TEV).

When Jesus "changed the arithmetic" from "retaliate" to "love your enemies" (Mt. 5:44) his hearers and all of us who have come after them (i.e., who are "informationally A.D."—see chapter 12) became accountable for a higher standard than was expected of the Hebrews of Moses' day. This higher standard is also illustrated in the matter of murder (i.e., hate now equals murder—Mt. 5:21–22) and with reference to adultery (i.e., lust equals adultery—Mt. 5:27–28). Perhaps the lowest revelational standard available to people is that referred to by Paul in Romans 2:14–16:

When Gentiles who do not possess the law carry out its precepts by the light of nature [culture?], then, although they have no law, they are their own law, for they display the effect of the law inscribed on their hearts. Their conscience is called as witness, and their own thoughts argue the case on either side, against them or even for them, on the day when God judges the secrets of human hearts through Christ Jesus. So my gospel declares (NEB).

It is clear, then, that human accountability before God is relative to the extent of revelation that human beings have received. And we end up with respect to revelation at the same point at which we ended vis-à-vis endowment—at a degree of accountability determined according to a supraculturally controlled given that differs from person to person and from group to group. Thus

the servant who knew his master's wishes, yet made no attempt to carry them out, will be flogged severely. But one who did not know them and earned a beating will be flogged less severely. Where a man has been given much, much will be expected of him; and the more a man has had entrusted to him the more he will be required to repay (Lk. 12:47–48 NEB).

3. A third aspect of biblical relativism (again partially overlapping with the other two) is the fact that God takes into account the cultures of the peoples with whom he deals. That is, God conditions his expectations for each society to take account of the cultural patterns in terms of which their lives are lived. True, God works with people for culture change. But he starts by accepting and even endorsing customs practiced by Old Testament peoples that he condemns or at least does not endorse in his dealings with Greco-Roman peoples. God's approach, then, is relative to the human cultures of the Bible. We assume that he deals with contemporary cultures in terms of the same principle. See Barney 1957 for a good contemporary illustration of this approach.

Leviticus 25:39–46, for example, sanctions the enslaving of Gentiles by Jews (though not of Jews by Jews). This was undoubtedly the prevalent custom. But God chose to work *with it* on the surface, while at the same time advocating other principles that would eventually do away with the custom. It seems to have died out by New Testament times. He seems to have chosen to refrain from making a big issue of such nonideal customs, probably to keep from diverting attention from more important aspects of his interaction with the Hebrews. He treated polygamy (see 2 Sam. 12:7–8) including levirate marriage (Deut. 25:5–6), trial by ordeal (Num. 5:11–28), and numerous other Hebrew customs similarly. In dealing with divorce Jesus makes explicit the reason why God chose to allow and endorse such less-than-ideal customs—it was because of the "hardness of their hearts" or, as the New English Bible translates it, "because [their] minds were closed" (Mk. 10:5) and God was patient (2 Pet. 3:9).

The most significant New Testament indication of biblical endorsement of a relativistic attitude toward culture, however, lies in Paul's statement that he attempted to be "all things to all men." This statement is buttressed by several illustrations of his application of this principle. In 1 Corinthians 9:20–22, for example, he indicated his movement back and forth over the cultural barrier separating Jews from Greeks:

To Jews I became like a Jew, to win Jews; as they are subject to the Law of Moses, I put myself under that law to win them, although I am not myself subject to it. To win Gentiles, who are outside in the Law, I made myself like one of them, although I am not in truth outside God's law, being under the law of Christ. . . . Indeed, I have become everything in turn to men of every sort, so that in one way or another I may save some (NEB).

This principle of approaching each situation in terms of its own special cultural circumstances is a constant supracultural principle of God's interaction with people. The principle, therefore, is not relative, but its application in the relative context of human culture illustrates once again the correctness of the "biblical relativity" understanding of God's approach to people. Both the supracultural principle and this understanding of biblical relativity enable us to explain a large number of apparent discrepancies in the working of God in the human context. The relative application of God's supracultural principle explains, for example, how Paul could object strenuously to Peter's compromising in a Gentile context under pressure from the Judaizers (Gal. 2:11–14). Yet, later, he himself, when in a wholly Jewish context, went through Hebrew rites of purification to demonstrate to them that he had not abandoned Judaism (Acts 21:20–26). Likewise, Paul could circumcise Timothy who had a Greek father but a Jewish mother, in order to give him an "in" with the Jews (Acts 16:3), yet not compel Titus, whose parentage allowed him no such "in" with the Jews, to go the same route (Gal. 2:3).

Nida helpfully summarizes this perspective by stating:

Biblical relativism is not a matter of inconsistency but a recognition of the different cultural factors which influence standards and actions. While the Koran attempts to fix for all time the behavior of Muslims, *the Bible clearly establishes the principle of relative relativism, which permits growth, adaptation, and freedom, under the Lordship of Jesus Christ.* The Bible presents realistically the facts of culture and the plan of God, by which He continues to work in the hearts of men "till we all come in the unity of the faith, and of the knowledge of the Son of God, unto a perfect man, unto the measure of the stature of the fulness of Christ" (Eph. 4:13). *The Christian position is not one of static conformance to dead rules, but of dynamic obedience to a living God* (1954:52). [Emphasis added.]

Far from being a threat to a Christian perspective (even a conservative one), the development of an understanding of biblical cultural relativism should be regarded as a part of the leading "into all truth"(Jn. 16:13), which is one of the important functions of the Holy Spirit today.

ADEQUATE, THOUGH NEVER ABSOLUTE,
HUMAN PERCEPTION OF SUPRACULTURAL TRUTH (Model 5a)

Perhaps the most basic problem in this whole area is the reliability of our perception of supracultural truth. Can we trust what we think we understand? If sincere specialists such as theologians are not exempt from cultural limitations in their understandings of supracultural truth, where does that leave the rest of us? Furthermore, if we adopt the position here advocated and open ourselves up to the validity of a diversity of culturally conditioned interpretations, can we be certain that any supracultural truth will survive at all? The answers lie in (1) coming to better understand how the Holy Spirit goes about leading culture-bound human beings "into all truth" (Jn. 16:13), and (2) the sufficiency of an adequate, though nonabsolute, understanding of supracultural truth.

The Spirit leads "into all truth" via the human perception of those to whom he speaks. Since the channel is culture-bound human perception, the receptors do not understand supracultural truth absolutely. Indeed, we are limited by at least five factors:

1. The limitations of the revelations (including "illuminations"). God has seen fit to reveal only certain things concerning himself, his plans, and his purposes. That which he has not yet revealed we cannot know.

2. Our finiteness. We are limited in our understanding of even that which has been revealed. We all study the same Scriptures but there are a multitude of differing interpretations of the meaning of much of what is there revealed.

3. Our sinfulness. Our perception and ability to understand and respond to God's revelation is, like every other aspect of our lives, affected at every point by sin. For this reason our motives are never completely pure nor our vision completely lucid.

4. Our cultural conditioning. The fact that we are totally immersed in a given culture conditions us to perceive of all reality, including God's revelation, in terms of that culture.

5. Our individual psychological and experiential conditioning. Even within shared cultural boundaries, the life experience of every individual is unique. This likewise conditions one's perception of the revelation.

The assumption here is that supracultural truth exists (with God) above and beyond any cultural perception or expressions of it. God reveals to us glimpses of this truth via the human languages and cultures of the Scriptures. Our perception of the various aspects of this truth may be barely acceptable to God at the start but may, during the course of our maturing as Christians, develop into a much more ideal understanding. This may eventually approach, though never quite reach, the supracultural ideal that lies outside culture and therefore beyond our grasp.

As receptors who are limited in these ways we interpret the Word and other (e.g., experiential) data at our disposal in terms of culturally organized models that incorporate and exhibit these limitations. Though we are not totally unable to see beyond what such cultural structuring channels us into, our tendency is to gravitate toward and to most readily understand those portions of supracultural truth that connect most closely with life as we already perceive it. How the faces of Africans light up as they hear that God endorsed levirate (Deut. 25:5–10), polygamous (2 Sam. 12:7–9), arranged marriages (Gen. 24:50–51; 34:10–12) and many other customs similar to theirs. But none of these Hebrew perceptions of God excited Luther, for German culture is related to and has been influenced by Greek culture. So it was those portions of Scripture couched in Greek thought patterns that caught Luther's attention. The Spirit, then, spoke most clearly to Luther via those portions.

In the original revelation of biblical materials God also worked in terms of culturally conditioned human perception. For each biblical writing participates completely in the context to which it is addressed. And the topics treated are dealt with, under the leading of the Spirit, in categories culturally and linguistically appropriate to the way a particular culturally and psychologically conditioned participant perceives of that situation and its needs.

It is not at all strange that large portions of the New Testament are phrased in terms of *Greek* conceptual categories (rather than in supracultural categories). For God wanted his message contextualized within the human frame of reference in such a way that it would be maximally intelligible to those within that frame of reference. So he led Paul and others to write about those things that they noticed and perceived to be important both to God and to their hearers. There are many questions that we twentieth-century Euro-Americans wish Paul had written about (e.g., race relations, the place of women, the relative importance of evangelism, and "social action"). But he, in his cultural setting, did not see the importance of providing a word from God on such issues. God will have to provide that word through people today whom he leads to be as concerned about these issues as Paul was about the issues he faced.

Nor is it strange that the writings of the Old Testament and those portions of the New Testament written to Hebrews show other authors dealing under the leading of God with other issues. Apparently it has always been God's plan to lead people via their concerns. What might be considered surprising is that so many very specific issues in both the Old Testament and the New Testament are of such wide general relevance to peoples of many other cultures, and are dealt with within Hebrew and Greek cultural matrices in such a way that people today can benefit from the scriptural treatments. Beyond the divine factors involved, we can point to two human conditions that God has exploited. The first is the high degree of basic similarity between peoples of different cultures (model 3g). So much of the Bible deals with basic issues of life that its relevance is assured at this level. The second of the human conditions is the great similarity between the cultures of the Bible and contemporary cultures. This is especially true of Hebrew culture throughout most of the world and of Greek culture and European cultures. Most of the Bible is couched in Hebrew thought patterns. Though those portions of the Scriptures are often less compelling for Europeans, the Spirit frequently speaks clearly through them to other peoples of the world.

The Scriptures are like the ocean and supracultural truth like the icebergs that float in it. Many icebergs show at least a bit of themselves above the surface, some lie entirely beneath the surface. Much of God's revelation of himself in the Scriptures is at least partially visible to nearly anyone who is willing to see it—though belief must precede "seeing" (Jn. 5:39). But much lies beneath the surface, visible only to those who search to discover what supracultural truth lies beneath the specific cultural applications in Scripture.

"PLAIN MEANINGS" AND "INTERPRETATIONAL REFLEXES"

Searching beneath the surface involves the process of interpretation (technically called "hermeneutics"). The fact that we are in a different culture from that in which the original events occurred causes problems, for our perception and our interpretation are affected by that different culture. We learn as part of our cultural conditioning a set of "interpretational reflexes"—a set of habits in terms of which we automatically interpret whatever happens. We don't think things through before we interpret in these ways. Our responses are reflexive in the same way that most of our muscular responses are reflexive. We need to develop hermeneutical techniques for getting beyond these reflexive interpretations into as close an approximation as possible to the perception of the original participants.

There is a sense in which a new or deepened approach to hermeneutics is the major subject of this whole book. Certainly the kind of alteration in our understandings of biblical communication and translation that this book aims to bring about implies an alteration in the way many interpret God's Word. The following is but a preliminary presentation of an approach to biblical interpretation that is developed in much greater detail as the book progresses.

Those unaware of the pervasive influence of their own culture on their interpretations often slip unconsciously into the assumption that arriving at most supracultural truth is simply a matter of accepting the "clear" or "plain meanings" of Scripture. A typical statement of this view says, "The plain meaning of the Bible is the true meaning" (McGavran 1974:65). Lindsell condemns those who disagree with his point of view by accusing them of developing "interpretations of Scripture *at variance with the plain reading* of the texts" (1976:39, emphasis added).

A plain-meaning position assumes that our interpretation corresponds with that of the authors of Scripture. There is, however, a major problem here, stemming from the fact that those who agree on large areas of cultural experience seldom discuss (or make explicit in other ways) these areas of agreement.

What everyone in a given context assumes (i.e., agrees on) is not mentioned. People conditioned by the same culture agree on, and therefore seldom if ever discuss, thousands of interpretationally (hermeneutically) significant understandings and perspectives. Hebrews, for example, assumed that God exists. The author of Genesis as a Hebrew writing to other Hebrews did not have to prove God's existence. Jesus could rightfully assume that his hearers understood what a mustard bush and its seeds looked like, that those who sowed seeds scattered them "broadcast" (rather than, say, putting each seed in a separate hole), that sheep could be *led* (rather than driven) by a shepherd, etc.

The interpretational reflexes of Jesus' hearers were conditioned by the same culture as his were, and so they did not need explanation of the assumptions and agreements underlying Jesus' words and actions. Our interpretational reflexes are conditioned by quite a different culture. Thus we are likely to find that any given portion of Scripture falls into one or the other of the following categories characteristic of any communicational situation that involves the crossing of a cultural border.

1. We, as readers, may not understand major portions of what is going on at all, since we don't know the cultural agreements. In the story of the Woman at the Well, for example, we are likely to miss entirely the significance of such things as Jesus' going through Samaria, his talking to a woman, the fact that the woman was at the well at midday, the necessity that she go back to get her supposed husband before she could make a decision, etc. For us to understand such things we need large doses of explanation by those who study the cultural background. We cannot simply trust our culturally conditioned interpretational reflexes. For the Scriptures are specific to the cultural settings of the original events. Sheep, mustard seeds and bushes, broadcast sowing, levirate marriage, and many other aspects of the life of biblical cultures fit into this category.

2. A much bigger problem of interpretation lies in those areas where the Scriptures use cultural symbols that are familiar to us but for which our cultural agreements are different. We are tempted to interpret according to what seems to be the "plain meaning"—as if we could get the proper meaning of Scripture as we would from a document originally written in English. To avoid this pitfall, many translation theorists are now contending that a faithful translation of the Scriptures must involve enough interpretation to protect the reader from being seriously misled at points such as these. Our interpretational reflexes tell us, for example, that a fox is sly and cunning. So, when Jesus refers to Herod as a fox (Lk. 13:32) we misinterpret the symbol to mean sly when, in fact, on the basis of the Hebrew cultural agreement, it was intended to signify treachery. Our cultural reflexes tell us that plural marriage is primarily a sexual matter, though in nonwestern cultures it seldom is. Our cultural reflexes tell us that Jesus was impolite to his mother when he addressed her the way he did in the temple and at the wedding feast. Our culturally conditioned interpretational reflexes lead us to understand "the faith

once for all delivered to the saints" (Jude 3) to be a system of doctrine rather than a relationship to God, and the "by faith" of Hebrews 11 to signify something somewhat less than behavioral obedience (faith=faithfulness or obedience in Hebrew categories). The culturally conditioned interpretational reflexes of the Nigerians I worked among misled them into thinking that Psalm 23 presented Jesus as insane, since in their culture only young boys and insane men tend sheep. The interpretational reflexes of the Sawi of New Guinea misled them into admiring the treacherous Judas even more than Jesus (Richardson 1974) and those of the Chinese to regarding positively the dragon of Revelation.

The point is that, for cultural reasons, we who are not a part of the biblical cultures cannot *trust* our interpretational reflexes to give us the meanings that the original authors intended. What are to us the "plain meanings" are almost certain to be the wrong meanings unless the statements are very general (see below). Therefore, we must engage in exegesis to discover what the original utterances meant to those whose interpretational reflexes were the same as those of the authors.

With respect to interpretational reflexes, there seem to be four principles:

1. If the culture of the original is at any given point very similar to ours, our reflexes are going to serve us fairly well. In these instances the interpretational principle that says, "The plain meaning is the true meaning" is a valid principle. Such a situation is rarely the case between Euro-American culture and the Hebrew and Aramaic portions of the Scripture. Certain Greek cus toms do, however, seem to be similar enough to Euro-American customs that our interpretational reflexes will give us the correct meaning. I think in this regard of the language of the track meet that Paul uses in Philippians 3. The same may be true of the language of economics that Paul uses earlier in that same chapter. The amount of biblical material where there is such close cultural similarity to our agreements is, however, distressingly small, and the fact that we cannot trust our interpretational reflexes in most places means that *we can never be sure of them unless we have independent evidence* that this is a place where their custom is close to ours.

2. If the scriptural statement is *a cultural universal*, however, our interpretational reflexes will enable us to get close to the intended meaning. Statements that exist, as far as we know, in every one of the world's cultures, e.g., the concepts in the Ten Commandments, are easy to interpret relatively accurately. There is a slight problem in the fact that each culture defines murder, adultery, etc. in its own way. But the fact that such commands occur in all cultures means that these statements are elevated out of the most difficult interpretational category—that of the culturally specific. Other parts of Scripture such as those dealing with eating together, injunctions like "Love your neighbor," and many of the proverbs are also in the cultural-universal category.

3. Similarly, if a scriptural statement relates to *experiences that are common to*

all humankind, our culturally conditioned interpretational reflexes can be of considerable help. When the Scriptures say "go," "come," "trust," "be patient," and the like, they are dealing with experiences that are common to all human beings and readily interpretable. Likewise, with respect to illness and death, childbirth and rearing, obtaining and preparing food, and the like.

4. But, as indicated above, much of the biblical material is presented in cultural forms that are *very specific to cultural practices quite different from ours.* Because of their specificity to the cultural agreements of the original hearers, these materials communicated with maximum impact to them. This is a major part of the genius of God and of his Word—that he speaks specifically to people where they are and in terms of the culture in which they are immersed. At the same time, this fact enormously complicates the task of the person immersed in another culture who seeks to interpret the Scriptures.

The fact that our interpretational reflexes are so limited when dealing with biblical materials argues strongly for the application of the sharpest tools available to the study of the cultural matrices through which God revealed his Word. The harnessing of the perspectives of anthropology and linguistics to this end of the interpretational task (as well as to the communication end) could be a real boon to the exegete. One important result of such harnessing is the development of faithful dynamic equivalence translations and highly interpretive "transculturations" of God's Word (see chapters 13 and 14). These aim to communicate God's message as specifically as possible in today's languages and cultures so that the members of these cultures will be able to trust their interpretational reflexes when they study the Scriptures.

BEYOND GRAMMATICO-HISTORICAL
TO ETHNOLINGUISTIC INTERPRETATION (Model 5b)

The statement of model 5b does not differ in essence from the ordinary hermeneutical principle of biblical theology that states that biblical passages are to be interpreted in their original contexts (see e.g., Ramm 1970: 138ff).[3] The method employed is often referred to by some such label as "the grammatico-historical method" (Ramm 1970:114; Mickelsen 1963:159; Fuller 1969, chapter 11).

The hermeneutical concern is for "extracting" or decoding from biblical texts the meanings that their authors encoded in those texts. The problem of biblical hermeneutics is thus the same problem as that faced by the receptor of any message in any context. It is therefore likely that the insights of contemporary studies into the nature of the ethnolinguistic setting in which communication takes place and into the nature and process of communication itself will be most helpful. Such insights enable us to go beyond the grammatico-

3. See Barr 1961 for a critique of certain of the methods of interpretation traditionally used by biblical theologians.

historical model as previously developed at at least two points: (1) the extent to which the linguistic (grammatical) and cultural (historical) factors are taken into account, and (2) the attempt to focus both on the central biblical message in the original linguistic and cultural vehicles (as that approach does) and on certain other important aspects of supracultural truth—especially those related to the processes God uses to convey that truth.

This approach attempts to see more deeply into language and culture both at the biblical end and with respect to their influence on the interpreter himself. We may refer to this approach as "ethnolingustic" (i.e., "culturo-linguistic") hermeneutics or even as "ethnohermeneutics."[4] The "context" of which we speak is not simply the literary or even the linguistic context in which an utterance occurs (Ramm 1970:138–39; see Nida 1964 and 1971:84–87 for further elaboration of this point); *it is the total cultural context* (including both literary and extra-literary components). And we focus not only on the central message of the Scriptures as expressed in the original linguistic and cultural vehicles (as important as that is), but also on the total process by means of which God seeks to communicate that and numerous other messages (both then and now) via language and culture. This approach, in keeping with the aims of biblical theology, emphasizes the pervasive importance of the cultural context but add considerations of process to those related to the product (the Scriptures).

At this point it is important to define, in at least a preliminary way, several of the key concepts that will be employed below. The complex relationships between information, message, context, and meaning will be in primary focus. By *information* we designate the raw materials from which messages and meanings are constructed (see also chapter 11). A *message* consists of the structuring of a body of information in a way appropriate to the ethnolinguistic context within which it is transmitted. The *context* is the structured and structuring matrix within which and according to the rules of which information is organized into messages that may then be reliably encoded, transmitted, and decoded to provide people with meanings. *Meaning* is the structuring of information in the minds of persons. It is frequently encoded into messages that are transmitted by communicators to receptors who decode the messages and, under the stimulus of those messages, restructure meanings in their own minds (see chapters 8 and 9). Though most of this will be explained in greater detail in the following chapters, it is important to deal here with the relationships for biblical interpretation.

The fact seems to be that messages and, by implication, the information they contain require structured contexts in order to be interpretable (i.e., to be transformed into meanings in the mind of the receptor of the message). As Hall states:

4. I am indebted to Mr. Phillip Leung, a Chinese student at the School of World Mission, 1976–78, for suggesting this term.

Information taken out of context is meaningless and cannot be reliably interpreted.
. . . [The] separation of information from context, as though the two were unrelated,
is an artifact of Western science and Western thought (1974:21).

"Information, context, and meaning are inseparably and dynamically linked to
one another" (Hunter and Foley 1976:45).

The following diagram (similar to that provided by Hunter and Foley
1976:46) is an attempt to depict this dynamic relationship.

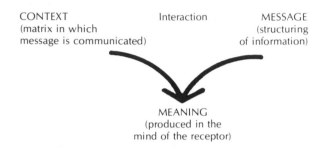

CONTEXT   Interaction   MESSAGE
(matrix in which   (structuring
message is communicated)   of information)

MEANING
(produced in the
mind of the receptor)

Fig. 7.2. The dynamic relationship between context, message, and meaning.
Read: In a given situation information is structured into a Message and
communicated within a Context to produce signals that a receptor transforms
into Meanings.

If this perspective is correct, there is no possibility of a message (a structured
body of information) making sense (i.e., taking on meaning) to a receptor
without participating in *some* context. Two questions arise, however: (1)
Which context, that of the originator of the communication, or that of the
receptor? and (2) In the interaction between the message and the context, what
does each contribute to the resultant meaning?

Model 5b holds that it is the interaction between the message and the *original*
context that determines the correct meaning—the meaning that the interpreter
seeks to ferret out. As discussed above, the biblical interpreter is hindered in
this process by interpretational reflexes conditioned to derive meanings immediately from messages interacting with a different cultural context. Such an
interpreter, to transcend this disability, needs to probe to discover the answer
to the second question.

The context contributes that part of the meaning deriving from the culture-
specific nature of an event. A certain amount of information implicit in the
context is a part of this contribution. The fact that a given event occurred in the
first century rather than in the twentieth, in Palestine rather than in America,

and in Hebrew culture rather than in American culture is extremely significant to the meanings of that event at every point. The context must, therefore,
be taken as seriously and analyzed as thoroughly as the message if the meaning
of the message is to be understood either for its own time or for ours. The
fallacy of the plain-meaning concept lies in the fact that it advocates simply
extracting the message as if it would mean the same in interaction with a
contemporary context *in that same form*. Such extracted messages "cannot be
reliably interpreted" (Hall 1974:21).

Nida points in this regard to the unsatisfactory way in which words are
traditionally dealt with by biblical scholars. He points to three fallacies (we
shall cite only two of these) that stem from certain deficiencies in the philologi-
cal and historical models commonly employed by such scholars:

In the first place, there has been the tendency to regard the "true meaning" of a word as
somehow related to some central core of meaning which is said to exist, either implicitly
or explicitly, in each of the different meanings of such a word or lexical unit. It is from
this central core of meaning that all the different meanings are supposed to be derivable
(1971:84).

Words are, therefore, regarded by many as *bearing meaning* independently of
their contexts. But words, like all information-bearing vehicles within culture,
derive their meanings *from* their interaction with the contexts in which they
participate. Nida goes on:

In the second place, a common mistake has been to regard the presumed historical
development of meaning as reflecting the "true meaning" of a word. . . . The so-called
etymology of a word is supposed to contain the key to the proper understanding of all its
meanings (1971:85).

The historical development of a word or other cultural form is occasionally
relevant to its meaning in the same way that a person's genealogy is occasionally relevant to his or her "meaning" (the nature of his or her participation) in a
given context. But again, it is the relevance of this aspect of the cultural form to
and in interaction with the context in which it occurs that determines its
meaning. *A cultural form does not have inherent meaning, only perceived
meaning—and this is context-specific.* "Valid lexicography must depend in the
ultimate analysis upon patterns of co-occurrence in actual discourse" (Nida
1971:85)—in actual situations. See chapter 18, below, for further elaboration
of this point.

As an example of the kind of contextual analysis here recommended, we
may choose two scriptural commands that ought to be treated the same
according to the plain-meaning dictum (though in practice they seldom are).
The problem is how to explain the difference between the command against
stealing (Exod. 20:15) and the command that a woman cover (veil) her head
when praying in public (1 Cor.11:10). In America I have heard the one

strongly advocated as it stands, while the other is explained away as "merely cultural." This approach is very unsatisfactory. The problem of the differential interpretation of these commands was vividly brought home to me by one of the Nigerian church leaders whom I was assisting. He pointed out to me that the Bible commands both that we not steal and that we not allow women to pray with their heads uncovered. He then asked why we missionaries teach that the one command be obeyed and the other ignored. Are we using a different Bible?

The fact is that both commands are expressed in cultural terms—that is, via cultural and linguistic forms or symbols. So both are cultural messages. But, since nothing in the Bible is "merely" cultural, we need to look beyond each command to discover how the word and custom symbols were understood by the authors and those to whom they were originally written. That is, we need to look for the supracultural meaning in each by getting beyond our own cultural conditioning (with its "plain meanings") to the interpretation of each within its original cultural context.

At this point we are in danger of being put off by the fact that our culture has a rule against stealing. We may, therefore, simply employ our interpretational reflexes and assume that we know what the command against stealing meant in its Hebrew context on the basis of what similar word symbols mean in our culture. We are wrong, however, since no cultural symbols have exactly the same meanings in any two cultures, owing to the differences in the contexts with which the symbols interact. Yet, since those words do have a meaning in our culture and that meaning is consonant with Christianity, most accept the meaning assigned to those words (that message) in our culture as the plain meaning of Scripture. They see no need to go into Hebrew culture to discover their original meaning.

With respect to the headcovering command, however, many take an opposite point of view—and appear to some to be "explaining away" the command. Since those word symbols and the whole context in which they occur have no plain meaning that seems to bear Christian truth in our culture, most American Christians feel compelled to study the Greek cultural background to discover the original meaning. Some groups, of course, are consistent at this point and interpret the headcovering command in terms of the meaning of those word forms within our culture. These groups make their women wear headcoverings.

We infer that the stealing command already existed in Hebrew culture (as, from cross-cultural data, we learn it does in every culture). It had specific reference, however, only to what the Hebrews of that time considered to be the unwarranted appropriation of certain of those things considered to be the property of another. In that kind of strongly kinship-oriented society it is unlikely that it would be considered stealing if a person appropriated his brother's goods without asking. Nor is it likely that a starving person who "helped himself" to someone else's food could be accused of stealing (see Mt. 12:1–4).

By interpreting in terms of the Hebrew cultural context, we find this command to differ only slightly from our own cultural understanding of it. This fact illustrates that, due to human commonality, meanings derived from the interaction of certain (general) messages with any cultural context are appropriate even in quite diverse cultures. The relative importance of context and message, however, varies from situation to situation. In situations such as this where the significance of the context in the determination of the meaning is less, the possibility is increased for transferring the message from one cultural situation to another in roughly its original form with *most* (never all) of its meaning intact. Truly "propositional" statements[5] in Scripture such as "God is love" illustrate this point. For this reason, even plain-meaning interpretations are fairly accurate for such statements.

When, however, the contribution to the meaning of implicit contextual information is high (as, for example, with the genealogies or the headcovering issue), it is necessary to interpret at a much deeper level of abstraction (see model 5c below) to ferret out the more general transferable meanings. Ethnolinguistic insight into the cultural and linguistic factors involved is especially valuable at this point. For there is much more meaning that God seeks to communicate through his Word than the surface level, context-specific messages so often in focus.

As for the headcovering command, analysis of the meaning of the custom in its cultural context does not lead simply to an alternative understanding of the same command. It leads, rather, to a *meaning* that demands *expression via a different cultural form* if it is to be understood in English. In the Greek culture of that day, apparently, the cultural form "female praying in public without headcovering" would have been interpreted to mean "this female is immoral," or, at least, "she is not showing proper respect to men" (see commentaries on 1 Cor. 11:10–12). Since that meaning was not consonant with the witness that Christians ought to make, Paul commands against the use of the head-uncovered symbol in favor of its opposite, the head-covered symbol. For only this latter symbol conveyed the proper Christian meaning in that culture —that Christian women were not immoral and were properly subject to their men. The theological truth then—a truth just as relevant today as in the first century—is that Christian women should not behave in such a way that people judge them to be "out of line" (whether morally or with respect to authority). (See Sproul 1976 for a useful discussion of this issue.)

DIFFERING LEVELS OF ABSTRACTION (Model 5c)

Such crosscultural analysis of the two passages shows that in comparing the two commands we are not comparing sames. For the commands are given at different levels of abstraction. That is, the relative importance of the specific

---

5. See R. Nash 1977 for an enlightened discussion of the pros and cons of using the term "proposition" as a designation for that which God has revealed.

cultural context to the meaning of the utterances differs. Those utterances that relate most specifically to their particular cultural contexts are at what is here termed the "surface" or "cultural-specific" level of abstraction. For correct understanding (interpretation) these depend greatly on implicit information embedded in the context with which the given custom interacts. Those utterances in which the specific context is less important to the meaning, and which, therefore, relate to pancultural human commonality, are at what may be termed a "deeper" or "general-principle" level of abstraction. These utterances are not so dependent on information implicit to their original contexts for interpretation. That the stealing command is at a deeper level of abstraction is evident from the fact that it does not refer to a specific cultural act but to a *category* of cultural behavior. The command is general rather than specific. Note, by way of contrast, the specificity of the tenth command. That command is at the surface level of abstraction (like the headcovering command) in that it specifies the proscribed cultural *acts* rather than (until the final phrase) generalizing them into an *overall principle* as we do when we refer to that command as a general command against "covetousness." Note the wording:

Do not desire another man's house; do not desire his wife, his slaves, his cattle, his donkeys, or anything else that he owns (Exod. 20:17 TEV).

The headcovering command is at this more specific level, where the embedded information in that particular cultural context is very important to the meaning. A corresponding specific stealing command would be something like "Don't take your neighbor's donkey without his permission." A headcovering command at the same level of generality as the stealing command would be something like "Don't appear out of line with respect to immorality or authority." Thus we see a specific cultural form/symbol level with the original context contributing relatively more to the meaning, and a deeper general-principle level in which the original context contributes relatively less. "Seesaw" diagrams illustrating these two possibilities are as follows:

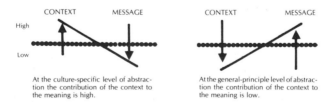

At the culture-specific level of abstraction the contribution of the context to the meaning is high.

At the general-principle level of abstraction the contribution of the context to the meaning is low.

Fig. 7.3. "Seesaw" diagrams illustrating the relationship between the context-message interaction concept and the levels of abstraction concept.

There seems, however, to be a yet deeper level of abstraction in Scripture. This is made explicit by Jesus when he summarizes the teaching of the law and the prophets in two statements:

"Love the Lord your God with all your heart, with all your soul, and with all your mind." This is the greatest and the most important commandment. The second most important commandment is like it: "Love your neighbor as you love yourself." The whole Law of Moses and the teachings of the prophets depend on these two commandments (Mt. 22:37–40 TEV; cf. Deut. 6:5; Mk. 12:29–31; Lk. 10:27).

These three levels correspond to some extent with the three levels charted in Figure 5.1: the level of specific customs, the level of worldview values, and the deep level of human universals. The universals apply to every person in every culture at all times. These may be regarded as transcultural or even supracultural ideals. The general principles (such as the Ten Commandments) seem, likewise, to apply universally. If these are seen as corresponding with the cultural worldview level (as suggested above) it is with the recognition that values such as these occur in the worldviews of every culture. At the level of specific custom, though, there is a considerable range of diversity expressive of the general principles.

There are occasional problems as to which of the levels to assign certain of the general statements of Scripture. We may advance Figure 7.4 (p. 142) as a step in the direction of developing this model more precisely. Note that a complete chart would show (even more than this one does) the fact that there are fewer categories at the Basic Ideal Level, more at the General Principle Level, and an enormous number at the Specific Cultural Form/Symbol Level.

In such expositions as the Ten Commandments (especially as Jesus summarizes them in Mt. 22:37–40), the Sermon on the Mount, the listing of the fruits of the Spirit (Gal. 5:22–23), and many similar statements, the Scriptures seem to us to come closest to a clear statement of a portion of the supracultural will of God for human conduct. The reason for the apparent clarity of these portions is that they are phrased at a level of abstraction that largely extricates them from specific application to the original cultures in which they were uttered. As one moves from specific cultural applications of supracultural truth (as with the headcovering command) back toward the most general statements of the truth, the statements require less understanding of the original cultural context to be accurately understood. They have more immediate (though general) meaning to us in another culture. The plain-meaning principle is therefore often adequate for interpreting information presented at this deeper level of abstraction.

Note, however, that the effectiveness of the communication (termed "impact" in chapter 8) is a matter of cultural perception. For the original hearers, it was presentations of supracultural truth in terms of specific applications (abstraction level 3) that communicated most effectively. For us, likewise, specific applications of scriptural generalizations would most effectively

1. BASIC IDEAL LEVEL	2. GENERAL PRINCIPLE LEVEL	3. SPECIFIC CULTURAL FORM/SYMBOL LEVEL
◄---------- More General	◄-------►	More Specific ------------►
A. Love your neighbor as you love yourself (Mt. 22:39)	1. Don't steal (Exod. 20:15)	a. Don't take your neighbor's donkey (Hebrew) b. Don't take your employer's money (U.S.A.)
	2. Don't covet	a. Don't desire another man's house . . . (Exod. 20:17) b. Same for U.S.A.
	3. Be free from partiality (1 Tim. 5:21; Jas. 3:17)	a. Treat Gentiles/blacks/women as human beings b. Rebuke whoever needs it (1 Tim. 5:20)
B. Love the Lord your God with all your heart . . . (Mt. 22:37)	1. Worship no God but me (Exod. 20:3)	a. Don't bow down to any idol or worship it (Exod. 20:5) b. Don't pledge primary allegiance to material wealth (U.S.A.)
	2. Seek by all means to save people (1 Cor. 9:22)	a. Live as a Jew to win Jews (1 Cor. 9:20) b. Live as a Gentile to win Gentiles (1 Cor. 9:21) c. Live as an African to win Africans
C. Everything must be done in a proper and orderly way (1 Cor. 14:40)	1. Leaders should be beyond reproach (1 Tim. 3:2; Tit. 1:6)	a. They must be self-controlled, etc. (1 Tim. 3:2)
	2. Christian women should not appear out of line	a. They should cover their heads when praying in Greek culture (1 Cor. 11:10) b. They should not wear their clothes too tight (U.S.A.)
	3. Christians should live according to the rules of the culture (as long as they don't conflict with Christian principles)	a. Women should learn in silence in Greek culture (1 Tim. 2:11) b. Women may speak up in mixed groups in U.S.A. c. Pay the government what belongs to it (Mt. 22:21) d. Obey governmental authorities (Rom. 13:1) e. Wives submit to your husband in Greek and many segments of U.S.A. culture (Eph. 5:22; Col. 3:18; etc.) f. Wives and husbands work coordinately in many
D. Other Ideals?		

Fig. 7.4. Illustrative chart of differing levels of abstraction model (5c).

communicate. But, since the Scriptures were written in terms of cultures other than ours, we are denied enscripturated applications of supracultural truth in our culture. The general statements, therefore, make more sense to us than the specific cultural forms through which these principles were applied in biblical cultures. And the more specific applications in the Scriptures are often the most confusing to us.

Throughout the Scriptures we are provided with glimpses of the supracultural, clothed in specific events taking place within specific cultures at specific times. Frequently, as with statements at the general-principle or basic-ideal level, we get the impression that we are looking at supracultural truth with a minimum of cultural conditioning. More frequently, however, we are exposed to supracultural truth applied in a specific situation in a specific biblical culture. The record of this comes to us only in translation, so that we see such truth as "puzzling reflections in a mirror" (1 Cor. 13:12 JBP). Among these "reflections," Smalley feels that

> those parts of Scripture which give us evaluations of human motives and emotions, human attitudes and personalities, give us the deepest insight into God's ultimate will, and that to understand the revelation in terms of God's will for our behavior we will have to learn to look behind the cultural facade to see as much as we can of what the Word indicates about those questions. The cultural examples given us are thereby not lost. They provide most valuable examples of the way in which God's will was performed in another cultural setting to help us see how we may perform it in ours (1955:66).

In this way it is possible for Christians to learn something of supracultural truth even though this, like all human knowledge, is perceived by us in terms of the cultural grid in which we operate. Though often puzzling and never total or absolute, such knowledge is adequate for God's purposes—the salvation and spiritual growth of all who give themselves to him in faith (Mickelsen 1963:353). We may then, under the leading of the Spirit, come to know something of how the Spirit desires us to live out these truths in terms of our cultural forms. See chapters 16–20, below, for further treatment of this topic.

"TWO-CULTURE DIALOGIC" INTERPRETATION (Model 5d)

As amply indicated in the foregoing, we are dealing with both the interpreter's culture and the ethnolinguistics of the biblical contexts when we interpret. Any model of hermeneutics that ignores the influence of the interpreter's culture on that person's attempts to understand the Scriptures is seriously deficient. Many who seek to employ grammatico-historical methodology are severely hampered by a failure to grasp the full significance of the culture-boundness of themselves and of their methodology.

The plain-meaning approach, though providing reasonably accurate interpretations at the most general levels of abstraction, is flawed by its simplistic approach to the original contexts. In reaction against that approach the grammatico-historical approach digs deeply into the original contexts. But it tends to overestimate the possibility of objectivity on the part of the contemporary scholarly interpreter. We have attempted, by means of the application of anthropological, linguistic, and communicational insights, to increase our ability to maximize the strengths of these approaches (especially the latter) while minimizing their deficiencies. It remains to deal explicitly with the dialogical nature of the interaction between the messages of Scripture in their contexts and the concerns of the interpreters in their contexts.

A concern for the contextualization of biblical messages is a concern that scriptural meanings get all the way across what might be pictured as a "hermeneutical bridge" into the real-life contexts of ordinary people. In a perceptive article dealing with hermeneutics from the perspective of one deeply committed to the contextualization of Christianity, René Padilla says:

Hermeneutics has to do with a dialogue between Scripture and a contemporary culture. Its purpose is to transpose the biblical message from its original context into a particular twentieth-century situation. Its basic assumption is that the God who spoke in the past and whose Word was recorded in the Bible continues to speak today in Scripture (1978:11).

If interpretation is done naively, as in the plain-meaning approach, meaningful dialogue between past revelation and present need is often prevented, owing to a premature application of hastily and superficially derived meanings. Scholarly approaches to interpretation, on the other hand, have prevented such dialogue by considering the biblical message in its original context in such a way that its meanings remain in "a world which is definitely not our world" (Padilla 1978:5).

A balanced approach takes both contexts seriously and gives both due weight.

The aim is that the horizon of the receptor culture is merged with the horizon of the text in such a way that the message proclaimed in the receptor culture may be a dynamic equivalent[6] of the message proclaimed in the original context (ibid.:6).

The hermeneutical process, then, involves a dynamic interaction or dialogue between an interpreter deeply enmeshed in his or her own culture and worldview (including theological biases) and the Scriptures. The interpreter has needs, some of which he or she formulates into questions, "asking" these questions of the Scriptures and finding certain of them answered. Other questions remain unanswered, since "there is a large number of topics on which Scripture says nothing or very little" (Padilla 1978:17). Still other questions are stimulated in the mind of the interpreter as a result of the

6. See below, chapters 13–17, for a detailed treatment of this concept.

person's interaction with Scripture. Meanwhile, in attempting to live life in a particular context, the interpreter's interaction with that context also stimulates new questions.

The richer and deeper the questions brought by the interpreter from the receptor culture, the richer and deeper the answers provided by Scripture. It follows that without a good understanding of the real issues involved in living in a particular situation there cannot be an adequate understanding of the relevance of the biblical message to that situation. Each new formulation of the questions based on a more refined understanding of the situation makes possible a new reading of Scripture and consequently the discovery of new implications of its message. If it is true that Scripture illuminates life, it is also true that life illuminates Scripture (Padilla 1978:17).

Hermeneutics is not, therefore, merely an academic game to be played by supposedly objective scholars. It is a dynamic process that properly demands deep subjective involvement on the part of Christian interpreters operating within the Christian community (which includes scholars) both with the Scriptures and with the life of the world around them in which they live. Hermeneutics is thus a kind of three-way conversation, proceeding according to the rules of communication (Taber 1978a:9ff), under the guidance of the Holy Spirit, issuing in what might be pictured as an upward "spiraling" of understanding of Scriptures, of self, of the world, and of the proper, God-guided interactions between the three at *this* time and in *this* setting. At the beginning of the "spiral" the interpreter goes with certain felt needs to the Scriptures under the guidance of God and with the assistance of the Christian community (in person or via published materials). Within the community, then, the interpreter moves from needs to Scripture, to application in the living of his or her life, to needs (some of which are newly perceived and at a deeper level), to Scripture (some of which he or she sees with "new eyes"), to deeper-level application in the living of his or her life, etc.

The life context with which the interpreter is interacting is critical to the whole process. If the life context to which the applications are made is merely an academic context, the nature of the insights derived from Scripture and their usability outside that context are vitally affected. This is what makes much of what goes on in academic institutions and scholarly writings unusable in life contexts other than the classroom. One of the damaging effects of such academicization of biblical interpretation has been the excessive informationalizing of revelation, of which I speak later (chapter 9). Given the "down-to-earth" nature of the Scriptures, it is often the unschooled interpreter who can best interpret them, in spite of the difficulty (discussed above) that one may have in understanding the more culture-specific passages. For, as discussed below, the Scriptures are *life*-related, not merely "religious discourse . . . couched in technical language" (Taber 1978a:12), as western exegetes have tended to assume.

This dialogical approach to hermeneutics is more serious than previous approaches in the place it gives to the interpreter and the receptor group in their respective contexts. It does not assume either unbiased interpreters or the universality for all times and places of the answers arrived at by previous interpreters in their times and places. It places real people with real needs in real-life contexts at the center of the hermeneutical process. It questions the ultimacy of academic, scholarly interpretation outside academic, scholarly contexts. (We would see this book, then, as an attempt within an academic context to free people from bondage to that context.) Dialogical hermeneutics draws its

concern for context from the Bible itself. And it recognizes in the multi-leveled character of biblical context the multi-leveled character of context in the process of understanding itself. What was that original context addressed by Jesus Christ when he called, "Repent, for the kingdom of heaven is at hand" (Matt. 4:17)? What was that context to which Matthew spoke as interpreter of Jesus when he used the words, "kingdom of heaven"? How was it different from the context of Mark who summarizes the same message of Jesus in terms of the "kingdom of God" (Mark 1:15)? What was the context Paul addressed as the re-encoder of the kingdom message at Rome, transposing "preaching the kingdom of God" into "teaching concerning the Lord Jesus Christ" (Acts 28:23, 31)?

A process of this kind can be liberating as the man of God wrestles with biblical context, his own, and those to whom he speaks and before whom he lives. Charles Taber writes that such an appeal to Scripture "can free indigenous theology from the bondage of Western categories and methodologies" (1978b: 71) (Conn 1978:45).

The concern for the importance of the contexts of interpreter and receptor must not diminish our concern for Scriptures as our "tether" and "yardstick" (see model 9, below). For the hermeneutical process is an interactional process with the Bible as the necessary point with which all else is to interact. More will be said concerning these matters, below. For in a real sense the remainder of this volume is a continuation of this discussion of hermeneutics. But now we turn to further theoretical input, this time from the field of communication theory.

8. Communicating Within Culture

In this chapter we shall continue our consideration of certain basic understandings (models) coming from communication theory and the insight they give us into God's workings. These models have been developed within a number of disciplines, including psychology, speech, anthropology, and the more recently developed discipline called "communications" or "communicology." In the first section of this chapter we present ten basic principles of communication. The four most basic of these are then discussed in subsequent sections of the chapter. They are the frame-of-reference principle (model 7b), the communicator-credibility principle (model 7c), the message-credibility principle (model 7d), and the discovery principle (model 7e).

BASIC PRINCIPLES OF COMMUNICATION

Of the many basic principles of communication theory that could be dealt with we present ten that seem to be crucial to the message of this book. The final four of these will then be elaborated upon with reference to God's use of them to communicate to human beings within culture.

PRINCIPLE 1: *The purpose of communication is to bring a receptor to understand a message presented by a communicator in a way that substantially corresponds with the intent of the communicator* (model 6a). There is always a degree of "slippage" between the participants in a communicational event, for there is much going on in a communicative event that may detract from this purpose. For one thing, there are always many messages being sent, most of which lie below the level of consciousness for both the communicator and the receptor(s). In addition to the main message, for example, communicators send information concerning their attitudes toward themselves, the message, the receptor, life in general, and the like. The result may be that one or another of these unconscious "paramessages" will become more important to the receptor than the message intended by the communicator. Often the receptor (R) is more impressed with the communicator's (C's) attitude toward himself or herself than with the message (M) itself. If so, what R understands may be far different from what C intended—unless, of course, C intended (consciously or unconsciously) simply to communicate such an attitude. The communicator's problem is to present the primary message in such a way that the receptor understands it in the way it is intended with a minimum of interference from paramessages. Due to interference from paramessages and slippage of other kinds, C allows R to understand within a "range of acceptable variation" (see model 9b). *An absolute identity between what R understands and what C intends is, apparently, never achievable.* Substantial equivalence within such a range is possible, however.

PRINCIPLE 2: *What is understood is at least as dependent on how R perceives the message (plus the paramessages) as on how C presents it* (see Nida 1960:34ff). Words, gestures, and the other cultural forms that C employs in communicating derive their meanings from the experiences with such symbols that C and R have had. The fact that the experiences of any two people, though they may be similar, never correspond exactly, leads to greater or lesser differences in interpretation of those symbols. This fact plus the presence of paramessages assures that R will never understand C's message with 100 percent accuracy even if C presents his or her thoughts in such a way as to, from C's point of view, have expressed these thoughts perfectly. For *the ultimate formulation of what is understood is done within R's head, not within C's* (model 6b). This fact seems to require some understanding of the communication process such as that presented in principle 3.

PRINCIPLE 3: *Communicators present messages via cultural forms (symbols) that stimulate within the receptors' heads meanings that each receptor shapes into the message that he or she ultimately hears* (model 6c). *Meanings are not transmitted, only messages.* For "meanings are not in the message, they are in the message-users" (Berlo 1960:175). The meanings and their organization into received messages come from the interaction between the stimulus of what C says and does and the experience-conditioned understanding facilities of R. The symbols employed function not to *contain* the meanings but to *stimulate* meanings within the mind of R that correspond as closely as possible with those in the mind of C. Information and, perhaps, other components of messages may come from outside R, but meanings and their ultimate organization into received messages come from within R.

The meaning . . . comes from a reservoir in which all of our prior experiences are contained. When we encounter a social stimulus, we dip into our reservoir and using our own unique thought process extract the meaning we deem appropriate and attach it to the stimulus (Samovar and Porter 1972:33).

The message received is, therefore, the product of R even more than it is the product of C, for R has the final say over how M is understood and what is done with such understanding. This being true, we must recognize that the M that R constructs mentally on the basis of the signals sent by C is *never identical with the M that C intended* to transmit. R always misses some things intended by C and adds some things not intended by C. *Wise communicators, therefore, settle for rough equivalence* in the understanding of their receptors rather than demanding exact correspondence. *Wise communicators, furthermore, give primary attention to their receptors* (principle 4) and the kind of stimulus or impact of their messages on Rs (principle 5).

PRINCIPLE 4: *The communicator, to communicate the message effectively, must be "receptor-oriented"* (model 6). In much communicational activity C is primarily concerned that what he or she says and does be accurate and correct. This is well and good but may be quite inadequate if C does not parallel it with just as great a concern for the *way* he or she goes about communicating. For it is R who will make the final judgments concerning what has been communicated. *Accuracy and correctness, then, will have to be evaluated at R's end of the communication process even more than at C's.* The cultural forms (symbols) that are employed by C to convey M, then, will have to be chosen carefully on the basis of C's best understanding of what their impact on R will be. It is entirely possible for C to present a true and vital M to R via cultural forms that minimize or obscure its truth and vitality from R. This C must avoid.

PRINCIPLE 5: *If the communicator's message is to influence the receptor(s) it must be presented with an appropriate degree of impact* (model 7). Messages that are simply intended to convey information (e.g., a news broadcast) may be appropriately presented without much concern for whether or not R feels the need for that kind of information. Messages that are intended to influence R's behavior, however, must be presented in such a way that the symbols employed stimulate within R the desired effect. A message that is strictly informative will not have high impact unless R perceives it to relate to a felt need. If R is already aware of such a need and hears something that relates to it, R may (or may not) make the connection without C's help. If, however, C perceives a need that R does not realize, it is C's task to present the message via such symbols as will stimulate R to make the desired connection and the desired change in behavior. Such stimulus is here termed "impact." As in all communication it is R who makes the final judgment concerning the impact of M and what to do about it.

PRINCIPLE 6: *The most impactful communication results from person-to-person interaction* (model 7a). It is the "rubbing" of life against life, not simply the sending and receiving of vocal, gestural, or printed symbols that makes for maximum effectiveness in communication. Even in mass communication where R has no opportunity for close contact with C, the impact of M is affected by whatever information R has concerning C as a person. *Messages are made credible or incredible by the nature of their relationship to the life of C, on the one hand, and to that of R, on the other.* Prolonged involvement of person with person (e.g., in a family) assures intensive and effective communication of a multiplicity of messages transmitted and received both consciously and unconsciously concerning a multiplicity of topics. The less personal the communicational interaction (e.g., in a public lecture or via radio), the more the communicational event is likely to devolve simply into a performance. While a great deal of information may be conveyed by such means, the permanent impact is likely to be low, owing to the reduction of the person-to-personness of the situation—unless R's felt need for the information conveyed happens to be high.

PRINCIPLE 7: *Communication is most effective when C, M, and R participate in the same context(s), setting(s), or frame(s) of reference* (model 7b). The sharing of cultural, subcultural, linguistic, and experiential frames of reference maximizes the possibility that the cultural forms/symbols employed to transmit messages will mean the same thing to both C and R. Differences in the frames of reference of C and R assure that at least some of the symbols employed in M will be understood differently by the participants. If C's frame of reference is adopted as that in terms of which the communication is to take place, R must be extracted from his or her own frame of reference and indoctrinated into that of C. If R's frame of reference is chosen, C must learn whatever is necessary to function properly in that frame of reference. See below for a fuller treatment of this and the next three principles.

PRINCIPLE 8: *Communication is most effective when C has earned credibility as a respectable human being within the chosen frame of reference* (model 7c). Lack of credibility on the part of C severely hampers C's ability to communicate the message. One of the greatest hindrances is the tendency of R to assign C to some isolating stereotype such as doctor, clergyman, expert, foreigner, fool, unintelligent person, high-class person, and the like. If such occurs, C has to discover how to win credibility with R by escaping from the stereotyped category of people into R's "human-being" category. One important way of accomplishing this is by C's acting unpredictably in terms of R's stereotype.

PRINCIPLE 9: *Communication is most effective when M is understood by R to relate specifically to life as R lives it* (model 7d). General messages may have general appeal but they have low impact. To have high impact M must be perceived by R to "scratch where it itches." Historical, technical, theoretical, and academic presentations may contribute to R's store of information but they rarely affect the person's behavior unless, via application and illustration, lessons are extracted from them and related to R's day-to-day life. Likewise with predictable, stereotyped messages. Personal experiences of C and case studies from the lives of others are often effective techniques for making messages specific to R's life.

PRINCIPLE 10: *Communication is most effective when R discovers (1) an ability to identify at least partially with C and (2) the relevance of M to his or her own life* (model 7e). This principle states R's ideal response to C's attempts to establish his or her own credibility (principle 8) and that of the message (principle 9). When C and M have the proper impact on R, the latter responds by discovering a life-changing relationship to both of them.

EMPLOYING THE FRAME-OF-REFERENCE PRINCIPLE (Model 7b)[1]

Human beings live in different contexts or frames of reference. And this causes communication problems, since all the symbols (cultural forms) by means of which people can communicate derive their meanings totally from the frame of reference in which they participate. There are no such symbols with universal meanings (Nida 1960:89–93). Thus, if effective communication

1. Kraft 1973c, 1973e, and 1974 include previous versions of much of the material in this and the following sections in this chapter and the first section of chapter 9.

is to take place, both the communicator and the receptor must be in a position to attach similar meanings to the symbols employed. This implies that they must be operating within a common context or frame of reference. For if persons speak no common language and have no culturally defined common agreements concerning the noises and gestures they use, their ability to communicate with each other will be virtually nil. An unbridged barrier to communicative interaction exists between them.

Sharing of a frame of reference will involve primarily a common understanding of cultural and linguistic categories. The common cultural involvement of persons of the same culture ordinarily means that each will be able to make a high proportion of correct assumptions concerning what the other person means to convey via the use he or she makes of linguistic and cultural symbols. When potential communicators employ specialized jargon, they risk the possibility of "losing" their hearers if the frame of reference in terms of which they are speaking is not shared by their hearers. Such is often the case when Christians attempt to witness to non-Christians by using such "Christian jargon" as "church," "be saved," "believe," "accept Christ," "justification," "sin," etc. When people belong to such different subcultures, the lack of agreement concerning the meanings of linguistic and cultural items severely hampers communication. If the distance between speaker and hearer is even greater, as between members of very different cultures (e.g., American versus an African culture), then the percentage of shared cultural and linguistic categories in terms of which communication is possible is severely reduced, even if one of them has learned the language of the other. Thus the possibility of misunderstanding is enormously increased.

The frame of reference chosen for the communication can be that of either participant but with a different impact, depending on whose set of categories is employed. *If the communicator demands that it be his (or hers), rather than the hearer's frame of reference* that provides the communicational categories, the approach may be labeled "extractionist." A primary concern of such communicators, then, is to convert receptors to their way of extractionist thinking. Communicators seek to teach receptors to understand and look at reality in terms of their own models and perspectives.

If, for example, an extractionist communicator believes that the Bible is inspired and authoritative but the hearer doesn't, this approach would demand that the hearer first convert to the speaker's understanding of biblical inspiration. This would be a prerequisite to the establishment of the frame of reference in terms of which they will operate. I once heard of a potential Christian witness being broken off very early in the conversation with words like these: "You don't believe the Bible is inspired? Well, then, I don't have anything more to say to you." If, for some reason, that receptor had badly wanted what the communicator was offering (salvation in Christ), he or she would have had to at least "go along with" the conviction of the communicator. For the latter was clearly designating his frame of reference as the only acceptable matrix for their discussion. If, however, the receptor did not care that much about the communicator's message, the receptor would simply reject it without a hearing in response to the would-be communicator's rejection of the receptor's frame of reference.

In a cross-cultural situation problems often arise when the western communicator's worldview holds that the physical environment is to be viewed as controllable by human beings, while the receptor's worldview holds an opposite point of view. An extractionist approach attempts to convert the potential receptor to the advocate's position as pre- or co-requisite to any intercultural communication involving these concepts. If, as often happens in missionary work, the missionary's culture is highly regarded by the potential receptors, while their attitude toward their own culture is ambivalent or negative, the receptors may well be intimidated into agreeing to the advocate's demands. The receptors will then convert to the latter's cultural understanding as a part of what they believe is necessary to become a Christian. They may in this way become genuine Christians—though understanding and expressing their Christianity in ways foreign to their indigenous culture. Or they may simply convert to the foreign culture without becoming Christian at all. In many other missionary situations (e.g., Islamic areas), where the receptors have a high view of their own culture and a lower view of that of the missionary, they are unlikely to respond in ways suggested above. For they are not positive toward a witness who seeks to extract them from their own cultural frame of reference in order to insert them into that of the missionary as a pre- or co-requisite to their conversion to Christ.

If, instead of this extractionist approach, *the communicator adopts the receptor's frame of reference* as that in terms of which the communication takes place, we may label the approach "identificational." In this approach communicators become familiar with the conceptual framework of the receptor and attempt to fit their communication to the categories and felt needs of that frame of reference. Communicators employing this approach first attempt to learn where their hearer is and what needs the hearer feels before attempting to present any answers. And then the answers are presented in such a way that they "scratch the hearer's itch"—not the speaker's. If the hearer is hurting because of loneliness or meaninglessness, this identificational approach attempts to apply the Gospel to these needs. It does not insist that the hearer first learn to desire heaven or to feel guilt as a sinner.

Suppose a Christian in a cross-cultural situation discovers that the potential receptors feel that God has gone far away, having left humanity helpless and hopeless. Identificational advocates, without denying the receptors' understanding (even though possibly regarding it as misguided), attempt to "fill in the blank" by initially communicating only that part of their understanding of God that answers the receptors' felt need. By this means communicators identify both themselves and their message with an appropriate part of the hearers' frame of reference and lead the hearers gently from their own keenly felt need to the Christian answer to that need. But this is accomplished without the extractionist's precondition that the communication take place within the communicator's (rather than the hearer's) frame of reference.

Thus in my own experience in Africa one of our favorite leading questions when witnessing was, "What did your people believe about God before the missionaries came?" One day in response to that question an old chief told us the following myth:

Once God and his son lived close to us. They walked, talked, ate, and slept among us. All was well then. There was no thievery or fighting or running off with another man's wife like there is now. But one day God's son ate in the home of a careless woman. She had not cleaned her dishes properly. God's son ate from a dirty dish, got sick, and died. This, of course, made God very angry. He left in a huff and hasn't been heard from since.

Then the chief looked at me and said, "White man, can you tell us how to get back into contact with God?"

An extractionist might well have answered that question by reading the account from Genesis 3 of how human alienation from God came about. The extractionist would have pointed out how wrong the chief's story was and attempted first to convert him to the correct story in Genesis. The missionary would then most likely have attempted to get the chief to feel guilty about his sins and in some western philosophic way tried to connect them with Adam's sin. If the missionary were successful to this point (and this just might happen—especially if the African had greater respect for the missionary's culture than for his own), he or she would go on to redemption, forgiveness, reconciliation and, one hopes, the decision of the chief to convert. Along the way, in order to "simplify" things and to assure that the chief got all the points straight, the missionary would arrange for him to join a "converts' class." At the end of that class, then, the degree to which he had been extracted from his own conceptual frame of reference and indoctrinated into that of the missionary would be tested.

An identificational approach, on the other hand, would take the chief's story very seriously. Without contradicting or correcting any of its essentials, this approach would address the communication directly to the expressed question. The real truths of the chief's story (e.g., the existence of God and his son, the alienation between people and God, the resultant description of human relationships) would be focused upon. The only additions would be God's plan of salvation and (if not at that time certainly eventually) the necessity for a faith-response to God as the means of restoring the original peaceful relationship. Since the missionary would have already learned that this society functions in groups rather than as individuals, any appeal for decision would be addressed to the chief and his group, not to him as an individual. For at every point the attempt to witness identificationally takes the receptor's frame of reference as the context for communication.

The aims of both the identificational and the extractionist approach are similar—to lead the receptors into an experience with God through Christ. Extractionism, however, requires a high degree of indoctrination involving a longish period of dependence upon the communicator for instruction in order to be effective. For the strange (to the receptor) frame of reference in terms of which the communication takes place must be carefully taught. Much Christian missionary effort has, unfortunately, adopted the extractionist approach. This is in spite of the fact that many of the major changes that this approach has effected in the thinking of receptor peoples have proved to be counter to the specifically religious aims of Christianity. That is, due to their extreme dependence on western schools teaching secular western curricula, they have typically produced a scientistic, naturalistic, secularistic frame of reference that is antithetical to Christianity, rather than a Christian supernaturalistic focus. It is an ironic fact that missionary schools have become the greatest secularizing force in the nonwestern world.

The identificational approach seems to be more in keeping with the approach of the early Christians. Christ himself, working on an interpersonal though not an intercultural level, started with the felt needs of his potential receptors, adopting their frame of reference as that in terms of which he operated. He dealt with Nicodemus in terms of his Pharisaic understanding, with the Samaritan woman in terms of her background, with the disciples in still other ways, with Zacchaeus differently yet. He told the rich young ruler to follow him (Mk. 10:21) but forbade the demoniac to (Lk. 8:38–39). Jesus was not being inconsistent—he was very consistent in his principle of working with each person in terms of that person's frame of reference. The apostle Paul, in keeping with the same identificational approach, determined to be Jewish when attempting to communicate with Jews and Greek when attempting to communicate interculturally with Greeks (1 Cor. 9:19–22). He provides a prototypical example of an identificational approach when he says, in speaking to a group of Athenian philosophers,

Men of Athens! I see that in every way you are very religious. For as I walked through your city and looked at the places where you worship, I found also an altar on which is written, "To an Unknown God." That which you worship, then, even though you do not know it, is what I now proclaim to you (Acts 17:22–23 TEV).

The frame-of-reference principle may be usefully summarized in the following diagrams. *Situation I* depicts the would-be communicator and the would-be receptor in entirely different frames of reference. Since there is no bridge between them, such a situation means that effective communication of person "a" with person "b" is impossible. *Situation II* shows the extractionist approach to bringing both communicator and receptor into the same frame of reference, while *Situation III* depicts the identificational approach that Jesus and Paul employed.

Frame of Reference A

Frame of Reference B

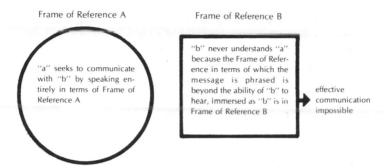

"a" seeks to communicate with "b" by speaking entirely in terms of Frame of Reference A

"b" never understands "a" because the Frame of Reference in terms of which the message is phrased is beyond the ability of "b" to hear, immersed as "b" is in Frame of Reference B

effective communication impossible

Situation I: Communicator and receptor exist in different frames of reference.

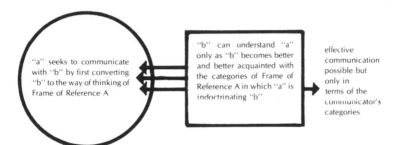

"a" seeks to communicate with "b" by first converting "b" to the way of thinking of Frame of Reference A

"b" can understand "a" only as "b" becomes better and better acquainted with the categories of Frame of Reference A in which "a" is indoctrinating "b"

effective communication possible but only in terms of the communicator's categories

Situation II "extractionist": Communicator extracts the receptor from receptor's frame of reference.

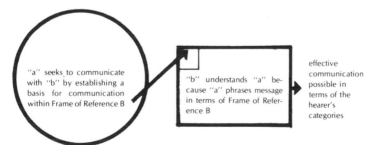

"a" seeks to communicate with "b" by establishing a basis for communication within Frame of Reference B

"b" understands "a" because "a" phrases message in terms of Frame of Reference B

effective communication possible in terms of the hearer's categories

Situation III "identificational": Communicator identifies with the receptor's frame of reference by learning and entering it.

Fig. 8.1. Three approaches to inter-frame-of-reference communication.

THE COMMUNICATOR-CREDIBILITY PRINCIPLE (Model 7c)

Once the frame of reference for communication is established, communicators must give attention to the matter of their credibility with those they seek to reach. They may unthinkingly simply accept whatever stereotype the receptors have of them. Or, disliking that stereotype, they may make an effort to reject it and to establish some alternative basis for interaction with the receptors.

A stereotype may be thought of as a technique for lumping people into a grouping for the purpose of saving oneself the time and energy that would be necessary to relate to each one personally. Stereotyping appears to be a necessary socio-cultural mechanism. It enables one to cope to some extent with large numbers of people that one could not possibly relate to individually. A serious problem arises, however, when one comes into person-to-person contact with a member of the stereotyped group and, instead of relating to that one as a person, relates in terms of the generalized understandings derived from the stereotype. Thus a dichotomy is set up between regarding and relating to a person in terms of the stereotype of the group to which that person belongs and regarding and relating to a person as an individual human being. Stereotypes depersonalize.

In attempting to communicate identificationally one can easily be crippled by allowing oneself and one's actions simply to be interpreted in terms of a stereotype—even if the stereotype should be a complimentary one. The stereotyped understanding removes a person from the realm of human-beingness. It interprets a person too predictably. It keeps that person at arm's length from the people he or she seeks to reach whether by according unearned respect (that is, unearned within the receptor's context), or by denying respect. Thus, in attempting to communicate to another person, a stranger who simply conforms to the receptor's stereotyped expectations operates at a low degree of credibility. For what the stranger says and does is predictable in terms of the receptor's stereotype of the person. If, however, what the person says and does is not predictable in terms of the stereotypic expectations of the potential receptors, the communication value of the person's message and overall credibility may be increased. All the person has to assure is that the unpredictability is in the direction of the receptor's definition of human-beingness.

If, for example, person A is initially perceived by person B as a *preacher*, person B automatically attaches to the former whatever expectations B's stereotype of a preacher might require. And if that preacher never says or does anything to shake the hearer's faith in the appropriateness of the stereotype, the credibility of A's message may be seriously compromised. This is especially true if a part of the stereotype is the conviction that any preacher is simply "out of it" as far as the real life issues of the hearer are concerned.

A university student once came to a professor's office to ask some minor question concerning a course she was taking from him. He invited her to sit down and they began to talk about various things. This went on for some time; then she seemed to lose track of the conversation for a moment. Finally she broke in with something like, "Gee, you don't act like a professor! You know," she continued, "since I've come to this university no professor has ever spent more than ten minutes with me. And nobody has ever shown the interest in me that you've been showing." A poor lost victim of what some have called the "megaversity" had finally found someone among the gods of that situation who had broken the stereotype. At least for that hour or so, the professor had begun to relate to her as she expected a human being to relate to her, rather than simply in terms of her stereotype of a professor.

A pastor whom I know, when straight out of college, accepted a call to a small New England church. Soon after assuming that pastorate he also took a job in a factory. The deacons of the church reprimanded him for this. They admitted that they weren't paying him the highest salary in the world but insisted that they expected him to devote all his time to the work of the church. "Oh," he replied, "it's not for the sake of the money that I took the job in the factory. In fact," he continued, "the church is welcome to whatever I earn. It's just that to this point I've spent all my time in school. Yet I'm expected to minister to people who spend from nine to five every day in the factory. If I'm going to minister effectively to these people, I've got to find out what it's like to be in their shoes." I rate this as one of the most constructive approaches to the ministry that I've ever seen. Though the pastor and his people were members of the same culture, he was able to recognize that in major ways they were operating within different subcultural frames of reference. He lived within an academic subculture while they lived within quite a different subculture, strongly influenced by their involvement in factory work. In this and other ways he was able to break through the stereotype that the church people had of a pastor. He was thus able dramatically to increase the effectiveness both of his preaching and of his overall relationship with the people.

On the cross-cultural level it was my experience that the Nigerians among whom I worked assigned such a high prestige to the missionary role that the missionary was virtually regarded as fitting into the "God" category, rather than into the "human-being" category. From their point of view beings are assignable to but one of two categories which may be labeled "human" and "supernatural." Human beings were easily assignable by analogy to themselves. That is, strangers coming into their midst were simply observed and, if they acted more or less like them, they were unthinkingly assigned to the "human-being" category. But they had a big problem with the assignment of westerners to that category. For so many of the things with which we are associated in their minds have not traditionally been associated with their category "human being" but, rather, with their category "supernatural."

Who but supernatural beings, for example, could possess magic powerful enough to produce automobiles, trains, airplanes, radios, western medicines, monstrous buildings, engines for grinding grain, fertilizers, western cloth and clothing, sewing machines, paved roads, fantastic bridges across uncrossable rivers, self-propelled boats, etc.? How could these beings be fitted into their category "human being"? They must belong to the "God" category with the rest of the incomprehensible, superhuman, supernatural beings. So these Nigerians said, "Fear God, fear the White Man," and assigned westerners, including the missionaries, to the "God" category. And this assignment, in the case of missionaries, is continually reinforced in the minds of many by the fact that the missionaries speak of God as if God were on intimate terms with them. Furthermore, they frequently act, to the Nigerian way of thinking, both capriciously and with a confidence considered unwarranted on the part of human beings. That is, missionaries behave according to the Nigerian stereotype of *God*, not according to their understanding of how human beings behave.

This type of stereotyping is perhaps the most disturbing thing about simply being assigned to a role such as "missionary." For it allows the people to whom missionaries go to understand them and their presence in their midst wholly in terms of whatever their stereotype of a missionary might be. That is, missionaries become in their eyes absolutely predictable, isolated from effective contact with them and depersonalized. In the case of the Nigerian situation referred to above (which is not at all uncommon the world over, especially in rural areas) this meant that missionaries were not expected to operate by the rules governing human beings. Missionaries were not considered to be restricted by the same limitations that human beings are restricted by, nor could they be approached in a manner appropriate to human beings. At each of these points (and many others) the analogy in the minds of those people as they sought to think about or interrelate with missionaries was not a human-to-human analogy but a human-to-God analogy.

In other parts of the world, especially in urban areas, the specifics of the stereotype may vary. But a similarly well-defined set of predictabilities resulting in a similar stereotype is generated. In many cases the stereotype of missionaries is a negative one. They may be regarded as subordinary human beings rather than as superhuman. They may be considered strange rather than respected. The same principles (see below) apply to both positive and negative stereotypes.

If missionaries simply conform to the people's stereotype of what missionaries should act like, the communicational impact of their activity is likely to be slight, unless their stereotype puts the missionaries within their frame of reference as full-fledged human beings. The missionaries may act unpredictably in terms of the stereotype, but in a manner intelligible to them in terms of their concept of human-beingness. In such a case the missionaries' credibility, the communication value of their message, and the potential for its acceptance are all increased. By thus identifying with the potential receptors and acting credibly (i.e., unpredictably in terms of the stereotype), hundreds of missionaries and others have endeared themselves to their hearers and effectively communicated the Christian message to peoples all over the world.

Such communicators have *earned* rather than *demanded* the respect they have received. They have followed Jesus' example in turning their backs on the assigned status, the expected role (Phil. 2:5–8), to risk the possibility that they may never be accorded any respect at all. They have attempted to understand the people to whom they go and to see life as they see it. They have empathized with those people, identified with them, participated in life with them. They have been life-involved with "their" people even to the extent of human-being-to-human-being "self-exposure" (Loewen 1965). And they have won a greater hearing as credible human beings than they ever could have as stereotyped semigods.

THE MESSAGE-CREDIBILITY PRINCIPLE (Model 7d)

The use of these two principles of effective communication prepares the way for the potentially life-changing interactions that are the focus of this and the next principle. The message-credibility principle observes that *a message has greatest impact if (1) it is not a stereotyped message and (2) if it is presented in very specific life-related fashion.*

The stereotyping of messages, like the stereotyping of communicators, considerably reduces their impact. A stereotyped message is predictable and therefore has little in it to attract receptors' attention. It may serve to confirm receptors in their biases and thus allow them to feel comfortable. But it will not induce them to alter their behavior. We may illustrate this fact by referring to an aspect of the English linguistic frame of reference.

If one says, "He winked his——" or "He shrugged his——," the impact of the information conveyed by the word "eye" in the completed first statement or the word "shoulder" in the second is exactly zero. For no other fillers of these blanks are allowable by English structure. Each word is absolutely predictable in its context (frame of reference), and adds no information to the message not already signaled. If, as someone says "He winked his eye," some noise blots out the last word, nothing is lost, since "eye" is 100 percent predictable in that context. The impact of that word symbol in that context is nil.

In statements such as "The——barked" or "He smacked his——," the predictability of the words filling the blanks is very high, but not quite 100 percent. For, were a word spoken in each of the blanks blotted out by some noise, one could not be sure whether it was a dog, a seal, or a baboon that barked or whether the person smacked his lips or his child. The "information value" and consequent impact of the word that fills the blank in either of these statements is, therefore, slightly higher than that of the fillers in the sentences in the paragraph above, since its predictability is lower. This principle may be pictured on a "seesaw" diagram as in Fig. 8.2:

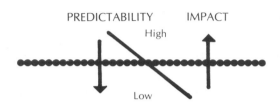

Fig. 8.2. Relationship between predictability and impact: high predictability = low impact; low predictability = high impact.

Note that any movement of the left end of the "seesaw" toward higher predictability forces the right end down toward a lessening of the impact of the message. On the other hand, any movement of the right end toward higher impact forces the left end down toward a lessening of predictability (always, of course, within the given frame of reference).

The message that is not predictable in terms of some stereotype, like the communicator that thus resists predictability, has greater impact on the receptors. This is the principle employed in developing newspaper headlines. And as our newspapers demonstrate, it is a principle that has to be employed carefully or it can damage rather than enhance credibility. For if the communication that follows the initial unpredictable "attention-getter" does not fulfill the promise of that headline, the credibility of the message (and of the communicator) may be destroyed—especially if this is done regularly.

Much more trustworthy in enhancing the credibility and impact of the message is its *specificity to the life of the receptor(s)*. The communicator needs both to become a specific human being in terms of the receptors' definition of human-beingness and to learn to communicate like a human being (from their point of view). Person-to-person life-involvement is ordinarily as crucial to high message credibility as it is to communicator credibility in most cultural contexts. However, should the receptors feel a great need for a given message, its credibility for them is assured, no matter what the circumstances. Usually, though, the message and/or the messenger need to generate enough credibility in the eyes of the receptors to win them over. Receptors usually have to be convinced that the message is specifically related to the needs they feel.

To relate the message to the real life of one's hearers, the communicator must learn to employ the communicational devices familiar to the receptor in ways to which the receptor is responsive. Credible messages start from where the receptor is. In many cultures this involves the knowledge and use of a variety of proverbs, aphorisms, and tales of various kinds. Such literary devices form important vehicles within their communicational system. In the majority of the world's cultures these devices will need to be used orally, since most of the world (an estimated 70 percent of the population) either cannot or cares not to read (P. Smith 1975:3). And even with those who do read, the credibility of the message is so closely related to the credibility of the messenger that personal oral presentation generally has greater impact than written communication. Messages that have to do with personal experience, furthermore, have greater impact than messages that simply intellectualize. This is true even if the personal experience consists of true-to-life stories rather than descriptions of actual events. Many of Jesus' parables are just such true-to-life stories. Credible messages deal with real life or true-to-life experience.

How wide of the mark is the kind of homiletic instruction that encourages a primary focus on a few generalized "points" with few if any allusions to personal experience. Often young preachers are encouraged to spend the majority of their time simply explaining ("expositing") biblical passages in the belief that only such preaching is truly biblical (see Ramm 1970:97). Such preaching, unless carefully related to the felt needs of the receptors and fully illustrated from real life or true-to-life experience, is often low-credibility communication. This is true in western culture where such preaching is widely practiced and, therefore, a practice to which many are accustomed. It is even more true, however, in cultures where such practices are totally foreign.

How sad it was for me recently to hear a whole sermon by an African pastor in the Hausa language without a single proverb, cultural aphorism, or even an illustration in it! And this in a language and culture that in ordinary conversation drives virtually every point home with at least one proverb. But this man had been taught to "preach from the Bible," not from life. Starting from the text in this way is extractionist, unless that is where the audience is. Jesus started from Scripture when speaking to the Pharisees and Satan. When speaking to the common people he started where they were. He dealt with topics of interest to them and employed communicational techniques (like parables) understood and appreciated by them. From real life, then, he moved to an application of the truths of God. Such specificity and life-relatedness invite receptor discovery (see below) and give credibility to both the message and the messenger.

It also *invites the hearer to identify with the speaker*. And human commonality seems to be such that even across cultural barriers (such as those between us and the persons whose case histories are recorded in the Bible or those between western missionaries and their hearers) a high degree of this *reverse* or *reciprocating identification* is possible if the communicator speaks in terms of common human experience rather than in terms of generalizations. Effective communication starts with an attempt on the part of the communicator to relate identificationally with the audience and succeeds best when they are able to relate reciprocally to both messenger and message. A potential communicator's living within the hearer's frame of reference in a way that is intelligible to the hearer contributes markedly at the specificity level (although these principles interdepend on each other to such an extent that any good illustration of one principle also illustrates each of the others).

I once asked a missionary if he didn't feel a bit guilty over having fixed up his house so nicely. He had not only made the house comfortable by American standards but had added a touch of luxury to it here and there. "No," he replied, "the Nigerians expect us to live this way." And he was absolutely right! But the *communication value* of his living condition was *zero*, since his actions were completely predictable (in terms of the missionary stereotype) and beyond the specific knowledge of his hearers. His communication resulted in very low credibility for both himself and his message. Another missionary locked up his mission home for a few weeks and moved his family and a few necessaries seven miles out into the African bush to live in an African compound. He hadn't been there very long when his African host asked, "What in the world have you come for? Why," he continued, "if I had a home like that, I wouldn't even poke my nose outside the door, much less come way out here to live."

This missionary had (1) put himself within the African's frame of reference, (2) broken out of the stereotype in such a way that the African was forced to reconsider his stereotype and the credibility of the missionary, and (3) become specifically known by the African. As the message of all of this began to sink in, it resulted in some very interesting questions and comments from the African host. One day the African came to him and said, "I know why you don't like our food. We don't like yours either!" The practice had been for each to offer the other a portion of his food whenever it was mealtime, and this sharing had resulted in quite a significant discovery on the part of the African. For to him the missionary had previously been not only distant, isolated, and unknown but also a source of envy. The African envied both his food and his home. But when the African began to experience the specificity of the life involvement with the missionary that that situation required, a new kind of understanding of the missionary and everything about him, including his message, began to break through via the process of reciprocal identification mentioned above. And this experience was doubly good, for the same sort of insight concerning what it is like to be inside the skin of an African was breaking through to the missionary as well. He was thus enabled to communicate more effectively from within the African's frame of reference. In another experiment in living in an African village another missionary was told, "We want to follow your God, not that of the [other] missionaries!"

A similar, though necessarily lesser, impact is carried by the specificity of life-related sermon illustrations, teaching examples, and personal testimonies (whether of Christian experience or by way of recommendation of a product, movie, teacher, etc.). See chapter 9 for a discussion of this principle with respect to the Bible.

THE DISCOVERY PRINCIPLE (Model 7e)

Though the three aspects of the communication process previously discussed all relate primarily to the activity of the communicator, the fourth relates primarily to the potential receptor. This principle suggests that communicational effectiveness is heightened considerably (1) if receptors have the impression that the new information or insight has come to them via their own *discovery* rather than as the result of their being told something by an outsider and (2) if receptors discover that they can identify with the communicator. *The effective communicator, then, seeks to lead potential receptors to the discovery of both the substance and the value of the message, rather than simply to provide for them "prefabricated" alternatives to their present understandings.* And, as pointed out above, by presenting the message via life involvement with the receptor, the communicator invites the kind of reciprocal identification that drives the message home with impact.

We who live in a day of prefabricated houses and preshrunk clothes are also constantly beseiged by predigested messages, often presented in "one-way conversations" such as lectures, books, and sermons. And much of the effect of all of this is to rob us of the opportunity of discovery. We are very privileged to read and hear of the discoveries of others. But we are often largely unable to avail ourselves of the insights that pass through our consciousness because, though we have heard much, we have not been allowed to discover much on our own. And it is in the process of discovery rather than in the simple hearing of the report of someone else's discovery, presented in predigested form, that the deepest, most abiding kind of learning takes place. This is likely the main reason why God's written Word is presented to us in experience-oriented casebook fashion rather than as a predigested theology textbook (see chapter 10).

This type of discovery-oriented learning provides the basis for the educational systems of a majority of the world's cultures and once had a much more prominent place in our own educational system. Education, for example, that makes much use of proverbs, fables, parables, and similar types of stylized recountings of the experience and accumulated wisdom of the community tends to be discovery-oriented. That is, the focus is usually on the deducing (discovery) of the kind of activity recommended by these techniques for immediate application in the life of the hearer rather than (as is often the case in our educational system) on the mere assimilation of information considered valuable for its own sake whether or not it is applicable to the life of the hearer. An additional value of this kind of educational technique is that it is learner-oriented rather than teacher-oriented. This kind of educational process is dependent upon learners deducing (discovering) what in the materials presented is of value to them and in what way it may be applicable in their life. *Basically, they are learning how to learn.* It does not matter whether the communicator of the information is regarded as a teacher. They learn from the teacher how to learn on their own; not, as in American society, only how to depend on teachers and other "experts" to predigest and even to apply the material presented.

This does not mean that the potential communicator refrains from articulating a message in hopes that the hearers will discover it on their own. On the contrary, the communicator speaks and lives as persuasively as possible, employing the principles described above as completely as possible but in a noncoercive manner. The communicator recognizes that the determinative role in the communication process is that of the receptor rather than that of the communicator. Receptors alone can make the recommended changes in their own perspective, and everything depends upon their feeling that whatever change they make is on the basis of their own choice rather than because of outside coercion. *Discovery, then, is the process within the receptors' minds by means of which they come to understand the relevance to them of the communication and begin to apply the new insights to their own felt needs.* Millions of non-Christians, exposed to effective communication on the basis of these principles, are yearly having revealed to them via discovery the relevance of the Christian message to their lives in the same way that happened to Peter (Mt. 16:15–17). Note that *what Peter perceived as discovery was labeled revelation by Jesus.* Apparently revelation and discovery are the divine and human aspects of the same process.

SUMMARY OF THE PRINCIPLES

Soon after a young missionary had taken charge of a mission station in Africa he was sitting chatting with the son of the local chief on the porch of the mission home. After some time the chief's son looked up at the missionary, asking, "How long have we been here?" The missionary calculated the time and said, "About an hour." The chief's son then asked, "Do you know how long I would have been here if your predecessor was still here?" The missionary answered, "No." "Five minutes," the chief's son replied. "Your predecessor would have come to the door when I called and asked me, 'What do you want?' I would have stated my business, gotten my answer, and been off again in about five minutes! Just look, we've been sitting here for an hour, and I didn't even notice that the time was passing!"

The previous missionary had made only one major blunder. He had acted in a way perfectly intelligible from within *his* cultural framework by stepping outside to meet the chief's son, extending to the African a few common greetings, and getting right to the point (so as not to waste too much time) by asking very politely but directly what the man wanted. The African, however, was interpreting all of these things from within his frame of reference. And his frame of reference regards a direct question such as "What do you want?" no matter how politely asked in that context, as an extreme breach of etiquette. It is about the equivalent of a punch in the nose. In his culture it is the prerogative of the one who comes to state his business in his own good time. It is a matter of common courtesy for the person visited to wait until the visitor gets ready to bring up the matter that brought him.

However, the chief's son had come to expect such breaches of etiquette on the part of missionaries. And this expectation had become a part of his stereotype of missionaries. Thus, it was not the actions of the first missionary that startled him. It was the fact that the newcomer was willing to sit and chat with him without asking what brought him. It was the humanness of the second missionary—humanness in terms of his African definition of human-beingness—that caused him to sit up and take notice. For that which he could define as courtesy in terms of his frame of reference was, in this situation, the unpredictable and the specific that led to a new discovery on the part of this chief's son.

The following outline of this material may be useful as an aid to understanding the whole process:

1. Establishing a frame of reference:

   a. If the approach is *extractionist:*

The communicator must: The receptor must:

| Teach his system via strong indoctrinational methods | ← | Convert to the communicator's system |

   b. If the approach is *identificational:*

The communicator must: The receptor must:

| Learn the receptor's system- Identify with the receptors | → | Adjust minimally |

2. If the communicator employs the receptor's frame of reference:

   a. The commnicator may *accept a stereotype:*

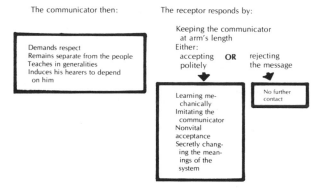

   b. The communicator may *reject the stereotype:*

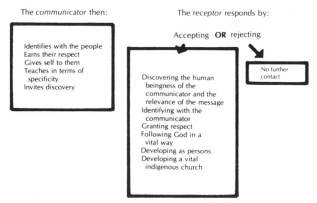

Fig. 8.3. Outline of key communicational principles.

PART IV
THE DYNAMICS
OF REVELATION

9. Receptor-Oriented Revelation

This section is devoted to the application of anthropological and communicational models to theological interpretation (models 8–10). These models yield exciting perspectives on revelation and inspiration. I believe the use of such models to assist us in understanding divine revelation is a step toward the kind of revision of our theories of revelation and inspiration that Bernard Ramm foresaw when he said:

> When . . . an immense amount of sober research has gone into the nature of language theory and communication, we might have to develop a whole new theory of inspiration and revelation. I am always haunted with the suspicion that *our* theories of inspiration and revelation are severely culturally conditioned *by our culture* and not, as we hope and think, by the Scriptures themselves. It may well turn out that when modern theory of communications is developed, we will find that Holy Scripture is far more in harmony with that than it is with the kinds of concepts of language and communication we have worked with in the past few centuries in developing an evangelical view of revelation and inspiration (Ramm 1971:55).

The perspective of this book understands God not as one who speaks or reveals "out into thin air," but as one who comes *all the way to human beings where they are.* In crossing the gap between himself and his creatures, God does not merely build a bridge halfway across, calling to us to construct a structure from our end to span the unspanned area. Rather, God employs our language, our culture, the principles of communication in terms of which we operate. *He reveals himself in a receptor-oriented fashion* (model 8a).

In this chapter we focus on the analysis of God's communication of himself in terms of the principles set forth in chapter 8. The Incarnation is then presented as a case study, a concept of dynamic revelation developed, and the place of the Bible as a measure of revelation discussed. The following chapters in this section elaborate on this concept.

COMMUNICATING ACROSS
THE SUPRACULTURAL-CULTURAL GAP (Model 8b)

How does one bridge a gap like that between the supracultural, absolute God and finite, sinful, culture-bound humans? We wouldn't know were it not for the fact that we have a written record of a large number of God's "bridg-ings" of that gap.

I have sought to demonstrate that (1) human beings are totally immersed in culture, while (2) God exists totally free of culture (except as he chooses to submit to cultural limitations), but that (3) God uses human culture as the milieu within which he interacts with human beings. One of the important implications of the first of these assertions is that humans are utterly depen-dent upon communication from outside of culture for information concerning what, if anything, exists there. "If we are authorized to say anything at all about the living God, it is only because of God's initiative" (Henry 1976:II, 8). This information, then, must be phrased in cultural terms if it is to be intelligible to human beings. For human beings cannot see supracultural truth apart from their cultures (1 Cor. 13:12). We see such truth only in terms of the perceptual categories of the cultural frames of reference in which we are immersed. God, in seeking to reveal himself to us, does so in terms of human language and culture, within the human frame of reference.

His primary method may be labeled "interactional" (model 7a). That is, God reveals himself by interacting with the receivers of his revelation (human beings). And whenever he interacts with humans, he, like a human being, reveals something of himself. He is not simply the God who *acted* (Wright 1952) to create the material universe and who now acts to sustain it—although he does perform these and, undoubtedly, a large number of other activities that have primary reference to material phenomena. He has revealed himself to us primarily as the God who gives himself to human beings in personal *interaction*. He must be more than what we know persons to be. But he assumes a form that we can understand. And in this personal interaction he has brought about the spanning of the gap that separates God from human beings.

There was and is a gap, though. God and human beings exist in utterly separate frames of reference. And we, limited as we are by our cultural context, would not even know God existed except for the fact that he took the initiative and revealed himself. *This he did, we assert, by employing the principles for communicational interaction between personal beings dealt with in the preceding chapter.*

God's revelation, then, can be understood in communicational terms. In accordance with the principles outlined in the preceding chapter, God (1) seeks to be understood, (2) recognizes that what R (the receptor) will understand depends as much on R's perception as on how he (God) presents the message, and (3) realizes that it is his task to stimulate the receptor to produce within the receptor's head the desired meanings. God, therefore, is (4) receptor-oriented in the way he goes about presenting his messages. He attempts to (5) present those messages with impact in (6) person-to-person interaction within (7) the receptor's frame of reference via (8) credible human communicators who (9) relate God's messages specifically to the lives of the receptors and (10) lead the latter to revelational discoveries.

God could, presumably, have done things otherwise. He might have simply ignored us. Or he might have developed some sort of heavenly language and culture and demanded that we learn it in order to make contact with him. But he didn't. Instead, he chose to work through the cultural vehicles at human disposal—often as if he, like us, were bound by the cultural frame of reference. He seems in this matter to abide largely by the rules by which human beings are bound.

When there is communicational interaction between human beings it is necessary, as pointed out in the previous chapter, that they adopt a common frame of reference within which they agree to interact. If persons speak no common language and have no culturally defined common agreements concerning the meanings of whatever noises and gestures they may use, their ability to communicate with each other will be virtually nil. An unbridged barrier to communicative interaction exists between them.

Thus it was between God and humans before God spoke to Adam. And thus it has become again every time humans have stopped listening to God. Often there has been enough information about God to *impress* the human beings on the other side of the gap. That is, *God has usually had a very good reputation* among humans. But he and humans operate within different frames of reference—until he speaks. For when God speaks he chooses to employ the cultural and linguistic frame of reference in which those to whom he speaks are immersed. And the result is that the supracultural-cultural gap is bridged and communication can take place.

He communicated in this way to Adam, to Noah, to Abraham, to Moses, to David, to the prophets, to the apostles, to us. He used the words, the expressions, the grammatical structures of human languages. He communicated directly through words, through dreams, through visions—employing vehicles that those he approached believed in. He also communicated indirectly via the receptors' observation of the lives of those who responded to him and through spoken and written records of their experiences and insights—again in ways that those he approached believed in. On occasion he communicated in more unusual ways, such as through a donkey (Num. 22), through an angel, or through some other miraculous event. But God's preferred way of bridging this gap seems to be by means of human-being-to-human-being interaction within the receptor's frame of reference.

Indeed, until God communicates within a human context his message cannot be perceived as relevant to human life, since it cannot be understood by human beings (see chapter 7). Nor can it provide any stimulus to action. And messages from God need to be perceived as relevant and to stimulate to action if they are to communicate adequately what God apparently desires us to know about him. God's revelation of himself is not, as many seem to assume, simply a matter of adding new information to that which human beings can already know (see chapter 11). God's revealing activity does add information but for a purpose that lies beyond the information itself in the stimulus to behavioral change that can result from the communication of messages with impact. *God's messages, like all effective communication, are not intended simply to impress or inform his audience.* They are intended to be "expressive" and "imperative" as well. God seeks to

present the message in such a way that people can feel its relevance (the expressive element in communication) and can respond to it in action (the imperative function) (Nida and Taber 1969:24).

So God enters into interpersonal relationships with us in terms of our frame of reference. It might have been expected that God would have kept quiet, not even attempting to communicate with us. Or, if he were to attempt to communicate with us, we might expect that someone with his reputation would simply content himself with giving orders, never allowing us, his creatures, to talk back to him.

But he has consistently done the unexpected, the unpredictable. He sought Adam in the cool of the day when he had every right to turn his back on Adam. He arranged for Noah's survival through the flood. He entered into a covenant with Abraham—an agreement that he refused to break even when Israel was unfaithful to its end of the bargain. He worked *with* (not apart from) Moses to rescue the Israelites from Egypt. He dealt lovingly, though firmly, with David in the Bathsheba incident. He even became a man in order to effect his ultimate communication with humans within a human frame of reference.

And in going beyond the predictable, God broke through the human stereotypes that would keep us from taking him seriously. He thus attracted human attention, became credible, and effected an impact on the lives of at least certain human beings that will never be reversed.

Furthermore, in interacting with human beings within the human frame of reference, God was very specific. He did not simply deal with humankind as a whole but with specific individuals and groups. The people he deals with have specific names, specific life histories, and specific cultural contexts, all of which are taken very seriously by God. And this specificity increases enormously the relevance and impact of the communication both to the original participants and to those of us who later hear and read their case histories.

In this process, further, the human participants are not simply passive. Human beings are invited to truly interact with their creator and thereby to discover what he wishes them to learn. In response to the communicational impact of such discovery (plus God's Spirit), human beings like the disciples were transformed from cowards into firebrands for Christ. In earlier days the same kind of transformation had taken place via the same kind of faith discovery in the lives of Enoch, Noah, Abraham, Isaac, Jacob, Joseph, Moses, Rahab, Samson, Samuel, David, the prophets, and many, many others (Heb.

11). For they had received God's communication with transforming impact to the extent that they committed themselves to both God and his cause.

THE INCARNATION: A CASE STUDY
IN RECEPTOR-ORIENTED REVELATION

To assess the communicational impact of the Incarnation properly, let us look at it from the receptor's point of view. By the time of Christ a vital interest in God seems to have been rare in Israel and even rarer outside Israel. To the Greeks "the gods were dead." To the Hebrews God and his message had largely become so formalized and ritualized that it was widely regarded as the property of a minority of religious specialists who disdained the common people (Jeremias 1969:267). In spite of his association with the Hebrews and his constant working in human affairs both within and outside the Hebrew nation, God had come to be regarded even by them as rather predictable, isolated from meaningful interpersonal contact with all but a very few human beings, and more or less depersonalized. But then, "in the fullness of time," God did something about the situation. In Jesus, the stereotyped God broke out of the stereotype. Jesus was God, and had every right to remain God. But he did not choose to remain God (Phil. 2:6). He was above humanity and powerful and majestic and worshipable, and had every right to remain that way. He had every right to accept the stereotype, to remain within it, accepting the assigned status, the prescribed role, the assured respect that the stereotype provided for him. In spite of all this, though, Jesus turned his back on his prerogatives as God, refusing any longer to cling to these rights. He laid aside both his rightful position and the power that went with it to become a human being (Phil. 2:7) for the purpose of coming to dwell among us (Jn. 1:14). That is, he broke out of the stereotype so that we could actually see, hear, and touch him as he dwelt not above or apart from us but truly *among* us.

To many people of that day (and this) God was regarded as very impressive. His power, majesty, and "otherness" made a deep impression on people. We might say that God had developed a very good reputation and lots of respect, but few of his creatures knew him well. He had many admirers but few friends. And much of what he said and did was subject to the same kind of suspicion with which we regard the words and deeds of the very rich or the very powerful—especially if their wealth or power has been inherited rather than earned. How could the Kennedys or the Rockefellers understand what I have to go through? we ask, since they have always had the wealth and/or the power to insulate them from these things. They could never understand our desires, our wants, our needs, we assume. For they, without struggle, were already in possession of the things that we are working so hard to attain. Just as we suspect that such people don't really understand us, so many humans had come to feel that God, being so far "out of it" with respect to the problems and difficulties of the human scene, could not possibly understand what human-beingness is really like.

Those who questioned his ability to understand were likely also to question whether or not he really cared. And if he didn't really care about humans, why should humans care about living up to what was called "God's standard"? So people assigned God to a status and a role (or nonrole) in relation to themselves. Humans fitted God into a stereotype that effectively insulated people from active concern about God or their relationship with God. This stereotype kept God securely at arm's length and allowed humans to go about their business with little or no concern about God. This was often as true of the professional religionists of that day (and of ours) as it was of the majority of the rest of the population.

But then God in Jesus broke out of that assigned status and role, rejecting the stereotype to which he had a right, and incarnated himself (Phil. 2:7; Jn. 1:14). He thus became a real human being *among* us—a learner, a sharer, a participant in the affairs of humans—no longer simply God *above* us. Nor did he then merely content himself to do God-type things *near* us. He spent approximately thirty-three years truly among us—learning, sharing, participating, suffering; seen, heard, touched; living as a human being among human beings and perceived by those around him as a human being. He learned, as the book of Hebrews contends, how to sympathize with human beings by allowing himself to be subjected to the temptations and sufferings of human beings (see Heb. 2:10, 17–18; 4:15; 5:8, and elsewhere).

"Preposterous," said the religious leaders of that day. "You can't expect us to believe a thing like that!" For they had studied the Scriptures and were sure they knew exactly how the Messiah would come. He would be above ordinary people. He would associate with religious, good people; he would assume political power; he would *demand* that people follow him.

"Mere mythology," say many religious experts of our own day who find the Incarnation but another attempt on humanity's part to deify itself. Jesus an incredible man, yes, but incarnate God? "Certainly not," they say.

And, we must admit, it was a rather incredible thing to do. What a terrible risk he took in thus making himself vulnerable, able to be talked back to, able to be criticized by people, able to be tempted. But in this process of rejecting the assigned status that he had a right to retain, he put himself in the position to *win* our respect (rather than to demand it—as he had a right to). He could *earn* (rather than simply assume) our admiration and allegiance on the basis of what he did and became among us. And, in the process, human beings discovered that God was even more impressive than their doctrine had told them he was. This discovery was doubly meaningful because it was based not simply on knowledge *about* God, but on experience *with* him.

Listen to the reaction of the disciple John to this incarnational approach to communication (reading between the lines of 1 Jn. 1:1–3):

Boy, wait till you hear what happened to us! This man came along, an impressive teacher. And I and several others became his students. For three years we lived together. We walked together, talked together, ate together, slept together. We both listened to his teaching and watched closely how he lived. And what an impression he made on us! For as we lived together we began to realize that this was no ordinary man—that when he spoke of God as his Father he spoke from firsthand experience, and when he spoke of what was in the hearts of men he really knew what he was talking about! For this man living among us was God himself! This man whom we called "Teacher," to whom we listened, with whom we lived—we discovered that he is the very God who created the universe. But he chose to come in human form to live with us, his creatures, to demonstrate what he is like to us in a way that we could not misunderstand. And this discovery has so shaken us up that we'll never be the same again!

In God's ultimate revelation of himself, we see him again employing the communicational principles outlined above. Note again that he chose a personal, interactional, receptor-oriented approach within the frame of reference of those he sought to reach. But this time God not only came, he *became*. He, in Christ, identified with his receptors. He not only traversed the infinite distance between heaven and earth to get close to us, he also covered those last couple of feet that separate person from person. He came all the way to identify specifically with us in the human condition in which we, but until this point never he, were immersed. *God in Jesus became so much a part of a specific human context that many never even recognized that he had come from somewhere else.* His enemies accused him of many things but never of being a foreigner (except, of course, in Jerusalem where he was identified as a Galilean). To most he seemed to be more the carpenter's son than one "come down from heaven" (Jn. 6:41-42). But because Jesus thus became specific and because the specific details of much of his life are available to us, the receptors, we are able to receive God's revelation through him in the most impactful way.

God employed these principles in order to effect impactful communication of his lifesaving message to humans. *He had a choice of the means he could employ.* He could have simply remained as God in heaven or he could have spoken a "heavenly language" and developed a "heavenly culture" to which we must all convert (see Fig. 8.1). Even if he had entered the human frame of reference but followed the extractionist course he could have come to earth as God and retained the respect and prestige that is his right as God. *He could have become a human being and simply announced that he was God.* He would, then, have continued to have admirers, but not friends. The risks would have been far fewer, but the real impact and credibility very low because the predictability would have been so high.

He could have come to earth and simply fitted into the stereotyped (i.e., predictable) understanding that humans had of God. This would have resulted in the completion of the following statements in highly predictable terms: "If God came to earth he would come as a ——," or "He would associate with —— people," or "He would go to —— places." The Pharisees, for example, thinking in terms of the stereotype, expected Christ (the Messiah) to come as a king, to associate only with good people, and to go to religiously respectable places. These were the predictable answers in terms of the stereotype produced by their frame of reference. And had Christ acted according to these expectations he might well have been accepted by the Pharisees. But the very predictability of his message lived in these terms would have meant that the communicational (and revelational) impact of his life would have been only slightly above the zero level, even for the Pharisees, but especially for the common people.

Note, though, the far greater communication value of filling the blanks above with unpredictable terms—terms that did not, and still do not, conform to the stereotype that most people have developed of God. Suppose, for example, someone said, "When God came to earth he came as a peasant," or "God associated with prostitutes and crooked, traitorous tax collectors," or "God went to a rowdy wedding feast." These statements make an impact today because they are so unpredictable, so out of line with the stereotype. They sound like headlines. They make you perk up your ears.

Jesus, furthermore, employed the specificity principle. As mentioned above, a communication presented in terms of "life involvement" in the actions, attitudes, and activities of real life makes a greater impact than a strictly verbal message. And even if the communication be verbal, a greater impact is made by specific, detailed descriptions of real life, or even by illustrative parables describing true-to-life events, than by generalizations or abstract propositions concerning those events.[1] For this reason Jesus, living truly among people and teaching in terms of life-specific parables and miracles, communicated infinitely more to us concerning God than would all of the theological abstractions, no matter how true, that could be developed concerning God's interest in people. This is how Christ not only taught truth, but presented it in such a way that it came across to his hearers and observers with impact. And the fact that the life of Christ has been recorded and transmitted to us in biographical, casebook fashion (see chapter 10), rather than in abstract theological textbook fashion, makes available to us even at this distance in time a large degree of that communicational impact of his life and teaching in first-century Palestine.

Jesus, then, invited discovery. He taught from within the framework of his society by means of living and verbal example. He employed familiar forms, such as the discipleship teacher-student relationship and the parable, as primary models for the presentation of his material. He then waited for discovery to take place. When, for example, John the Baptist inquired from prison as to whether or not Jesus was the promised Messiah (a question raised in John's mind because Jesus did not fit the stereotype), the Master did not provide a

---

1. See Trench (1874), chapter 2, "On Teaching by Parables," for an older treatment of this insight.

predigested Yes or No answer. He told the messenger simply to report to John the "things you have seen and heard . . . " (Lk. 7:22), so that John could make his own discovery of the truth. And even at Jesus' trial before Pilate, the question "Are you the King of the Jews?" was answered by a return question—a question designed to probe and challenge Pilate to discovery (and that, incidentally, indicated that Jesus regarded Pilate as fully adequate as a learner). Jesus did this rather than simply providing an answer based on a predigestion of the information to be taught, to provide Pilate the opportunity of really confronting his own question and of possibly discovering real truth in the process.

Some critics of Christianity, speaking from within western culture, have maintained that Jesus' refusal to teach in terms of predigested, easy answers is to be interpreted as a denial on his part of his deity. Such critics do not seem to realize that this discovery-oriented approach to communication was culturally appropriate in first-century Palestine and, in fact, is recognized by many modern-day western educators to be superior to the majority of educational techniques presently employed within western culture. The effectiveness of his learner-centered, discovery-oriented teaching method is vindicated by the thoroughness of the change it made in the lives of his disciples. Such change or transformation is seldom, if ever, effected except on the basis of profound discovery by the person changed. An example of the early stages of such discovery is provided by the response of Peter (on behalf of all the disciples) to Christ's question, "Who do people say that I am?" The Holy Spirit was active in the whole process, leading the disciples into (i.e., revealing to them) truth. But we do injustice both to Scripture and to our understanding of Christianity to ignore that part of the process that Peter was most aware of (and, therefore, didn't need to have Jesus mention)—discovery.

Surrounding, interpenetrating, and tying together all of these factors is one further aspect of receptor response. Human beings identify with other human beings. Jesus made use of this fact by becoming a human being in identification with humanity. But his credibility, though made possible by his identifying with us, was cemented by the fact that *we can identify with him*. As the book of Hebrews (esp. 2:18, 4:15, and 5:8) points out, he suffered to learn what we have to learn. That is, he learned in the same way that we do. *We can identify with him in learning*. Likewise, we see him living in the Gospels in such a way that *we can identify with him in living*.

The Kennedys with all their wealth have seemed to be too high above most Americans for us to identify with. Yet that family has been struck time after time by tragedy—tragedy that for many Americans removes them to some extent from their godlike position and makes it possible for us to identify with them. And this "reverse identification" creates a bond between receptor and communicator that often transcends the isolating influences of privilege and wealth or, in Jesus' case, divinity and glory.

It is a shame that our theologies have often been so impressed with Jesus' divinity that they have seriously jeopardized the ability of many to receive the full impact of the incarnational message. For it is at the point where he sorrowed, wept, was lonely, was abandoned, was tempted, had to struggle to be understood, arranged for his mother to be cared for, prayed to be released from his agreement, died unjustly, that we can identify with him and cement the communication bond in such a way that we will never recover from the impact.

God became human in terms of his hearer's definition of human-beingness. God broke through the isolating stereotype to become specific. Those close to Jesus discovered that this one who had invited them to get close to him, who had earned their respect and undying admiration and yet had called them "friends" could actually have *demanded* all of this but had refused to. For he was God, even though it was as a full-fledged man, a man with whom they could identify from within the human frame of reference, that he demonstrated it. This is the ultimate of receptor-oriented revelational activity.

Such impactful communication, then, invites the receptors to commit themselves to the cause of the communicator. Because Jesus identified with us, and because his life has been recorded for us, we are able to reciprocally identify with him in imitation of both his life and his approach to communicating God's message.

REVELATION: STATIC OR DYNAMIC?

God does not act without revealing something of himself. Whenever God's messages are conveyed via new vehicles (whether new people, new languages, or new cultures), however, *certain completely new things happen* (model 8c). In the first place, the *conveying of God's eternal message by a new person* involves both the necessity of Spirit-guided interpretation and Spirit-guided presentation of the message on the part of that person. These are new events in the stream of history. Second, such communication of the eternal message involves *new receptors and new meanings stimulated within their heads.* These are new events in the stream of history. Third, such communication involves *cultural and linguistic vehicles that have never been used in precisely that way before.* Since the media of communication always interact with the message and affect it in some way, the result is additional newness that has never before happened in history. And fourth, the *application of God's message in and to a new situation results in a new event* in the course of history.

Not only were the communicational events recorded in Scripture new in history; every communicational event is new. And when these communicational events convey accurate messages from God they may stimulate genuinely revelational meanings within the heads of the participants in those events—meanings that have never before happened in just that way in history. Every Bible translation, every new church, every conversion, every attempt at theologizing is a new event in human experience. And each such event, though involving models and meanings that have occurred before, results in new questions that have to be faced and answered, new applications of supracultural truth, new understandings of God and his workings.[2]

But is it correct to speak of such newness as new revelation? Not if one's model of revelation is static.

Western culture places an extremely high value on information for its own sake. Information and the increase of knowledge are thought to be good in themselves whether or not the knower is able to do anything with that knowledge. We buy and sell information through our school systems, via literature, via mass media, and in many other ways. We honor those who know, whether or not they use their knowledge to be worthy of honor. *In keeping with this emphasis of western culture, we have both accepted the informationalizing of revelation and often lost our ability to imagine that it could be anything else.* We have done the same thing with truth—and in the name of the One who made a point of the fact that truth is not informational but personal.

Jesus said, "I am . . . the truth" (Jn. 14:6). And personal truth and revelation are not static. A true person will speak truly. But *our understanding of truth (especially in the biblical sense) should not be reduced to a concept of "true information."* Philip Holtrop points out that if we want to be biblical in our definition of truth we must use the "strange language" of Jesus and speak of "doing the truth," "living the truth," "abiding in" or "being in the truth" (see Jn. 18:31–36; 15:10–11). "Christ is called the Truth," he says,

because he is the great Act of the Father toward us. He is not the Truth in a "metaphorical" or "allegorical" sense. He is the expression of the Father's covenantal fidelity. . . .

A biblical theology of truth and joy, in contrast to scholasticism, has to do with living relations and not primarily abstract definitions and essences. That theology must provide support and direction for dynamic circumstances in which we are called to be responsible, faithful or true before the face of God (1977:9,13).

As Jesus did the truth, related truly in living the truth, he truly and truthfully revealed *God*—not simply information about God. We need to learn to *distinguish between such dynamic revelation (and truth) and the information that is inevitably a part but never the whole of either* (model 8e).

William James at the turn of the century aptly described the process by means of which dynamic, life-related, even life-transforming events are intellectualized into arid, static philosophical propositions. He suggests that the intellectual endeavor of the westerner "consists almost wholly in his substitu-

2. See Coleman 1972:73–105 for a perceptive discussion of the issues that divide liberals from evangelicals concerning revelation. Footnote 31 on page 96 deals well with the matter of newness in revelation. My focus on divine-human dynamics plus that on the unchanging method (model 10a) and message (model 10b) of God (Mal. 3:6) lead me to attempt to work the traditionally liberal concept of continuing revelation into an evangelical system.

tion of a conceptual order for the perceptual order in which his experience originally comes" (Kallen 1925:77). It is the dynamic world of perception, a world filled with what James terms "percepts," in which life is really lived. To me, it is in dynamic interaction within that world that the impactful, life-transforming revealing activity of God takes place. In the static, intellectualized world of information and knowledge, however,

trains of concepts unmixed with percepts grow, . . . and parts of these conceptual trains arrest our attention just as parts of the perceptual flow did, giving rise to concepts of a higher order of abstractness, . . . and these formations have no limit. Aspect within aspect, quality after quality, relation upon relation, . . . different universes of thought thus arise, with specific sorts of relation among their ingredients. The world of common-sense "things"; the world of material tasks to be done; the mathematical world of pure forms; the world of ethical propositions; the worlds of logic, of music, etc., all abstracted and generalized from long forgotten perceptual instances, from which they have as it were flowed out, return and merge themselves again in the particulars of our present and future perception (Kallen 1925:77–78).

But such a retreat into the world of generalized concepts of an ever higher order of abstraction, though a common thing in western culture, especially among academics, is very misleading when it becomes the perspective in terms of which God's interactions with human beings are interpreted. For it produces static, nonspecific, lifeless models incapable of properly interpreting living reality. Such models turn living events into cadavers, capable of being dissected but no longer capable of life. Concepts (models) are, of course, necessary. But they must be dynamic models, in vital touch with reality, if they are to relate properly to life. For in real life concepts and perceptions constantly

interpenetrate and melt together, impregnate and fertilize each other. Neither, taken alone, knows reality in its completeness. We need them both, as we need both our legs to walk with (Kallen 1925:78).

Thus when we observe that in any world of discourse (such as attempts to characterize God's revelational activity) "nothing happens," something has to change. For, James contends, in spite of (or perhaps because of) the fact that "the static nature of the relations in these worlds . . . gives to the propositions that express them an 'eternal' character" (Kallen 1925:88), their accuracy is not thereby proved. *This "eternal character" of such propositions does not, as many assume, prove the truth of the propositions but, rather, their inappropriateness to real life*—at least until such a time as they are perceived to be appropriate at the level where life is lived. But when even eternal truths are so perceived, it is not their eternalness but their dynamic relevance to the life of the receptor that is perceived. For, continues James,

the significance of concepts consists always in their relation to perceptual particulars. . . . Made of percepts, or distilled from parts of percepts, their essential office . . . is to coalesce with percepts again, bringing the mind back into the perceptual world with a better command of the situation there. Certainly whenever we *can* do
this with our concepts, we do *more* with them than when we leave them flocking with
their abstract and motionless companions. It is possible, therefore, to join the
rationalists in allowing conceptual knowledge to be self-sufficing, while at the same
time one joins the empiricists in maintaining that the full *value* of such knowledge is got
only by combining it with perceptual reality again (Kallen 1925:80–81).

Current evangelical Protestant models, except for those of Pentecostalism,
seem to assume that revelation is primarily a matter of knowledge and information (Fuller 1969:ix–20). Even worse, evangelical attempts to support "intellectually" their views on the authenticity of Scripture often devolve into complete
trivializing. Ramm describes "the ideal concept of authenticity which evangelicals have worked with" as follows:

if we know the author, date, nature of composition of a book of the Bible, it is then
authentic. It can be considered inspired and authoritative and therefore part of the
Sacred Canon. It is not possible to do this directly with every book of the Bible for we
do not know the authors of many Old Testament books. So we build up our case as
much indirectly as we do directly (such as noting that the New Testament sanctions the
entire Old Testament as the Word of God) (Ramm 1971:55).

Perhaps more is intended in valuable statements such as the following, but
the knowledge/information orientation of western cultures inhibits our ability
to understand any but the intellectual, knowledge, and information aspects of
the matter:

All merely *human affirmations* about God curl into a question mark. We cannot *spy out the
secrets* of God by obtrusive curiosity. Not even theologians of a *technological era*, not even
Americans with their skill in probing the surface of the moon, have any special radar for
penetrating *the mysteries of God's being and ways.* Apart from God's initiative, God's act,
God's *revelation*, no confident basis exists for *God-talk.* "The things of God none
knoweth, save the Spirit of God" (1 Cor. 2:11b, ASV). If we are authorized to *say anything*
at all about the living God, it is only because of God's initiative and *revelation.* God's
disclosure alone can transform our wavering *questions concerning ultimate reality* into
confident exclamations!
   Human beings *know* only what God has chosen to *reveal* concerning the spiritual
world. "Things which eye saw not, and ear heard not, and which entered not into the
heart of man . . . unto us God *revealed* them through the Spirit" (1 Cor. 2:9–10, ASV).
Revelation is always *God's communication;* in John the Baptist's words, "a man can receive
nothing, except it have been given to him from heaven" (John 3:27, ASV) (Henry
1976,II:8). [Emphasis added.]

I like this statement very much and find myself in hearty agreement with it.
But note our culturally inculcated tendency to interpret each of the italicized

expressions totally in terms of the *information* that they refer to. When we think of "human affirmations," "secrets," "mysteries of God's beings and ways," "revelation," "God's disclosure," "questions concerning ultimate reality," "God's communication," etc., we focus on intellectualized knowledge and information.

We know, if we stop to think about it, that knowledge and information are not proper ends in themselves. They are valuable only insofar as they provide understanding and stimulus to some kind of desired behavior. And yet, especially those of us who are considered intellectuals buy and sell knowledge as if it were itself the most important commodity in the world. As a result, we tend to define revelation in terms of the *information* that it contains rather than in terms of the much more important *stimulus* that God's revelatory activity provides to induce its receptors to respond to him. *We define revelation as God's supplying of information that would not otherwise be available to us.* Even Geerhardus Vos, in an otherwise very helpful statement, submits to this temptation in stating, "The most important function of Special Revelation . . . consists in the introduction of an altogether new world of truth" (1948:20). With respect to both revelation and truth we are pressured by our culture to reduce them to synonymity with but one of their important components—information.

But note certain aspects of even the statement above by Henry that our cultural perspective tends to allow to remain out of focus. It is possible to make affirmations via behavior as well as via words. "Skill in probing . . . " and "radar for penetrating . . ." are phrases indicating that knowledge has been put to work. "God's initiative, God's act" imply behavior that goes beyond the mere imparting of information. The scriptural use of the term "know" (1 Cor. 2:11, quoted above by Henry), shows it to have a much more behavioral meaning than the American usage implies. *"God's disclosure" consists of far more than mere information. God's disclosures of himself stimulate to action.* The 1 Corinthians 2:9–10 passage deals primarily with perspective, not knowledge. "Communication," including God's revelational communication, is more properly defined as a matter of *stimulus to action* than as the mere transmission of information. Henry's statement is not necessarily to be faulted for what it says. The problem I see lies in the perspective (model) in terms of which the statement is likely to be interpreted.

Perhaps, if we are to resist such cultural pressure toward the emasculation of our understanding of God's revelatory activity, we will have to employ something other than the English word "know" in our discussions of revelation. For

the concept of "knowledge" here is not to be understood in its Hellenic sense, but in the Shemitic [sic] sense. According to the former, "to know" means to mirror the reality of a thing in one's consciousness. The Shemitic and Biblical idea is to have the reality of something practically interwoven with the inner experience of life. . . . God desires to be *known* after this fashion. . . . The circle of revelation is not a school, but a "covenant." To speak of revelation as an "education" of humanity is a rationalistic and utterly un-scriptural way of speaking (Vos 1948:8–9; see also Bultmann on Hebrew *yadah* 1964: 696–703).

A western focus on knowledge as information combines with the underlying fear of subjectivity (see Allen 1956) and the desire to know absolutely (be like God?) to lock many evangelicals into totally static models of revelation.[3] In critique of such positions Coleman records liberals as contending that an evangelical

must explain how revelation can be conceptualized without being subject to historical relativity. More specifically, he must demonstrate how revelation can be cast into human and historical forms which reflect a particular culture and still provide propositions which are universally valid (1972:89).

Coleman (articulating the liberal position) continues to point out the inconsistency of maintaining that God utilized "human modes of thought and speech" to reveal himself, but in a way that does "not falsify or misrepresent God in any way."

But if revelation is not complete, then it must be . . . theoretically possible of improvement . . . [for] partiality necessitates nonobjectivity and indirectness. It may be that the biblical authors did not substantially misrepresent God by the literary and cultural forms they used, but it does not follow that their forms or propositions are absolute or incapable of development. To maintain his argument the evangelical must disregard the onward thrust of human thinking and deny revelation the benefit of later inspiration which adds to the very core of divine truth new insight, precision and understanding. The evangelical is also caught in the inconsistent argument that God accommodated himself by using historical forms but that certain men at certain times received God's word so perfectly as to transcend human and historical limitations (1972:89–90).

At issue is the model(s) in terms of which we are to understand revelation. My suggestion is that *revelation be seen as both information and stimulus to understanding* (model 8f), *rather than simply as information*. Revelation, like all communication, is a matter of information structured into messages designed to stimulate response. That which brings about proper response to God is revelatory, whether or not it involves the communication of new information. Such stimulus to divinely led revelatory understanding may result from personal contact, from a change of perspective, from remembrance of something past, from experiencing something present, from anticipating something future, or from the receiving of new information. But in each case it is the *kind of stimulus* rather than the newness of the information transmitted via the activity that is the key to its revelatory nature.

3. See Bromiley 1968 for an informed evangelical statement that both states well the problem of relativity and exhibits the fear that drives many evangelicals to static models of revelation.

What are ordinarily referred to as "general" and "special" revelation are but the very important informational components that may be employed by God in revelational interaction with human beings. We have *general information* concerning God and his activities coming to us from cultural and transcultural sources via cultural vehicles. We have, further, enscripturated, inspired, *special information* concerning God and his activities coming to us from the supracultural God via cultural vehicles. But it is the proper *use* of that information by God as communicator and by human beings as receptors that is revelatory. *Revelation is,* as Vos points out, *"a divine activity," not simply "the finished product of that activity"* (1948:5). Revealing results when personal beings interact with God. One important type of revelational interaction occurs when persons under the guidance of God's Spirit interact with the products of previous revelational activity (e.g., the Scriptures). The desired output of God's revelational activity is that the meanings stimulated in the receptors' minds correspond with the intention of God for them at that time and place.

Revelation seen as receptor-oriented is not like the sermon about which it was said, "That man is saying all of the right things, but he isn't saying them *to* anyone" (from a lecture by John V. Taylor). God's revealing is always *to* someone. This fact is clearly demonstrated in the Scriptures (see chapter 10), for they record for us case after case of God's revelatory activity. Thus, while the Bible is the inspired product of God's revealing, it points beyond itself to the contemporary re-creation within contemporary hearers of the process that it records. Therefore, though the Bible is today a most important means to revelatory ends, it should never be itself regarded as the only end of the revelatory process.

Revelation is not merely "objective" and complete, it has a subjective and continuing dimension as well (model 8g). Some, in keeping with their static models of revelation, see God as simply revealing himself, as if without reference to his receptors and the range of variation that is obvious at the receptors' end. They think somehow that God's revelatory activity is better represented if it is described without reference to those to whom it is directed. Thus Vos compares revelation to redemption but suggests that only the latter has a "subjective and individual" component to it. He says:

Redemption is partly objective and central, partly subjective and individual. By the former we designate those redeeming acts of God, which take place on behalf of, but outside of, the human person. By the latter we designate those acts of God which enter into the human subject. We call the objective acts central, because, happening in the centre of the circle of redemption, they concern all alike, and are not in need of, or capable of, repetition. Such objective-central acts are the incarnation, the atonement, the resurrection of Christ. The acts in the subjective sphere are called individual, because they are repeated in each individual separately. Such subjective-individual acts are regeneration, justification, conversion, sanctification, glorification (Vos 1948:6). [Emphasis added.]

I like what this statement says concerning redemption because it is balanced in its representation of both the once-for-all components of divine-human interaction and the receptor and context-specific components. Both aspects need to be dealt with at all points in our attempts to understand God and his works. Vos does not, however, treat the subject of revelation with the same balance. On this subject he says that "revelation comes to a close where redemption still continues" (ibid.). In keeping with orthodox Protestantism, he claims only the objective-central function for revelation. In recognition of the subjective-individual aspects of the same process, however, he speaks also of "enlightenment" (others would call it "illumination"). But this he sees as limited to the interpretation and application of the Bible. Vos says:

Now *revelation accompanies the process of objective-central redemption only*. . . . To insist upon its accompanying subjective-individual redemption would imply that it dealt with questions of private, personal concern, instead of with the common concerns of the world of redemption collectively. Still this does not mean that the believer cannot, for his subjective experience, receive enlightenment from the source of revelation in the Bible, for we must remember that continually, *alongside the objective process, there was going on the work of subjective application, and that much of this is reflected in the Scriptures* (1948:6). [Emphasis added.]

Note that Vos recognizes, at the end of this statement, that God once revealed subjective applications. These are now "reflected in the Scriptures." In the second sentence of the quotation above, however, he dismisses the possibility that one could define as revelation anything that dealt with "questions of private, personal concern." From this point of view revelation can deal only with "the common concerns of the world of redemption collectively." I would like to suggest that this model, though orthodox, is neither required by Scripture nor consistent with Vos's own treatment of the parallel process of redemption. We highlight the inconsistency in this model in Figure 9.1.

Could it be that Protestant orthodoxy has drifted into this kind of position in over-reaction against the Roman Catholic position that seems to Protestants to elevate ecclesiastical tradition above the Bible, and out of an exaggerated northern European cultural reverence for written documents? The latter value seems to press Euro-Americans to regard "objectified" written documents as objective.[4] This attitude often combines in Euro-American culture with a

4. I use the term "objectified" here to signify something that is regarded by people as an object or entity *in and of itself*. Written documents and certain historical events are often focused on (objectified) in such a way that the context in which they occurred is blurred or completely ignored and the document or event invested (usually implicitly) with a kind of timeless, eternal character. The tendency to reverence written materials (especially if they are ancient) has, I believe, led many to regard such objectified materials as objective (i.e., unbiased and virtually unaffected by the real-life context in which they are produced). This bestows on written documents a value that is often undeserved. Certain events are objectified by being recorded in written documents. In the case of scripturally recorded events we may consider such objectified events as (1) unconditioned by their cultural contexts and (2) beyond the possibility of contemporary parallels.

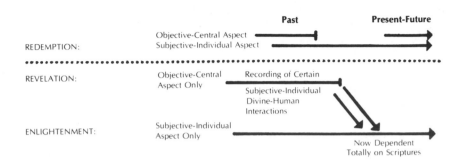

Fig. 9.1. Vos's position relating the objective and subjective dimensions of redemption and revelation/enlightenment to past and present-future time (see Vos 1948:6).

perspective on historical events that tends to regard what happened long ago as quite different from what is happening today. Objectify a written record of ancient events regarded as sacred for people with these values and, I suspect, one could predict an attitude such as the foregoing that regards the biblical events as *different in kind* (i.e., revelatory) from anything today that appears similar (i.e., enlightenment.)

Perhaps existentialist positions on revelation (e.g., Kierkegaard, Bultmann) that seem to evangelicals to go too far in emphasizing the subjective-individual dimension of revelation are reacting against this kind of overbalance. *For such models as the foregoing imply a radical change in God as soon as the last book of Scripture was written* (though this apparently wasn't discovered until after the canon was closed). At that point, orthodox, static views of revelation imply, God ceased to reveal himself and turned exclusively to "enlightening" or "illuminating" people who search the Scriptures.

But has he so limited himself today? Has he totally gone back on Jesus' promise to send the Holy Spirit to lead us into (further?) truth (Jn. 16:13)? Or is there another model or models in terms of which to understand and balance the objective dimensions of revelation/enlightenment with the subjective dimensions? I believe that the perspective presented here provides a better answer to these questions.

It sees revelation as both objective and subjective. Furthermore, it sees revelation as paralleling redemption at every point (Ramm 1961:71). Since even old messages in new persons and contexts are at least partly new, and since God has not stopped working (and, therefore, revealing himself) we can adopt a balanced dynamic model at this point in place of the traditional unbalanced model. This could be pictured as follows:

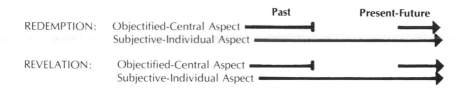

Fig. 9.2. A balanced dynamic model of redemption and revelation.

THE BIBLE AS THE MEASURE OF REVELATION

One further model needs to be introduced at this point to clarify the relationship between the Scriptures and the contemporary applications of scriptural principles. The problem facing us if we admit that God has, in fact, continued to reveal himself since the completion of the writing of Scriptures may be phrased in the question, "How do we know if a given 'revelation' is from God or not?" How do we know if the purported revelations of our contemporaries or, for that matter, of supposed "heretics" such as Joseph Smith, Muhammad, or Mary Baker Eddy are from God or not? The answer lies, I believe, in the "measuring" of that purported revelation by what we know of God's past revelatory activity from the inspired record of some of that activity in the Scriptures.

God will not (we believe) contradict himself. We can therefore use an assuredly inspired collection of his revelations, often accompanied by inspired interpretations of them, as a measuring device against which to test and evaluate contemporary data. Recognizing that the Bible shows us a range of ideal, subideal but acceptable, and unacceptable behavior and belief, our task is to discern whether or not there is an equivalence between items of contemporary behavior and belief and those recommended in the Bible. If contemporary behavior is functionally equivalent in meaning within its cultural context to what the Bible shows to have been acceptable (even though, perhaps, subideal) behavior in its cultural context, the measurement has proved positive. This may be termed "dynamically equivalent revelation" (model 8h). (See chapters 13–17 for an elaboration and application of the dynamic equivalence model, i.e., model 11.) If, however, the contemporary behavior equates in meaning in today's context with that of behavior recorded biblically as having conveyed unacceptable meanings, the judgment is negative.

For measuring such equivalence or nonequivalence we suggest a *Bible-as-yardstick model* (model 9a). This (I believe) is essentially the same as that currently employed by evangelicals to test "applications" of scriptural truth. Perhaps the only novel aspect of this model (for evangelical Protestants, though not for Pentecostals and others who believe in continuing revelation) is that *it labels and measures a contemporary application as divine revelation, not as something that is qualitatively different from God's revelatory workings in the past.* This model does not claim to have solved all the knotty problems of how to make such evaluations but, unlike traditional (evangelical Protestant) approaches, it faces the issue of the similarity (equivalence) between what God is doing today and what he has done in past times. It also alerts us to the fact that revelation is an *ongoing activity* of God, not simply the record of part of that activity.

The Bible is no less important from this perspective than from traditional perspectives. Here, however, *we distinguish between what the Bible is and how it is used.* To regard the Bible as inherently revelatory regardless of how it is used is to evaluate it in terms of only one of its *potential* uses. For the Bible, like any other cultural form, can be used to evil ends as well as to good ends. *The information contained in what we call the Word of God if used improperly is neither revelation nor God's Word.* If, further, the meanings stimulated in the minds of the receptors do not fall within the range of the variation that God approves of as the end-product of his revelatory activity, the result is not revelation at the receptor's end of the bridge. (See chapter 11 for further elaboration of this perspective.)

Here we will turn to a consideration of the fact that *the Bible as yardstick allows for a range of variation in the understanding and application of God's truth* (model 9b). The Bible clearly shows that God is content to accept human behavior, including understandings of himself and his truth, that fall within what we will here term a "range of acceptable variation" (see also model 10c, starting point plus process, below). Owing to the limitations of such factors as culture, individual experience, and sin, human beings seldom if ever live or understand at the ideal level. Even through inspired Scripture, therefore, it is highly unlikely that any, much less all, people will perceive exactly the same meanings from any given portion. It is here postulated, however, that certain meanings are within a range of allowable variation as measured by the Bible yardstick—reasonably equivalent to the original intent but not corresponding exactly. This principle is true to what we know of ordinary interpersonal communication where, since the meanings are stimulated in the receptor's head via message symbols rather than transmitted directly, the result is never more than approximately the same as the intent (see principle 3, chapter 8). This is true even when both C (communicator) and R (receptor) participate in the same frame of reference. The lack of correspondence between intent and interpretation is even greater when there is a large frame of reference gap, such as a culture and/or a time gap between C and R.

In ordinary communicational interaction people attempt to compensate for the lack of correspondence between intent and interpretation in four ways:

1. Communicators seek to build into their message enough repetition and reiteration (technically known as "redundancy," Berlo 1960:202–3; Nida

1960:74,199) to guide the hearer as close as possible to the main points. In ordinary speech it has been estimated that "successive sequences are usually about 50 per cent predictable" (Nida 1960:74). Good communicators make use of this fact and may even increase the percentage of reiteration via creative restatement. Technical writing is quite different from ordinary speaking and writing in that it is characterized by a severe reduction in redundancy. This fact makes technical writing seem strange in comparison to ordinary speaking and writing. It also makes technical writing much more difficult to understand. The Bible, by the way, is largely informal, almost never technical writing.

2. Communicators attempt to elicit "feedback" from their receptors to see how well the receptors are getting the message. If C discovers thereby that they are not understanding well, C adjusts the message by rephrasing, providing additional information, explaining more elaborately, etc., in order to bring about greater correspondence between C's intent and R's understanding.

3. Communicators settle for approximate (rather than exact) understandings of what they seek to communicate, as long as the understandings are reasonably close to what is intended. C makes a statement, R restates it in his or her own words, and C agrees to accept that restatement as close enough (i.e., within an acceptable range of variation).

4. Communicators may judge that a matter misunderstood by their hearer(s) is not sufficiently important for them to devote any more effort to explicating. C may feel that the surest way for R to keep from being distracted out of the allowable range is simply to drop the misunderstood subsidiary point, even if R's misunderstanding is allowed to continue.

In interpreting the Scriptures we are, of course, cut off from the ordinary approach to eliciting feedback from the original authors. Through prayer, however, we ask the Original Source (God) to lead us into (i.e., to reveal to us) greater understanding. He frequently answers such prayers by leading us to read in Scripture or to hear or read otherwise reiterations and/or creative restatements of the message that puzzles us, for such redundancy is a major characteristic both of the Bible and of Spirit-led extra-biblical interpretations of the major themes of the Bible. Or God may answer such requests for further explanation by guiding us back to more central issues, even though our misunderstanding remains, in order to keep us from turning away from major points to focus on peripheral issues.

The communicational (revelational) focus of God (via the Bible) appears to be on a fairly small number of crucial items. These are either assumed or continually reiterated (often via case-study illustrations rather than mere verbalizations). Denial of such scripturally basic concepts as the existence of God, human sinfulness, God's willingness to relate to humans on certain conditions, the necessity of a human faithfulness response to God as preconditional to salvation, and the like would put one outside the biblically allowed range of acceptable variation. These are the deep-level core constants that form the basis upon which the historical (cultural) interactions between God and human beings take place. They are, thus, not debatable as items in the revelation of God to which the acceptable range model is applicable at the more surface level of interpretation or perception.

Nor can we debate the biblically recorded historical outworkings of these constants in such contexts as the life of Israel, the life and ministry of Christ, the experiences of the early Christians, etc. The range of acceptable variation model applies only to the receptors' culturally and psychologically conditioned *perceptions* of the intended messages of God concerning his core constants communicated via culture, some of which are recorded (called "holy history") in the Bible.

For example, though the existence of God is not debatable (Heb. 11:6), we see in Scripture a range of understandings of him allowed. Likewise with sin, the understanding of the nature of humans (one, two, or three parts), understandings of the spirit world, etc. The problem is to determine which contemporary understandings of such things fit within the scripturally allowed range and which fall outside. Within the allowed range are both the intent of God and that of the human author, but these are not always the same. In prophetic utterances, for example, the human author was often unaware of the later use God would make of those utterances (e.g., Isa. 7:14).

In ordinary human communication the perceived understanding of the message on the part of the receptor is affected by several things in addition to the communicator's primary message. Such "paramessages" also affect the interpretation of God's communications. Human beings have particular culturally inculcated preconceptions concerning God and his activities, the method of communication (e.g., written or oral), the human communicators involved, the place in which the communication takes place, the tactics employed, historical material, the language used, "religious" communication in general, etc. All such preconceptions affect R's perception of the message of God by altering and widening the range of meanings that R perceives in any given communicational situation. God's Spirit is, of course, at work to see to it that what is understood is adequate. But the presence of such factors demands a range of allowable variation within which the Spirit works.

One such preconception that strongly influences a number of conservative exegetes is the assumption that in the Bible God uses human language in a more precise way than this model suggests. In order to support such an assumption, however, these interpreters find it necessary to contend that God perfects language and that he has changed his way of working at some time after the events recorded in the Bible. A good bit of what I say here and elsewhere throughout this book is intended to dispute those contentions (though not to disallow that they are within the range of interpretation allowed by God). In support of my position, I believe that we have evidence within Scripture that God worked within a range in the way New Testament authors employed quotations from the Old Testament.

Calvin long ago noted the apostles' use of "freer language than the original" and the fact that "they were content if what they quoted applied to their subject, and therefore they were not over-careful in their use of words" (on Rom. 3:4). In another place Calvin says that the apostles

were not overscrupulous in quoting words provided that they did not misuse Scripture for their convenience. . . . As far as the words are concerned, as in other things which are not relevant to the present purpose, they allow themselves some indulgence (on Heb. 10:6; cited by Rogers 1977).

This lack of a "fixed mode" for citing the Old Testament in the New speaks of an allowable range of variation. So do most of the alleged discrepancies in the Bible.

J. W. Haley (1874, republication 1953) has published nearly four hundred pages full of such alleged discrepancies. Hodge says of these discrepancies:

These apparent discrepancies, although numerous, are for the most part trivial; relating in most cases to numbers or dates. The great majority of them are only apparent, and yield to careful examination. Many of them may be fairly ascribed to errors of transcribers (1871–73:1–169; quoted with approval by Haley 1874:49).

Note that the perspective in terms of which such examples are labeled "discrepancies" assumes an exactness of statement in the Bible that we do not demand either in ordinary conversation or in any but the most technical writing. *Most of the Bible is, however, written in a nontechnical or even an informal style according to the standards of other cultures. It should not, therefore, in context be judged by standards set up by Euro-American cultures for technical writing* (see Taber 1978a:12).

Recognition that the Bible allows a range of variation, especially at the culture-specific level (see chapter 8, above), is required if we are to be true to the culture-specific nature of the Bible. For it is in the area of cultural variation in the receptors' perception of the Gospel message and its implications that this model is best illustrated. Numerous scriptural illustrations cited throughout this volume could be adduced (e.g., marriage customs, concepts of God, understandings of the Ten Commandments, concepts of leadership). Application of this model with respect to sin concepts is presented in chapter 12.

One further picture of the relationship of the Bible to the allowable range of variation may usefully be introduced at this point. We will label it *the Bible as tether model* (model 9c). A tether is a means such as a rope or chain "by which an animal is fastened so that it can range only within a set radius" (Webster's *Dictionary* 1967:912). A tether, then, provides both a circle within which one moves and a point at the center of that circle to which one is tied. The Bible is the "in-culture" point of reference that provides the "set radius" within which contemporary revelational encounters may occur and in terms of which all claims of divine revelation are evaluated. The range of allowable variation within which we work interpretationally and experientially is the biblical range. The yardstick and tether by which we measure is the inspired record of certain of God's previous interactions with human beings.

SUMMARY

Though we will in succeeding chapters attempt to broaden our understanding of how to employ the Bible to measure, there are, I believe, only two novel elements in this approach to the matter. These are (1) the labeling of what evangelical orthodoxy terms "application" as at least potentially revelatory, and (2) the concept of the allowable range of acceptability. Essentially the same leeway for variations in interpretation (and the same exegetical problems) attach to this model as to the traditional model. Full development of the dynamic-equivalence model (model 11, below) will assist considerably with this problem.

The basic elements of this perspective on revelation so far presented are: (1) to see God's revelational activity as a dynamic process rather than to reduce it to a static product; (2) to see revelation as incomplete unless it reaches *to* someone—revelation is therefore receptor-oriented; (3) to distinguish between information, even that recorded and preserved under divine inspiration and the revelatory use of that information; (4) to see revelation as consisting of a balance between objectified-central information (data) and subjective-individual experience; (5) to see Scripture as a "yardstick" for measuring the equivalence of contemporary revelation to assured past revelation; (6) to understand that God accepts receptor perceptions that fall within a range of variation with respect to their equivalence to his original intent; (7) to see Scripture as providing the "tether" in terms of which the range of allowable variation in interpretation and experience is gauged.

A perspective that includes these elements is more balanced than static models, less open to the accusation that it implies a drastic change in God's method of communicating himself when the last book of Scripture was written, and more open to the contemporary validity and usefulness of the whole Bible (including the Old Testament) than previous models. Certain aspects of these elements will be developed further in the next three chapters.

These considerations inevitably raise the problem of the canon of Scripture. The production of the canonical Scriptures was, I believe, the aim of what we here call the objectified-central aspect of God's revelational activity. The Holy Spirit led the early Christians to use, value, and collect certain writings above others that were available. These writings (as detailed in chapter 10) were considered by the church to be "classics" in their presentation of "salvation history" and were therefore regarded as of the highest degree of helpfulness in stimulating others to respond to God's revelation. Undoubtedly, the choice of many of the New Testament writings was motivated (humanly speaking) by the fact that they were written by eyewitnesses of the Incarnation (Cullmann

1967:295–96). But this principle cannot be made to carry the whole burden for explaining the present Scriptures. It cannot, for example, explain the inclusion of the Old Testament, and it is stretched too far with respect to certain New Testament writings as well (e.g., Luke-Acts, the Pauline epistles, Hebrews). Furthermore, if late dates for certain New Testament writings should be proven, the limited usefulness of the principle will become even more evident.

I believe the majority of traditional approaches to the explanation of "Why these writings and no others?" participate in the same staticness that largely characterizes evangelical views of revelation and inspiration. Such explanations tie us to unbending a priori assumptions concerning how God *must* have worked, rather than allowing us the freedom to observe how he works today and analogizing from those observations to theories concerning how the unchanging God worked in the past. The dynamic models here presented help us to keep from getting enmeshed in such problems.

We turn now to a more detailed look at the Bible as God's inspired casebook.

10. God's Inspired Casebook

We have sought to establish an understanding of God's communicational activity, including that called revelational, by using the models of communication science. Informed by these models plus the more broadly anthropological models introduced earlier, we have attempted to deal with God's activity in crossing the supracultural-cultural gap. We have postulated that in attempting to bridge that gap God has engaged in revelatory activities that, in the past, "built bridges" all the way across the gap and that, in recorded form, provide materials from which he and his receptors can build bridges all the way across today. In an attempt to suggest a more balanced orthodoxy in this regard we have suggested that what has traditionally been termed "revelation" and what has traditionally been labeled "illumination" or "enlightenment" are but objectified and subjective aspects of the same process. It is time now to make explicit another model that has to this point been implicit and to discuss certain horizontal dimensions of God's communicational use of cultural vehicles.

This chapter starts by dealing with God's constancy with respect to the methods he employs in revealing himself (model 10a). We then turn to a discussion of the Bible as an inspired, classic casebook (model 9d). We see the Bible as a human word as well as God's (model 9e), present a dynamic view of scriptural inspiration (model 9f), and we view the Word as a presentation of truth with impact (model 9g).

CONSTANCY OF METHOD (Model 10a)

The Bible, the source of the data that we are attempting to analyze, is a more wonderful book than evangelicals have often realized. It has been customary to look to it as the source of the *message* we are to proclaim. That message we regard as inspired. *There is, however, more to the Bible than just its message. It shows us also the* method *of God in dealing with that life-transforming message.* That method is always personal, interactional, and according to the principles set forth in chapter 8. His method involves both a giving on God's part and a receiving on humanity's part. It involves a frame of reference which, by God's choice, is a human culture and language. God's constant method is what we have described above as the dynamic process of his revelation of himself to humanity.

Another name for this same process is "leading." In view of the foregoing discussion (chapter 9), some might accuse me of a "low" view of revelation.

Such is far from the case. I have, rather, a "high" view of the continual operation and effectiveness of the leading of God in the human arena. I see God as in constant, effective interaction with his people both individually and corporately to bring about ends that he and his people mutually agree upon. A key to this leading activity is the process of subjective-individual revelation—the process by means of which God's bridge is built all the way across the gap.

This leading involves a leader, a follower, and a setting (frame of reference). The leader, of course, is always God. But on certain occasions he has manifested himself as God the Father. In the Incarnation he manifested himself as God the Son. And since Jesus' ascension his primary manifestation of himself is as God the Holy Spirit.[1] Each of these manifestations of himself, geared as they are to the human frame of reference, are met with particular perceptions of God and responses to him on the part of the human participants. In this interaction between God as he manifests himself and the persons to whom he manifests himself, and who in turn perceive and respond to God in particular culturally conditioned ways, both his self-disclosure and his leading take place. For we do not know God's nature apart from his interaction with us occasioned by his leading activity. Wright (1952:90) quotes Brunner on this point:

The Bible says nothing of a God as He is in Himself and nothing of a man as he is in himself, but only of a God who from the first is related to man and of a man who from the first is related to God (Brunner 1943:58).

We gain insight into the nature of the one who leads us as we interact with him. For God "communicates himself by revelatory happenings" (Wright 1952:89). We have, therefore, come to understand this revelational leading as divine-human communication. We have focused on the fact that there are messages, or communications, that pass between the participants. This process, too, is an interactional one, involving both a sender and receivers of the messages. And though our tendency is to focus largely on God the sender of messages in the divine-human communicational interaction, the receptors' part is also crucial. For, though God may be the initiator in focus in the

1. Speaking of God as "manifesting himself " as I do here is not to be taken as a blanket endorsement of the second- and third-century theory of the nature of God called "modalism," "Sabellianism," or "modalistic monarchianism" (see Brauer 1971:563). As a protection against polytheism, that position has impressive strengths that might be well employed today to counteract the tendency within trinitarianism to regard the three Persons as totally separate individuals. Modalism however, does not deal well with the apparent distinctions within the Trinity at the same point in time (e.g., when Jesus spoke to God the Father). I find Nida 1959 the most helpful presentation of the matter. He admits (as I think we all must) both that we cannot understand all that we would like to concerning the single God and the three names we use for him, and that "the Bible contains neither a description nor an explanation of the Trinity" (p. 53). He then suggests that we think of God as one in form but three in function or activity with respect to the human cultural and historical milieu.

scriptural records to which we look for our information about this process, there are always particular concerns, particular needs, particular questions on the part of the human participants to which he addresses himself. Quite often these needs are verbalized by the human beings (as in prayer or in the questions the disciples addressed to Jesus). Often, though, they remain latent and unverbalized (e.g., Nicodemus' need for new birth, David's need for reconciliation over the Bathsheba affair) until pointed out by God, usually through a human representative. The information, in the form of the existence of the need, is there before God communicates the stimulus for the receptor to build his or her part of the bridge.

Thus the divine communication by means of which God reveals himself is based as solidly on the needs of human beings as on the desire of God to reveal himself. The result is a continuous process of a human being feeling a need and God addressing himself to that need. No matter what "objectified-central" revelational materials God may employ in the process of meeting that need, *the need is not met, the leading is not effected, the "revelation" is not revelatory until the subjective as well as the objective component of the process is actualized.* This principle is true both to Christian experience and to the analytical insights of the behavioral sciences. For it has been often demonstrated that until persons or groups feel the need for something it is very unlikely that they will even accept helpful advice concerning it, much less seek help. As Barnett, who labels felt needs "wants," states:

. . . change for the sake of change is a relatively infrequent motivation for innovation. . . . A large number of wants call for satisfactions that require change if they are to be realized, but . . . the aim is not newness, freshness, or modification . . . (1953: 152).

The aim is, rather, the attainment of a more satisfactory solution to a felt need. For "only felt-needs move individuals to borrow new ways" (Luzbetak 1963:287). The basis of revelation and leading in human felt needs is a part of God's constant method.

God seldom addresses himself to that need directly. True, at many points in the Scriptures (e.g., in the early Old Testament records and in the person of Christ), God speaks directly to humans. But in most situations (e.g., through the prophets, in the New Testament epistles) he leads human beings who are in close contact with him to become concerned about the issues at hand and to speak on his behalf to those issues. God thus reveals himself and his will on occasion directly, but most frequently indirectly, in cooperation with Spirit-led human beings. And these human beings frequently perceive the Spirit-led formulation of the answer they have articulated to be the result of *discovery* on their part.

What is communicated is more than mere information about God, which, though interesting, might easily be dismissed as not vital to real life. Rather, the messages are addressed to specific issues (needs) that surface to human awareness in specific situations. And God typically addresses himself to these needs from within the frame of reference in which they develop. He does this through concerned servants of his whom he leads to discover and communicate his Word to those particular situations. Thus the message comes with a relevance and an impact (both on the deliverer and the hearers) that would most likely be minimized if at every point God broke in, disrupting the normal flow of events to deliver his message personally. In such a process God's Spirit works with the hearers as well, so that both at the delivery end and at the receptor end the fact is confirmed that the message delivered is from God.

We reiterate that since God's revelation of himself is an interpersonal thing, it regularly conforms to the ordinary requirements for effective interpersonal communication. It carries relevance and impact as well as information (Nida and Taber 1969:24). It fits the specific situation, as well as the overall plan of God, being life-related and addressed to a human felt need that surfaces in that situation. Since this revelatory process is interactional, human beings are not passive. Rather, we actively participate in the process at every point. Perhaps the model for this participation is made clear to us by Jesus' statement to his disciples in John 15:15:

I no longer call you slaves, for a master doesn't confide in his slaves (LB). Instead, I call you friends, because I have communicated to you everything I heard from my Father · (TEV).

Accounts of this primary interpersonal revelational divine-human interaction have been written down under the guidance of God's Spirit. They have been collected under the same guidance and translated and transmitted to us—again under the guidance of the Holy Spirit. Thus the selection of interpersonal revelational events on which we most often focus is that which has come down to us in written form—the Bible. By applying the "yardstick" of the Scriptures to the analysis of contemporary divine-human interactions we can speak of the *constancy of God's method* of relating to human beings.

Certain theological positions, of course, deny the constancy of God's method (e.g., dispensationalism and evolutionary understandings of "progressive revelation"). Such models are, it seems to me, overly influenced by western cultural ethnocentrism. They thus are prone to focus more on the differences in the cultural forms God employs at the receptors' end than on the constancy of his adaptation to his receptors in their cultural contexts. Paul articulates this latter principle in 1 Corinthians 9:19–22. Since western interpretations of culture history tend to be evolutionary, the forms of ancient Hebrew culture (being older and most different from ours) are regarded as inferior to those of Greek culture. On this basis such theologies imply that God continually abandons inferior (Hebrew) methods in favor, eventually, of superior European (Greek) forms. I shall attempt to show the way out of such ethnocentric positions in the next chapter.

THE BIBLE AS INSPIRED CLASSIC CASEBOOK (Model 9d)

When we seek to reveal ourselves and our thinking to others in book form, we sit down (as I am doing here) and attempt to produce a single, unified, treatise. But God did not do it this way. He did not, in the first place, write anything at all (perhaps because he is more aware than we are of the extreme limitedness of writing as a vehicle of communication). And second, the product is anything but a unified treatise (though there is a unity of theme to it).

Rather, what he led others to do ("horizontally" from human being to human being) was to record in written form certain of the divine-human interactions to produce what has come to be called a "casebook." A *casebook*, or book of case histories, is a collection of descriptions of illustrative real-life exemplifications of the principles to be taught. Such descriptions may (should) include interpretations (as the Bible frequently does, Ramm 1961:77ff; Mickelson 1963:58ff), but as a part of the case studies or in response to a larger situation (case) not fully described in the case study. For

the primary means by which God communicates with man is by his acts, which are the events of history. These events need interpretation, it is true, and God provides it in his Word by chosen heralds or messengers. But the focus of attention is not upon the Word of God in and for itself so that it can be frozen, so to speak, within a system of dogmatic propositions. The Word leads us, not *away from* history, but *to* history and to responsible participation *within* history. It is the accompaniment of history. The Bible thus is not primarily the Word of God, but the record of the Acts of God, together with the human response thereto (Wright 1952:107).

The Bible presents both the drama of the events it records and the perspective in terms of which those events are to be interpreted. Dramatic presentations that are not interpreted (such as most of the drama to which we are exposed in popular culture) become mere entertainment. And biblical events taken out of their contexts (as, for example, by Hollywood film-makers) easily become simply entertaining. On the other hand, mere interpretation of God and his workings without "eventness" (such as in most sermonizing) is dead. The proper balance is attained only when there is both event (drama) and perspective-building interpretation. In the Bible, even the most theological portions (e.g., Romans) participate in the "eventness" of the fact that they were written as letters from specific persons to specific persons to meet specific needs. In using them today we must not ignore this fact and fail to "repersonalize" these writings (see chapters 11 and 14). Likewise, the most event-laden portions of the Scriptures (e.g., Old Testament historical books, the Gospels) are laced through with interpretive comments designed to build the desired perspective. As a casebook the Bible is balanced in this regard.

I remember vividly my first exposure in college to a casebook used as a supplementary textbook in a sociology course. I remember that I soon developed a negative attitude toward the primary textbook, which presented the theoretical material in treatise form (i.e., without drama). My attitude toward the casebook, though, was just the opposite. That volume came to life for me. It provided drama and eventness, for it was filled with descriptions of real-life stories of difficult situations to which sociological insights were applied by real-life caseworkers.

The casebook described real life. The theoretical presentation in the textbook, on the other hand, so abstracted from life that it was difficult to make the connections to my own experience that would have cemented the learning. Yet, though American education seems to feel that the most effective way to teach is to present the principle and allow the students to perform the supposedly less difficult application, God knew better. He seems to have realized that *the process of analogizing is easier from the specific to the general* and thence again to the specific than if one starts from the general principles alone. So he has provided us with a casebook rather than with a theology textbook. And, it seems to me, both the process of theological education and that of understanding what the Bible is are infinitely complicated by the constant attempts of preachers and theologians to give the impression that the Bible is a theology textbook (Welbourn and Ogot 1966:137).

"Give me an illustration," our students say in an attempt to get us to bring the teaching down to earth for them. And when we do, the teaching gets across, because they are then equipped to start with specifics rather than simply with generalizations. Similar to this is the custom formerly followed in our culture, and still followed in many cultures, of teaching through fables. The story is related in specific detail, and only when the story is complete and the result reported is the generalization, the "moral of the story," stated, if it is stated at all. Jesus, in teaching this way, employed a pattern both fully appropriate to his culture and, apparently, also much more widely applicable. It seems, in fact, that this method of teaching is effective in every culture (even American, which is the most different)—a cultural universal.

The various disciplines that deal with communication point out that all interpersonal communication is by analogy. We cannot know absolutely what it is like to be in the other person's shoes. Nor can we communicate our own experience absolutely, since the other person has never been in our shoes. We can, however, in attempting to get across to the other person, describe how the point we are trying to relate has been experienced in our, or someone else's life and thinking. And since the range of human experience in all cultures is similar (Nida 1960:90–93), a person may thus enter into our experience, or that other one's experience, analogically. In this way the recipient of the communication is able to "get the point." "Why, you know *just* how I feel," a girl once said to me after she had described to me her desperate plight and I had countered by describing the most desperate situation that I had ever been in. By my estimate her situation was worse than mine had been, but by her estimate we stood on common ground and an adequate foundation had been laid for my giving and her receiving help. She, the hearer/learner, had perceived the appropriateness of the analogy and experienced the "reverse identification" spoken of in chapter 8.

The effectiveness of such use of analogy[2] in the communication process is predicated on three bases: (1) the closeness between the experience of the communicator or recommended model and that of the potential receptor, (2) the appropriateness of the analogy, and (3) the ability of the receptor to identify through the analogy with the personal model being recommended. In a caseboook the assumption is that: (1) there is an appropriate degree of closeness between the receptor and the persons whose experiences are being described, (2) the analogies are appropriate to the lessons being taught, and (3) the reader is apt enough at learning to be able to identify sufficiently with the participants in the experiences being described to learn the lessons being taught.

The Bible assumes that, in spite of significant differences in culture, there are impressive basic human similarities between peoples (see chapter 5, above). It assumes, further, that these are sufficient to provide the necessary experiential commonality to make the cases of divine-human interaction described appropriate analogies. It also assumes that the hearers/readers are good enough at the job of learning by analogy to be able to deduce the principles being illustrated and to "transculturate" them (see chapter 14, below) into their life within their culture.

The physician John Hercus, author of a slim volume entitled *Pages from God's Case-book*, apparently had an experience similar to mine while he was a student. He records how "by the time we were in our fourth year we had some knowledge of some diseases, though we had never as yet seen actual cases" (1962:15). Then the fledgling doctors were taken into the wards and introduced by their instructors to real-life situations about which they had merely theorized to that point. Hercus says:

This was an entirely new method of teaching, one where we were learning from the cases themselves. We were no longer learning pneumonia from test-tubes and microscopes and bottles, but from the thing itself, from the cas · of pneumonia (1962:16).

This method of teaching was a directly interactional one. Hercus and the other trainees were coming face to face with those to whom they must apply their insight. Only slightly removed from this directly interactional approach, however, is that which employs a casebook describing in detail what the learner would have observed in person had he been there at the time. Hercus continues:

2. A useful parallelism between terms is pointed out by Rogers: "The word 'analogy' functions in theology in roughly the same way that 'metaphor' functions in literature and 'model' functions in the sciences" (1976:69).

Now in His Textbook God has used this teaching method perhaps more than any other. He has recorded case after case, to teach us how he encounters men, to teach us what He wants from this encounter. It is as though He has given us access to a lavish selection of case histories, so that every aspect of truth is demonstrated. Here is the greatest ward-round any student can undertake. All are cases needing treatment, and every aspect of their need, as of their treatment, may here be studied in the official clinical records. Temperature charts? X-rays and blood counts? Autopsies? Yes, they are all there, even a number of fatal cases, with the full relevant post-mortem findings. Complications? Oh, yes. All the complications. Some of the cases are recorded only as the complication—like empyema, where you must pre-suppose the causative pneumonia.

Yes, they are there, one after another. That is why the Bible is not just a history book; rather it is a *case history* book (1962:16–17).

As pointed out above, though, case histories are useful as teaching devices only insofar as the reader is able to identify with one or more of the personal participants in the cases. This fact requires that the Bible be regarded as "classic casebook." Those who develop and teach from casebooks produce at least two types of casebooks. Ordinary casebooks typically include a variety of case studies. Some of these studies are so specific that analogous situations are hard to find. They are, therefore, of rather limited applicability beyond the particular type of situation that they describe. Others, however, are qualitatively different from the rest in that they exemplify more widely applicable principles and thus come to be regarded as "classic" cases. These get collected into "classic casebooks."

This fact points up another characteristic common to casebooks and the Bible: they are selective. The Bible does not record all the divine-human interactions that have ever taken place. Even though it may legitimately be called "the heart and soul of special revelation" (Ramm 1961:169), it is by no means a complete record. It is selective. John makes this fact explicit when he notes that if all that Jesus did were written down "the whole world could not hold the books that would be written" (Jn 21:25). Ramm helpfully points out this fact when he says:

The *graphē* is not the corpus of all revelations, nor is it the exhaustive history of the divine action in the world. According to Hebrews 1:1 the Old Testament possesses a fragmentary and partial character. The problem of Cain's wife is a perpetual reminder to the Church that the Church has only a partial and representative document in her *graphē*. Scripture is not the wholy story; and the people of God do not need the whole story. The book of Acts is so suggestive of the character of all Scripture. *It is a few acts of a few apostles at a few places during a few years.* But the few disciples were the very important ones; the few acts were the decisive ones; the few years were the gestating years; and the few places were hinges of history (1961:169–70).

The Bible may thus be usefully seen as an *inspired classic casebook* and the process of canonization as the Spirit-guided process of selecting those cases to be preserved as classic cases. Note that, as in the case of the classic casebooks, the process by means of which the Bible came into existence involves four major steps: (1) the occurrence of certain events, (2) the recording of many of the events, (3) the experimental use of a number of the recorded events among a constituency, and (4) the selection and publication of those case studies felt by the constituency to be most valuable. When the period of time during which the case studies are experimentally used is lengthy and the size of the constituency large and varied (as with the Scriptures), the likelihood is increased that the cases chosen will be truly classic. Add to this the leading of the Holy Spirit throughout the whole process and all the requirements have been met for the production of an inspired classic casebook.

Identifying with the participants in classic cases is not much of a problem, since human beings and their life experiences have so much in common. For, as Goldschmidt states, even across cultures "people are more alike than cultures" (1966:134). Thus, even in a multicultural casebook such as the Bible, it is possible for a given reader to identify with a good many of the participants whose case histories are recorded. And the fact that it is multicultural, along with the fact that the classic cases largely deal with universal human problems, makes it certain that *anyone of any culture can identify with at least certain major portions of the material recorded.*

And as you thus read it you may come to see better what God has in mind for your life. And wonder of wonders, your name (and mine) may in the ages to come be found in the Lamb's Book of Life, as one of Successful Cases (Hercus 1962:17).

By virtue of the fact that the inspired record is in classic casebook form, the revelation remains very personal even though it comes to us in written form. It also has another advantage—an advantage stemming from the fact that, in true casebook fashion, it is primarily descriptive rather than hortatory. That is, it is a record of events that have already happened, rather than a book addressed directly to the reader exhorting him or her to do this or that. The advantage in this is that such an approach invites the reader by indirection to identify with participants and to involve the self thereby in the kind of discovery that produces the most effective kind of learning. As the authors of a more recent casebook state, "Our concern is not to tell the answer, but to help the reader to discover the process by which the resolution was attained" (Rogers, Mackenzie, and Weeks 1977:8). In involving the self with the subjects of the case study, of course, the reader also becomes involved in the kind of participation with the Holy Spirit in which the participants were involved.

A HUMAN WORD AS WELL AS A DIVINE WORD (Model 9e)

Scripture is a joint product, the product of divine-human participation, involving leading and revealing. For although "all Scripture is given by inspiration of God" (2 Tim. 3:16), all Scripture is also written by human beings and from (Spirit-guided) human points of view. It is human perception that is recorded (albeit under the inspiration of God), even when God's communication is most direct (as in the giving of the law). And in terms of the perceptions recorded, a major proportion of the material is far from that degree of directness. That is, the Bible is not only God's Word, it is a human word as well.

Closed conservatives have often felt uneasy and threatened by this recognition of the human element in Scripture. They tend to see divine-human relationships in terms of an either/or, competitive model. If Scriptures are "God-breathed," they contend, they cannot be human. If human, they cannot be of God. However, the interaction-participation model employed here for all divine-human leading/revealing (including the production and canonization of Scriptures) specifically denies that the either/or, competitive perspective and the fear that admitting the humanness of what we term "God's" Word is doing an injustice to God. God gave himself to redeem human beings. If he has that high regard for humanity and has, furthermore, invited human beings to participate with him in his redemptive activity (2 Cor. 5:20; Jn. 17:18; 20:21), how can we fear to recognize human participation *with* (not *in place of*) God in the production of Scripture?

Closed conservatism (fundamentalism and closed evangelicalism),

> in its eagerness to maintain Holy Scripture's divinity, does not fully realize the significance of Holy Scripture as a prophetic-apostolic, and consequently human, testimony. . . . They allow their apologetics to be determined by the fear that emphasis on the human witness may threaten and overshadow Scripture's divinity. . . . The result is that their apologetic, which is meant to safeguard Scripture's divine aspect, threatens in many respects to block the road to a correct understanding of Scripture . . . by ignoring and neglecting its human aspect (Berkouwer 1975:22–23).

In producing the Bible, as in many (most?) of his other activities within culture, God has permitted human beings to participate with him.

The written record of God's interaction with human beings is in human language. To some, such a statement is so obvious that it need not be restated. But unfortunately, many still

> have an exaggerated view of the Biblical languages. Hebrew is regarded as a special esoteric tongue for the theologians, and Greek is a "mystery" or "the finest instrument of human thought ever devised by man." On the contrary, Greek and Hebrew are just "languages," with all the excellencies and liabilities that every language tends to have. They are neither the languages of heaven nor the speech of the Holy Spirit (Nida and Taber 1969:6).

Furthermore, the evidence suggests strongly that these were completely normal people who wrote in their own vocabulary and their own ways of expression. They all employed their own grammatical and dialectic idiosyncrasies. God worked *with* and in terms of their normal cultural, psychological, and intellectual limitations rather than against them. Thus, though the inspired meanings that flowed through their words transcended their intent, the forms in which these meanings were conveyed were characteristic of the authors themselves. Each Gospel writer records the life of Christ from his own perspective, in terms of his own interests, concerns, and perceptions. And when to Mark it did not seem important to distinguish the words of Malachi from those of Isaiah (Mk. 1:2–3) or to identify correctly the high priest from whom David received consecrated bread to eat (Mark calls him Abiathar when in fact it was Ahimelech; compare Mk. 2:26 with 1 Sam. 21:1–6), God does not step in to straighten Mark out.[3] Rather, both the language and the humanity are demonstrably intact throughout the pages of this book, even as they are when God leads human beings today. His method today is the same.

Note, however, that the recommendation here implied is that (with Berkouwer 1975:197ff) we understand the nature of the Scriptures by analogy to the way God works with imperfect, though usable, human beings. Inerrantists have a very different model in mind. They hold that since Jesus was without sin, the Bible must similarly be without error. The relationship between God's inspiring activity and the activity of the writers would therefore be analogous to the activity of the Spirit in the Virgin Birth. The result, then, would be sinless, errorless language, just as the result of Jesus' birth was a sinless human being.

The problem with attempting to understand Scripture in terms of the inerrantists' analogy is that the more one learns concerning language and culture in general and the ethnolinguistics of the Scriptures in particular, the more difficult it is to believe that God perfected the ethnolinguistic vehicles he there employs. If one admits, though, that scriptural language is not perfected (i.e., not free from all error) must one, as the inerrantists claim, go to the opposite extreme and claim that the Bible is full of errors and therefore not inspired? The answer is No, if one can simply replace the inerrantists' model (imperfection is to scriptural languages as sin is to Christ) with the model recommended here (imperfection is to scriptural language as sin is to Spirit-led human beings). In the case of the latter model, both scriptural language and Spirit-led human beings are trustworthy, adequate, usable vehicles for God's

---

3. This statement is made on the assumption that these and the majority of the other similar discrepancies in the best extant Greek and Hebrew source texts just might be authentic. It is, from my point of view, unlikely that (1) we do right to hold the biblical authors, who wrote in cultures and times other than ours and largely in nontechnical style, accountable for "inerrantist" standards of how God's Word *ought to have been written*, and (2) all of the so-called discrepancies would vanish if we ever discovered the original manuscripts. Though it is *possible* that the original manuscripts did not contain such discrepancies, I regard it as more likely that the inspired message was presented in a way that the original receptors would regard as reliable, authoritative, and adequate in terms of *their* criteria. We need, I believe, to understand in context God's specificity in accommodating to the expectations and limitations both of the original receptors and of the human communicators.

working in the world, though neither is perfect (see below in this chapter for further discussion of this point).

This conception of how the Bible is inspired sees no difficulty in maintaining that the totality of the Bible (forms as well as meanings) is inspired. The Bible, though fully human as well as fully divine, is all Word. God has inspired and still inspires (some prefer to say "illumines") the whole Bible. He is not, however, limited to the Bible in his workings with people. In fact, in the Bible we see clearly that God works in a wide variety of ways—through circumstances, through people, through special revelations of various kinds. Thus, though the Word is all Word, it is not the only communication of God. God's other communication will not, however, contradict the written Word, the canonical Scriptures. In this way, the Bible provides for us a "yardstick," a "plumbline," or a "norm" by means of which to measure other purported communications from God (model 9a).

A DYNAMIC VIEW OF SCRIPTURAL INSPIRATION (Model 9f)

This perspective focuses on the similarities between the divine-human activity which produced the Scriptures and that which results in any other leading of humans by God. Many views, for philosophical reasons, cannot allow for such a similarity. I believe that the primary reasons for static views of scriptural inspiration lie in certain values of Euro-American culture. In cultures such as ours, which accord such a high place to material that gets into print, it is only natural that our focus would become fixed more on the written (biblical) descriptions of divine-human interactions than on the dynamics of the interactions themselves. We may, however, mention three additional cultural emphases that contribute to the attractiveness of a static view: (1) the excessive idealization ("mything") of historical events that sees them as quite different from what happens today, (2) a negative attitude toward human beings that sees humans as so totally affected by sin (or some secular equivalent) that they cannot be trusted today, and (3) a depersonalized (mechanized) view of human beings. Put these four factors together and it becomes possible to explain on cultural grounds both the strong drive of some to defend a mechanistic view of inspiration that reduces the authors of Scripture to the status of impersonal instruments which could not err while this process was taking place, and the almost exclusive focus on and idealization of the written accounts of historical events.

Seeing such positions as simply the result of their advocates' uncritical following of the pressures of our culture may seem a bit harsh for the positions of people who are true sisters and brothers in Christ. The need to straighten out or at least balance such perspectives is (from my point of view), one of the more pressing needs of our time. For the mechanistic views of scriptural inspiration to which fundamentalists and closed evangelicals subscribe form an important part of that cultural brittleness spoken about earlier. Such views prevent closed conservatives from considering and adapting to new insight, while forcing them to defend ultimately untenable positions (e.g., Lindsell's attempts to deal with discrepancies in Scripture, 1976:161–84; see especially his fanciful approach to Peter's denials—six of them!—pp. 174–76). If, though, such Christians begin to take seriously informed views concerning language and culture, they may feel they have no way to go except the way of the liberals or the naturalists. For such liberals and naturalists (e.g., the so-called linguistic school of hermeneutics), having faced such facts and found no viable alternative within orthodoxy (such as the one I am attempting to develop here), have frequently opted for subjectivistic naturalism.

Bruce Vawter, a Catholic scholar who would be considered an evangelical if he were Protestant, contends that, in the light of new understandings, it is incumbent upon us to re-examine our conventional idea of biblical inspiration

in the light of the findings of various modern linguistic studies. We have often forgotten that *as a means of communication literature is only an extension of language*, and not always an adequate extension at that. Before it comes to be written the word must be first spoken, if only in the mind and not on the lips. Any theory of inspiration that manifests interest in a sacred text ought, then, to have as one of its prime areas of investigation the process by which the text first emerged as language within the minds of its authors. It may be replied that . . . traditional theology . . . always tried to investigate just that. According to its lights, no doubt it did. But its investigation was inadequate and even misdirected, for many reasons. For one thing, it was concerned with language formation only to the extent that it was a presupposition of the Biblical text, which later it *identified rather mechanically with the inspired word*. In turn, its idea of word and of language was *entirely static*; it thought in terms of the elaboration of words that were then once for all put down on paper, *not of words as means whereby the Spirit continues to speak to men* and makes "colloquium" with God a possibility. . . . Furthermore, even with all its best intentions to the contrary, *the language it contemplated was more oracular than real, more assumed to fit the hypothesis* than recognized as a human reality with a life and a history of its own (1972:113–14). [Emphasis added.]

One major point that I would like to demonstrate is that *it is possible as an evangelical Christian to look squarely at the facts of language and culture and to come up with an understanding of how God reveals himself that is neither mechanistic nor naturalistic*, neither oblivious of cultural and linguistic realities nor of the reality of continuous divine-human interaction. I believe strongly that the Scriptures are inspired and that this inspiration may properly be labeled "verbal" (that is, inspiration attaches to the wording employed) and "plenary" (that is, the *whole* Bible is inspired). These terms label what is inspired (i.e., all the words). But the words are inspired almost incidentally. For the primary focus of inspiration (as of all ethnolinguistic communication) is on the meanings. *Only in a culture like ours that, under the influence of simplistic views of language, has chosen to focus almost exclusively on words, would one get theories of inspiration that concentrate almost exclusively on words.* At Christmas should we be so interested in the wrappings that we virtually ignore the gifts inside? As Barr (1961) and

Nida (1971) correctly point out, it is an uninformed approach to biblical interpretation that devotes itself almost totally to word-level analyses. I contend that a word-focused doctrine of inspiration is also inadequate.

My primary concern here, however, is to probe the *dynamics* of inspiration—the *process* by means of which God and Spirit-led humans produce inspired utterances. As indicated above, I believe that this is a continuing process, a part of the leading of God. I believe, further, that one of the major purposes of the Bible is to provide us with insight into the process, the dynamics, of God's continuing leading. The Bible, from this perspective, is not simply notable for its propositional content (a static concept), though this is a very important part of the revelation. It also shows us what to do with that and the rest of its content. It provides a magnificent display of the dynamics of divine-human interaction. And this is a continuing interaction in which we are invited to participate in our time and culture in a way dynamically equivalent to that displayed therein—and on the basis of the same principles employed as God participated with the authors of Scripture. This interaction has the potential, at least, of the kind of output that God's Spirit will lead others to perceive as God's revelation to them.

Because of the multicultural nature of the Scriptures (see chapter 11) and its demonstrable applicability to enough basic human needs adequately to serve what we understand to be the purposes of God, I have no expectation that further Scripture will be written. This is because we don't *need* any more, not because there are no more inspired things happening. The Scriptures are here seen as adequate in fulfilling God's purpose to provide necessary guidelines. They are not regarded as different in *form* from anything that now occurs. As I see it, those who have attempted to support their doctrine of biblical inspiration by contending that there are demonstrable differences in form (e.g., linguistic, literary, or in their means of compilation and transmission) between the Bible and any other book, and/or the events recorded in the Bible and any other events have not made their case (see Rogers 1974:98–105 for a discussion of Warfield and others who fell into this trap). They have also, unwittingly, driven to an opposite extreme many who see the fallacy of such views but who are unable to see any alternative between outright acceptance and outright rejection.

Thus one is tempted to react against rigid positions such as those of John Warwick Montgomery (1974), Harold Lindsell (1976) and, formerly, Clark Pinnock (1967) by fleeing into the arms of what Pinnock called the "naturalistic" theologians. For the positions of these men allow for only two alternatives—theirs and that of subjective rationalism. They fail to take seriously the livingness of God and the contemporariness and personalness of God's revelational activity. They thus can do nothing else than contend that anyone who disagrees with their extreme position is in fact denying that God has revealed himself at all. They correctly condemn the biblical critics for treating the Bible "like no other book, by bathing it in the acid solution of their scepticism and historical pessimism" (Pinnock 1967:23). Yet they attempt to defend their position by loudly asserting their a priori assumption that the *form* of the Bible is "like no other book" or any other communication that ever came in terms of human language and culture. They prove to me that "fanatical 'objectivizing' of Scripture can be as detrimental to its proper understanding as a frightful 'subjectivizing' " (Ramm 1961:99).

In defending the Bible's inspiration, such closed conservatives feel compelled to sink or swim on the basis of an equation between inspiration and inerrancy. This is a "chancy" kind of decision at best, given the fact that such an equation is based on philosophical presuppositions, *not* on scriptural statements, for the Bible, though claiming inspiration (2 Tim. 3:16), never claims inerrancy. Furthermore, the very number and diversity of the theories advanced to explain what the Bible claims but never explains should be warning enough against locking oneself so tightly into such an equation. If God did not see fit to inspire an explanation, should we not allow for a range of understanding? Perhaps a principle employed by certain Christian groups is useful here: "Speak out when the Bible speaks out, remain silent where the Bible is silent." Though I have not in this book followed that advice, I have attempted to present my assumptions (models) in such a way that readers can disagree with or reject them if they so choose.

Nevertheless, it is possible, to my way of thinking, to agree to the use of a term like "inerrant" if it is defined as a technical term. Such is done with the word "myth." The latter term has a popular meaning that is widely different from its technical meaning. Clark Pinnock, who once took the belligerent posture of Lindsell and Montgomery, has recently chosen not to fight over the term (which he still prefers in 1976b but not in 1976a) and to define it as a technical term in a way that conforms to, rather than being imposed on, the scriptural data. Pinnock states that

according to this understanding of inerrancy, the Bible is *not* free of all "errors" in its whole extent, but free of errors where its intended teachings are concerned. . . . Inerrancy when understood in this way . . . does not suspend the truth of the gospel upon a single detail . . . (1976b:12).

Pinnock thus qualifies the term "inerrancy" to refer *technically* to the absence of biblical error in all that the Bible affirms. With respect to the necessary kinds of qualifications, he says:

The qualification can be illustrated in cases such as these: *where the biblical writer pictures the natural world in the modes of expression current in his day*, scientifically precise references neither being intended nor made; *where the degree of historical precision correlates with the author's intention*—in confusing the facts of the Abraham story in Acts 7 we fault neither Stephen for citing the facts as he recalled them nor Luke for recording what he believed Stephen said; where Job cites the errant opinions of liars; where the chronicler recounts figures quite different from those in parallel passages, his intention being only to set forth the record as he found it in the public archives; where the *ipsissima verba* of Jesus are handled with a certain freedom depending on the purpose of the redactor evangelist, or where Paul cites the Old Testament freely in line with some concept he wishes to teach us. In all these cases, and in many others, *inerrancy is being applied in a qualified sense, relative to the intended assertions of the text.* Even Warfield, always taken to be the champion of the strictest possible view, wrote: "No objection (to inerrancy) is valid which overlooks the prime question: what was the professed or implied purpose of the writer in making this statement?" (Pinnock 1976b:12 [emphasis added]; see also Warfield 1881:245, and Packer 1958:98).

When the term "inerrancy" is used as a technical term and qualified in this way so that it fits the scriptural data to which it is applied at the contextual-meaning level, I have no problem with it. Since, however, many people who use the term are in fact using it with its popular connotations (e.g., Lindsell 1976), my preference is to avoid it. I prefer simply to use the scriptural term "inspiration."

As noted above, many of those who most strongly support the use of the term "inerrancy" (in the popular sense) do so on the basis of an analogy between Jesus and the Scriptures (i.e., as Jesus was God in perfect human form, so Scripture is God's Word in perfected human language; see Berkouwer 1975:197ff for a critical discussion of this view). The analogy is likely to be misleading unless we carefully distinguish where it applies from where it does not apply on the basis of a consideration of the scriptural documents themselves—not on the basis of prior philosophical assumptions. Closed conservatives seem to assume that since God is all-powerful and *could* have produced a perfect, inerrant Bible, he therefore *must* have. Berkouwer cites Warfield in this regard as follows:

Warfield writes that "in both cases divine and human factors are involved" and "even so distant an analogy" shows that it can be said both regarding Christ and Scripture that "by the conjoint action of human and divine factors, the human factors . . . cannot have fallen into that error, which we say it is human to fall into" (Berkouwer 1975, citing Warfield 1948:162).

It has become increasingly obvious from a study of the actual form in which the Scriptures have come to us that God has not perfected the *form* of the linguistic vehicles in which his Word is presented to us. The languages appear to be human languages used in ways that are comprehensible to us (within our frame of reference) from our study of how human languages are used by human beings. The *function* that scriptural linguistic forms serve and the *meanings* conveyed through them when they are used properly are, apparently, the only things that distinguish the language of Scripture from other uses of human languages. And it is in this sense that the analogy between the Scriptures and Jesus is helpful. For *he came in human form* not merely for the sake of sanctifying human form but *for the sake of the function that he could carry out and the meanings he could convey by this means.* And in this function the ministry of Jesus parallels that of other (imperfect) human beings through whom God has worked.

This fact suggests a better analogy than that between the sinless form of Jesus and the suggested sinless (errorless) form of Scripture. This would be an analogy between the God-ordained function of the ministry of Jesus and that of countless fallible Spirit-led human beings, on the one hand, and of the function of Scripture on the other. The sinless Christ can be worshiped as God. Fallible human vehicles (whether human beings or human words), though they may be greatly honored for their faithfulness in ministry (their function), should never be worshiped. The Scriptures, like human beings who serve God, are to be valued for the function they perform and for the meanings they convey rather than for the perfection of their form. For the form itself minus the participation with it of the Spirit of God is nothing.

Berkouwer speaks helpfully in this regard of the "servant-form" of Holy Scripture (1975:195–212). This concept has also been developed by Calvin who (in Ramm's words)

speaks of this great condescension of God in which he bends down and, lowering himself, lisps that we might hear and understand him. Just as the Son of God emptied himself and lowered himself to our estate, so revelation comes to us in a humbled, lowered form that we might cradle it in our minds (Ramm 1961:33; see Calvin 1953,I:xiii,1).

This functional understanding of the nature of Scripture keeps us from being "embarrassed by the marks of humanity and humiliation which it bears" (Ramm 1961:34, after Thornton 1950). For Scripture's purpose, like that of Christ, is to function as a servant. Abraham Kuyper, on whom both Berkouwer and Ramm lean at this point, articulates well this functional perspective:

As in the Mediator the Divine nature weds itself to the humans, and appears before us in *its* form and figure, so also the Divine factor of the Holy Scripture clothes itself in the garment of our form of thought and holds itself to our human reality . . . when, on Sinai, God with his own finger engraves in human words His law upon the tables of stone, and the revelation remains not absolutely transcendent, but makes use . . . of the human as instrument. All the shadows and types bear the same mixed character. All of sacred history rests upon the same entwining of both factors. And even in miracles, the Divine factor remains never purely transcendent, but in order to reveal Himself, ever enters into human reality. . . . As the Logos has not appeared *in the form of glory*, but in the form of a servant, joining Himself to the reality of our nature, as this had come to be through the results of sin, so also, for the revelation of His Logos, God the Lord accepts *our* consciousness, our human life *as it is.* . . . The "spoken words," however much aglow with the Holy Ghost, remain bound to the limitation of our language, disturbed as it is by anomalies. As a product of writing, the Holy Scripture also bears on its forehead the mark of the form of a servant (Kuyper 1954:478–79).

I fear that closed conservatives will not be likely to accept this functional view, because of their "low" view of humanity. If one believes that, by definition, what is human, and therefore tainted by sin, cannot be of God, one will have difficulty with each aspect of the "high" view of humanity that I am presenting. Closed conservatives typically view humans as vying with God in competition for centrality in all such cases of divine-human interaction. They thus become reactionary "because of their fear that the divine nature of revelation will suffer in an overemphasis on its human nature" (Berkouwer 1975:23). The models here developed—where we see human beings as elevated by God to function in a participatory status in a wide variety of his activities (including revelation and inspiration) and where distinctions are made between forms, functions, and meanings—should help greatly to clarify this issue and, one hopes, to alleviate fear. For God's pattern is not a competitive one where he jealously seeks to exclude human beings from appearing in center stage. It is, rather, one in which he joins humanity in center stage, respecting, honoring, adjusting, and bending to our creaturely existence, mediating himself to human beings via human-beingness (Ramm 1961: 34).

In being critical of those who use inerrancy with its popular connotations, I do not wish to question either their sincerity or their right to hold to their particular theory of inspiration. In fact, I agree with most of their major conclusions concerning the inspiration and normativeness of Scripture. I also agree that it is important to hold and defend a "high" view of scriptural inspiration and authority. But I do not believe that such closed conservative positions as those of Lindsell, Montgomery, and Francis Schaeffer are "high" enough. For they are *based on static philosophical presuppositions* that don't seem to fit the dynamic livingness either of the Scriptures or of vital Christian experience. The kind of behavioral insights that have been developed over the past couple of generations make their supporting arguments very difficult to accept. For, in their writings,

the concept of inerrancy, in practice at least, has almost demanded as its correlative a notion of Biblical truth fixed once for all in a single point of time, and therefore, a notion of word that is essentially lifeless, historical in the sense of archival only. Yet no theory of Biblical truth . . . should have been permitted to envisage an inerrant letter that would, logically, rule out the possibility of a Sermon on the Mount updating the Law and the Prophets or constitute St. Paul's law of faith an heretical attack on the Law given through Moses. For that matter, it can hardly envisage any kind of verbal inerrancy or sufficiency that would declare Rom. 13:1–7 the ultimate Biblical word on civil obedience or make of Mk. 12:17 the Bible's definitive and adequate teaching on Church and State. *Biblical truth . . . is evidently far less concerned with words than with the word: its witness is not to formulations that can be bent to new situations only by an appeal to senses that were unknown to and unintended by an inspired author, but to the historical continuity of a Biblical message that was, at some stage, undeniably his* (Vawter 1972:155). [Emphasis added.]

That is, in coming to a theory of inspiration (and we are simply discussing theories—I and even those I am quoting negatively all agree on the *fact* of scriptural inspiration), we must take adequate account of the continuing processes to which the Scriptures witness. *Static views have tended to focus only on the result, or product, of the revelatory process,* and to suggest that God employed a radically different method of revealing the contents of Scripture from what he employed before or has employed since. And yet the very events recorded in the Scriptures witness clearly to the fact that, over thousands of years, God has interacted in a revelatory way with any human being who would respond to him. It does not appear to me reasonable to believe that as soon as the last New Testament document was committed to writing, he totally changed in his method of operation to such an extent that he now limits himself to the written record.

But if such defenses of a static theory of scriptural inspiration are difficult to agree with, I find the kind of approach that sees inspiration attached only to portions of the Scripture even more deficient.[4] To my way of thinking the whole Scripture is inspired—that is, Scripture is the product of the Spirit-led recording and canonization of divine-human interactions. Yet—and here is a point where much confusion has developed—not all Scripture, by virtue of the fact that it is inspired, should be understood to consist of novel information. Indeed,

> not all the statements of the sixty-six books, which are verbally inspired, concern . . . revelational matters. In Scripture there are statements or aspects of statements about matters which fall within the range of what men can know by themselves. That Emmaus was about seven miles from Jerusalem (Lk. 24:13), that the emperor Claudius commanded all the Jews to leave Rome (Acts 18:2) . . . these are examples of Biblical propositions that we can know the truth of without having to have them revealed to us (Fuller 1969:ix–20).

But inspiration and revelation are not synonymous terms. *Inspiration* relates to a quality of God's leading of human beings. It may involve a person in saying and/or doing certain quite ordinary things which God employs as the vehicle of his communication to others. Inspiration thus is the process by means of which God reveals himself indirectly. He does this primarily through human beings to other human beings and secondarily through written records proceeding from such interactions. *Revelation* always happens when God leads people. In events labeled "inspired," God reveals himself both to and through the human agent with whom he participates. Inspiration is the quality of leading that happens to that person as God participates with that person to communicate (reveal) himself through him or her to others.

This view assumes, with respect to biblical inspiration as with respect to all other leading of people by God, that: (1) we are dealing with a God who lovingly *interacts* with human beings; (2) God chooses to employ human

---

4. See Vawter 1972:134–35 for a discussion of several such views.

culture and language as the milieu of his interaction with humans; (3) it is in the process of this interaction between God and human beings within the human cultural context that the events now recorded in Scripture took place; (4) God has, in working with humans, led certain of them to record certain of these God-human interactions as well as certain other materials specifically relevant to these interactions (including inspired interpretations of many aspects of the interactions);[5] (5) a selection of these recorded materials has been preserved by the people of God and, following God's leading, elevated to the status of Scripture; (6) these writings are therefore inspired in at least four senses, only the third of which (c) is unique to the Scriptures: (a) the original interactions between God and humans participated in the same kind of inspiration that God's leading and a person's positive response to it always do (2 Pet. 1:21—God led people to speak), (b) God led certain persons to record these divine-human interactions (2 Tim. 3:16—God led people to write), (c) God has led the church (and Israel before it with regard to the Old Testament) to preserve and employ these particular materials in a unique way in their attempts to discern and follow God's leading, and (d) the Holy Spirit is active in interacting with the readers and hearers of these materials.

TRUTH WITH IMPACT (Model 9g)

The Bible, the inspired casebook, is seen to be as much the record of a dynamic and continuing process of divine-human interaction as it is the repository for divinely revealed truth. It is indeed the latter, as static models of the nature of the Scriptures contend. But it is considerably more.

The Bible presents in casebook fashion a long series of communicational events by means of which God has made himself successively better known to his people (Israel in the Old Testament, the church in the New Testament). But the receptors of the messages and the processes of communication employed are as in focus as the messages themselves. And the diversity of the means of communication (e.g., direct speech, visions, seemingly spontaneous utterances, written documents, church councils) and of the literary devices employed to record these communications is as evident as the essential unity of the total message.

Truth is there. And it often includes information that could not have been known other than as the result of God's revealing it to people. History is there—accurate, trustworthy history that records many of the most important events by means of which God worked out the details of our salvation. Information concerning the most astounding event of all time is recorded

---

5. The fact that a majority of the scriptural writings preserve for us a record of "holy history" is of very high significance, since it thereby reveals to us a large number of the details by means of which God worked out our salvation. But this content, as important as it is, does not in itself assure inspiration. The leading of God that results in inspiration, and that process rather than the content conveyed by means of it, is what is here in focus.

there—the incarnational entrance of God into a single human culture at a specific point in time to demonstrate conclusively, in a way that cannot be misunderstood, the extent of his commitment to and involvement with human beings.

But even the excitement that the revelation of this new information engenders in us must not obscure the facts concerning the process by means of which it is conveyed. It is information presented in particular hearer-oriented ways—in ways designed to have maximum relevance to and high impact on the hearers, for effective communication does not consist merely of information. It is not simply the truth value of material presented that gets it across. Many have been the times (as, alas, Christian preachers have discovered too often) when utterly true and necessary information has been presented but has not gotten across.

It is an unfortunate fact of our cultural conditioning that we have ordinarily learned to think of processes such as teaching, preaching, writing, and reading primarily in terms of the kind and/or amount of knowledge thereby transferred from one person to others. For example, we often evaluate classroom teaching in this light rather than in terms of the much more significant concern as to how great the motivational impact of that knowledge might be. Thus our schools regularly churn out millions of young people with great amounts of information in their heads, which they are largely unable and unmotivated to use because it has not come to them with relevance or impact. Far better would be less fact or truth communicated over a longer period of time in such a way as to be relevantly applied to questions that the students are asking. It would thus motivate rather than stifle them.

The Bible goes considerably beyond revealing merely intellectual truth or information. It demonstrates how truth is effectively gotten across. It proclaims the fact that the expressing nature of God (often termed "word" in our English translations) "is alive and active" (Heb. 4:12) and must be looked to and depended upon by the Christian in every event of life. Our God is there portrayed as mainly a God of dialogue who interacts with us, not simply a God of monologue who makes pronouncements above us. And he did not change when the last biblical book was completed.

God's communication with humanity is depicted in the Bible as coming to humans in familiar, expected ways (though the message itself was often unexpected). To people who believed that he would speak through dreams and visions, he spoke through dreams and visions. To those who looked to prophets for word from him, he spoke through prophets. To those who looked to written documents, he employed written documents (e.g., Neh. 8:1ff). And to many (e.g., Israel, the early church) who expected God to reveal himself in all these ways, he employed all these ways. My point is that God has not now limited himself to working only through the written word—though to those who (for cultural reasons) limit themselves to seeing God only via the written word he largely accommodates himself to their expectations.

Furthermore, *God's method of self-disclosure is demonstrated to be participatory*. He worked *with*, not simply above, those to whom he revealed himself. He participated with people and with groupings of his people (e.g., Israel, churches) to bring about discovery of himself, his leading, his revelation. He employed any means available to, and considered appropriate by, those with whom he was working. And he has not now changed simply because the Bible is complete.

Lastly, *we observe God's revelatory activity as recorded in the Scriptures to be situation-specific*. The number of highly generalized, cosmic pronouncements (e.g., the Ten Commandments, the Sermon on the Mount) is limited. And even these were addressed to specific persons at specific times and places and for specific immediate purposes. The fact that such pronouncements are more widely applicable is a function of our human commonality activated by our ability to identify with the needs of the participants to which these pronouncements were originally directed. God is not simply "playing to the grandstand" and using the original people as "props" for the purpose of getting across to someone else somewhere else. Thus, most of the biblical records deal with events that are even more demonstrably specific than these cosmic pronouncements. The prophet Nathan speaks directly to David concerning a specific sin, Paul writes to the Corinthians concerning a series of specific concerns, Jesus chooses and devotes himself to a specific twelve students, etc. My contention is that God's method is still the same today, dynamically (functionally) equivalent to his workings in the past. He continues to reveal himself in such specific ways.

From this point of view, God is just as alive and active in his process of self-revelation now as he ever was. And when he communicates truth about himself he still communicates it with impact. He communicates in familiar, expected ways by means of participation with human beings in specific situations to which the revelation is immediately applicable. Since God is self-consistent, such contemporary revelation of himself will never contradict scripturally recorded revelation.

Having discussed these several horizontal dimensions of God's revelatory process, we turn to an elaboration of certain of them.

11. The Components of Revelation

God has not left humanity helpless and hopeless. He has not left himself without witness, even in the muteness of his subhuman creation (Rom. 1:20; Ps. 19:1–6). He has witnessed powerfully in and through human beings and supremely in and through *the* Human Being, Jesus Christ. He has employed the whole spectrum of cultural vehicles of communication, showing a special preference for personal, interactional means. And he has led human beings to commit certain accounts of his workings to writing. God's Spirit, then, works with and through all these vehicles to reveal God and his messages to human beings.

Revelation, from this perspective (models 8f above and 8j below), is like certain strong glues that require the mixture of two substances at the time when they are used. I have used an "epoxy" glue and a "plastic steel," each sold in two containers. The one container holds the "base" and the other a kind of "activator." Neither of these substances will work by itself. When they are mixed, though, they powerfully bond the substances to which they are applied. In the process of revelation, the informational component is the "base," while the Holy Spirit, usually in partnership with a human being, is the "activator." *Without both components, revelation is only potential, never actualized.*

In what follows we look at certain additional aspects of model 8: (1) the informational base of revelation, (2) the activators, and (3) the receptors' will and the problem of human sinfulness as it affects the revelational process. We then relate the constancy of the message (model 10b) to the multicultural nature of the Scriptures (model 9h) and the cumulativeness of the revelational information therein contained (model 8k).

THE INFORMATIONAL BASE OF REVELATION

Revelation is ordinarily conceived of as of two types: general revelation and special revelation. Communicationally it seems preferable to regard these as general and special revelational messages or, getting down to their most basic components, as *general and special revelational information* (model 8i). Information in and of itself is powerless. Certain information, however, can be predicted to have high impact on virtually any receptor whether or not it is well communicated. The message "Your house is on fire," for example, will ordinarily have high stimulus value for any receptor if it is true. But the impact

216

of the message comes from the receptor's perception that that information is relevant to (meets a need felt by) him or her at that particular moment. You, the reader, for example, probably did not respond very excitedly to that statement as you read it. For you did not perceive it to be either true *for you* or relevant to your present situation.

Such is the nature of both general and special information about God and his activities. They are both inert unless activated by the receptor. There is no magic in the information itself. Though some messages have more potential for high impact on any receptor (e.g., "fire" vs. 2 + 2 =4), it is still the function of the receptor to transform a message from inert information into impactful, action-producing meanings. This fact has important implications for the way we look at the various sources of information concerning God.

General revelational information concerning God and his activities is defined by Ramm as "God's witness to himself for all men" (1961:17). It is "a revelation universally given in nature, in history, and in the reason and conscience of every man" (Henry 1976,II:9).

It is general in two senses: (i) It is a general revelation for all men, i.e., it is not restricted to a specific man or people. (ii) It is a general kind of revelation. In the correct translation of Psalm 19:4 general revelation is not in the form of speech or words; *no voice is heard*. The theologians have appealed to the glory of God in the heavens by day and by night (Ps. 19:1), the witness of the created thing (. . . Rom. 1:20), the pre-incarnate logos (. . . John 1:9), the inner moral dialogue (Rom. 2:14–15), and the goodness of God in his providence (Acts 14:17) as examples of general revelation (Ramm 1961:17).

Much general information of this nature appears to be passed on via natural cultural processes—though perhaps not every culture possesses the same selection of data. Some things appear to be a part of all cultures, while others may be present in some but missing in others. I have asserted (chapter 5) that among the basic human needs cultures seek to meet are spiritual needs, including the need for a relationship with the supracultural God. It is well known that some sort of religious quest, some sort of search for entrance into a "symbolic eternity" (Goldschmidt 1966:136), is a part of every culture. If we rightly understand passages such as Romans 1 and 2 and Acts 10:34–35, there is communication from God embedded in every culture. The psalmist points to the heavens and claims that there exists a declaration of God's glory for all to see (Ps. 19:1). Going beyond the psalmist, Paul states:

Ever since God created the world, his invisible qualities, both his eternal power and his divine nature, have been clearly seen; they are perceived in the things that God has made (Rom. 1:20 TEV).

There is, for example, a great similarity between the proverbs of many peoples (e.g., Higi and Hausa of Nigeria) and those endorsed as a part of the revelational information in the Scriptures. Applying our yardstick model we find that these fall well within the biblical tether (model 9c). Many (most?) Euro-American missionaries have, however, been so New Testament oriented, so competitive in advocating our understandings in place of theirs, and so much attached to special revelational information that they have often neglected the possibility of using indigenous proverbs as stepping stones to bringing such peoples to faith.

This communication or revelation from God in nature and basic cultural heritage may be seen as vouchsafed to humanity at creation and passed on through natural cultural processes. The Old Testament Hebrew view is that the existence of God and knowledge of his will are self-evident and universal (Gartner 1955:103). A lack of response to God was seen, not as a lack of knowledge but as resistance to or turning from him (ibid.:235). In the New Testament, Acts 14:17 seems to imply that God has never allowed a culture to go without some witness to him. It is apparently possible for men to "stifle" the purpose of this information (see Rom. 1:25), but not possible for them to obliterate it completely (Rom. 2:11–16). And human beings are to be held accountable for it. According to Paul, it is possible, by means of this information, to glimpse at least "God's invisible attributes, that is to say his everlasting power and deity . . . in the things he has made" (Rom. 1:20 NEB) and, apparently, on this basis to carry out the precepts of the law (Rom. 2:14). The religious quests of human societies may be seen, then, as attempts to respond to that culturally embedded communication called "general revelation."

It appears from these passages that such general information supplies enough knowledge to provide by itself the basis for revelational activation. Some with a knowledge-information concept of revelation have argued for the sufficiency of natural revelation as a basis for salvation. For example, "Rome believes in natural theology as a system, 'a rational system which is sufficient unto itself' " (Berkouwer 1955:39). Maurier, a Roman Catholic, says that

men are able to reach a certain knowledge of God (Rom. 1:19–20). They carry within themselves the lights of the natural law (Rom. 2:14–15). They are judged according to their consciences and what they have been able to know. Finally, God does not withhold his grace from one who does what is in his power; no man "in flesh and bone" is irreversibly on the way to damnation (1968:5).

Evangelical Protestants, though recognizing the presence and importance of such "natural knowledge of the Deity" (Henry 1976,I:323ff), have tended to conclude that such knowledge (called "revelation") is in itself insufficient to bring a person to salvation. While affirming "that men stand everywhere and always in direct knowledge relation to the living God" (ibid.:324), evangelicals generally recognize that there is something missing to activate that knowledge in such a way that a saving faith relationship with God is the result. Though human sinfulness is seen as the real culprit, evangelicals often give the impression that humans *also need more knowledge* than is provided by "general revelation." Even Berkouwer, who sees clearly that the real need is for divine stimulus to overcome the sin problem, allows one to infer that humans also need additional knowledge (1955:285). Henry, likewise, though again seeing the sin problem as the primary reason for "man's reductive dilutions and misconstructions of" general revelation, sees enscripturated revelation as taking "priority over general revelation" because it "republishes the content of general revelation objectively" (1976,I:223).

There is so much truth in these statements that I do not want to dissociate myself from them entirely. Yet I feel that we should not be allowed to turn to a consideration of "special revelation" as if we are turning from a flawed type of information to an unflawed type of information that somehow has greater (even magical) power *in itself*. I agree that there is potentially a qualitative difference between this special information and the general information but suggest that it *lies in the difference in the stimulus value of information that is specially related to the felt needs of specific human beings*. That is, the use by personal communicators of special revelational information with the kind of stimulus value of the message (if true), "Your house is on fire" makes a *qualitative* difference in the communication. "General revelation" of the "2 + 2 = 4" type does not ordinarily have that quality of impact.

But note that for one who is desperately in need of the solution to the "2 + 2 = ?" question, the answer "4" can be very relevant and impactful. Likewise, as noted above, even the "Your house is on fire" message is not very impressive to one who does not perceive that it relates to his real needs. Thus, *the important differences* between general and special revelational information lie *not so much in the information itself as in the way that information is used*. There is *no magic in the information*. There is, however, a great difference in potential impact (or potential impactful usage) between messages that are predictable and general (and, therefore, less easily "repersonalized" in a present situation) and those that are unpredictable and specific to the felt needs of the receptors in the present situation (see above, chapter 8).[1] *General revelational information is*, from this point of view, *not deficient* even as a basis for salvation (see below). But it is so general and so predictable that it is *unlikely to attract the notice of most people* unless more stimulus is added to it.

The very predictability of the processes of the universe is too great (in terms of information theory) ever to reveal with certainty the uniqueness of the God and Father of our Lord Jesus Christ. . . . The creation confirms God, but does not define Him (Nida 1960:221–22).

Yet throughout history (part of which is recorded in the Old Testament) there have been (many?) people who have responded to God in faith without the benefit of the special information presented in the Scriptures. Even a large

1. We could point to another distinction in potential that relates to the receptors' ability to imagine the impact of that message on them if they were in a situation where that message would be appropriate. Such imaginative repersonalization of the message could lead one to postulate an inherently greater impact resident in the "fire" message than in the "2 + 2" message.

number of those whose stories are recorded in Scripture fit into this category. *As important as the Scriptures are to us, it seems evident that God has worked throughout most of history and over most of the world's geography without the receptors' being aware of the special revelational information contained in the Book.* What should we conclude about this fact? Has God refrained from working in all of these times and places? Or has he provided extra-scriptural special information in other places and times? Or what?

We will leave these questions up in the air for now and turn to the source of information called "special revelation."

Special revelational information concerning God and his activities consists of information that God has revealed by means of special intervention in human contexts. Ramm speaks of this information (though he doesn't use this term) as "the products of special revelation" or "the deposit of special revelation" (1961:125). These products, he says, exist in the form of language (both spoken and written), in knowledge of God, in sacred Scripture and in translations of Scripture. "Special revelation is longer and wider than Scripture, but Scripture is the heart and soul of special revelation" (ibid.:169). Ramm, in his excellent treatment, details the "modalities," or processes and vehicles, by means of which special revelation comes to us. Then he contrasts those processes with the informational product as follows:

Something is said in revelation, and what is said is the root and ground of our knowledge of God. Or to put it otherwise, in revelation God is known, God is experienced, but we are also given a true word of God which can be reproduced—reproduced as witness, reproduced as preaching, reproduced as tradition, reproduced as Scripture. That which the modalities of revelation convey is a product, a deposit, which itself can be called revelation (1961:150).

Though it appears that Ramm would agree with me that revelation is more than simply information, he properly cautions against denying the informational, conceptual component.[2]

Revelation cannot be restricted to "encounter" or to "event" or to "illumination." If a theologian is to be loyal to the full witness of Scripture, he must grant that the conceptual side of the word of God is also revelation (1961:151).

This product or deposit, centered in the Scriptures, is supracultural Truth in cultural trappings. Enscripturated, it consists of information concerning revelational events and their interpretations. Both the events and their interpretations consisted of information plus stimulus when they happened. They therefore meet my criteria for labeling them revelational (model 8f). But recording them informationalizes them again. By this definition, revelation involving these reports does not again take place until they are "fertilized" or

2. See Coleman 1972:86–104 and Pike 1962:46–53 for good discussions of the liberal-evangelical debate over these issues.

activated by the stimulus of what may be termed "repersonalization" (see below). This repersonalization may happen via the communicational activity of another person or via the readers' ability so to identify with the participants in the events about which they are reading that they personalize God's message through the participants for themselves (under the continuing influence of the Holy Spirit).

Ramm, and evangelical orthodoxy, want to call this informational product of God's past revelational activity "revelation." And so it is *in a potential sense.* But the tendency to label forms, even forms that are intended to be used in Christian ways, is so often disastrous and even idolatrous that I question the wisdom of employing the term "revelation" for anything less than the total process by means of which God and human beings participate in the actualizing of the potential inherent in either general or special revelational information.

The pitfalls into which the Pharisees, Judaizers, and many closed conservative Protestants and Roman Catholics have fallen and continue to fall are always with us in this regard. *When the product is misinterpreted and mislabeled as if it were the process, idolatry is not far behind.* Jesus said to the Pharisees:

You study the Scriptures, because you think that in them you will find eternal life. And these very Scriptures speak about me! Yet you are not willing to come to me in order to have life (Jn. 5:39–40 TEV).

The Pharisees' very reverence for the product of God's past revelational activity was allowed by them to get in their way so that they missed participating in the process of God's continuing revelational activity. They, like many of us today, were so impressed with the form(s) of past revelation that they turned to preserving and elaborating on that form, rather than using it for its intended purpose—once again to recreate, in combination with Spirit-guided personal stimulus, impactful, revelational meanings in the minds and hearts of contemporary receptors of God's messages.

In the Pharisees' use of the Scriptures the meanings that God intended to be revelational were transformed into idolatry for them and oppression for the recipients of their messages. Such is always the result when reverence for "information about" is substituted for vital "participation in." *For information and knowledge in themselves are lifeless means to be used by personal beings, not ends to be bowed down to.* They, like the Sabbath, were made to be used for the good of human beings, not for their enslavement (Mk. 2:27). They, like the misuse of the written law, can result in death if not activated by the stimulus of Spirit-guided repersonalization (1 Cor. 3:6).

But this fact does not give warrant to go to the opposite extreme. As Ramm points out, "Revelation cannot be restricted to 'encounter' or to 'event' or to 'illumination,' " as some have tried to make it (1961:151; see Coleman 1972:94–96). The need for something/someone to provide stimulus to go along with the information (whether general or special) is clear. But there *must be some information,* for *stimulation alone cannot be revelational.* The quantity of information about God and his workings may be very small or, as in general revelational information, very general and predictable. But there must be some information present. Perhaps the least information that God can use is that stated in Hebrews 11:6:

. . . anyone who comes to God must believe that he exists and that he rewards those who search for him (NEB).

The Bible is unique as a source of special information. Its uniqueness lies in the fact of its inspiration (see chapter 10) and in the specialness of the information that it provides. For the theme of the Bible is redemption. The Bible, though informational, introduces "an altogether new world of truth, that relating to the redemption of man" (Vos 1948:20). This is why Christians have felt led to preserve it. Perhaps Vos and especially Ramm (below) mean to include what I am calling stimulus in their concept of redemption. Ramm says:

The proper relationship between redemption and revelation must, however, be carefully maintained. Unless this is done, revelation appears as sheer didactic impartation of knowledge, and not as the word of life. Redemption is prior to special revelation (1961:70).

The uniqueness of the Bible as the source of special information is that it presents us with information focused on the redemptive process—a process "that centers in the redemptive acts of Hebrew history from the exodus to the resurrection of Jesus of Nazareth and in the communication of the meaning of these saving acts in both the prophetic and the apostolic word" (Henry 1976, II:10). *Though the Bible is a product, it recounts for us the same process that is the intended result of the recombination of revelational information plus stimulus.* The focus on the process of redemption and the re-creation of that process today must, therefore, take precedence even over a focus on the inspired document that is intended to be so central in the recreation of that process.

The danger in any discussion of inspiration is that an *excessive preoccupation with the subject matter is apt to blind the theologian to this logical and axiological priority of redemption over revelation.* This is the basic reason why strong books on inspiration seldom change anybody's convictions. *Redemption carries inspiration, and not the opposite.* Revelatory words apart from the great acts of redemption are abstractions and carry little spiritual power (Ramm 1961:80–81). [Emphasis added.]

ACTIVATING REVELATIONAL INFORMATION

A dynamic view of revelation requires something besides the "intellectual product" that provides the "base" component for additional revelational events. The Bible or any other source of special information about God (e.g.,

Ramm lists dreams, visions, the lot, angels, etc., 1961:44–48), if it is to serve its purpose, needs to be used by personal beings to stimulate revelational meanings (model 8j). Mickelsen (after Childs) refers to this stimulus as "actualization" (1963:175). This is "the process by which a past event is contemporized for a generation removed in time and space from the original event" (Childs 1962:83). We will discuss later (chapter 13) the "dynamic-equivalence" aim of such actualization. There are, however, several characteristics of such stimulus to dynamically equivalent Christian meaning and behavior that should be treated here.

First, the actualization of revelational information requires *repersonalization*. As emphasized repeatedly above, effective, impactful communication is always from persons to persons (model 7a and elsewhere). *Knowledge and information in themselves are not communicative.* Indeed, they may be deadening. People characteristically know more than they make use of in their behavior. How will they live up to even what they now know if they are not stimulated by someone to do so? This is, I believe, the question beneath the surface of Romans 10:14. For, "in both content and form, God's revelation is uniquely personal" (Henry 1976,II:10).

There are, however, *two kinds of personal stimulus, two kinds of "actualizers," or activators.* The most obvious kind is external to the receptor. The second kind is entirely internal to the receptor and involves the fascinating capacity that human beings have to carry on internally both ends of an imaginary conversation. Both kinds of stimulus interact with the receptor's feeling of need for whatever is recommended. And the decision as to the results of such stimulus is up to the receptor.

Though we may speak of general and special revelational information, *all revelational stimulus is special* in that it is always "in a concrete form to a specific person or group" (Ramm 1961:17). Such stimulus may work from either general or special revelational information but always within the tether of Scripture, for God's general information can never contradict his specially revealed information.

External actualizers of revelation will ordinarily be Spirit-guided human beings called and empowered to witness persuasively concerning their interactions with God. Success in such witnessing activity depends on the receptor's relating the message of the witness to his or her own felt needs. These needs may have already been a part of the receptor's awareness or be brought to consciousness in the witnessing interaction. (Human agency in this regard is treated in chapter 14.) The partnership between human beings and the Holy Spirit is, however, crucial. Henry refers to the Spirit's position as that of "supervision of the communication of revelation" (1976,II:14). Henry's static model of revelation allows for "no new truth" to be conveyed. He also makes the traditional distinction between revelation and illumination (though, I feel, very unconvincingly). He does, however, helpfully contradict his static model and open the way for the more dynamic model presented here when he says:

The Spirit illumines persons by reiterating [stimulating?] the truth of the scriptural revelation and bearing witness to Jesus Christ. Spirit-illumination centers in the interpretation of the . . . sense of Spirit-breathed Scripture (1976,II:15).

The *internal process of actualization* ordinarily requires both a high level of felt need and an inclination and ability on the receptors' part to "repersonalize" the message for themselves. Though learning to "carry on a conversation" with a book is a difficult skill to learn, many do in fact develop it.[3] The casebook form of the Bible, by making it easier for receptors to identify with those concerning whom they read, facilitates this internal actualization for those with good reading skills. For the 70 percent of the world with minimal or no reading ability (P. Smith 1975:3), however, the written word alone is not likely to suffice. There need to be personal communicators as well.

In quotations such as those from Henry above, we see exhibited the traditional fear that leads evangelical orthodoxy, on the one hand, to staticize revelation by reducing it to the written records of holy history and, on the other, to reduce the Holy Spirit's activity to a form of activity called "illumination" that is of lesser status than the activity called revelation considered to be now terminated. He fears that "unless priority is given to the objectively inspired content of Scripture, Spirit-illumination readily gives way to private fantasy and mysticism" (1976,II:15). Without denying the fact that much of what purports to be "Spirit-illumination" may be misguided, I believe that Henry and evangelical orthodoxy are giving up too much in the attempt to gain an "objective" scheme for measuring revelational truth. For the real problem they are struggling with is not whether or not God is working in contemporary life in the same way as he did historically, but how to identify beyond the shadow of a doubt whether, in fact, any given instance purported to be God's working is of God or not.

To avoid the necessity of measuring contemporary events, then, they reduce revelation to the static information concerning "objectively inspired" (or better, objectified) past revelations. Those events that happen today due to divine-human interaction, though they may be of the same nature as the events recorded in Scripture, are labeled by a lesser term, "illumination." This distinction is not demanded by the difference in quality in the events but, rather, by the *fear* on the part of the theologians lest they misevaluate something that is not of God as being of God. Actually, *the term "illumination" might usefully be employed to designate what I am calling "stimulus." It could then be recognized to be an essential part of all of God's revelational activity whether past (and recorded in Scripture) or present.* By labeling one set of similar events "revelation"

---

3. It should be noted that in cultures and subcultures without the kind of reading tradition that encourages such "conversations" with books it may not even occur to people that such internal repersonalization is possible. We who have such a tradition dare not assume that others, especially those who don't read well or who are members of cultures without a highly developed tradition, are able to read in this way.

and another "illumination," however, evangelical orthodoxy, on the one hand, reduces God's dynamic revelational activity to its static informational component and, on the other, diminishes the status of the activating component of all revelation—the Spirit-led stimulus or illumination.

With respect to the difficult task of evaluating whether or not given contemporary understandings, "illuminations," or (using my term) revelations, are, in fact, from God or not, I have offered model 9a. The introduction of this model does not necessarily eliminate fuzziness in attempting to make such evaluations. It is hoped, though, that we have thereby made an advance over previous approaches. But even if we have not made an advance in our ability to evaluate potential revelations with certainty, we are at least no worse off than previous approaches in this area. Indeed, we have gained considerably on them with respect to understanding the dynamics of God's revelational activity.

If the validity of continuing revelation is accepted, there is one aspect of the Bible as tether model (model 9c) that can usefully be made explicit here. It is important that whatever contemporary events and utterances are evaluated be measured by the tether of the Scriptures, not by that of some tradition of scriptural interpretation. This makes the evaluational process quite difficult, and probably almost impossible for those who are outsiders to the culture in which the events and utterances took place. *For we never see the Scriptures except within some interpretational context.* Yet the attempt to counteract such biases must be made, for the history of Christianity is replete with illustrations of the substitution of measurements of interpretation and repersonalization traditions for those of the biblical tether. The result is the kind of oppression for which Jesus scored the Pharisees. The object of translational activity (see chapter 13) and the other activities designed to communicate the Scriptures (chapter 14) is to enable people to have more direct access to and remain within the radius of God's tether. When people are enabled to look directly to the Bible, they are able to get beyond the staticizing influences that always accompany the imposition of an outside tradition.

THE WILL OF THE RECEPTORS

The desired impact of inspired information, even when fertilized by personal stimulus, is affected by another factor—the will of the receptor(s). Before the fall, we as human beings presumably wanted to see things God's way. In our sinful state, however, we, like the disciples, though having eyes and ears, so often fail to "see" and "hear" (Mk. 8:18). Human perception of reality has been distorted by the effects of sin on our wills so that we refuse to "will to do God's will," and therefore do not perceive God's evidence in a convincing way (Jn. 7:17). This influence of sin on the human will affects the response both to revelational information (general and special) and to revelational stimulus.

Theologians have taken a variety of positions concerning the relationship between the knowledge of God and his purposes and the distorting influence of sin on this knowledge. Typical of much evangelical thinking on this subject is the position of John Calvin, which, as outlined by Carl Henry, holds that

God's objective revelation in nature no less than in Scripture is clear and adequate. What interferes with man's eager reception and appropriation is not some weakness in the revelation, but man's own perversity. The majority of those immersed in error are "blind amidst the opportunity of seeing" and "notwithstanding all the displays of the glory of God, scarcely one man in a hundred is really a spectator of it" (Calvin 1953: I,5,8). "The manifestation of God . . . is . . . clear enough; but . . . on account of our blindness, it is not found to be sufficient" (Calvin 1961, commentary on Romans 1:20). The revelation itself is adequate for its divinely intended purpose; hence man is both accountable and guilty for this disposition of it (Henry 1976,I:337–38).

While I find myself in general agreement with the overall thrust of such explanations, there is a certain lack of preciseness with respect to the dynamics of the processes they assume. Given the universality of knowledge of God and the universality of the effects of sin, *what differs in the situation of those who respond to the revelation from the situation of those who do not respond?* I find singularly unsatisfying those positions that postulate the capricious counteracting of sin-blindness by the Holy Spirit for some persons but not for others. Is not the "wooing of the Holy Spirit" as much as a constant as his revealing activity? To me the proffering of salvation must be as universal as the revelation and human sinfulness. For God does not will that any perish (2 Pet. 3:9).

The difference must lie today as ever in the human will which, though infected by sin at every point, has not lost its capacity to respond to God's revelational activity. God, in his revealing activity, however, is able to break through the sin barrier, at least for some. For the activating of the inspired information by the Holy Spirit takes place within the receptor(s). Those who, in spite of the effects of sin on their wills, somehow receive the Spirit's stimulus, then, experience at least enough of God's revelation to respond in saving faith to him. We who love him see "things beyond our seeing, things beyond our hearing, things beyond our imagining, all prepared by God for those who love him (1 Cor. 2:9 NEB).

Response is the desired end of receptor-oriented revelation. It is directed *to* people today just as specifically as the scripturally recorded revelations were directed to Isaiah, to Jeremiah, to Amos, to Theophilus, to the Galatians, to Timothy. But revelation "does not bring to salvation all who comprehend it. Without personal appropriation God's revelation brings salvation to no one" (Henry 1976,II:44). But those who *will* to adopt God's model (Jn. 7:17) and to respond to it in faith (Heb. 11) will be saved, not by their *knowledge* but by their *faithfulness* to the One who stimulated their response to himself (Rom. 1:17).

In revealing himself and those other things that God wants human beings to know, he makes use of general and special information plus personal stimulus to pierce through the sin-affected human "will barrier." In doing this God seeks to elicit a continuing faith response that is initially saving and from that point leading on toward spiritual maturity (see chapter 17). Glimpses of this process as it occurred in many lives are recorded in Scripture. In the Book we see specific events occurring in the lives of specific persons acting out and/or interpreting their interactions with God in accordance with the specific cultures in which they were immersed.

These recorded interactions took place with a variety of persons at various times and places in a variety of cultures. The constants in the process were (1) God, (2) the underlying commonalities of human beings, including sin, (3) the constant method (model 10a), and (4) the constant message (model 10b, see below) of God. *He employs the same processes to reach the same kinds of people via the same kinds of culture using the same message and method to bring about the same results today.*

THE CONSTANCY OF THE MESSAGE (Model 10b)

When the *forms* through which a message is communicated *call attention to themselves*, it is easy for the receptor(s) to *focus on those forms and to miss much of the message*. Whether the forms disrupt or facilitate the flow of the message is, however, a matter of the receptor's perception of them. To the members of western culture the forms of Hebrew culture are perceived as so strange that they draw our attention to *themselves* rather than to the message of God and its effects. But in the Pauline epistles we see God's message phrased in first-century thought forms similar at many points to those of contemporary Europe. Though many things are different from the way we think and do things, there is enough similarity between Greek thought forms and ours that we see the message with much less distraction resulting from the forms in which it is phrased. Because of our cultural similarities to Greece, then, God's message comes to us quite clearly through the Pauline epistles but indistinctly, if at all, through the Old Testament.

As a result of these cultural influences, many westerners have concluded that God changed his message when he turned to the Gentiles.[4] It is not uncommon at the popular level for people to assume that the Old Testament way of salvation was via adherence to the law, while the New Testament way is via faith in Christ. Hebrews 11 comes to them as quite a shock. For the strangeness (from a western point of view) of Hebrew culture has obscured their view of a salvation-by-faith message in the Old Testament. Yet Hebrews 11 contends that all of the Old Testament "heroes of faith" were saved by means of the same faith allegiance to God that they (we) have considered to be a New Testament message.

---

4. See Bright 1953:192–98 for a convincing assertion (though with a slightly different focus) of the singleness of the biblical message.

Two other western cultural biases also obscure our view of the message of Scripture: (1) western culture's bias toward *information for its own sake* (see chapter 9), and (2) western culture's tendency to *interpret history evolutionarily*, with western culture at the top and all other cultures judged to be inferior because (we think) they represent stages of culture that we have now outgrown (see below on cumulative information, model 8k). To us, therefore, the greater accumulation of information evident by the later stages of the New Testament, plus the obvious "superiority" (i.e., similarity to our perspective) of the material there presented lead us to value those portions (with their Greek context) more highly than the earlier portions (with Hebrew contexts). We will deal with this in more detail below.

We tend to assume that those Scriptures that have greater communication value to the members of *our* culture have greater revelational value to the members of *every* culture. What a shock it was for me to learn that the Nigerians with whom I worked actually saw many aspects of God's message more clearly in the Old Testament than in the book of Romans. I had been taught to see Romans as the epitome of God's revelation to humanity. Like Packer (and many others), I felt it was "the fittest starting point" in Scripture (1958:107). I was anxious to lead these Nigerian church leaders into the depths of the riches of God there recorded. But their perception of Romans differed from mine. I had fallen into the pitfall spoken of by Snaith of ignoring the Hebrew understandings of God that form the basis of Christianity, in favor of Greek "speculation" (theologizing). This, he says, is a "characteristic feature of the history of Christian thought" (1964:14). Snaith continues:

Christians have been tempted to regard the Old Testament as being but one of the many sacred books which the world has known. They have thought therefore that it was of small account for the Christian, who would do well to save his time in a busy, thronging world and begin with the Gospel according to Matthew (ibid.).

My background had led me to assume that the Old Testament should be treated as merely an interesting historical foundation for the New Testament but without much contemporary value. I had learned that

the former revelation lays the foundation for later revelation. The law prepares the way for the prophets; the earlier prophets lay the foundation for the later prophets; the total Old Testament is the preparation for the total New Testament. The life of Christ is the necessary backdrop for the Acts and the Epistles. And the Book of Revelation presupposes the fullness of interpretation of the Person and work of Christ as this is contained in the Epistles (Ramm 1961:104).

Such a statement does point up an important aspect of the unity of the Scriptures. But if one's cultural perspective leads one to downgrade in value those components of Scripture that are earlier in the procession and to overemphasize those portions that come later, one is likely to miss a very important fact: *the essential message of the Bible is the same from beginning to end.* For one is likely to take more notice of the differences between the Hebrew and Hellenistic matrices (the contextual component dealt with in chapter 7) than of the sameness of the message(s) (the informational component) couched in these matrices. Note that, in terms of the interaction between context and information (chapter 7), in a case like this the cultural strangeness of the context interferes with the clarity of the intended message. The message a western reader receives is more influenced by contextual features than the original author intended that it be. The resultant message for the western reader of the Old Testament is, therefore, likely to be quite different from what the author intended.

The people of another culture (or subculture), however, may see God's essential message more clearly in Hebrew dress than in Hellenistic dress. To them the philosophical, cognitive approach of the apostle Paul in Romans may be as distracting and confusing as genealogies and Palestinian agrarian, fishing, and herding analogies are to us. Even if Romans should contain more precise revelational information, one needs to ask whether it is presented in a form which the intended receptors can readily grasp. Romans was not simply written, it was written *to* someone. It participated in a real interaction between a real communicator and real human receptors. It was therefore produced in such a way as to have maximum communicational impact on *that* audience. This means that, even though as a classic case it has been preserved for all, it will have greatest impact on contemporary audiences that most approximate the original receptors. It will have less or different impact on contemporary audiences that are less like the one to which it was originally directed. For them the contextual component of the Romans presentation of the message will interfere in the same way that the Hebrew contextual component interferes for Euro-Americans.

The Nigerians who saw less value in Romans than I did were not rejecting the message of Romans. They were simply responding to the fact that they could see the message of Romans more clearly through portions of Scripture that were originally written to communicate the message to people in cultures more like theirs. That is, in order to see clearly that same constant message of God that the Scriptures present in a variety of cultural forms, they preferred different case studies than I did—for cultural reasons.

A conversation between a Gentile and a Jewish student of Old Testament studies at Brandeis University illustrates the same point. The Gentile asked the Jewish student what his favorite passage of Scripture was. His immediate response was, "The first eight chapters of First Chronicles." These are Hebrew genealogies. From my (Gentile) point of view I have often wondered why God allowed so much space in his Word to be "wasted" on such trivia. But to a Hebrew (and to many other kinship-oriented societies around the world) genealogical lists of this nature demonstrate in the clearest way the specificity of God's love and concern that lies at the heart of the Gospel.

Before turning to a discussion of the multicultural format of the Bible (model 9h) and the cumulativeness of the information (model 8k) therein presented, I want to attempt to define the central, constant message. Looking at that message through the biblical materials (as we must), we see what Ramm terms "the one organic word of God" (1961:101). He sees this "word" (or message) as paralleling the oneness of the "people of God throughout the different historical periods," and points out:

The different forms and conditions under which the people of God existed do not fracture the people of God into a collection of individuals; neither, then, do the different modalities of special revelation fracture it into many words of God (1961:101).

Ramm denies that the information contained in the Scriptures should be seen as "a series of dots running across a paper" or as "unrelated telegrams from heaven to earth" (1961:102).

Even though revelation is ineradicably particular in the sense that the word of God always comes to some particular man, it is not a miscellany of words. Each word of God which came to the prophet or apostle is part of the one word of God. . . .
   Revelation is a whole and is therefore organic. It is a *membered* revelation. It does have parts, i.e., members. . . . But the parts of revelation when added together form an organism (1961: 102; see also M. Bavinck 1928:409–10, cited in Rogers 1977).

There are differences between the New Testament and the Old Testament, to be sure. There are, as noted above, differences in cultural matrix and differences in the extent of the understanding afforded concerning God and his activities in relation to human beings. As we move through the Scriptures we gain greater insight into what God is doing and how he is doing it. But we must guard against assuming that the *message* is changed when (1) God (like Paul—1 Cor. 9:19–22) adapts his communicational approach to the receptors or when (2) more information concerning the message is presented.

We learn from the New Testament, for example, how God went about making it possible for him to be legitimately just and, simultaneously, to justify Old Testament peoples and New Testament peoples alike on the basis of faith alone (Rom. 3:26). However, such justification was never based on *knowledge* of how God worked it out. Abraham, who had no way to know the details of God's work through Christ, was saved by faith (or rather, by faithfulness) just as we are (Rom. 4:3, 9; Gal. 3:6; Jas. 2:23). He, like us, was saved *through* Christ—for there is no other way to God (Jn. 14:6). There is no other "name" through which salvation can be granted (Acts 4:12). But note that "name" in such contexts signifies the *authority* of the person of the bearer (Christ), not any magic that might attach to the knowledge and utterance of a word.

My point is that, though the inspired information concerning *how* God brought about our eternal salvation is extremely valuable, *God's message is no different since the occurrence and Spirit-guided interpretation of those redemptive events than it was in Abraham's or Adam's time.* It was then, and still is today, the message of the eternal God who exists and who "rewards those who search for him" in faith (Heb. 11:6). "What, then, was the difference between" Old Testament and New Testament believers? asks Anderson.

> It was not that godly Jews were saved by "works" or by their obedience to the law, for no one can ever be saved by "works" and no Jew ever succeeded in keeping the law. Believers under the Old Covenant were saved by grace through faith, just as we are: that is, through the grace of God in Christ. . . . Their knowledge was deficient, their assurance often fitful, but their forgiven status identical with ours (1970:99).

God holds people accountable for what they *do* know, rather than for what they don't know (Rom. 1:32; 2:14–16). I believe, therefore, that we can assume that those whose understanding of God's message today is more like Abraham's than like ours will be held accountable for the response they make to the message as they understand it. *People are not required to respond to a different message today simply because we, interpreting it from our cultural perspectives, may understand it to be a different message.* Information concerning God's righteousness, his love, his redemptive activity, human sinfulness, and all the rest is of the highest value. But the fact that we now possess such information should never be allowed either to obscure that basic message or to be interpreted as having changed that message. The information revealed to us concerning these details has high value if used to stimulate a saving faith relationship between human beings and God. But it distorts the essential message if the information becomes the *end* rather than a *means* to faith. The task of the Christian witness is to stimulate the receptors' to faith on the basis of whatever knowledge they have, plus any information that the witness can helpfully contribute and that is accepted by the hearers. The witness does not do the proper thing if he or she distracts the receptors' attention from the message to the supporting (or subsidiary) information.

That we are saved through faith in *Christ*, whereas Old Testament peoples pledged their allegiance to *God*, is a point that is sometimes made to indicate a change in the message. But this is a change only if we heretically believe that God and Christ are two Gods rather than one. If "they" are one God, faith in Christ the Son is the same as faith in God the Father—and vice-versa. Faith in God through the work of Christ as a human being is, furthermore, an elaboration on our understanding of the way God has always brought about human salvation, not an alteration of that way. That is not a change in the basic message. Insight concerning the historical facts relating to the work of Christ and their inspired interpretation can have high stimulus value in the communication of the essential message. But even the potential for this knowledge does not change the message.

This relationship between knowledge and faith is difficult for westerners to sort out due to their cultural conditioning, for this cultural conditioning has led westerners to see the biblical presentation in terms of the differences in the information presented rather than in terms of the constancy of the message. We as westerners have, in keeping with our cultural values, produced written theological schemes to interpret and transmit the meanings of revelational events rather than developing ritual, ceremony, and person-to-person oral transmission techniques. Our way is similar to the Greek way, while the ritual-and-ceremony route is the way preferred by Hebrews and Hebrew-like cultures.

There is, as discussed below (model 8k), an increasing accumulation of information concerning God's redemptive activity in the Scriptures. We have been much impressed by this. But perhaps our focus on these informational differences has obscured our view of the change in the cultural context in which the essential message is couched. The message of a saving faith relationship centered around covenant, tradition, and tribe expressed ceremonially looks very different to us from that same message centered around grace and freedom interpreted philosophically. Yet in many ways tradition ("law"), tribe, and ceremony in Hebrew culture were the functional equivalents of grace, freedom, and philosophizing in Greek culture. The latter are not necessarily superior ways of expressing the Gospel, just different culturally.

The apostle Paul was specifically attempting to reclothe God's constant message in Greek cultural clothing (see von Allmen 1975). His effort should not, therefore, be understood by us as a denial of the validity of Hebrew-type cultural clothing for the Gospel. Our own cultural preferences should not be allowed to prejudice us against certain (Hebrew) portions of Scripture as they did Martin Luther. I believe it was unconscious ethnocentrism on his part (like that with which we all struggle) rather than, as he thought, a concern over authorship that led him to be negative toward the books of Hebrews, James, Jude, and Revelation. Luther placed these books at the end of his New Testament. Note the probable ethnocentrism in the following statements from Luther's preface to the New Testament written in 1522:

From all of these books, you can, in a flash . . . distinguish which are the best. John's Gospel and St. Paul's epistles, especially the one to the Romans, and St. Peter's first epistle contain the true kernel and marrow among all the books, for in these you do not find Christ's deeds and miracles described very much but you find emphasized in a most masterful way how faith in Christ overcomes sin, death, and hell, and gives life, justification, and blessing—which is the true nature of the Gospel. If I should have to choose between the deeds or the preaching of Christ, I would prefer to leave the deeds go, for these don't help me, but his words are the words of life. . . . Therefore John's Gospel is the only Gospel which is delicately sensitive to what is the essence of the Gospel and is to be widely preferred to the other three and placed on a higher level. Likewise, the epistles of St. Paul and Peter are to take precedence over the three gospels of Matthew, Mark, and Luke. To sum it all up—St. John's Gospel, and his first epistle, St. Paul's epistles, especially those to the Romans, to the Galatians, and to the

Ephesians, and St. Peter's first epistle—these are the books which show you Christ and teach everything which is needful and blessed for you to know, even if you don't see or even hear any other book. . . . Wherefore St. James' epistle is a true epistle of straw compared with them, for it contains nothing of an evangelical nature (Reuss 1891:322, 329, quoted by Fuller 1969:IX,10).

The only New Testament book traditionally thought to be directed to a Hebrew audience that Luther seemed to respect was 1 Peter. He is hard on Hebrews, James, Jude, Revelation, and the Synoptic Gospels, all of which either have been understood as directed to Hebrew audiences or (like Mark and Luke) center on the events in the life of Christ lived in a Hebrew context. Luther is similarly hard on the Old Testament (see Fuller 1969:IX,13). Note his preference for preaching and theologizing over Hebrew-type recording of events. Fuller (ibid.) quotes similarly ethnocentric statements from the Scofield Bible. And Madvig (1977) critiques Carnell (1959:58–59) for similar, though better reasoned, tendencies.

As we study the Scriptures our cultural perspective is like a magnet. It draws to us, as it were, those portions of Scripture in which God's message is presented in ways most meaningful to those of our culture. Those portions written to people within Greek culture, therefore, tend to speak most clearly to us Euro-Americans, since we have been so strongly influenced by Greek thinking. Thus we gravitate toward the Pauline letters for cultural reasons. This is predictable and, I believe, a part of God's plan, since in this way we are able to hear God's message with a minimum of cultural adjustment. Because of this fact, however, we can be misled into serious error.

Such Euro-American Christian positions as those of Luther and Scofield seem to have fallen into the assumption that, because the Pauline letters speak most clearly to us, they are therefore more inspired or more adequate in their presentation of God's revelation than other portions of Scripture. Note Lindsell's position in this regard:

All Scripture is profitable and all parts of it afford us knowledge and insight into God's self-revelation, but the didactic books such as Romans and Galatians, that open up to us the great teachings about justification by faith, are *of more significance* than some of the genealogical tables, or the details of the history of the kings, or some aspects of the journeys of the apostle Paul. The teaching books are *more important* to us than some of the material contained in the apocalyptic books. The latter are surely important, but *less so* than some of the other parts of the Word of God. The Proverbs of Solomon do not rise to the level of the gospel records. All of Scripture presents truth, but some truths are central, other peripheral; *some parts are of the first magnitude* in the scale of values and others of the second (1976:38–39). [Emphasis added.]

Luther's, Scofield's, and Lindsell's ethnocentric views are specific examples of a position that afflicts all of us who study the Scriptures from our position within western culture. The differences between Old Testament and New

Testament seem great to us. And we recognize that much of the interpretation of the greatest of God's redemptive acts (the Incarnation) is focused on by that part of the Bible closest to us culturally (the Pauline epistles). We are easily led to deny the value for anybody of the Old Testament and, like Luther, even of the Hebrew portions of the New Testament, simply because we don't feel their great value for us.

This is the result of a culturally inculcated evolutionary understanding of revelation. There is *some truth* to such an understanding but it ignores the fact that one's cultural conditioning has much to do with one's ability to understand and appreciate the various sections of the Bible. If such views are absolutized they become serious detriments to Christian understanding and communication. It is predictable for cultural reasons, as mentioned above, that Euro-Americans would be more attracted to the Pauline epistles. Africans and many others, however, with cultures more similar to Hebrew culture than ours is, are more attracted to the Gospels and the Old Testament. For their preference, unlike Luther's, is for narrative presentations of events rather than for philosophical analyses of their significance.

But what about those who see God's essential message more clearly, rather than less clearly, via the Hebrew portions? What about those who, like certain Kikuyu people of Kenya, felt the Old Testament to be the final revelation? After all, it was translated *after* the New Testament and it made *much more sense* to them! Does this mean (as some contend) that their understanding of Christianity can never be as adequate as ours until they learn to love the Pauline epistles as we do? Certainly not! It is enough that God appeals to them forcefully through those portions of the Scriptures that are written in terms of cultural perspectives more similar to theirs.

Could it be because of this kind of ethnocentric understanding of biblical revelation that Bible translating in nonwestern languages often virtually ignores the Old Testament? Commonly, in spite of the fact that a given culture may be concerned over kinship and genealogies, the first book to be translated is Mark rather than Matthew. Then Acts, perhaps John, and on through the whole New Testament. For many cultures this provides much that speaks to them only minimally, while ignoring much (e.g., the Old Testament) that would carry revelational truth to them with greater impact.

This gives us a different perspective on the fact that many Africans want the Old Testament more than missionaries have been willing to provide it for them. I have heard missionaries interpret this preference, and the allied observation that many African independent churches make great use of the Old Testament, as due to perversity or other sub-Christian motivations on the part of the Africans. Could it be, though, that it is *need*, rather than perversity, that leads Africans to the Old Testament? What about Africans and those of the hundreds of other cultures that could see God's message more clearly in Hebrew dress than in Greek? Should they perhaps be provided with at least *some* of the Old Testament before they receive all of the New Testament? The remarkable similarities between the God-inspired book of Proverbs and the proverbs of many peoples, for example (in spite of Lindsell's opinion), can powerfully communicate messages from God to those of other cultures in terms maximally meaningful to them.

Could it be that the *whole* Bible is inspired and usable today? Could it be that every portion of God's multifaceted Word can still speak to someone, somewhere, if allowed to? God has provided a multiculturally useful witness to himself because its contents originate in, and therefore speak to, many cultures.

CUMULATIVE INFORMATION IN MULTICULTURAL FORMAT
(Models 8k and 9k)

The supracultural, transcendent God has, as we have seen, chosen to reveal himself in terms that are comprehensible to humans from within the human cultural context. He has, then, chosen to transmit the record of certain of his revelations of himself, and his supracultural message to human life, in human language and culture in order to effectively communicate with human beings.

Thus the Old Testament records the supracultural God communicating himself to Hebrew people in terms of Hebrew thought patterns. He accepted from them typically Hebrew responses to his supracultural message which, for their sakes, he had clothed in Hebrew language and culture as the

best minds and spirits of Israel adopted and adapted those elements of their cultural heritage and environment—myths, customs, laws, institutions, literary forms, and vocabulary—that were useful in expressing their view and experience of God (Blair 1975:389; see also Kautzsch 1904, Hooke 1938).

In the Old Testament, therefore, God is perceived primarily in terms of majesty, power, and justice, attributes that are both true characteristics of the supracultural God and characteristics expected of God from a Hebrew cultural perspective. God, however, also went beyond Hebrew expectations (Wright 1950; Snaith 1964)[5] and revealed himself, in addition, as a God who enters into covenant relationships with people. For, though covenant relationships were already an important part of Hebrew culture and in that sense not new, the employment of such a concept with regard to the relationship between God and humans appears to have been very new and in that sense "beyond Hebrew expectations." Even when communicating this (and other)

5. Snaith, while admitting the importance of setting Hebrew religion "in focus with respect to Semitic religion generally," states that "it is high time" to awaken from "the desire for comprehensiveness and broad-mindedness" and to focus also on Old Testament distinctiveness (1964:12–13). My position is that we should strive to focus on *balance* and *process*. We should recognize the great similarities in the forms employed but never neglect the fact that, with Israel, there was a distinctive *use* of those forms (with and for God) that resulted, over time, in greater and greater differences between Israelite religion and neighboring religions, which were once quite similar.

nonexpected revelation, God started where the Hebrew recipients of the revelation were (see model 10c, below). From that point he then revealed new insights in a manner comprehensible to them through the voices and pens of thoroughly Hebrew preachers and writers.

In the New Testament, likewise, we see this method of God's revelation of himself both in terms of first-century Palestinian culture (Gospels, Acts, Hebrews, James, Peter) and in terms designed to appeal to those immersed in Greco-Roman culture (Paul's epistles). In each case we see God starting (though not ending) where people are culturally for the sake of revealing himself to them comprehensibly. The apparent differences between the loving God of the New Testament and the stern judgmental sacrifice-demanding God of parts of the Old Testament are not to be interpreted as indications that God changes his approach to humans every few thousand years (as some seem to imply). They indicate, rather, that the unchanging supracultural God usually (not always) chooses to reveal himself in such a way that the members of various cultures may focus in on those aspects of God's nature and activity most amenable to their cultural expectations as to what God should be like. They then respond to him in faith (a supracultural requirement) expressed in ways appropriate to their cultures.

The special information recorded in the Bible should not be looked upon as a linear, evolutionary type of presentation of God and his workings with human beings (Bright 1953:193–94). For it did not start from a simple concept and proceed evolutionarily to a more complex concept *within a single cultural framework,* as the concept of "progressive revelation" (see Ramm, Henry, Mickelson, etc.) is likely to lead one to believe. That information is presented, rather, in a series of "zoom-lens" views of God's interactions in a variety of cultural settings. The Bible focuses at different times on quite different cultural understandings of God's constant message and its implications, each of which is Spirit-guided. And the accumulation of information developed from studying these insights tends toward a comprehensiveness of under- standing of God that far exceeds what could be given in terms of any single culture. Hebrew culture, for example, allows for certain insights into the nature of God that Greek culture is not so strong on (e.g., God's majesty). Greek culture, on the other hand, allows for insights that Hebrew culture is not so strong on (e.g., God's grace). And Euro-American and Asian and Latin American and African cultural insights also have, under the leading of the Holy Spirit, important contributions to make to the comprehensiveness of the truth that God seeks to reveal concerning himself and his interactions with humans. Indeed, as Jacob Loewen (1974) suggests, we may never see the full richness of God's revelation (the full range of his allowed variation in human perception of his ways) until we are able to participate in the multitude of different perspectives brought to it by the multitude of languages and cultures in the world.

The Bible is a multicultural document with something to appeal to everyone in terms of cultural conditioning; and the message of each part of the Bible is essentially the same qualitatively, though there are differences in the quantity of information available. But that message is packaged in terms of differing cultural and psychological matrices, for, as Hebrews 11 (also Rom. 1:17; Hab. 2:4) points out, it is in terms of a single faith-response to God that God's people have always operated, in spite of differences in culture and in the extent of the information concerning God and his works that had been revealed to them.

One way to make more explicit this view of the written revelation is to portray it "horizontally" to show the buildup of the quantity of information concerning its single message within a diversity of the cultural frames of reference in terms of which that message and the responses to it are illustrated. This accumulation of information is what has been traditionally labeled "progressive revelation" but is here termed "cumulative revelational information." It is signified on the following chart by the ascending line.

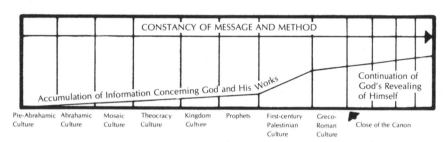

Fig. 11.1. A "horizontal" view of the accumulation of the revelational information.

From this perspective the greatest number of distinctions between the various parts of the Bible are cultural rather than theological. This is a *quantitative* statement and as such does not refer to the obvious fact that there is a *qualitative* difference between God's revelation of himself via Jesus Christ and that via ordinary human beings or angels (Heb. 1:1–4). The statement is intended to alert us to the danger of mistaking quantities of cultural differences for qualitative differences. For God is the same yesterday, today, and forever; he interacts with humankind on the basis of the same set of principles yesterday, today, and forever. There are informational differences, to be sure, and human beings are held accountable for the differences in the information available to them and the amount of that information that they are able to comprehend.

With respect to the continuing revealing activity of God, it must be emphasized that such revelation is never new in the sense that it changes the essential message or contradicts anything that is in the canonical Scriptures. It may and frequently does confirm and elaborate on scriptural information but it will never contradict it. Furthermore, the range of variation in perception of God's revelation demonstrated in Scripture shows the dimensions of the range within which contemporary revelation can take place. The Bible is our "yard-stick" (model 9a) and our "tether" (model 9c)—the latter to show the radius within which we range, the former to measure whether any given potential revelation is in or outside that range. Such perspectives are needed to deal adequately with (1) the fact of the well-nigh infinite diversity of humanity, (2) the fact that the living God operates today as he always has by adapting to that diversity even in his leading and revelational activity, (3) the fact that, though the Scriptures are entirely adequate and normative, they are not complete in the sense that they reveal to us everything that it is possible to know about God, and (4) the fact that they do not anticipate all that is necessary to know for us to make all the necessary contemporary applications of Christian truth. We need the constant revelational leading of the Holy Spirit and the Spirit's human partners to assist with that.

12. Revealed Through Culture

In this the final chapter of the section on the dynamics of God's revelation of himself in human culture we focus on the way God works within the limitations of human culture. God's choice to work within such limitations, plus God's method of starting where people are, leads to the introduction of the very important "starting-point-plus-process" model (model 10c). The use of this model is illustrated first by a case study dealing with the concept of sin in a Papua New Guinea tribal situation and then by a consideration of the position of those who are today chronologically A.D. but "informationally B.C." (model 10g).

STARTING POINT PLUS PROCESS (Model 10c)

We have noted that God starts working with human beings where they are, solely on the basis of their faith commitment to him. This new allegiance issues in a series of changes in the converts' behavior. The conversion process and the effects of these changes on the converts' culture will be treated in detail in chapters 17–19. It will be helpful here to introduce briefly the "starting-point-plus-process" model in relationship to God's revelational activity.

Western Christianity has characteristically taken a hard line on human sinfulness. We have been impressed with the evilness of human beings and the wide disparity between human behavior and God's ideals. There is, of course, plenty of scriptural support for a negative posture toward human beings. We have "gone astray" (Is. 53:6), sinned and fallen short of the glory of God (Rom. 3:23). When we have sought to be righteous we have produced nothing more valuable than "filthy rags" (Isa. 64:6). We deserve judgment and eternal death (Rom. 6:23).

As true and impressive as this negative teaching of Scripture is, however, I believe the message of God's love and acceptance to be even more impressive. It goes beyond the stereotype that people have concerning God and is, therefore, communicationally most impactful. How is it that God steadfastly refused to break his agreement (covenant) with Israel even though they continually broke their part of the bargain? How is it that God expressed himself to us through his supreme act of love even "while we were yet sinners" (Rom. 5:8)? God starts with us in the basis of faith and counts that faith for righteousness (Rom. 4:5, 22; Gal. 3:6; Jas. 2:23). But what then? Does he accept subideal behavior on our part? He must. But on what basis?

There are at least two ways to look at a topic such as this that deals with both

239

points and processes. One way is to focus on the *positioning* of the points, the other is to focus on the *direction of movement* involved in the processes. The first focus gives one a grouping or what mathematicians call a "set" made up of the items positioned at the various points. A border can then be drawn around that grouping to distinguish it from any other grouping, or "set," of points. The other focus is not so concerned with the position of the points themselves as with the direction in which the items are moving with respect to a central point or goal. This perspective leads to a categorizing of items (for our purposes, Christians) not in terms of their *static positioning* vis-à-vis those in other positions, but in terms of the *directions* in which they are moving with respect to that central point or goal. Those moving *toward* a given goal would therefore be in one category, no matter how great the distance between them and the goal, while those moving *away from* that goal would be in another category, no matter how close they might be to that goal.[1]

I would like to suggest that the basis on which God interacts with (and reveals himself to) human beings is what I will call a *directional* basis rather than a *positional* one (model 10d). Faith/faithfulness is, of course, both the starting point and the sine qua non for a continuing relationship with God. But the Scriptures lead us to believe that those who, like the thief on the cross (Lk. 23:42), simply reach out in faith at the last possible moment are as completely accepted by God as those who have expressed and developed their faith over decades. Jesus' illustration of the kingdom by the use of the story of the laborers who were all paid the same amount for unequal amounts of work (Mt. 20:1–16) would also seem to indicate that God has an attitude different from ours toward who is "in" and who is "out."

As Euro-Americans, our tendency would be to assume that there are two compartments, one labeled THE SAVED, the other labeled THE UNSAVED. We think, then, of people as being *positionally in one or the other compartment*. We think of those who commit themselves in faith to God through Christ, and who therefore move "from death to life" (Jn. 5:24; 1 Jn. 3:14), as moving from a position in one compartment to a position in the other compartment. We tend to see those in the Christian compartment as distinct from those in the compartment of non-Christians in terms of both their faith and their behavior. In dealing with non-Christians who are considering the possibility of converting to Christianity, then, we are likely to lead them to believe that when they commit themselves to Christ and "all things become new" (2 Cor. 5:17), their behavior will immediately change radically because they have somewhat mysteriously moved from one compartment into another.

And yet in actual experience we find it impossible to distinguish which

---

1. I am indebted at this point to my colleague at the School of World Mission, Paul G. Hiebert, for input from the thinking of mathematicians concerning "sets" and "fuzzy sets" (see Zadeh 1965). This input has sharpened my ability to formulate the ideas that follow. What I call here a *positional* basis, or model, corresponds roughly with a mathematical "set," or "fixed set," where positioning within certain borders is determinative for categorizing. What I call a *directional* basis, or model, corresponds roughly with what Zadeh calls a "fuzzy set," where the direction of movement with respect to a given goal is determinative for categorizing.

compartment people are in on the basis of their behavior. We can even be sure of great uncertainty in this regard with respect to evaluating those who belong to Christian groups. Jesus pointed to one of the most dedicated groups of his day (the Pharisees) and called them "hypocrites" (Mt. 23 and elsewhere). He suggested that there will even be those who have cast out demons and performed miracles in his name to whom he will say, "I never knew you" (Mt. 7:22–23). And he forbade that the disciples attempt to pull up the "tares" (the unbelievers) in the wheatfield lest they inadvertently pull up some of the wheat (the believers) (Mt. 13:24–30,36–43)

Perhaps Jesus was getting at the fact that it is impossible for humans to distinguish Christians from non-Christians on the basis of their behavior because such evaluations lead to the positioning of all of those with similar behavior in the same compartments. His basis, however, would seem to place the emphasis on the *direction* in which people are going. Some may (like the young wheat) behave very much like non-Christians. But, since they are growing in the direction of greater Christlikeness, they are among the saved. Others may (like the tares) look very much like Christians on the outside. But they are growing away from Christlikeness and are therefore among the lost. We might picture the human scene as follows (each arrow represents a person):

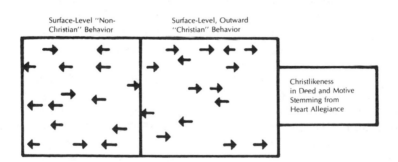

Fig. 12.1. Directional versus positional understandings of those "in" Christ and those "outside" Christ. Read: The *positional* understanding of Christianness sees all those in the compartment on the left as positioned outside Christ and those in the compartment on the right as in Christ. The *directional* understanding sees all those who are *moving toward* greater Christlikeness as saved, no matter what position they may occupy in the behaviorally defined compartments.

Note that, though there may actually be a majority of those headed toward Christlike commitment and behavior in the right compartment and a majority of those headed away from such Christlikeness in the left compartment, it is the direction, not the position, that is determinative. It is the *direction of the process* in which a person is involved that is crucial, not the *position of the point* at which he or she stands. Not that behavior is unimportant, for it is the deep-level allegiance and motive behavior of those headed toward Christ at the extreme left that save them and the deep-level allegiance and motive behavior of those headed away from Christ at the extreme right that mean that they will be lost. But surface-level behavior may be quite misleading as a test of deep-level saving commitment.

I do not intend to suggest that God is unconcerned with the surface-level behavior of his people. For it is surface-level behavior that others read to attempt to discern the deep-level motivations and allegiance of his people. Indeed, we may conclude on the basis of passages such as Galatians 5:22–23 that God wants his people to manifest "the fruits of the Spirit." But these fruits develop as the result of a process of growth in a certain direction. The behavioral starting point for such growth differs from person to person, however, for God accepts people where they are behaviorally on the basis of their faith commitment to him. *He thus accepts a range of variation in the behavioral starting points at which he begins his transforming work with human beings.* This he does both on the cultural level and on the individual level. On each level we can postulate that God has an ideal type of behavior that he would like the individual or the culture to practice habitually. But he accepts people before they reach that ideal and refuses to abandon them even if, after a period of time, they have not arrived at ideal behavior. Yet many people in partnership with God make a considerable amount of progress from where they start toward God's ideal during the course of their Christian experience. Likewise, there seems to be movement toward God's ideals on the part of whole cultures under the influence of God (see chapters 18 and 19).

At this point we need to remind ourselves that we are not simply discussing cultural forms. We are, rather, dealing primarily with the meanings and usage of cultural forms and only secondarily with the forms.

The following diagram (Fig. 12.2) will provide the grid in terms of which we will discuss and illustrate this matter. To show how it works we will plot on it the starting point plus process of an imaginary individual with respect to several of the "fruits of the Spirit" (love, patience, kindness, and self-control—Gal. 5:22). Note that we are indicating both a range of starting points and a range of approximation to God's ideal once the process of movement toward the ideal has begun.

Our imaginary individual, at the time of coming into a faith relationship with God, is found to be totally impatient, selectively loving, kind only to friends, and undisciplined. Note that this individual starts at a different distance from God's ideal at each point. During, say, ten years of Christian experience, improvement to occasionally patient, loving most people, kind to nearly all, and greater self-control occurs. Each of these movements is in the right direction, toward God's ideal. This person might (at least theoretically)

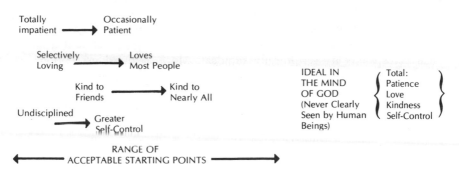

Fig. 12.2. Starting-point-plus-process model applied to four fruits of the Spirit.

have regressed or remained stationary at certain points in surface-level behavior. Only if this betokened a change of direction in deep-level allegiance, however, would the person be lost. The greater likelihood is that the deep-level movement in the direction of greater faith commitment to God will bring about movement at the surface level toward greater behavioral Christlikeness.

On the cultural level we may illustrate from biblical data in quite a number of areas, for the Bible gives us a good bit of insight into both the ideals of God and the places where he has historically started his work with human beings. I infer from this that God is willing to work with people today who fall within the scriptural range of acceptable (though subideal) behavior and to work with them toward the same ideal goals.

Figure 12.3, below, plots certain aspects of human understanding of, and response to God as deduced from scriptural data. According to Kautzsch (1904) and many others (see McBane 1976), the early Hebrews believed in the existence of many gods. The commandment "no other gods before me" (Exod. 20:3) and Jonah's assumption that he could avoid having to follow God's command by running away from God's territory (presumably into the territory of some other god) are among the scriptural evidences for this interpretation. Since God accepted people who had this subideal belief, we include it on the diagram in the acceptable category. In another scriptural glimpse of God's attitude toward human response to him, though, we find God rejecting those who worship Baal rather than him (1 Kings 18). Apparently God was (and is) willing to tolerate *belief in* other gods but not *devotion to* them. God demands that he alone be the object of human allegiance. We thus enter "Allegiance to Another God" as an unacceptable starting point. Such an allegiance demands a "power encounter" (Tippett 1973:88–91), resulting in the radical replacement of the old allegiance with commitment to God, before God's process can even start.

Perceptions of God as distant, judgmental, to be feared, and perhaps even despotic are also plotted on the diagram as subideal, though acceptable at the start of a people's experience with God. I do not wish to suggest that there is no truth in these perceptions of God. I suggest only that unless balanced by a consciousness of God's personalness, lovingness, forgiveness, and the like, such perceptions are scripturally subideal. More balanced perceptions are implied in analogies such as "shepherd" (Ps. 23), "father," and "friend" (Jn. 15:15). A far less balanced view, indicating regression rather than development, is represented by the unscriptural American "Santa Claus" analogy.

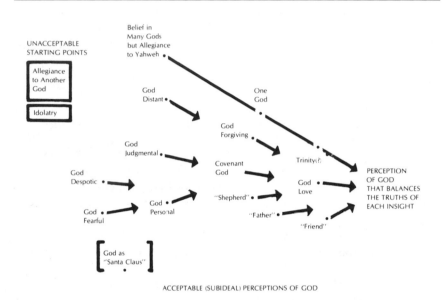

Fig. 12.3. Starting-point-plus-process model applied to scriptural perceptions of God's nature.

Similar diagrams could be devised for a large number of additional categories relating to understandings of, for example, God's workings, human nature and behavior, doctrines such as sin, salvation, faith, and the like. Since God has not changed his method of operation, the scripturally allowed range of starting points is still available today. So is the process by means of which God's Spirit leads us toward his ideals. We will deal in more detail with the change process later (chapters 17–19). It needs to be noted here, however, that fallible human beings neither start at the same points nor move uniformly toward Christian ideals at the same rate when they pledge their allegiance to God through Christ. A given person or group will at the start of the conversion process be at one point with respect to one of the fruits of the Spirit and at another point with respect to another of them (see Fig. 12.2). One individual may already be very kind but quite lacking in self-control. The people of a whole culture may, likewise, already be characterized by a high degree of patience (as are those of many African cultures) when they come into Christianity. Thus the starting points at which people actually begin vary among themselves in their distance from the ideal.

People, then, do not focus uniformly on all of the areas in their behavior that need development toward greater idealness. Thus, while a given person or group may, after ten years, have made considerable progress in one area, he/she/they may not even have noticed the need for change in several other areas. Americans, affected as they are by the value their culture places on competitiveness, may not even notice the unloving way in which they often compete with each other. Members of cultures that strongly focus on politeness in interpersonal relationships may fail to notice their lack of truthfulness in many situations.

WHICH IDEALS? A CASE STUDY
IN A CROSS-CULTURAL APPROACH TO SIN

A question raised by this consideration is: What ideal(s) does God hold people initially accountable for—his or theirs? It is commonly assumed that God takes only one set of ideals into account—his. If this is so, Christian witnesses have but to present their best understanding of God's ideals and leave it at that. But if what we have been saying concerning God being receptor-oriented is accurate, we need to consider the possibility that God takes seriously any discrepancy between his ideals and those of his receptors.

I shall argue here that God endorses a two-step process in leading people into greater approximation to his ideals. The first step is to lead and empower (by the Holy Spirit) people to *live closer to their own ideals* (model 10e). It is a second step to lead and empower them to *raise their ideals to approximate God's ideals* (model 10f). They then claim the power of the Spirit to assist them in living up to God's ideals.

T. Wayne Dye (1976) has written a very important article on this subject, stimulated partly by a course based on a previous version of this book, partly by Pike 1962:35–45. In it he presents an approach to sin that seeks to be cross-culturally valid. He illustrates this approach and its results from his decade of missionary experience among the Bahinemo people of Papua New Guinea. In what follows I lean heavily on Dye's presentation.

How do cross-cultural Christian witnesses respond to the differences in their perception of sin and those of the people to whom they go? As Christian leaders in their home country they have developed (on the basis of culture-specific interpretational reflexes) an awareness of the discrepancies between God's ideals and the sinful practices of their own people. Adopting the role of prophet, they feel they have a special ability under God of "sensing what is wrong for others by noting what is wrong for [themselves]" (Dye 1976:27). They take this habit and these instincts with them to the foreign culture, of course, but often fail to distinguish properly between the usefulness of this ability in their home culture and its effect in a culture that is strange to them and, therefore, not amenable to their interpretational reflexes. *They are likely to assume that their ability to judge discrepancies between God's ideals and the actual practice in one culture will carry over to the new culture.* Sin is always sin, isn't it?

But no matter how hard he tries to adapt externally, Joe goes to another culture with a heavy load of internalized "cultural baggage." Many of the things which he naturally assumes to be right, sensible, and natural are not in fact biblical ideals at all, but simply part of his own culture. For instance, American values such as efficiency, punctuality, and cleanliness are very important to many American Christians, though hard to document from Scripture. Joe is probably most aware of those things in the host culture which would be wrong at home (Dye 1976:28).

The receptor culture, being human and sinful, will, of course, need to be judged by God's standards. There will be plenty in that culture and in the lives of its people that will need to be dealt with. And the more involved the missionaries get in the culture, the more of these things they become aware of. But their tendency is to work (as they did at home) on the basis of the reflexes developed in another cultural context. They have probably never really analyzed how they made their judgments or even whether the judgments were always appropriate to groups within their culture outside the Christian community in which they developed the reflexes. They probably never learned, even at home, to distinguish between the values they hold as a part of their culture and those that they hold as Christians. Such judgments are intertwined in their experience and not differentiated when they make evaluations of other people's behavior. As they learn the new culture and add evaluations of that behavior to their store of evaluations of home-culture behavior, it is likely that they will attempt to be consistent. For they have been taught as American Christians that God's ideals are constant and unchanging. They believe, furthermore, that they as Christian experts see and apply those ideals accurately and consistently.

So missionaries (or American Christians working among those of another American subculture) constantly speak to their receptors concerning the parts of the latter's behavior and belief that seem worst to them. The receptors, of course, may not be much concerned at all about those things missionaries label "sin." Though the receptors soon become aware of the things a missionary disapproves of and though they have things in their own experience that they feel are morally wrong, it may never occur to them that the Christian witness is talking about moral wrong. Though there are things that they feel guilty about, the cross-cultural witness probably has not touched on many of them and they see no need to feel guilt over the items that upset that witness. Some hearers, often for motives unrelated to the sin problem, may respond and submit to the indoctrination concerning what they are to label as sin. Many have thus learned to "dutifully 'confess' things about which they feel no guilt" like smoking, drinking, polygamy, and dancing. They then become Christians often "without ever repenting of the things which most trouble their consciences" (Dye 1976:28).

For example, in one area with which I am familiar, the local evangelical missionary is extremely concerned with the problems of polygamy, betel nut chewing and smoking. In the thinking of the local people, good behavior is much more a matter of avoidance of discord in the village than it is of what they "eat." Therefore, disobeying husbands and leaders, refusing hospitality and inter-clan payments, and expressing anger are to them far more serious sins.

The local missionary is eager to do what is right, but this is not always communicated to the people. He is extremely stingy with things they would normally share; he doesn't even care enough to learn about their kinship obligations. Furthermore, he appears to be angry ("frustrated," as he sees it) fairly often, so they perceive him as frequently sinning. Local leaders seldom listen to him. Many of his converts have not grasped the meaning of living in obedience to God, and several have fallen into sexual sin.

As a result, this missionary is convinced that he himself must be the judge of the converts, for they do not show enough evidence of real repentance to be trusted. He told me that he focuses on the relatively external matters of smoking and betel nut chewing because he doesn't know the people well enough to ascertain whether they are really loving, etc. These external matters were the only "fruits meet for repentance" that he could easily identify (Dye 1976:28–29).

What can Christian witnesses do differently? Should they "compromise" Christian convictions by "lowering their standards"? Or is there another way that will allow faithfulness to the Scriptures and, at the same time, kindness to the people to whom God has called them? The key lies, I believe, in distinguishing, as the Scriptures distinguish, between God's ideals and the way those ideals are communicated to and responded to by sinful humanity. For God works with and within relative human cultures to promote his supracultural ideals. And we must learn, as Peter has stated, that when God works with humans, patience is not laxness (2 Pet. 3:9). God, rather, exhibits the patience and loving concern that he recommends even while he leads (not drives) us toward his ideals.

Since God is receptor-oriented he takes seriously where his receptors are as well as where he would like then to be eventually. In Scripture we learn about definite standards or ideals that God has set up. Falling short of "God's glory" is sin (Rom. 3:23). Wholehearted love for God and neighbor is the ideal toward which humans are to aim (Mt. 22:37–40). The purpose of Hebrew law and tradition was to bring people to this love (Rom. 13:8–10; 1 Jn. 3:4). To help us to see this aim the Bible presents (1) negative commands (Exod. 20:1–17) and specific sins to be turned away from (Mk. 7:21–23; Gal. 5:19–21), and (2) positive examples such as those of Jesus and others committed to God and verbalized ideals (1 Cor. 13; Gal. 5:22–23). Though these ideals are articulated in terms of the specific cultural contexts in which the biblical events occurred, there is enough evidence in what we have learned of the cultures of the world to suggest that most of these ideals are universally known. But are they universally obeyed?

Dye records his discovery of this fact:

Back before they had had Christian teaching, I tried to translate Jesus' list of sins in Mark 7. As each sin was described, they gave me the local term for it. They named other sins in their culture.

"What did your ancestors tell you about these things?" I asked them.

"Oh, they told us we shouldn't do any of those things."

"Do you think these were good standards that your ancestors gave you?" They agreed unanimously that they were.

"Well, do you keep all these rules?"

"No," they responded sheepishly.

One leader said, "Definitely not. Who could ever keep them all? We're people of the ground" (1976:39).

This kind of knowledge of the ideal, accompanied by the frustration of a felt inability to live up to the ideal, appears to be a worldwide phenomenon. I have experienced it in Nigeria. Dye has found it in the Philippines as well as in New Guinea. "Prohibitions against lying, stealing, murder and adultery are virtually universal, though exactly what constitutes each can vary from culture to culture" (Dye 1976:30). The anthropologist Beals documents similar norms in India (1962:50–52). *People don't seem to need more ideals* (especially foreign ones) to increase their feelings of guilt and frustration. *What they need in the first instance is assistance in dealing with their own ideals.* Even if the missionary or other witness is able to present only biblical ideals (rather than some mixture of these with his own cultural ideals), the result on the receptors can be demoralizing frustration rather than Christian hope. For if they are already discouraged over their inability to live up to their own cultural ideals, how much more discouraging it is to discover that God's requirements are even higher.

We have four sets of ideals to sort out, with partial overlap between them: (1) God has supracultural standards that he has revealed to us in his Word. (2) The revelational information comes to us clothed in the perspectives of the biblical cultures. God's ideals enscripturated are, therefore, mixed with the ideals of the biblical cultures. This fact enables us to gain an understanding of the range of application of God's ideals in human cultures (model 9b). (3) Then we find that we have mixed our perception of God's ideals with the ideals of our own culture. (4) Further, the culture to which we go has its own ideals.

Though these universal moral principles seem clear enough, the actual realization of them is partly determined by each culture. Exactly what actions manifest kindness, humility, peace, or self-control (Gal. 5:22–23)? An executive in an industrial country is being patient if he waits for someone ten minutes. A Bahinemo of Papua New Guinea would think nothing of waiting two hours. In one village in southern Mindanao, my daughter and I were given gifts equal to a month's wages, as a demonstration of their hospitality. In the U.S. the most lavish hospitality to a stranger seldom adds up to a day's wages.

Even such clear statements as the Ten Commandments have as it were, fuzzy borders. For instance, is it [defined as] stealing to pick up a child's toy from a suburban sidewalk? Yes, in the United States. No, in Mexico. In ancient Israel one could pick and eat fruit while passing through another man's orchard, but that would be recognized by everyone as theft in present day Southern California. Many Papua New Guineans see my culture's practice of leaving the care of the elderly to the state as a clear violation of the fifth commandment. My Balinese brethren do not see taking a second wife as adultery, but it would be for me. It seems that the essence of each commandment is clear, but the edges are defined differently by different cultures. God's universal standard must be realized in different situations by different behavior (Dye 1976:30–31).

One major problem in dealing with matters such as these is that we so often unconsciously employ the plain-meaning model (see chapter 7) instead of the Bible-as-tether model (model 9c) plus the dynamic-equivalence model (model 11).[2] Thus we often end up with a procedure such as the following:

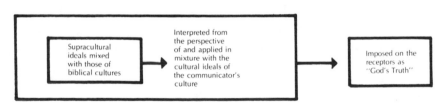

Fig. 12.4. Improper procedure for applying God's ideals.

Another, more scriptural, approach is, however, available. This starts where God starts—with the context of the receptors, rather than with that of the communicator. Romans 2:15–16 shows God's approach in a previous cross-cultural situation. The Gentiles of that day, as well as of this, had enough of God's ideals "written in their hearts" that they had a known standard in terms of which to measure their behavior. Using that standard in the same way that the Hebrews used theirs (the "law"), they found that "their thoughts sometimes accuse them and sometimes defend them." This is the standard, according to Paul, that God will use to judge "all the secret thoughts in men's hearts." Apparently, in spite of strong influences of culture and sin on human understanding of God's ideals, God will judge on the basis of that understanding.

The guilt that God seeks to work from is that which results from perceived

2. Not formally introduced yet; see chapter 13.

discrepancies between *one's own ideals and behavior*, not from the imposition of someone else's ideals. Note Jesus' words in this respect concerning the forgivableness of a *lack of guilt* on the part of those who don't know (Jn. 9:41; 15:22; Lk. 12:47–48). The Galilean towns that refused to repent even after they had seen Jesus' miracles were, however, to be judged severely (Mt. 11:20–24, 12:41–42). *God's judgments are based on the understanding of the receptors* (see also Jas. 4:17).

Within the Christian community the Holy Spirit works with these individualized and communal understandings to enlighten the understandings of truth we already possess, to bring to our awareness truths that are new to us, and to enable us to have the power and the will to live closer to his standards than previously. John 2:27, Romans 8:5–6, and many other passages inform us about these activities of the Spirit.

Even an unbeliever's inner awareness of what is right for him may be more demanding than he admits. His inner standard is brought into play on all sorts of occasions in daily life, and God will use this standard to judge him (Rom. 2:1–8). This explains some other words of Jesus. "God . . . will apply to you the same rules you apply to others" (Matt. 7:2). Why? Because you are aware that it is wrong or you wouldn't use it as a standard for others. "Everyone will have to give an account of every useless word he has ever spoken. For your words will be used to judge you, either to declare you innocent or to declare you guilty" (Matt. 12:36–37).

Francis Schaeffer explained this concept in *Death in the City* (1969:112–13). He compared it to a tape recorder built into every person's brain. At the judgment, God will cause this to play back, contrasting occasions when a man made moral judgments of other people, with other occasions when he himself did what he had condemned. Out of our own mouths we shall be condemned (Dye 1976:32).

People can and do warp and disregard their consciences, of course (1 Tim. 4:2). Culture likewise affects conscience.

It therefore cannot be exactly the same as the Holy Spirit's voice, nor can it be a reliable guide to God's ultimate will for an individual. On the other hand, it is each person's point of awareness of right and wrong, and the principal channel through which the Spirit convicts and enlightens (Prov. 20:27). Knowing this, Jesus appealed to the consciences of the hypocritical Pharisees. As a result they couldn't bring themselves to condemn the woman taken in adultery (John 8:7–9). It is the same way today. Preaching which results in conviction must deal with the issues which are already bothering the consciences of one's hearers (ibid.:32–33).

Within Scripture we see Paul allowing for the cultural conditioning of people's consciences in 1 Corinthians 8 "where the man who perceives an idol as alive sins if he eats sacrificial meat" (Dye 1976:33). To Paul an idol is not a real entity (1 Cor. 8:4). "But only the person who understands this would be free to eat such meat" (ibid.:33). In Romans 14 Paul sums up his approach to the whole matter, saying,

It is not the act itself which is important, but the underlying character of one's relationship to God (Romans 14:17). A man must do what he believes pleases God or be condemned (Rom. 14:12,18, 22,23). Different people will do different, even opposite, things to please God (Rom. 14:2,3,5,6).

God not only judges each of them differently, but actually makes each one succeed in pleasing Him (Romans 14:4). Therefore, we must not be contemptuous of those who feel obliged to follow rules that seem irrelevant, nor should we feel we are more spiritual than those who do not live up to our ideals of Christian behavior (Romans 14:10). Put another way, each of us is answerable to God, not to others. Only the Master knows exactly what He wants each servant to do. We should not judge another person because God may be leading him to obey in quite a different way. Nevertheless, we must be careful not to do things which are wrong for others and will tempt them to follow our example (Romans 14:13–15, 20–21) (Dye 1976:33).

God's (and our) acceptance of culturally inculcated ideals as his starting point does not, as static models would lead us to believe, imply either a lessening of his standards or an absolutizing of those of the culture. For *his starting point is followed by a process*—a process exemplified in the Scriptures. This process is twofold: (1) involving converts in living closer to their own ideals, and (2) the gradual raising of those ideals (as Jesus did in Mt. 5) to more closely approximate God's ideals. Missionaries may have been personally experiencing the first of these for so long that they have forgotten the frustration they felt as non-Christians over their knowledge of high ideals without the power to live anywhere close to them. Furthermore, they may have been brought up in a culture where long ago many of the culture's ideals had, at the surface level (often in form only), been made to appear similar to Christian ideals. They may, thus, be aware only of the *products* of Christian commitment and remain rather ignorant of the *dynamic Spirit-guided processes* by means of which these products have come about. In the new situation, however, it is the ability to initiate and work with those processes that they need.

The problem that most of us have inherited from our background (which includes the inculcation of monocultural, static theological models) is that we try "to hold a universal standard for sin," which we equate with our perception of sin. We not only believe in God's ideals but we feel that we know them well enough to impose them on others. Yet the missionary

has come to understand sin in quite a different way than his hearers do. He finds it hard to believe that God is not even speaking to those people about behavior which would for him be clearly sinful. Without disciplined application of the above principles, the only thing he knows is to preach about "sins" for which they do not feel convicted, and which in fact may not be sin at all for them. At the same time he ignores other sins which are real problems for them. In effect [the missionary] unintentionally takes on the role of the Holy Spirit, instead of cooperating with the Holy Spirit in His work.

In spite of all this, converts are won with such preaching. But they still face some difficult problems. For one thing, they may have a very long struggle learning what God wants for them, since they hear through their consciences. One result may be a slavish obedience to *everything* the missionary suggests or does, including brushing one's teeth and putting flowers on the dinner table. This inability to function independently greatly delays the development of an indigenous church.

Eventually, if the converts are taught the whole range of Scripture, or if they have the Bible for themselves, they may come to see how different is the teaching they have been given from their own sense of what is right. The result is a breakaway, independent church. Barrett (1968) found that among the more than 6000 independent churches in Africa, a common reason given for separation was: The missionaries were living inconsistent lives. In terms of Romans 14, the Africans were tired of trying to live by someone else's conscience.

One group of New Guinea highlanders responded to the mission teaching and were baptized. For several years they tithed, attended church, and followed the mission's "Christian" behavior. Then one day the leaders told the missionary, "We ought to have done enough by now to repay Jesus for his death" (Irwin 1972). They thereupon reverted to paganism. Or did they? Had they ever known real conviction of sin and forgiveness? Or had they only heard about the things that would have been sinful to the missionary if he were living there (Dye 1976:37)?

Dye then goes on to suggest how cross-cultural witnesses can "cooperate with" the consciences of their receptors. Witnesses must first become learners. Nothing in their background has provided them with the reflexes to guide them to react properly in the new cultural world. These they can develop (as Jesus and Paul did) only by long and intensive learning, if then. Such learning, combined with knowledge of scriptural ideals, will enable them to *better* sort out those areas within the receptor culture where God wants to start from other areas (such as those that immediately attract attention because they differ so much from the witness's own culture). Such an investigation will likely show areas in which the Holy Spirit has already begun his convicting work and will certainly show many "points of contact" (Nida 1960:211–15) and many "redemptive analogies" (Richardson 1974) that can profitably be used in the communication of the Gospel. The missionary will also find that most of the culture is quite compatible with and usable in Christianity.

There will be areas, though, where biblical norms conflict with cultural ideals. In such areas God wants to work in and through the culture for change. The missionaries' problem is to learn to work in God's way, even against their "natural" (i.e., cultural) instincts. Dye suggests the following steps:

1. Learn the ethical system of your potential hearers.

2. Compare your findings with your own culture and with the Bible. Become sensitive to the strengths and weaknesses of yours and theirs. This helps overcome blind spots and ethnocentrism.

3. Learn to live a loving life by their cultural standards . . . as a witness to them without going against your own conscience (II Cor. 4:2). For each decision you make, remember which cultural framework you are thinking in: your own culture, their culture, or the New Testament culture. Make decisions within the appropriate cultural framework.

4. Preach repentance for areas in which the Holy Spirit is already convicting. . . . Begin to teach with patience about God's concern and standards for actions which, though cultural, are in conflict with the Bible. Pray that you will be able to accept those aspects of the culture which, though galling, are compatible with the Christian faith.

5. Expect the Holy Spirit to be working, too. Keep getting feedback to find out how He is working, and also as a check on whether you are really communicating. Learn to trust the insights of new converts.

6. Teach the converts to obey and rely on the Holy Spirit. Teach them how to keep their consciences clear so the Holy Spirit can use their consciences to teach them new truths. Expose them to the Bible, not just the "pre-digested" form of your lesson plans Teach them to take from it the principles they need for wise and truly Christian answers (1976:38–39).

Dye started with God where the Bahinemo people were to use their culture with and for God. He explained to them the expectations of God and his disappointment in them in terms of the differences between their behavior and their own ideals. He then pointed out that God's redemptive activity had been performed for the purpose of reuniting them with him so that they could thereby live up to those ideals. Dye says:

This was a crucial step toward their conversion. For the first time the Scriptures were linked to what God was telling them through their consciences. Within a year most of the people in that village had committed themselves to Christ.

Since that day in 1967, they have never lost the awareness that in the Bible God is concerned about their daily behavior and not just talking about strange taboos. Since then, they have changed their source of authority from inherited tradition to the Scriptures, and they have been learning how Christ through His Spirit can come inside them and give them the power to attain the standards they could not keep before. All this has led them into a vital relationship with God and produced a strong indigenous church (1976:39–40).

Would that all missionary endeavor were as dynamically equivalent to the accounts in the book of Acts!

WHAT ABOUT THOSE WHO ARE TODAY "INFORMATIONALLY B.C."? (Model 10g)

Given that God starts his process of transforming those who hear of Christ from the point at which he encounters them, what are the processes that he employs for those who have never heard? If the issue is initial saving faith for those who have never heard rather than the transformation of the behavior of those who respond, what is the process by means of which God reveals himself in and through culture? To deal with this issue we introduce a model (model 10g) that distinguishes between the chronological position of those who have never heard and their position with respect to revelational information.

Revealed information (both general and specific) is necessary for people to respond to. But such information is ineffective unless activated by repersonalization, sometimes by the receptor but perhaps more often by someone else. Spirit-guided witnesses are, therefore, important, but not because people *cannot* know enough to enlighten or condemn them (see Rom. 2). Witnesses are needed basically to provide the *stimulus* that the mere possession of information cannot provide. The witness frequently stimulates both by repersonalizing information already known and by adding information previously unknown to the receptors.

"Paganism" is, according to Maurier (1968), the point at which God starts his saving process. Maurier claims that paganism has today enough information in it, as it has ever had, so that the addition of the proper communicational stimulus can lead people to saving faith in God through Christ. Paganism thus, in some sense, stands in continuity with the Christian Gospel. We have usually assumed discontinuity and antagonism between Christianity and paganism. Yet it was *within* paganism that God stimulated Abraham (and countless others whose stories are not recorded in the Bible) to faith based largely on the knowledge they already possessed. In the Old Testament mention is made of a few of those outside Israel who apparently came to saving faith. Among them were Melchizedek (Gen. 14:18; cf. Ps. 110:4; Heb. 7), Abimelech (Gen. 20), Jethro (Exod. 3), Balaam (Num. 22–24), Job, and Naaman (2 Kings 5). These came within paganism rather than within Israel to the same faith-allegiance to the true God that those saved within Israel experienced. In the New Testament, too, we get a glimpse of such a possibility when, in Acts 18:24–19:7, we see that there were roving bands of John the Baptist's disciples making converts without, apparently, even having heard of Jesus.

If the message and method are the same today as they were in biblical times, we must ask the hard question concerning the necessity of the *knowledge* of Christ in the response of contemporary "pagans." Can people who are chronologically A.D. but knowledgewise B.C. (i.e., have not heard of Christ), or those who are indoctrinated with a wrong understanding of Christ, be saved by committing themselves to faith in God as Abraham and the rest of those who were chronologically B.C. did (Heb. 11)? Could such persons be saved by "giving as much of themselves as they can give to as much of God as they can understand?" I personally believe that they can and many have.

If this is so it in no way excuses Christians from the necessity of communicating the Gospel, however. It is fully consonant with the strong scriptural imperative to communicate God's message persuasively to all peoples. That communication, though, is for the purpose of *stimulating the hearers to action* (in this case, faith commitment to God). It is *not simply for the purpose of imparting new information* (as with a news broadcast). If this perspective is accurate, people in nonwestern cultures, like those in western cultures, are *not lost for lack of information* but for *lack of willingness to respond* properly to what they may already know. The task of the cross-cultural communicator of the Gospel is therefore, like that of the pastor at home, *to stimulate those who know enough* to employ their wills to respond to the God who has not left them without knowledge of him. While cross-cultural witnesses may and should use information that is new to their hearers, they should be careful to (1) start from what their receptors already know, then (2) focus on those portions of biblical information that will be most acceptable and/or most impactful in stimulating the receptor(s) to respond in faith to God.

Though this view does not in the least diminish the imperative to witness for Christ to the ends of the earth, it does change our understanding of the *aim* of Christian witness. It focuses our attention on the proper function of witnessing—stimulation to faith—rather than on the lesser end to which our western predilections would likely lead us—to inundate our hearers with new information. I, as a stimulator who both know the revelational information concerning Christ and have experienced the revelational stimulus that comes from the repersonalization of that information, need to repersonalize that knowledge for my hearers within their frame of reference. Even though I may accept the fact that God continues to save in the same way as in Old Testament times, I dare not let that belief either allow me to fall into universalism so that I assume that people can be saved without making a commitment of their wills to God, or lull me into assuming that because people *could* come to salvation without specific knowledge of Christ that, therefore, many will. People at all times seem to reject God even when they have plenty of knowledge of him.

No one is, of course, saved in any other way than *through* Christ. There is no other authority ("name") by means of which salvation is possible (Acts 4:12). But the same was true for all Old Testament believers, whether or not they knew it. Salvation through faith allegiance to God through the authority and the saving work of Christ is a constant of biblical revelation, rather than a discontinuous feature of the movement from Old Testament to New Testament. The discontinuity from our perspective is in fact that chronologically A.D. people *could* know whereas B.C. people could not know. The fact that such knowledge now exists means, however, that it is available for use as a *stimulus* to faith, not that it is now (unlike in the past) the *only* informational basis for faith. There is no magic in knowing Jesus' name.

A helpful analogy is that of an electric light. One can turn the switch and the light goes on, whether or not the person turning it on knows how the electricity got from its source to the light bulb. Even so, God's requirement for salvation is now and ever has been the turning on of the switch of faith commitment to him. He does not require us to know how that faith activates the relationship between God and humankind. It is important that there be experts (theologians) who study and know as many details as possible concerning the process that results in salvation, just as in electricity it is important that there be electricians who know about the process by means of which the electricity gets to the light bulb. But neither the lighting of the light bulb nor the salvation of the believer depends upon the one who turns the switch having detailed knowledge of how the power gets to its destination.

The clearest exposition of this position that I know is provided by J.N.D. Anderson (1970). He quotes Peter, who discovered "that God has no favorites, but that in every nation the man who is godfearing and does what is right is acceptable to him" (Acts 10:34–35 NEB). Anderson continues:

This cannot mean that the man who tries to be religious and strives to be moral will earn salvation, for the whole Bible denies this possibility. But does it not mean that the man who realizes something of his sin or need, and throws himself on the mercy of God with a sincerity which shows itself in his life (which would always, of course, be a sure sign of the inward prompting of God's Spirit, and especially so in the case of one who had never heard the gospel), would find that mercy—although without understanding it—at the cross on which Christ "died for all"? (Anderson 1970:102).

G. Campbell Morgan, in his commentary on Acts 10:34–35, writes in the same vein that morality cannot save, nor can knowledge. For

no man is to be saved because he understands the doctrine of the Atonement. He is saved, not by understanding it, but because he fears God and works righteousness (Morgan 1945:220, quoted by Anderson 1970:102).

Anderson cites Zwingli and George Goodman (a popular Brethren Keswick Convention speaker of his day) as holding this view as well (see also C. S. Lewis 1956 and 1970:102, and W. White 1969:207–8). "Can we doubt," Anderson says,

that God is able to speak directly to the human heart, and particularly so when neither human messenger nor printed page is available to bear their testimony? What of Melchizedek or Balaam, for example, in the Old Testament, who from outside the covenant people clearly heard and obeyed (or, in Balaam's case, in part obeyed) the voice of God? What of the warnings given in dreams to such persons as Nebuchadnezzar and Abimelech? What, indeed, of the call of Abraham the Aramaean? (Anderson 1970:103).

Goodman asks whether a person can be disqualified from grace merely for lack of knowledge. "If so, where in Scripture do we have the exact amount of knowledge required set out?" If one is to have *assurance* of his salvation, knowledge is important; but "for grace it is not so much knowledge as a right attitude towards God that matters" (Goodman n.d., quoted in Anderson 1970:104). God's message and method are constant.

This position with respect to the place of knowledge should not, we reiterate, result in diminution of missionary activity or urgency. It should, however, help us to recognize that we must go *as those who stimulate to faith by witnessing—not as those who merely convey information* and knowledge. We must go, not (as we may ethnocentrically assume) because our hearers *could not* be saved (for lack of knowledge) but because they, like those in our home country, *will not* ordinarily respond in faith to God on the basis of the knowledge and stimulus they now have. In recognition of this fact, God places us "under orders, explicit and unequivocal, to go to all the world with the good news" (Anderson 1970:106) concerning salvation by faith alone. Any time we exchange that good news concerning faith for bad news concerning lack of knowledge or bad news concerning the necessity of prior adoption of one particular set of understandings (ours), we have betrayed the cause of the One who has called us.

We have now completed our discussion of the dynamics of God's revelation of himself in culture. We next turn to viewing God's constant message in certain alternative forms.

PART V
THE CONSTANT MESSAGE
IN ALTERNATIVE FORMS

13. Dynamic-Equivalence Translation of the Casebook

As the preceding chapters have attempted to make clear, God has manifested an intense desire to see himself communicated to humanity. In this chapter we seek to illustrate and develop that concept by discussing the translation of the Bible. Translation is basic to all kinds of worldview change, including paradigm shifting, conversion (whether Christian or not), and transformational culture change. All appeals for such changes require that the recommended change be communicated via conceptual translation to the receptors within their linguistic and conceptual frame of reference. Even in "scientific revolutions" that result from paradigm shifts, Kuhn states,

what the participants in communication breakdown can do is recognize each other as members of different language communities and then become translators (1970:202).

How much more important is effective translation in stimulating conversion to Christianity (or even to the perspective presented in this book). For since translation allows the participants

to experience vicariously something of the merits and defects of each other's points of view, it is a potent tool both for persuasion and for conversion (Kuhn 1970:202).

Translation, in addition to its value in channeling new concepts to new hearers, has also an important impact on the translators. For they must face their own material in a new way. "A translator must be able to describe the world to which the language being translated applies" (Kuhn 1970:200, fn. 17, based on Nida 1945). If translators are translating the Bible (or other ancient materials) they need to understand the cultural worlds of the Bible as well as that of the receptor language (whether their own or another). The language and culture expertise that this demands of the translators is enormous.

One major purpose of this book is to enable Christian communicators both to realize the importance of developing translational expertise and to increase their ability to develop such expertise. The insights that have come to the author in these areas from his study and practice in Bible translation are woven throughout this book. In this chapter we focus more specifically on these germinal insights and especially on the important concept of "dynamic" or functional equivalence. The changes taking place in understanding of what good translation is are both very instructive and crucial to the perspective being developed here. I will first introduce the change in perspective, then critique the literal or "formal-correspondence" model as a backdrop for our discussion of the dynamic-equivalence model.

HEARER-ORIENTED TRANSLATION

God's desire to communicate himself to human beings has involved him in a variety of interactions with humans. One important result of this, as mentioned above, has been the production of the Bible in the original languages Hebrew, Aramaic, and Greek. For by now

the Christian Church has spread into the entire world where thousands of languages are spoken. Is the Christian revelation restricted to its original languages and to those people who know them or is it capable of universal distribution? The answer is that the Christian revelation is universal and it achieves its universality concretely by the medium of translation so that the translated Scriptures becomes *one of the products of special revelation* (Ramm 1961:188).

God's desire to convey his message to humans within the human cultural and linguistic frame of reference necessitates the translation of God's casebook. God's Spirit has therefore been very active through the years in leading people to translate the Bible. Ramm suggests that such extensive involvement in Bible translation is demanded (1) because of "the universal character of Christianity," (2) "in order to fulfill 'the stewardship of the Bible' " that results from the fact that "the Church is the custodian of the Scriptures," and (3) because God intends that each national regional church possess its own scriptural "product of special revelation . . . the Christian *graphē* in its own language" (1961:188–207). The dynamic nature of Christianity requires that Christians constantly give themselves to the translation and interpretation of the Scriptures so that "what is said in special revelation may be eventually said in all the languages of the world" (ibid.:195). Though "the Christian Church can never grant any version the same status as it does the *graphē* in its original Hebrew, Aramaic and Greek" (ibid.:200), it is possible for good translations to be "authentic products of special revelation" (ibid.:196). For "content of special revelation is not dependent upon the language into which it is *first* cast for its truthfulness" (ibid.:197).

With the number of languages in the world presently standing somewhere in the vicinity of six thousand, the attempt to translate God's Word into every one of them is indeed a formidable undertaking—especially since the task of translation is so demanding. Nevertheless, United Bible Society figures show that by the end of 1974 the whole Bible had been translated and published in 257 languages, the whole New Testament (but not the Old Testament) in 368 more, with some lesser portions in an additional 924 languages. Thus, some portion of the Bible exists in a total of 1,549 of the world's languages, with translation work in process in several hundred additional languages. This makes some part of the divine casebook available to approximately 97 percent of the world's population. The total number of speakers of the remaining several thousand languages comprises but 3 percent of the world's population (United Bible Societies 1975:83).

But the question must be asked concerning just how adequately these translations are conveying the message of God to those for whom they are intended. For, even beyond the tremendous handicap to intelligibility that widespread illiteracy and semiliteracy presents, it must be observed that many of these translations are not giving the impression that God has really mastered the language into which his Word has been translated. The readers of such translations, therefore, often assume that God is a foreigner or out of date or, perhaps, that he has a speech defect (e.g., he can't say "has," only "hath"). Thus when, during World War II, J. B. Phillips asked a group of British youth if they thought God understood radar, their instinctive answer was No (Phillips 1954:65). They had the impression that God was at least three hundred years behind the times—"an old gentleman who lived in the past and was rather bewildered by modern progress" (ibid.). The Bible translation that they continually heard and that provided the language of prayer and church ritual (the King James Version) could leave them with no other impression.

Phillips, however, perceiving that such an impression was not the one that God intended, endeavored to produce a translation that is "hearer-oriented." In dealing with "essential principles of translation," he states:

There seem to be three necessary tests which any work of transference from one language to another must pass before it can be classed as good translation. The first is simply that *it must not sound like a translation at all.* If it is skillfully done, and we are not previously informed, we should be quite unaware that it is a translation, even though the work we are reading is far distant from us in both time and place. . . . I would . . . make this the second test: that a translator does his work with the least possible obtrusion of his own personality. The third and final test which a good translator should be able to pass is that of being able *to produce in the hearts and minds of his readers an effective equivalent to that produced by the author* upon his original readers (Phillips 1958b:ix). [Emphasis added.]

The task of the translator as Phillips (and more recent translation theorists) sees it is to "incarnate" the written word in the language of the receptors. It should (1) sound natural to them, and (2) have an impact upon them as equivalent as possible to that experienced by the original readers of the original writings in the original languages. This process of necessity involves translators in interpretation. They are to be divinely led interpreters of the words and thoughts of the original authors to those of another culture and time. Their interpretation is not properly done if it is simply "a manipulation of the words of . . . Scripture to fit some private point of view" (Phillips 1958b:x). The interpreting is, rather, to be like that of "skilled interpreters in world affairs [who] do not intentionally inject any meaning of their own" (ibid.:x). As Phillips sees it,

the translator's function is to understand as fully and deeply as possible what the New Testament writers had to say and then, after a process of what might be called reflective digestion, to write it down in the language of the people today (1958b:x.).

The task of the Bible translator is, therefore, the same in essence as that (1) of God when he seeks to communicate in language across the cultural-supracultural barrier, (2) of any witness (such as the authors of Scripture, a missionary, or a "personal worker") who seeks to communicate the message of God to any person or group who stands on the other side of a cultural and/or psychological barrier, or (3) of any preacher who seeks correctly and helpfully to interpret and apply the message to the lives of his hearers. All, if they are to communicate effectively, must be hearer-oriented, presenting their (i.e., God's) message with relevance and impact according to the basic principles of communication science discussed above (chapters 8 and 9).

FORMAL CORRESPONDENCE: AN INADEQUATE MODEL

The once prevalent literalistic, or "formal-correspondence," model of translation is based upon a very limited understanding of translation. The focus of this understanding is on the surface-level linguistic *forms* through which the message is conveyed. Primary attention is given to the words employed, and the specific details of the grammatical structures of the source language. The major concern with respect to the receptor language is often little more than to discover the corresponding word forms in that language and to render the original as literally as possible. Since those who translate literally see languages as merely alternative codes for the same reality, they seek insofar as possible to render each word in the source language by a single word in the receptor language. In the name of consistency, then, they attempt always to render a given source-language word by the same receptor-language word. Even the word order of the source language is often followed.

The focus on the minute analysis of the linguistic surface structure of the source language is not a wrong emphasis but a partial one. It tends to minimize the attention paid to the deep-level cultural context in which words participate and from which they derive their meanings. Word-for-word translation and the consistency principle are, however, the result of misunderstandings of the nature of language and of the translation process itself. The results of such emphases tend to be wooden and foreign-sounding. The literalists' focus sees but dimly the livingness of the original encoding of the message. Furthermore, it often ignores completely the contemporary cultural and linguistic involvement of any but the most theologically indoctrinated of the readers. Its aim is to be "faithful to the original documents." But this "faithfulness" centers almost exclusively on the surface-level forms of the linguistic encoding in the source language and their literal transference into corresponding linguistic forms in the receptor language. As discussed previously, however, when the forms are retained from culture to culture and language to language, the meanings are inevitably changed.

Among the typical characteristics of formal-correspondence translations are the following:

1. Formal-correspondence translations aim *simply to transfer the word forms* of the source language into the corresponding word forms of the receptor language. When Paul employs a word that in Greek is used as the name for "bowels," the King James Version renders it "bowels" (e.g., Phil. 1:8; 2:1). In spite of the fact that the term is clearly being employed figuratively (signifying "affection" or "kindness") in these passages, the King James translators felt bound to what they understood to be the basic meaning of the word.

Other examples of such inadequate literalism shared by the King James, American Standard, and Revised Standard versions are found in Mark 1:4, where the English word forms "baptism of repentance" are employed to express what would more naturally be conveyed in English by an expression such as "turn away from your sins and be baptized" (TEV); Matthew 3:8, where "bring forth . . . fruits meet for repentance" is used to express what in Greek signified something like "do the things that will show that you have turned from your sins" (TEV); and Luke 20:47, where "which devour widows' houses" is the literal rendering of what in English would have to be represented as "who take advantage of widows and rob them of their homes" (TEV).

2. In addition, a formal-correspondence translation attempts insofar as possible *to render each given word consistently* in the source language more or less mechanically *by the same term in the receptor language.* Thus the Revised Standard Version translates the Greek word *soma* as "body" in each of the following verses: Matthew 6:25; Mark 5:29; Luke 17:37; Romans 12:1; and Colossians 2:11, since "body" in English may be taken to be the main "literal" meaning of the word and the translators wanted to be consistent. What they did not seem to undertand is that the Greek word and the English word are far from exactly equivalent to each other. That is, the Greek word *soma* covers a different area of meaning from the English word "body." If, therefore, the English translation is to be true to the Greek meaning, *soma* should be differently rendered whenever the context so indicates. In Mark 5:29, for example, the English rendering that most naturally conveys the Greek meaning of *soma* in that context will be "(her)self," rather than "her body" (RSV, KJV, ASV, NIV). In Luke 17:37 a more meaningful rendering would be "corpse"; in Romans 12:1 it would be "selves" and in Colossians 2:11 it would be something like "lower nature" (rather than the RSV's puzzling but literal "body of flesh").

Nida and Taber instructively chart this contrast by citing the relevant portion of these verses as rendered by one formal-correspondence translation (RSV) and two dynamic-equivalence translations (NEB and):

---

1. Matthew 6:25

RSV: about your body
NEB: clothes to cover your body
TEV: clothes for your body

2. Mark 5:29

RSV: she felt in her body
NEB: she knew in her self
TEV: she had the feeling inside herself

3. Luke 17:37

RSV: where the body is
NEB: where the corpse is
TEV: where there is a dead body

4. Romans 12:1

RSV: present your bodies
NEB: offer your very selves
TEV: offer yourselves

5. Colossians 2:11

RSV: putting off the body of flesh
NEB: divested of the lower nature
TEV: freed from the power of this sinful body

Fig. 13.1 Illustrative translations of the Greek word *soma* (literally, ''body''); from Nida and Taber 1969:15.

For further exemplification of this point compare the translations of the words *(sarks* and *dikaioo)*—in a formal-correspondence translation such as King James, American Standard, or Revised Standard and a good dynamic-equivalence translation such as Good News for Modern Man (TEV), Phillips, or New English Bible (see Figs. 13.2 and 13.3).

Literally thousands of such illustrations can be produced from the King James, American Standard, and Revised Standard versions. These formal-correspondence translations from Greek and Hebrew, on the one hand, obscure and sometimes obliterate the intended meanings and, on the other, appear unnatural to or mislead the reader.

3. Formal-correspondence translations are produced in adherence to *nineteenth-century concepts of the nature of language.* These concepts saw each

	ASV	NEB	TEV
1. Luke 24:39	flesh	flesh	flesh
2. II Corinthians 7:5	our flesh had no rest	poor body	we
3. Romans 11:14	mine own flesh	men of my own race	people of my own race
4. Acts 2:17	all flesh	everyone	men
5. Romans 8:3	through the flesh	lower nature	human nature
6. II Corinthians 10:3	in the flesh	weak men	world . . . worldly
7. I Corinthians 1:26	according to the flesh	human standard	human point of view

Fig. 13.2 Illustrative translations of the Greek word *sarks* (literally, "flesh"); from Nida and Taber 1969:17.

	RSV	NEB	TEV
1. Matthew 12:37	justified	acquitted	declared innocent
2. Luke 7:29	justified	praised (God)	obeyed (God's righteous demands)
3. Luke 16:15	justify	impress . . . with righteousness	make yourselves look right in man's sight
4. Romans 3:4	justified	vindicated	be shown to be right
5. Romans 3:24	justified	justified	are . . . put right

Fig. 13.3. Illustrative translations of the Greek word *dikaioo* (literally, "justified"); from Nida and Taber 1969:18.

language as an alternative code made up of a different set of labels for the *same reality*. Early in this century, however, anthropologists and linguists began to recognize that understandings of reality are structured differently by different cultures and that these differences are strongly reflected in their languages.[1] There is, therefore, no such thing as an exact correspondence between a given word in one language and the most nearly corresponding word in another language. If we depict cultures (including their languages) as geometrical figures divided by lines to indicate the way these cultures segment reality, we can in very oversimplified fashion indicate the differences between the older concept and the modern one.

Since cultures and their languages do not correspond exactly with each other, formal-correspondence translations frequently are found to create the misimpression that God requires us to learn a foreign (i.e., Hellenized or Hebraicized) version of English before we can really understand him. They do this by employing English labels (words) to designate the segments into which the Greek or Hebrew languages are divided, not those into which English is

1. See especially the writings of Edward Sapir and Benjamin Lee Whorf. A valuable corrective to the temptation to carry "the Sapir-Whorf hypothesis" too far is provided by Nida 1971.

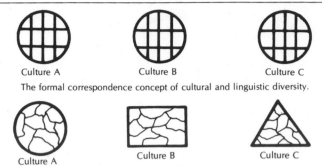

Culture A   Culture B   Culture C

The formal correspondence concept of cultural and linguistic diversity.

Culture A   Culture B   Culture C

The modern formal noncorrespondence understanding of cultural and linguistic diversity.

Fig. 13.4. Differing understandings of cultural and linguistic diversity.

---

divided. Preachers using literal translations, then, have to devote much of their time to explaining that the apparently English words don't, in the Bible, have their normal English meanings. They, rather, have Greek and Hebrew meanings, which only those who have studied the original languages can properly understand and explain.

An oversimplified diagram of the formal-correspondence understanding of the process of translation would look like this:

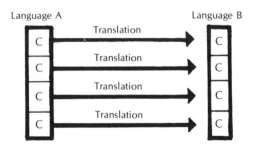

Fig. 13.5. The formal-correspondence understanding of the translation process; C=concept.

Attention is given by the translator to understanding the concept linguistically and to transferring it literally into the receptor language in, as far as possible, the same number of words as were required in the source language.[2]

2. The RSV translators, for example, naively pride themselves on the fact that the RSV is "terse," containing "fewer words than the former authorized versions, and certainly fewer than . . . Weymouth, Moffatt and Goodspeed" (Weigle 1946:56–57).

If the cultural and/or linguistic situation contains implications that the reader of the receptor language cannot understand (and it always does), it is considered invalid to add even brief explanatory phrases (paraphrase) to the translation. For the process of translation is conceived of (in keeping with certain values of western culture) as basically word-centered rather than idea-centered. Any such addition of words is considered paraphrase and, therefore, not allowed in a translation.

Such an approach to translation means (among other things) that the reader of the receptor language is held accountable for a good bit of knowledge of the source culture from which the linguistic structures derive their meanings. If, for example, Hausa is the source language, a formal-correspondence translation into English of one of the most common types of question-answer situations would be intelligible only to one who knows Hausa (or another language whose culture shares this particular characteristic). An English speaker who does not already understand Hausa will get exactly the opposite of the intended meaning via a literal translation of the following exchange:

Question: "Isn't there any work for me?"
Answer: "No."

An English hearer/reader of this literal translation would assume that there was no work for the questioner, since the literal translation of the answer is "no,"—unless, of course, the English speaker knows enough Hausa to be able to ascertain the true meaning in spite of the translation. What is actually being said, in the proper Hausa manner, is:

Question: "There is no work for me is there?"
Answer: "Not true. On the contrary, there *is* work for you."

Some such expansion of the words is absolutely necessary and entirely appropriate in order to make the meaning of the translation equivalent to that of the original, for the differing impact of the corresponding linguistic forms in the two different cultural contexts needs to be compensated for in the translation. A translation that requires the hearer/reader to fill in the necessary additional understanding or to depend on experts for the true meaning is inadequate.

THE DYNAMIC-EQUIVALENCE MODEL

Informed translators, however, attempt to produce translations that do not require the readers to supply such additional understanding or expertise. They aim to produce translations that are so true to both the message of the source documents and the normal ways of expressing such a message in the receptor language that the hearers/readers can, by employing their own interpretational reflexes, derive the proper meanings. In formal-correspondence translations such as the Revised Standard, American Standard, King James, NASV, and, largely, NIV, there is a non-English flavor because the translators have not carried their task far enough. They have not made sure that the English renderings function equivalently to their referents in Hebrew,

Aramaic, and Greek. The impression is of stiltedness and foreignness, since it does not represent the way people talk and write in English. Informed translators have come to recognize that "a so-called word-faithful translation may well result in a meaning-faithless translation" (Ramm 1961:203).

The great difference in such translations as Phillips, Today's English Version, New English Bible, and the Living Bible[3] is due to the fact that their translators got beyond the mere surface-level word-and-grammar forms both in the source and in the receptor languages. Those translators had to dig more deeply into the source cultures and to carry their renderings more totally into the kind of expression that is natural to the receptor language and culture. To do this, Phillips states that

I have found *imaginative sympathy, not so much with words as with people,* to be essential. . . . I have attempted, as far as I could, to think myself into the heart and mind of Paul, for example, or of Mark or of John the Divine. Then I tried further to imagine myself as each of the New Testament authors *writing his particular message for the people of today.* . . . This has been my ideal, and that is why consistency and meticulous accuracy have sometimes been sacrificed in the attempt to transmit freshness and life across the centuries (Phillips 1958b:xii). [Emphasis added.]

The "consistency and meticulous accuracy" to which Phillips refers, and which he says he sometimes sacrificed, however, were only those defined in terms of the formalistic, literalistic translation theory that he was breaking away from. In another, more important, sense Phillips was demonstrating consistency and accuracy. He was attempting to produce a translation consistent with the aims of God and the authors—to communicate. *He aimed to be accurate with respect to the use God and the authors sought to make of language.* He aimed to use language as a vehicle for the message, not as something that needs to be studied microscopically to wrest from it its meaning.

These writings, says Phillips,

are alive, and they are moving—in both senses of that word—and their meaning can no more be appreciated by cold minute examination than can the beauty of a bird's flight be appreciated by dissection after its death (1958b:xi).

The new aim is to go *beyond* the focus of the earlier translation theory. There is still focus on words, grammar, and expression—but for the purpose of building a communicational bridge between the author and the contemporary hearer. And building such a bridge must take into account the cultural and linguistic involvement of both the ancient author and the contemporary hearer. The informed translator *endeavors to be faithful both to the original author*

---

3. Though these translations are all receptor-oriented, they are of two types. Phillips, TEV, and NEB are *inter*language translations from the original languages into English. LB, however, is an *intra*language translation, from one style of English (that of the ASV) into another style of English—a receptor-oriented style. Both types of translation are valid.

and message and to the intended impact that that message was to have upon the original readers. Such a translator seeks to elicit from contemporary readers of the New Testament a response equivalent to that elicited from the original readers of the slangy, communicative Koine (=common people's) Greek. Thus, in recognition of the nonequatability of languages, informed translators seek renderings that go beyond mere correspondence in form. They use receptor-language constructions that function in the receptors' cultural world to convey meanings that are equivalent to the original meanings in the New Testament Greek-speaking world. Due to the nonequatability of the forms of languages and cultures, these meanings will never exactly duplicate the original meanings in the Greek world. But they should carry an *equivalent impact* in English. Such a dynamic-equivalence translation is described as "the closest natural equivalent to the source-language message." It is "directed primarily toward equivalence of response rather than equivalence of form" (Nida 1964:166). The quality of such a translation (as of any translation) is to be evaluated

in terms of the degree to which the receptors of the message in the receptor language respond to it in substantially the same manner as the receptors in the source language [responded to the original]. This response can never be identical, for the cultural and historical settings are too different, but there should be a high degree of equivalence of response, or the translation will have failed to accomplish its purpose (Nida and Taber 1969:24).

An important concomitant of this dynamic view of Bible translation is the fact that effective translation involves more than simply the conveying of information. According to Nida and Taber,

It would be wrong to think . . . that the response of the receptors in the second language is merely in terms of comprehension of the information, for communication is not merely informative. It must also be expressive and imperative if it is to serve the principal purposes of communications such as those found in the Bible. That is to say, a translation of the Bible must not only provide information which people can understand but must present the message in such a way that people can feel its relevance (the expressive element in communication) and can then respond to it in action (the imperative function) (1969:24).

This understanding of what is involved in translating the Bible is considerably more aware than previous understandings of the complexity both of language (and culture) itself and of the process of moving concepts from one language to another.

The new understanding of what translation involves recognizes that *the central aim is communication, not mere literalness* for its own sake (or out of reverence for words regarded as too sacred to change). The biblical writers, however, intended to be understood, not to be admired or to have their writings so highly thought of that they would be transmitted in unintelligible or misleading forms. Faithful translation involves doing whatever must be done (even including a certain amount of explanatory paraphrase, such as in the Hausa example above) in order to make sure that the message originally phrased in the words and idioms of the source language is faithfully phrased in the functionally equivalent words and idioms of the receptor language.

For the real issue in translation lies outside the mere words of the source and receptor languages in and of themselves. It lies in the *impact* of the concepts embodied in the linguistic forms *on the reader/hearer*. If the impact is such that it results in wrong understanding, misunderstanding, or lack of understanding on the part of the average, unindoctrinated reader/hearer, the translation has failed. Thus it is that a primary question asked by the new approach is, "How does the receptor language require that this concept be expressed in order both to be intelligible and to convey an impact equivalent to that experienced by the original readers/hearers?" Whatever of paraphrase must (because of the requirements of the target language and culture) be included in the translation to make it equivalently intelligible and impactful is legitimately to be called "translation." It should not be dismissed as "mere paraphrase" (in a negative sense) or (as in KJV) italicized as if it were optional matter inserted at the whim of the translator.

Such a revision in our understanding of translation theory has been made possible by a plethora of new insights into the nature and functioning of language and the linguistic capacities of humans. In this area the conclusions (models) of anthropologists, linguists, psychologists, and other behavioral scientists are coming to be regarded as more realistic than the speculations of the philosophers and philologists, on which most theological conclusions concerning language have been largely based.

These insights provide us with new and instructive perspectives on both linguistic communication and the process of transference (translation) from one language to another. Following Nida and Taber (1969:3–8) we may summarize several of these insights as they relate to our topic:

1. *Each language has its own genius*, its own distinctiveness, its own special character. Each has its own grammatical patterns, its own peculiar idioms, its own areas of vocabulary strength and its own weaknesses and limitations.

2. *To communicate effectively in another language one must respect this uniqueness* (both the strengths and the weaknesses) and work in terms of it. Attempts to "remake" languages to conform to other languages have been monumentally unsuccessful. The effective translator is, therefore, "quite prepared to make any and all formal changes necessary to reproduce the message in the distinctive structural forms of the receptor language" (p. 4).

3. *Anything that can be said in one language can be represented adequately (i.e., within the allowable range) though never exactly, in another*, unless the form is an essential element of the message. Thus, as with poetry, when the form is essential to the full meaning, one might say that translation is impossible. However, this is simply an extreme example of the fact that a translation can

never mean exactly what the original did. There will always be losses of information (largely contextual) contained in the original and gains of information due to the requirements of the receptor language. And this fact of translation is an example of the fact that "no communication, even within a single language, is ever absolute (for no two people ever understand words in exactly the same manner)" (p. 4). But though translation and communication can never transmit the original intent absolutely or exactly, they may be adequate if the focus is on the content to be transmitted rather than on the mere preservation of the literal forms of the source language.

4. *To preserve the content of the message the form must be changed.* It is a fact that different languages express quite similar concepts in very different ways and no concepts in exactly the same ways. The faithful translator, therefore, in attempting to convey an equivalent message in terms of the genius of the receptor language must alter the form in which that message was expressed in the original language.

If an equivalent meaning is to be conveyed, the forms employed must be as appropriate for expressing those meanings in the receptor culture as the source forms are in the source culture. The appropriate forms should be largely those that are natural (with respect to the given meaning) in the receptor language, rather than those that happen to correspond in some formal way to the source-language words. Heavy borrowing of terms with which the receptors are not familiar is also to be avoided. If the source language and the receptor language participate in fairly similar cultures (as do, e.g., English and any of the European languages) changes of form in going from one to another will usually not be great. But *the greater the linguistic and cultural distance between the source and the receptor languages, the greater the number and extent of the formal changes required to preserve the meaning.* This principle has had an interesting effect on even the literal translations. The greater cultural distance between Hebrew and English has forced the translators to prepare better translations of the Old Testament than of the New. They have to translate well or the result makes no sense at all. The smaller cultural and linguistic distance (often more apparent than real) between Greek and English has, however, given rise to greater literalism in New Testament translation, since literal translations from similar languages *seem* to make good sense.

Distance between languages need not, however, always be distance along a "horizontal" axis as, for example, between contemporary English and contemporary Zulu or Hindi. It may as well be distance along a "vertical" or nearly vertical axis as, for example, between contemporary English and seventeenth-century "King James" English, or between a contemporary European language and a first-century European language like Greek.

5. *The languages of the Bible are subject to the same limitations as any other natural languages.* They are, therefore, not rightly regarded if they are treated as too sacred to analyze and truly translate in the modern sense. The biblical languages are no more perfect or precise than other languages for, according to

Nida and Taber (1969:7), some seven hundred grammatical and lexical ambiguities have been counted in the Greek Gospels alone! Biblical languages, like all others, show great strengths in certain areas and great liabilities in other areas. Furthermore, as is true of all languages, the Greek and Hebrew vocabulary, idiom, and grammar that we see employed in the Bible participate fully in and have their intended meaning *only* in terms of their interaction with the culture in which these languages were used. The authors did not invent unknown words or use them in unknown ways except as anyone is allowed by his or her culture to innovate on occasion to convey new insight. "All the vocabulary was itself rooted in the finite experience of men and women, and all of the expressions must be understood in terms of this type of background" (p. 7). That is, *it is the message of the Bible that is sacred, not the languages themselves,* even though it is in terms of these finite, imperfect, culture-bound languages that the sacred message is conveyed.

6. *The writers of the Bible books expected to be understood.* To many Americans, accustomed to hearing and reading God's Word from a literal translation and accustomed to hearing preachers forced to use great amounts of their pulpit time trying to explain into intelligibility the strange-sounding "translationese" of these versions, the idea that the authors expected to be understood comes as a shock. Yet, "the writers of the Bible were addressing themselves to concrete historical situations and were speaking to living people confronted with pressing issues" (p. 7). They were not trying to be obscure. The translator, therefore, to keep faith with the original authors and the God for whom they spoke, is obligated to attempt to produce a translation that makes the same kind of sense in the receptor context that the original writing made in the source context.

7. *The translator must attempt to reproduce the meaning of a passage as understood by the writer.* It is the writings of Matthew and Luke, for instance, that we are to translate, not, as some have contended, the deduced Aramaic words of Jesus that these authors are reporting in Greek. And this is true even when there are apparent contradictions, as when in the Beatitudes Luke quotes Jesus as saying, "Blessed are the poor" (Lk. 6:20), while Matthew refers to the "spiritually poor" in the parallel passage (Mt. 5:3). Nor should the translator read back into the author's words *subsequent meanings* of these words, as has often been done. This was the case when the King James Version translators read back into the Hebrew *almah* ("young woman") in Isaiah 7:14 the meaning "virgin." They were influenced in their translation by the fact that several hundred years after that passage was written the "maiden" (Jerusalem Bible's rendering) to which that prophecy referred was in fact a technical virgin. Thus, when Matthew refers to that prophecy (1:23), he employs the Greek term for virgin. A similar "reading back into" has resulted in the Living Bible translating John 21:15–17 in such a way as to draw a sharp distinction between the two Greek words for "love" used there by John. The translation of these words into English should not differ, however, since throughout his writing John employs *phileo* and *agapao* interchangeably, and English covers the whole area of

meaning with one word. The Living Bible translation is influenced by the subsequent historical fact that the Christian church came eventually to employ *agapao* to the exclusion of *phileo* to refer to God's love.

This dynamic-equivalence model of translating goes far beyond the formal-correspondence model in its understanding of language, the cultural setting of language, and the complexity of the translation process itself. This leads to a new and more demanding set of procedures, which contrast markedly with the simplistic direct approach to translation of the literalists. The procedure may be briefly indicated by the following diagram:[4]

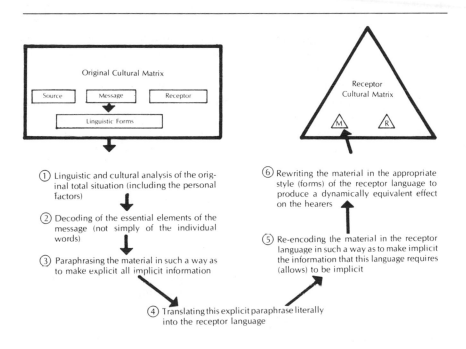

Fig. 13.6 Dynamic-equivalence translation procedure.

Even good, dynamically equivalent translations of the Bible cannot do the whole job of communicating the Christian message, however. There must be, as explained above (chapter 11), repersonalization of the message in the receptor's frame of reference. There must also be frequent explanations of cultural backgrounds, applications to present situations, and the like that are not properly a part of translation. These we term "transculturations." We now turn to this aspect of our treatment.

4. Modeled after certain of the diagrams in Nida 1960.

14. Dynamic-Equivalence Transculturation of the Message

Behind the meanings of the Bible and Christian experience that can be translated lie deeper meanings that can be expressed only in greater life involvement between communicators and receptors than translation allows. This life involvement includes linguistic communication but is not, at its most effective, limited to mere verbalization. The verbalization that does occur (and there may be much) is most effective when it is most closely related to the personal experience of the participants.

A translation is tied to the historical setting in which the original events occurred. A translation, even a dynamically equivalent one, dare not change the cultural setting of the original events. In most attempts to communicate the Word, however, the essential messages of God need to be "transculturated" into the receptors' cultural setting (model 11b). For today's receptors, Jesus needs to walk their paths, eat in their homes. The receptors need to live and learn, as the original disciples did, in Jesus' presence today. For this they need dynamic witnesses, living and speaking a dynamically equivalent message in terms of the receptors' perceptual grids. That is what this chapter is about.

WE PARTICIPATE IN GOD'S COMMUNICATION

Like those with whom the Master shares his plans, we are "in the know." Like those who have received the full Spirit-guided impact of effective communication from God, we are transformed into those committed to the cause for which he gives himself. Like those who share a commitment with God, we are called to participate in his communicative activity. We "stand in Jesus' shoes" today. "As the Father sent me, so I send you" (Jn. 20:21), said Jesus. And Paul admonishes us to go, characterized by the attitude of Christ and following his example (Phil. 2:5). We are to continue the personal, interactional communication that God has carried out with and through his people through the centuries.

God undoubtedly can still communicate to humanity directly, as he apparently did with Adam, Abraham, Moses, and many others. But for some reason he chooses not to much of the time. Someone has said, "Without him we *can't*, but without us he *won't*." He calls us to participate with him in his desire to cross communicational barriers to get his message across to humanity. As he

276

once came as a human being, so he continues to reach human beings through human beings. We go with God in Jesus' stead (2 Cor. 5:20). His method is still incarnational.

We are God's *agents* and *partners*. We are also his *ambassadors* (2 Cor. 5:20), his *heralds* (translated "preachers" 1 Tim. 2:7; 2 Tim. 1:11), and his *witnesses* (Lk. 24:48; Acts 1:8)—witnesses for Christ. As ambassadors, heralds, and witnesses we are responsible persons, possessed of a degree of freedom and self-determination but linked inseparably to the source of our authority and that to which we testify.

As *witnesses* we are pictured as those who have been personally involved in an experience and, having been involved, can faithfully testify (as we would in court) to the occurrence and details of that event. As *heralds* we give reports in "good voice" that have not originated with us. For behind our report

stands a higher power. The herald does not express his own views. He is the spokesman for his master. . . . Heralds adopt the mind of those who commission them, and act with the plenipotentiary authority of their masters (Friedrich 1965:688).

In the ambassador analogy, the focus is on the fact that we are official representatives "of the highest rank," as those who are "accredited to a foreign sovereign or government as the resident representative of his own sovereign or government" (Webster's *Dictionary* 1967). Thus we stand accredited by God as his official representatives to the world from the "kingdom of God." And in this we stand "in the shoes" of the Son of God himself.

An attempt to understand and apply these three analogies uncovers several valuable insights:

1. *We are to be ambassadors, heralds, and witnesses for Christ, not for ourselves.* Witnesses may speak on their own behalf, though in court at least one is under oath to speak "the truth, the whole and nothing but the truth" as the person perceives it. But heralds or ambassadors cannot speak for themselves alone. For they speak or act on behalf of another—the ruler and/or government that they represent. They must frequently consult with their leader and attempt as faithfully as possible to apply the leader's solutions to the problems at hand. And even when, on occasion, a herald or ambassador might say, "This is my opinion, not my leader's," the hearers are unlikely to grant him or her the privilege of an independent opinion. Thus we treat Paul when he makes similar statements (1 Cor. 7:6; 2 Cor. 11:17).

2. *Our witness is to be to our experience with God.* Here, under the more widely employed witness analogy, we are a bit more free than if we were simply heralds or ambassadors. At this point John and the other New Testament writers both state and show the way. We are to testify concerning "that which we have seen and heard" (1 Jn. 1:3). But, because of the uniqueness of the experience of each of us, we are not to be conformed to a single "party line."

Indeed, in a law court, if two witnesses present their stories in too similar a fashion they will be suspected of collusion and their testimonies discounted. People are not the same and no two people will perceive even the same event in exactly the same way. There is a range of allowable variation, and their accounts of the event will differ at significant points—unless they have gotten together ahead of time and agreed to parrot the same story. Such collusion and harmonization of accounts involves, according to Paul D. Fueter, the "mythologization" of the account. This drive to harmonize and to arrive at a single "authorized" (and mythologized) version of any given event or set of events he sees as a natural human tendency. And there is plenty of evidence, especially from the folklore of every culture, to support his point.

It is significant to observe that the biblical writers manifest a wide variety of individual perspectives. We can be certain, therefore, that they did not get together to mythologize their impressions into a single harmonized account. They spoke as individual witnesses. Fueter suggests

that the biblical authors, whether priests or prophets, apostles or evangelists consistently fought against man's natural tendency to mythologize. . . . The very fact that four different Gospels and not a harmony were recognized as fundamental by the Early Church proves that it was concerned about historical events as seen through several eyes. When one is aware of the human tendency to mythologize any great man's sayings and life, one must be amazed at the deliberate effort of the evangelists to situate the time and place of the events they are recording. Luke's introduction, Papias' description of how Mark's Gospel came to be written, John's statement as to his purpose, Matthew's composition, all point the same way. *The Early Church did not mythologize as some schools of theologians want us to believe,* but controlled the media at its disposal. *It wanted to curb the religious enthusiasm for legend and hero worship* (1971:444). [Emphasis added.]

The impact of the unharmonized testimonies of a wide variety of individuals, all witnessing according to their own perception concerning a transforming relationship with God, whether in biblical days or in our own, powerfully supports the validity of the message. And an important concomitant of such variety of witness is to "de-legendize," or demythologize, the witness.

3. We not only witness for God and in terms of our individual perceptions of our interaction with him, *we also are to witness for the sake of others.* We are, according to Jesus, sent into the world just as he was sent into the world (Jn. 17:18). We, like him, are not "to be served, but to serve" and to give our lives for others (Mt. 20:28). Our witness, like John's (1 Jn. 1:3; Jn. 20:30–31), Luke's (Lk. 1:1–4; Acts 1:1–5), Paul's (2 Cor. 5:20), and that of the other writers of Scripture, is for the sake of others.

Indeed, both the witness and the herald/ambassador analogies must have been chosen because they show the necessity of receptors as well as the necessity of a source. For both witness and herald/ambassador are obliged to speak and act relevantly as well as truly. A witness who does not present testimony intelligibly or in such a way that it is perceived by the hearers as bearing on the case is a worthless witness. Likewise, heralds/ambassadors whose representation is perceived as unrelated to the interests of the country in which they serve.

To employ for the moment an impersonal analogy, we are to function like electric cords that are as well plugged in at the "human end" as at the "God end." Otherwise there is no way that the "current of God," the message that we are called to live and deliver, can get to those around us for whose sakes we were commissioned ambassadors. Unfortunately, all too often the impression given by those who train people for witness is that if we are careful to plug in solidly at the God end, the other end will take care of itself. Such however, is not the case, as thousands of theologically sound but irrelevant-to-hearer sermons, Bible studies, Sunday school lessons, books, "personal" witnessing encounters, missionary efforts, service projects, and the like amply testify.

In this connection it is worth repeating John V. Taylor's heartbreaking statement made in a 1971 lecture at the School of World Mission, Fuller Seminary:

When my son decided to give up on the Church, he said to me, "Father, that man [the preacher] is saying all of the right things, but he isn't saying them *to* anybody. He doesn't know where I am and it would never occur to him to ask!"

Our witness is to be for the sake of others (as well as for the sake of God). Bitter experience, such as this has, however, time and time again demonstrated the ease with which a message that is intrinsically the most relevant, needed communication the world has ever known can be perceived as irrelevant. And this can happen even when that message is handled by very devoted witnesses. As witnesses (God's electric cords) we are to be plugged in tightly at *both* ends.

4. *We are to witness persuasively.* And here scriptural teaching concerning our role transcends the witness analogy. A herald or ambassador, however, frequently has to speak persuasively on behalf of "a higher power" to see that the master's or government's best interests are served. For, as Paul emphasizes throughout the fifth chapter of 1 Corinthians, our consuming desire to please God (v. 9) commits us irrevocably to speak a message the aim of which is the reconciliation to God of those to whom we speak (v. 19). It is for this reason that we attempt to persuade people (v. 11). Indeed, we "implore" them to "be reconciled to God" (v. 20 NEB).

Approaches to witness that consider mere "presence" or "dialogue" without persuasion as sufficient have not taken the herald/ambassador analogy seriously (see Tippett 1973). Nor have they taken the example of Jesus and his early followers seriously. In reaction against certain very real excesses—such as proselytization aimed at simply converting the hearer to the culture of the speaker (see chapter 17)—they have abandoned the ultimate aim of the Gospel message, the reconciliation of people to God. In place of this ultimate end of our ambassadorship they have turned to a marvelous *means* for accomplishing the end. They have focused upon the fact that in order to serve our Lord properly we have to genuinely be *with* those whom we serve (this is called "Christian presence"). In this context, then, we are to enter into the kind of sympathetic "dialogue" with them that shows them we are as willing to learn from them as we are to teach them.

Dialogue is a marvelous methodology, which provides a much needed corrective to the self-centered, "I have all the answers, you have none" spirit that Christians have often manifested. But the discovery of a better means of presenting the message of God to which we have been called to witness does not warrant the abandoning of the aim of the message—the reconciling of people to God. We are to get genuinely "with" those to whom we witness and we certainly have much to learn from them. But our primary model for witness is Jesus Christ, and he had something of supreme value to communicate as well as something to learn (Heb. 5:8).

A DYNAMICALLY EQUIVALENT MESSAGE

We have now dealt with both the human witness and how properly to translate the written witness. In each case this approach recommends a primary focus on the receptor, in addition to the traditional importance accorded to the divine source of the message. But what should the message itself look like to the receptor?

Just as a translation should be dynamically equivalent in its impact to the original writings, so should the message that flows through either the personal or the written witness. As I have attempted to prove above, the effective communication of that message involves both a credible witness and a good translation. But in order to be properly perceived by the hearer that message has to be "transculturated" in a dynamically equivalent way.

The term "transculturate" is intended to signify with respect to culture what the term "translate" signifies with respect to language. Transculturation includes translation in the same way that culture includes language. But translation, as important as it is, is only the first step toward transculturation. For even though, as suggested in chapter 13, the translation cannot avoid a certain amount of interpretation, the translator is not free to provide the degree, extent, and specificity of interpretation required to establish the message solidly in the minds of the hearers. Nor is it within the province of a translator to elaborate on the written message to approximate that of spoken communication. The translator is not free to give the impression that Jesus walked the streets of twentieth-century American cities. A translation is tied to historical facts. In transculturation, however, the aim is *to represent the meanings of those historical events as if they were clothed in contemporary events.* Transculturation is the task of the Spirit-led communicator of the message. The clearest scriptural statement concerning this role is in Romans 10:14–17 (my translation):

. . . how can they come to faith if they have not understood the message? And how can they understand if the message is not communicated to them? . . . For faith results from a person's responding to an understanding of the message, and the message results from someone communicating Christ.[1]

The idea of transculturating the message is not new, though the label we use may be. There are, however, certain dimensions of the process that may be clarified and elaborated by approaching them from this perspective. (1) Transculturation starts with the process that every faithful interpreter of the Scriptures goes through in seeking to exegete from these documents the meanings that the original authors sought to communicate to their hearers. (2) It then involves the would-be communicator in an attempt to understand the relevance of these meanings for his or her audience. (3) It involves the interpreter in the communication of the message to the hearers in a manner dynamically equivalent to the manner employed by the original participants (whose stories are recorded in Scripture).

Translation aims to provide a faithful written record of the biblical events. Transculturation attempts to take both speaker and hearer behind that record into a re-creation of equivalent events in today's cultural context. Frequently, within western and westernized churches, the major approach to transculturation is via monologue preaching. This is unfortunate, for there are a number of other communicational vehicles that facilitate transculturation and repersonalization more effectively than monologue. Among these we may list drama (including film), storytelling, musical presentation (including ballad), and the powerful transculturation that takes place in and through the living involvement of dedicated Christians in the Christian life. Whenever and however the biblical meanings are abstracted from the Scriptures and re-created as original events in new places and times (even when stimulated from outside), there we have transculturation. Translation is a limited form of transculturation and, as noted above, can be an important first step toward effective, vital transculturation. Poor translation can block effective transculturation.

If would-be communicators are members of the same culture and subculture as their hearers, they may communicate very effectively if they transculturate by simply "speaking to themselves." If, however, the hearers participate in one or more cultures or subcultures different from the communicators' own, the latter must devote considerably more effort to putting themselves "in the place" of the hearers—within their frame of reference (see chapter 8). In the first case, communicators engage in a one-step process of transculturation

---

1. It is a pity that even the better English translations (e.g., TEV) employ misleading terms such as "preach" and "proclaim" rather than "communicate" in contexts such as these. The "almost exclusive use of 'preach' " to translate nine more frequent and twenty or more less frequent Greek words results in "the loss of something which was a living reality in primitive Christianity" (Friedrich 1965:703).

from the biblical cultures into their own. In the latter case the process involves two steps: the attempt to understand the message in terms of the communicators' cultural frame of reference, and the attempt to understand it from the hearers' point of view. The less obtrusive the communicators' own cultural understanding is in the application of the message within the hearers' frame of reference the better. (See the next section of this chapter for a discussion of perceptual problems in transculturation.)

New insight into this process may be gained if it is thought of in terms of the dynamics of the following three situations:

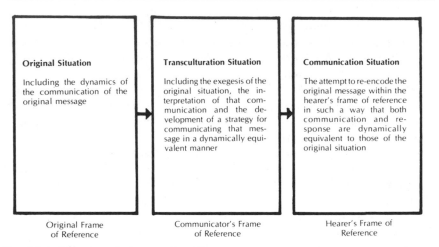

Original Situation

Including the dynamics of the communication of the original message

Transculturation Situation

Including the exegesis of the original situation, the interpretation of that communication and the development of a strategy for communicating that message in a dynamically equivalent manner

Communication Situation

The attempt to re-encode the original message within the hearer's frame of reference in such a way that both communication and response are dynamically equivalent to those of the original situation

Original Frame
of Reference

Communicator's Frame
of Reference

Hearer's Frame of
Reference

Fig. 14.1. The steps in transculturating.

It is important to note at this point that the process of transculturating should not be limited simply to discerning information from the Scriptures and preaching it. We are, rather, to analyze the total source situation, not merely the informational portions of it, and to do a total job of equivalently communicating the original message(s) in the contemporary situation. We must study such things as the relevance and impact aspects of each situation, the personnel involved and the interpersonal dynamics of the interaction, and the cultural factors, including the understandings and expectations of both the communicator(s) and the recipient(s) of the communication. Transculturation involves contextual understanding of both the original and the contemporary situations and contextual communication. The basic approach to transculturation should, therefore, be that recommended for all communication in chapters 8 and 9, above. The message of God lived out intelligibly and credibly in the life of the Christian communicator within the receptor's frame of reference is the most impactful form of transculturation.

There are, however, several other forms. Much more effective transculturation could often be done in preaching services by endeavoring to involve the congregation in the process of transculturation. We might, for example, lead a congregation to *attempt to understand and imitate the process Luke went through in producing his Gospel.* When considering this Gospel book for communication to a group of Christians we must first consider whether we want our audience to identify with Luke or with Theophilus. If with Theophilus, do I, the communicator in this situation, take Luke's position? Or do we all together identify with one or the other? Or do we simply "look over their shoulders," as it were, and not really become participants in a dynamically equivalent situation? Much of what goes on in most churches takes the latter attitude. *We so often focus only on the product of communication, rather than on the process, that it is difficult for us even to imagine what might be involved in another alternative.* But let us attempt a suggestion or two.

Suppose I, the communicator, decide to play Luke's role and to put the audience in that of Theophilus. My transculturation of the situation might well involve props such as a desk, a desk lamp, paper, and writing supplies. I would be sitting at the desk as if writing. If this were done in a church service it would probably require a microphone hung unobtrusively around my neck. My attempt to re-create the situation would likely start with some such words as:

Dear Mr. Jones,

There have been several others who have written accounts of the events that we have recently experienced around here, including the reports of those who were eyewitnesses from the beginning. But none of these accounts has been written specifically for you. So I felt, knowing your great interest in these matters, that you'd appreciate a detailed account. Accordingly, I have done my best to investigate every aspect of the events surrounding the birth, life, death, and resurrection of Jesus of Nazareth so that I can write them up especially for you—so that you can be assured that your understanding of these events squares with the facts.

The message could consist of a typically American-type (as opposed to Luke's Greek-type) presentation of selections from the Gospel. Luke's aim was primarily to provide information as a historian does. The selection and presentation of the events recounted should be such as to convey that information, but it needs to be conveyed with the degree of relevance and impact appropriate to the conveying of information via the kind of vehicle being employed (apparently an extended letter or even a short book).

If, in our attempts to transculturate, we chose to focus upon (1) a single event recorded in the Gospel, (2) our joint participation as a Christian pastor and a Christian congregation in the task of transculturating one portion of the total

Christian message, and (3) the fact that the message we are dealing with is badly needed by the outside world, we might approach it as follows:

Sunday morning. A church. The preacher is in the pulpit. . . . He invites the faithful to take into their hands a duplicated sheet and says:

We are Christians, and as such, are committed to the task of communicating the Good News of Jesus to people around us. But this means two things: first, to translate the biblical text into a language immediately understandable by those among whom we live. Second, *getting this translation into their own culture so that they can discover, with us, what it means.*

This is no easy task. Your pastor cannot do it for you. *He does not really know the language of your non-Christian neighbours.* Neither does he know your particular cultural situation. He can only help you to do this.

So this morning, *we have not gathered as "consumers of the Gospel"* to listen to it for our comfort and help. No, we have come to read together a passage of the New Testament in our new common language translation *in order to learn how to communicate it to others.*

We shall then ask ourselves the question, "How can we communicate this biblical text to others?" To do this, we shall *try to understand the communication situation which the passage reveals,* to whom Jesus speaks, what their attitudes are, what media and methods he uses. . . .

After reading Luke 15, the preacher asks questions already set out on the duplicated paper (on which the text is written out in full) and a lively exchange ensues. *Congregation and pastor together transculturate the story of the prodigal son,* looking for cultural equivalents of the two sons, of the far away country and of the feast. And a great joy comes over them all . . . (Fueter 1971:437). [Emphasis added.]

Such an experiment endeavors to involve the congregation in the dynamics of the *process* that was important to Luke (and to God). We have available to us the product that he produced in his situation. Transculturation asks the question, "How would he have done it if he were in our shoes?" That is, what should a product dynamically equivalent to Luke's product look like today? The pastor in the example above is inviting his congregation to join him in re-creating for a modern-day Theophilus (the name means "lover of God") an equivalent presentation of the message that Luke (and God) recorded in the Scriptures.

A transculturation is not tied to the historical facts of the original, as a translation is. In a translation it is inappropriate to give the impression that Jesus walked the streets of Berkeley or London or Nairobi. But a transculturation, in order to reach its target audience effectively, may do exactly that.

Two printed products of the transculturation process are the *Letters to Street Christians* (1971) and *The Cotton Patch Version* of several portions of the New Testament (Jordan 1968, 1970, 1973). Each of these "cultural translations" goes beyond simple translation in an effort to transculturate the message, aiming at alienated groups who are put off by much of what comes across to them in the standard translations. These groups are characterized by a kind of social and historical isolation that leaves them either unimpressed with or negative toward translations laced with references to historical, geographical, and cultural phenomena that are strange to them.

The idea of transculturational presentations of the biblical materials makes especially good sense for "Street Christians" and blacks, and for many additional groups both within and outside of the western world. I believe that the production of transculturations should in many cases be a higher priority than production of even the best kind of translations.

The Cotton Patch Version of Matthew interprets Matthew 2:1–6 as follows:

When Jesus was born in Gainesville, Georgia, during the time that Herod was governor, some scholars from the Orient came to Atlanta and inquired, "Where is the one who was born to be governor of Georgia? We saw his star in the Orient, and we came to honor him." This news put Governor Herod and all his Atlanta cronies in a tizzy. So he called a meeting of the big-time preachers and politicians, and asked if they had any idea where the Leader was to be born. "In Gainesville, Georgia," they replied, "because there's a Bible prophecy which says:

'And you, Gainesville in the state of Georgia,
Are by no means the least in the Georgia delegation;
From you will come forth a governor,
Who will wisely guide my chosen people.' "

In this version the major departures from strict translation are in the personal and place names. Jordan, who was a fine Greek scholar, goes back to the original context and, to make that specifically meaningful to his audience, renames most of the epistles. Thus, Romans becomes "The Letter to the Christians in Washington," 1 Corinthians becomes "A Letter to the Christians in Atlanta," Galatians becomes "The Letter to the Churches of the Georgia Convention," while Philippians becomes "The Letter to the Alabaster African Church, Smithville, Alabama."

In the salutations at the ends of the various epistles, Jordan "updates" the personal names. Thus he renders "Columbus" (Colossians) 4:10: "Rusty, my fellow jail-bird, sends his greetings to you, as does Mark, Barney's cousin"; "1 Atlanta" (1 Cor. 16:19): "Adrian and Prissy . . . send special greetings"; Philemon v.23: "Pat, my cell-mate in Christ Jesus, sends his greetings, as do Mark, Rusty, Damon and Luke, my co-workers."

The "Two Brothers from Berkeley" who produced *Letters to Street Christians* to reach a very different group, with a very different orientation toward history and geography, felt compelled to leave out the "personal historical references" (1971:8). They have avoided all reference to places and specific persons (except Jesus and God), numbered rather than named the epistles, and even kept from referring to slavery in the letter to Philemon (letter 13). Note their handling of the following passages:

James 2:15–17: Like if a brother or sister doesn't have any clothes or enough to eat and you say "see ya around, keep warm and eat right." If you don't give them any food or clothes, what good is all your rhetoric? A plastic trust in Jesus that doesn't cause you to act like Him is DEAD.

1 Cor. 13:17: God's love can take anything that's thrown at it; it never stops trusting and never gives up hope; it just never quits. In fact, man, when everything else is smashed, God's love still stands.

Col. 2:2–3: Get your joy from being tied to the rest of the family by the Father's love. Get your heads into God's secret plan: That's Jesus, the source of all wisdom and all true knowledge.

Both of these printed attempts at transculturation are masterful in their approach to the problem (though they are strictly limited because they are in written rather than personal form). They dare to be *specific to their audiences and free to be true to God's imperative to communicate rather than simply to impress.* In this they demonstrate the deep concern of their authors for the total communicational situation, not simply for one or another aspect of it. This total concern is also a feature of the previous examples. In each of these illustrations, the focus and the major effort in preparing for the presentation is a dual one. *Both the original situation and the contemporary situation must be in view at all times* just as is true in Bible translating. Incidentally, it is worth noting that the translators of each of the "cultural translations" exemplified above worked from the Greek as well as "to the American."

Unfortunately, too many attempts to communicate the Gospel (either in print or orally) get bogged down for one or more of the following reasons: (1) The focus may be almost totally on the information ("the truth") contained in the Scriptures rather than on the *truth as communicated* with which the case-history deals. (2) The focus may be (as in much preaching) so totally on the explanation of the details of the original situation that the result is merely a history lesson that takes the hearers back to Bible days. Such presentations do not bring the biblical message relevantly and impactfully to life in the experience of the contemporary hearers. (3) At the other extreme, the focus may be so completely on the contemporary situation that any device is resorted to, from prooftexting to completely ignoring situational similarities between biblical and contemporary events. This, too, divests the Scriptures of the dynamic nature of their message. (4) The form of presentation may be so impersonal (e.g., lecture or "propositional" preaching style) that few of the hearers would ever suspect that the message originated in real-life situations and is meant to be expressed in real-life situations today. (5) The application of the message may be so generalized that it never "hits" anyone in the audience. In these and other ways the impact of the communicational event is reduced to that of mere oratory or other types of *performance in front of people* in place of the intended meaningful *communication to people.* Effective transculturation of the Gospel message demands the kind of identification (Hesselgrave 1973) and "culturally relevant witness" (Beekman 1957) that have been advocated throughout this volume.

Just as in the divine casebook we have a balance between event and interpretation (Mickelsen 1963:58–65), so effective transculturation needs to be balanced. *Mere dramatizing without applicational interpretation becomes simply performance.* At the other extreme, however, *mere interpretation (as in much sermonizing) without any "eventness" to it is arid.* Transculturation that is dynamically equivalent to the scriptural balance will not go to either extreme.

Theologizing (see chapter 15) and all other attempts to adapt Christianity to indigenous cultures should be a form of transculturation like that in which the Apostle Paul (and other scriptural authors) involved themselves. Unfortunately, though, Paul's successors have often ignored the fact that the message must be transculturated into cultural forms appropriate to each new generation. Most often the forms of the group in power have simply been imposed upon any new receiving groups (whether the children of the group in power or the members of a different culture or subculture).

Paul, however, in reaction against the lack of proper transculturation, opposed the "orthodox" Judaizers (Acts 15). These were members of "the establishment,," not the new believers who were actively transculturating the Gospel (von Allmen 1975:49). Jesus, too, waged a running battle for culturally relevant transculturation against the "orthodox" retainers of the old cultural forms. Later, following the examples of Jesus and Paul, Roman churches opposed "the establishment" of their day to transculturate Christianity into Roman forms, Luther and others resisted the Roman "party in power," Wesley broke from Anglicanism, the Nazarenes split from the Methodists, and more than 5,000 African denominations have broken from western mission churches (Barrett 1968).

The lack of proper attention to the transculturation of the message by orthodoxy stems, I believe, from the same kind of insensitivity that often characterizes those in power. Even Christians when in power often simply label as "heretics" any who transculturate the Gospel into the forms of cultures or subcultures other than those of the group in power. There was and is, of course, genuine heresy that should be identified and eschewed. But by one knowledgeable estimate, at least half of the early church controversies labeled "heresies" by the "Orthodox" ought rather to be seen as valid cultural adaptations (like those of Jesus and Paul).

PROBLEMS OF DIFFERENTIAL PERCEPTION
IN TRANSCULTURATION

A distinct benefit of living and working outside of one's culture is that one learns so much about one's own culture, frame of reference, and way of doing and looking at things. One becomes aware that people of other cultures actually perceive reality differently, and so one comes to recognize the deep truth of anthropologist Edward Sapir's statement that people of different cultures, speaking different languages, are not simply attaching different linguistic labels to elements of the same real world but are actually operating in terms of *different realities* (1929:209). That is, reality at the perceptual level is culturally and subculturally defined rather than being a function of biology or environment. And this is just as true of Euro-American culture as it is of the cultures of Asia, Africa, and Latin America. Our own perception of reality is pervasively affected by our culture and by such subcultural perceptual frameworks as an academic discipline or an occupational or residential social grouping.

In an absolute sense, reality and truth remain one. But, as pointed out previously, it is a fact of life that perceptions of that reality and truth differ greatly from culture to culture, from subculture to subculture within each culture, and even from individual to individual within a given subculture.

What, for example, does the word "church" signify? It all depends on whom you talk to. For one group the word signifies such things as the "body of Christ," a fellowship of believers, God's people, "the elect" or a house of worship. For another, though, "church" signals religious fanatics, hypocrites, pious "out of it" people, spoilers of fun, strict rules, irrelevance or superstition. Which of these lists most nearly captures the contemporary attitudes of the majority of Americans toward the church? And what does this fact suggest with regard to the perception that most Americans carry around with them concerning Christianity?

Such an experiment could be conducted for any number of terms commonly employed by evangelical Christians, such as, "be saved," "believe," "preaching," "Sunday school," "hymns," and "Christian." The result will be very similar to that regarding the word "church," and will demonstrate the wide difference between the perception of Christianity that the "indoctrinated" carry in their minds and that which outsiders and even unindoctrinated insiders hold.

E. A. Nida starts his excellent book on the communication of the Christian faith, *Message and Mission*, by saying:

> The major difficulties in communication result largely from the fact that we take communication for granted. Whenever we hear someone speak, we tend to assume that what is meant is precisely what we understand by these words. But words do not always mean what we think they mean, even in our native tongue (1960:1).

The problem is complicated enormously when we attempt to translate or transculturate our concepts into other languages and cultures. For the "hearing" or perception of the message is at least as dependent on the way in which the receptor "decodes" it as it is upon the way the would-be communicator phrases it (Nida 1960:34).

Unless the communicator is very careful to take adequate account of the hearer's perception at every point, the potential for miscommunication is great. And even if the communicator is aware of the perception factor, the audience may include such a mixture of people that some will still mishear the message. The greater the difference between the perception of a given matter by communicator and hearers, the greater the likelihood of misperception of the matter by the hearers. This is why we of western cultures have greater difficulty understanding and transculturating Old Testament messages than New Testament messages (especially from the epistles of Paul). The Greek perception employed by Paul is closer to (and has had more influence on) our cultural perception than that of the Hebrews. This also explains why Luther preferred Romans (with a European setting) to James (with a Hebrew setting).

The book of Acts records several striking examples of cross-cultural miscommunication in attempts to transculturate Christianity. These likewise were due to culturally defined differences in perception. Among them were the experience of Paul and Barnabas at Lystra (Acts 14:8–18) and of Paul at Athens (Acts 17:18). In the healing of the cripple at Lystra, Paul and Barnabas were attempting to communicate by deed and word something like, "God is concerned with alleviating the suffering of a crippled man." The people of Lystra, however, interpreted this message in terms of their (rather than Paul and Barnabas') cultural frame of reference. That frame of reference assumed that only the gods could heal. Since these "men" had healed someone, therefore, they must actually be gods masquerading as humans. Their conclusion was, "The gods have come in human form." And they proceeded to worship Paul and Barnabas. In the Athens example, certain Athenian philosophers apparently overheard Paul preaching in the marketplace and noted the frequent occurrence of the terms "Jesus" and "resurrection" in his preaching. This led them (basing their judgment on their own cultural background) to understand that Paul was advocating the addition of two new gods (named "Jesus" and "Resurrection") to the pantheon. For those who wanted to hear more are recorded as saying, "He seems to be setting forth new gods."

Fortunately, in both of these cases Paul was able to get the kind of feedback that enabled him to see that his message had been wrongly understood. On the basis of such feedback he was able to adjust and/or amplify his message to bring about a greater degree of conformity between what was heard and what was said. Even so, the record states that the people of Lystra were scarcely restrained from offering sacrifices to them. Most of the Athenians, on the other hand, once they got the message straight, either derided it or lost interest in it.

Similar examples can be multiplied endlessly from contemporary times. A young Liberian who had received his western schooling under missionary auspices once told me that his understanding of John 3:16 was something as follows: "God so loves Europeans that he accepts as Christian any African who turns his back on his own customs and becomes converted to western culture." No missionary had ever said such a thing to him. But the total effect of his understanding of the missionary operation was such that he heard the Christian message in just such a vastly distorted form. Unfortunately, in this and many similar cases, little was done to remedy his culturally conditioned misperception (as Paul did at Lystra) until it was too late. For, he told me, "Having understood Christianity to be simply the religion of western culture, when I decided to reject western culture, I rejected Christianity with it."

The missionaries, speaking from within their conceptual framework and, therefore, failing to transculturate, had spoken of Christ as the ways to a right relationship with God and the source of real life and power. The Liberians, however, heard of a competing foreign religion promising new life and power via European culture. The missionaries set up schools and hospitals to show God's concern for the Liberians. The latter heard, however, messages concerning God's endorsement of these institutions as vehicles for condemning their institutions and Europeanizing them as persons.

These and many other misperceptions came pouring forth from this man as we talked—misperceptions that were largely predictable in terms of his cultural conditioning. But the real tragedy lay not in the misperceptions themselves, as wide of the mark as some of them were, but in the fact that they were allowed to go uncorrected. Apparently the missionaries did not take his culturally conditioned perception of their message seriously. Nor did they solicit the kind of feedback from him that could have led on their part both to an understanding of the perceptual differences and to the kind of adjustment that Paul and Barnabas sought at Lystra. For they,

tore their clothes and rushed into the crowd, crying at the top of their voices, "Men, men, why are you doing these things? We are only human beings with feelings just like yours!" (Acts 14:14–15 JBP).

Essential to the process of transculturating the Gospel message are both the necessity for taking the hearers' perception seriously and the determination on the part of the communicator to correct whatever misperception occurs. These facts are true both of the communication of the Gospel and of the communication of Christian theology. We now turn to that kind of transculturation labeled "theologizing."

15. Dynamic-Equivalence Theologizing[1]

Theologizing is a matter of dynamic-equivalence transculturation and of witness to Christianity in terms of culture. All theologizing is culture-bound interpretation and communication of God's revelation. Good theologizing is Spirit-led, even though culture-bound. In spite of the impression often given that theology is an absolute, once-for-all kind of thing, theologizing is a dynamic, continuous *process*. Static, once-for-all theologies are dead theologies. *Dynamic-equivalence theologizing is the reproducing in contemporary cultural contexts of the theologizing process that Paul and the other scriptural authors exemplify.* Any time that theologizing devolves into the mere "buying and selling" of past theological products (as it often does), it fails to serve its proper function.

In the following pages we deal first with producing theology. Models 12a, b, and c are developed to aid our understanding of this process. We next turn to the important process of communicating theology. Theologizing and culture-bound perception is the next topic. We conclude with a case study of nonwestern theologizing.

PRODUCING THEOLOGY

The academic field of study known as theology is defined by F. R. Tennant as the discipline that

sets forth the contents and implications of the revelation of Christ. It consists of a systematic exposition of doctrine and of the course of its development, . . . the histori-cal, critical and exegetical study of the Bible and the history of the church, its institutions, etc. Thus theology is a science, or a group of connected sciences, that, on the one hand, is in touch with general philosophy . . . and, on the other hand, is more or less isolable in that it deals with the deliverances of distinctively religious experience and its pre-eminent manifestations (1962:61B).

Theology as we know it is a disciplinary perspective on, or perception of, reality. It is the product of a specific historical process within western culture, and this history includes a specific deep and abiding relationship between western theology and western philosophy. This relationship between theolog-

1. A previous version of some of this material has been published in *Theology, News and Notes* (Kraft 1972b and 1972c).

ical inquiry and the very vital and leisured culture of western Europe, on the one hand, and the vitality of the discipline of western philosophy, on the other, has resulted in a large body of extremely insightful perceptions of the portion of reality revealed to people by God in and through the Christian Scriptures. But this body of perceptions cannot be exhaustive for at least three reasons: (1) the perceptions have been generated almost totally from within a single culture (and this in spite of the fact that the source materials were recorded in terms of the thought patterns of very different cultures—Hebrew and Greek); (2) the perceptions have been generated almost totally within a single academic discipline, or group of disciplines, within that culture; and (3) even within this strictly limited frame of reference, understandings differ, change, and develop—i.e., they are *never absolute understandings* even though they are attempts to understand the absolute God.

We do not mean simply to criticize when we point to the fact that theology as we know it has been generated almost totally from within a single culture, but it is a point that must be kept in mind in discussing theologizing. If we are tempted to absolutize the perceptions of our culture-bound understandings of the revelation of God, we are culturally taking a position equivalent to that of individuals who regard none but their own understandings of truth to be absolutely correct, and we accuse such individuals of egocentrism. None of the revelation about which we theologize took place within western European culture or was recorded in a western European language.[2]

However, this cultural limitedness does not obviate the value, especially for those immersed in western culture, of the perceptions of absolute truth thus gained. It does, though, mean that *any monocultural perspective* on truth is no more complete than the single perspective of any given individual. And this is true even if we are dealing with revealed truth, and even if the perspective be that of Hebrew, Greek, or western culture.

The same can be said concerning the perspective of a single academic discipline. Every discipline focuses in on certain things by specializing in its own perspective (as do cultures and individuals). But, as a byproduct of this specialization, it becomes unable to see other things clearly, if at all. Like individuals who gain things by becoming right-handed but, in the process, lose the potential to do certain things with their left hands, so disciplines and cultures both gain and lose by specializing.

What we are observing is that western cultural approaches to theologizing, though of great value to those specialized in western ways of interpreting reality (western worldviews), are "ethnic theologies" (model 12a)—specialized for westerners. They are not necessarily transculturally applicable perspec-

2. The Greek languages stand by themselves within the Indo-European family of languages. They show neither an alignment with the I-E language groupings to the east of them nor with the groupings to the west and northwest that one would ordinarily regard as western European (e.g., Romance, Germanic). Hebrew and Aramaic, of course, belong to a completely different family from I-E, recently renamed Afroasiatic (Greenberg 1966).

tives (the aim of "ethnotheology"). Model 12 postulates a distinction between culture-specific and cross-culturally valid theologizing. There are, to be sure, cross-culturally valid insights within such limited perspectives due to the fact that (1) they are based on a single set of revelational documents inspired by the one God, and (2) they relate to human beings at the basic level where the influence of cultural diversity is least important. But insights from any narrow, ethnic theology, be it western, Asian, African, or any other, need to be compared with those of other ethnic theologies to discover the transculturally valid expressions of the revealed truths of God.

Another, more technical, way of understanding this fact would be to apply to it one or both of two anthropological models commonly employed to distinguish between the understandings of a single culture and those that are cross-culturally valid. The first (and older) of these focuses on the difference between the *description* of a particular culture (termed "ethnography") and the *generalizations* that can be made concerning culture in general on the basis of comparision and analyses of data from many cultures (called "ethnology") (see Hoebel 1972:11–12). Applying this model to theologizing (model 12b), we may speak of the description of a specific cultural (or subcultural) approach to Christian theologizing as a *Christian theography*. The term "Christian theology," then, would be reserved for theological generalizations based on comparisons and analyses of a large number of single-culture Christian theographies such as those produced within western cultures. Note, however, that we are speaking here only of Bible-based *Christian* theographies—never of indigenous, non-Christian understandings of God that might also be labeled theographies, though not *Christian* theographies.

The second anthropological model of value here is the distinction originally applied to cultural data by the Christian linguist Kenneth Pike (1967:37–72; 1962:35–45) between *etic* perspectives and *emic* perspectives. An emic perspective is the "folk perspective" (Hunter and Foley 1976:52ff) of inside participants in a given culture. An etic perspective is that of outside analysts of many cultures (see also Pelto 1970:67–88 and Harris 1968:568–604 for detailed discussions of the etic-emic distinction). *Outside analysts* develop a series of categories in terms of which they view the specific data of many cultures. They speak of the religion, politics, economics, social structure, worldview, etc. of cultures in general and illustrate each from *their understanding* of the specific emic (insider) varieties of what they consider to be the religion, politics, etc. of the given culture. *The insiders* may not use these categories at all, since they are not necessarily comparing them with similar practices in other cultures. But the analysts need such categories to facilitate their cross-cultural comparisons. As model 12c we may suggest that we speak of *emic* (insider) *Christian theological understandings* and *etic understandings* (analytic comparisons by outsiders). *An emic Christian theology*, then, would be a specific cultural variety of Christian theology, appropriate for those immersed in it but lacking in comparative perspective (like monocultural western theologies). *An etic approach to Christian theologizing,* on the other hand, attempts to compare and discover universally applicable theological categories of Christianity on the basis of analyses of many emic varieties.

These three submodels of model 12 are designed to highlight the distinction between the important, though narrow, specific ethnic, emic theographic types of understandings of God and the broader etic, cross-culturally valid ethnotheological understandings that this book aims to point to. Model 12b would admit only the latter to be labeled "theology," since it alone is based on comparisons between culture-specific perceptions from a variety of cultures. There is, to date, very little of this kind of theologizing being done. The case study on sin in chapter 12 is a good example of the kind of data on which such theologizing must be based.

The subcultural differences in theological understandings within western culture provide a small glimpse of what broader cross-cultural theologizing would look like. For even within a single culture and a single discipline the perception of truth is anything but monolithic. The history of western theology is full of individual and group (subcultural) differences. These were often labeled "heresies" if they didn't seem to square with the perceptions of the group in power. But such differences often stimulate reactions. And both the original differences/deviations and the reactions are studied by succeeding groups. The original differences, the reactions, and the subsequent study of them, then, provide learning experiences and a broadening of theological perspectives for those involved. And these learning experiences result in a deepening of their understandings of Christian truth and the range of legitimate perception of that truth.

Theologizing, therefore, is *a process* taking place at the human perceptual level. This process, indebted to diversity of perspective and approach, is helped when the participants in the process are granted the freedom to dissent and to pursue the discovery of truth in terms of their own frames of reference. *Theologizing is a dynamic discovery process engaged in by human beings according to human perception.* It is not simply the passive acceptance of a doctrinal product "once for all delivered." It proceeds according to the rules of Spirit-led human interaction with God, rather than by means of simple indoctrination. And this is true even though we are dealing with the divine revelation of a portion of absolute truth.

Theology, then, must always be seen as the result of a dynamic process of human theologizing. It should not be confused with the changeless, absolute truth that remains in the mind of God. That divine truth is beyond our reach in any total sense (1 Cor. 13:12), even though God has seen fit to reveal an adequate amount of insight into it via the Spirit-led perceptions of that truth recorded by the authors of Holy Scripture.

In an attempt to make explicit the importance of seeing theologizing in this way, Robert McAfee Brown discusses ten propositions that affirm "the value of experiential-contextual theologies" (1977:170). Among the points that he makes are the following: (1) "All theologies are contextually conditioned"; (2) "there is nothing wrong with theology being contextually conditioned"; (3) "it may take others to show us how conditioned, parochial or ideologically captive our own theology is"; (4) we should be excited rather than upset when we hear such alternative theological perspectives, for they expand our understandings; (5) even if we could once ignore such voices, we can no longer; (6) contemporary alternative theologies are reminiscent of certain theological innovations in western cultures; (7) the point of contact between our traditions and these new theologies is Scripture; (8) we should "take the same kind of critical look at our own traditions" that we take at those of others; (9) "only in creative tension with the widest possible perspective can we develop theologies appropriate to our own particular situations"; and (10) since within the church the ultimate loyalty is not simply to nation, class, or culture, the church is uniquely suited to provide the context within which the task of creative theologizing can take place (1977:170–74).

In an attempt to discover and make explicit the process by means of which theology is produced Daniel von Allmen has studied Paul's part in what he calls "the birth of theology." He sees all theologies (theographies), including Pauline theology, as the result of "contextualization" done by certain people within a group to meet the needs of that group. Missionaries, translators, and those who "sang the work that God had done for them" (1975:41) provided the raw materials for theologizing in the early churches. These consisted of expressions of need, translations and transculturations (including preaching) of the message in Greek, and partial preliminary formulations in culturally appropriate fashion.

The Greek mystery religions apparently provided much of the matrix for the early theologizing. Von Allmen points to Paul's mysticism, rites based on the unity of the initiate with the divinity through death and rebirth, and a "dying rising god" as examples of this fact (1975:45). Paul saw those who opposed this process as heretics.

Putting it provocatively, one may say that the heretics in the New Testament are not those who preach the Gospel by becoming Greeks with the Greeks but rather the conservatives who, because they hesitate to win a new culture for the service of Christ, run the risk of being drowned by that very culture (1975:49).

Most important, though, is to recognize that what was going on in those days was not simply "a contextualization of an existing theology."

Any authentic theology must start ever anew from the focal point of the faith, which is the confession of the Lord Jesus Christ who died and was raised for us; and it must be built or re-built (whether in Africa or in Europe) in a way which is both faithful to the inner thrust of the Christian revelation and also in harmony with the mentality of the person who formulates it. There is no short cut to be found by simply adapting an existing theology to contemporary or local taste (1975:50).

If we are to be true to the dynamism of the early days of the Christian movement, we should be involved both in producing new theological formulations and in encouraging others to do the same. We are to some extent unfaithful to our calling when we become simply "consumers" of theological products and teach students simply to be consumers as well. "That is why," says von Allmen, "we should look upon theological education as the communication of working techniques and building materials" (1975:51), rather than as simply making available to students the past products of the efforts of "expert" theologians.

Rather than teach a theology (even a theology that claims to be a "New Testament theology"), what we should try to do is to point out what the forces were that governed the elaboration of a theology on the basis of the material furnished by the primitive church. This is the reason why, in my opinion, the study of the history of traditions in the early church is of capital importance in Africa even more than elsewhere. In so far as this study takes us back beyond any already developed theology to the stage at which the theology of the New Testament was still being worked out, it should enable us to uncover the forces that governed the making of that theology, in order that we may in turn let ourselves be guided by the same dynamism as we set about creating a contemporary theology, whether it be in Africa or in Europe (von Allmen 1975:51).

This present volume should be seen both as encouraging a study of the dynamics of the production of theology and as itself an effort to suggest and lay the foundations for a new approach. The major dimension of the approach here advocated—the cross-cultural perspective—is the key to carrying out what von Allmen is recommending. For it is this perspective that provides us with the tools with which to get at the processes to which contemporary theologizing should be dynamically equivalent. In seeking to derive lessons from "the history of traditions in the early church," for example, we need to look very carefully at the cultural factors at work. We need to ask which of those varieties of theology branded "heretical" were genuinely out of bounds (measured by scriptural standards), and which were valid contextualizations of scriptural truth within varieties of culture or subculture that the party in power refused to take seriously. *It is likely that most of the "heresies" can validly be classed as cultural adaptations rather than as theological aberrations.* They, therefore, show *what ought to be done today* rather than what ought to be feared. The "history of traditions" becomes intensely relevant when studied from this perspective.

We are dealing, then, with the perception of supracultural truth and with the understanding of the process by means of which the perceptions are analyzed and systematized so that they are regarded as relevant by the hearers. For theology, like every other presentation (transculturation) of the Christian message, must be *perceived as relevant* by the hearers if it is to fulfill its proper function within the Christian movement. Theology perceived as irrelevant *is* irrelevant. Theology that is merely passed from one cultural context to another, rather than being developed within that context, is frequently judged as irrelevant whether in Euro-America, in Asia, or in Africa. In America, theology perceived by the hearers as mere academic philosophizing is often judged to be irrelevant not on its own merits, but simply because the hearer judges irrelevant the framework in terms of which the theology is proclaimed. That is, *theological truth must be re-created like a dynamic-equivalence translation or transculturation within the language and accompanying conceptual framework of the hearers if its true relevance is to be properly perceived by them.* Theologizing, like all Christian communication, must be directed *to* someone if it is to serve its purpose. It cannot simply be flung out into thin air.

For this reason the missiologist Bengt Sundkler states that

theology is, in the last resort, translation. It is an ever-renewed re-interpretation to new generations and peoples of the given Gospel, a re-interpretation of the will and the way of the one Christ in a dialogue with new thought forms and culture patterns . . . (1960:281).

COMMUNICATING THEOLOGY

Theology is, therefore, not only to be produced but to be communicated. And culture and subculture pervasively affect this process at three points: (1) in the theologian's understanding of God's revelation, (2) in the communication of these understandings, and (3) in the receptor's perception of that communication. If, then, Christian theology as we know it in western philosophic garb is to be of value (i.e., perceived as relevant) to Latin Americans, to Asians, to Africans, it must be transculturated into the concepts and language framework in terms of which they operate. If, likewise, theology is to be of value to psychologists, to sociologists, to chemists, it must be "transdisciplinated" out of its present western philosophico-historical mold into the conceptual and linguistic frame of reference of these disciplines. If, further, theology is to be perceived as relevant by factory workers, by farmers, by engineers, by youth, by hippies, by blacks, by women's libbers, it must be translated into terms and concepts meaningful to each group. And the responsibility for this lies on the would-be communicator—in this case on the theologian. For too long have many theologians simply paraded an unintelligible static theological product before their public on the assumption that there is nothing more relevant than theology. The fact is, however, that *relevance is as relevance is perceived.*

The process of transculturation of theology is not new, but it is a very serious matter today. There is ample evidence both within and outside the western world that Christian theology is very often either misperceived or perceived as irrelevant (see, for examples, Bennett 1975 and Cox 1973). Yet this is not because the content of theology *is* irrelevant in and of itself, or even because people are unconcerned. It is simply because theology has so often been presented in terms meaningful only within the would-be communicator's frame of reference, rather than transculturated or transdisciplinated into that of the hearer.

Theology must be "deprovincialized" (Cox 1973:171; Ramm 1961:23). It must be understood that the task of theologizing is the privilege and the responsibility of *every* Christian person and of *every* Christian group. For the Christian world is seriously deprived as long as it continues to allow theologizing to remain the private preserve of a single discipline within a single culture. We need the emic-ethnic theologizing of Africans, of Asians, of Latin Americans, of psychologists, of sociologists, of chemists, of factory workers, of farmers, of engineers, of youth, of hippies, of blacks, of women's libbers. We need to enter into the Spirit-guided perceptions of these and a vast number of other cultural, subcultural, disciplinary, and occupational groups to come to a broader and better balanced etic, ethnotheological understanding of God's truth. For this truth transcends the capacity of any single individual, or group, or discipline, or culture to grasp fully even that portion of it that has been revealed to us. Every individual, group, discipline, and culture has much to offer the rest by way of insight and specialized understanding.

Missiologist A. R. Tippett, for example, testifies that it was his experience as a missionary to the Fiji people rather than his study of western theology or his experience in western churches that taught him most of what he understands to be a sound doctrine of the church.[3] A western cultural perspective, focused as it is on individuality, seems peculiarly blind to a large number of important aspects of this doctrine which, among other things, recognizes the human need for well-integrated groupness. This need Fijian culture seems to have long provided for, though western behavioral scientists are just now coming to assert it. When groups within such community-oriented cultures come to God, they immediately understand much more about many dimensions of "people of Godness" (i.e., the church) than most members of individualized western cultures know. After hundreds of years of experience with Christianity, we westerners have learned a few intellectual things about the church. These things may well be helpful to more communally oriented peoples if we share them in the proper way, but we need also to learn from them those aspects of open, communal interpersonal interinvolvement that are a part of biblical models of churchness but tend to be de-emphasized within western cultures. In this way participation in other emic-ethnic understandings of God's revelations can instruct us as outsiders concerning the dimensions of the etic, ethnotheological perspectives that we need if we are to present God's message effectively in a multicultural world.

Likewise, many of us who have served in Africa can point to a heightening of our understanding of and respect for the Old Testament (even the genealogies) as a result of our African experience. It is exciting to begin to enter into the

3. Private conversation.

riches of the majority of God's Word by beginning to see these portions through the eyes of people closer to Hebrew culture than we are. The message of the Old Testament and the New Testament is the same (model 10b). But many westerners need to be shocked into understanding this by exposure to the response of nonwestern peoples to that message in Hebrew cultural garb. Westerners then learn to view the Old Testament as a fully valid, fully inspired, and still usable record of divine-human interaction.

Similarly, theologian and psychologist Thomas Oden has discovered new dimensions of theological understanding by attempting to view theological truth from a psychological point of view. Oden, in teaching theology, has discovered how difficult theology phrased in the language and concepts of traditional theology (i.e., the philosophico-historical frame of reference) is for even his theology students to understand. Theology phrased in the language of psychology, however, gets across to them very well. Apparently, he says, "psychology is their home territory linguistically" (Oden 1974:36). He has found it necessary to trade one type of emic-ethnic conceptualization of theological truths that is, at least for those students, now out of vogue, for another emic conceptualization of the same truths that is in vogue. Neither emic understanding is inherently better than the other. Each is best for those immersed in it.

Theology, if it is to be perceived as relevant by students such as these and by a significant proportion of the rest of America's student generation, must be translated/transculturated into the (emic) linguistic and conceptual framework of the behavioral sciences—for this is where these students are. For them there ought to be one or more behavioral-sciences-based theologies rather than simply philosophy-based theologies. And if there are not such emic theologies today, Christian psychologists, sociologists, anthropologists, and others with both behavioral science and theological credentials should be encouraged to develop them.

What is here being advocated is, *first*, the need to recognize the limitedness of the cultural and disciplinary perspective of what is presently known as theology. This limitedness affects both the understanding and the transmission of Christian theological truths. *Second*, we need to develop (in some cases to continue a development already started) a diversity of cultural, subcultural, and disciplinary approaches to the study and presentation of theological perceptions of God's truth. We have always recognized, of course, that truth of one kind or another is discoverable from within the framework of a multiplicity of disciplines and cultures. But we must recognize that much of this truth is of high relevance in the understanding and communication of God and his works. The breadth and depth of theological truth available to us in the revelation of God is simply not attainable by or containable in a single culture or a single discipline.

Third, we need to learn to communicate Christian theological insight in a receptor-oriented, emically valid way to each particular group of recipients.

Unfortunately, many theologians (and preachers) take an extractionist approach to communicating theology (see chapter 8). They steadfastly refuse to budge from the presentation of theology in traditional western theological terms, for they have often come to regard these traditional formulations as sacred. How different is this approach from that of our Lord and the apostle Paul, who adopted the linguistic, cultural, and situational frames of reference of their hearers. Many missionaries, likewise, insist that their converts convert not only to Christ but to a particular western emic, ethnic understanding and verbalizing of Christian theology (see Kraft 1963). Jesus' approach, however, was to phrase theological truth in terms of whatever emic conceptual framework was appropriate to his hearers. He employed certain kinds of parables with the masses, life involvement (including a variety of verbalizations) with the disciples, reserving the overt use of Scripture largely for the Pharisees and Satan. Paul articulated the same approach when he stated that he sought to be a Jew to Jews and a Greek to Greeks (1 Cor. 9:19–23).

THEOLOGIZING AND CULTURE-BOUND PERCEPTION

As pointed out in chapter 2 and elsewhere, there is always a difference between reality and human culturally conditioned understandings (models) of that reality. We assume that there is a reality "out there" but it is the mental constructs (models) of that reality inside our heads that are the most real to us. God, the author of reality, exists outside any culture. Human beings, on the other hand, are always bound by cultural, subcultural (including disciplinary), and psychological conditioning to perceive and interpret what they see of reality in ways appropriate to these conditionings. Neither the absolute God nor the reality he created is perceived absolutely by culture-bound human beings.

It is, however, as already pointed out, possible to perceive God *adequately*. For he has revealed himself to human beings within the human cultural context. Furthermore, he has guided certain people to record their perceptions of experience with him and guided his people to preserve and pass on certain of these records. This preservation and passing on of the records is for the benefit of other people, most of whom participate in quite different cultural, subcultural, and psychological frames of reference from those whose perceptions have been preserved. And because, beyond the diversity of human frames of reference, human beings participate in a pervasive common humanity, because the perceptions recorded in the Scriptures focus on the same unchanging message from God, and because God's Spirit is active in guiding people into God's truth, the study of this inspired casebook yields understandings adequate for human salvation and sanctification.

This study has traditionally been labeled "theology." Since theological inquiry, being human and therefore culture-bound, yields culturally conditioned differences of perception, it seems proper to speak of "theologies" at this perceptual level. At this point it may be useful to distinguish between these theologies and the absolute theological reality that lies outside culture in the mind of God himself. This latter is only knowable to human beings in adequate, though not absolute glimpses, as through a dirty window (1 Cor. 13:12).

The object of theologies is to come to ever more adequate, accurate, understandable (by the group in focus), and communicable perceptions of the glimpses of God's absolute Truth (with a capital T) embedded in the inspired casebook. But, since perception differs so from culture to culture (and even from subculture to subculture and discipline to discipline), emic understandings perfectly satisfactory for one group are frequently perceived as somewhat less than satisfactory by another.

Witness a change that is taking place in at least certain segments of American culture from a predominant concern for quantity of life (i.e., everlastingness) to a much greater concern for quality of life (i.e., in terms of meaningfulness). Unfortunately (for modern Americans) the previous quantitative emphasis continues to be catered to in Bible translations and, often, in evangelical preaching and theologizing. This leads to a comparatively greater use in translation, preaching, and theologizing of quantitative expressions such as "eternal" or "everlasting life" than of qualitative expressions like "abundant," "real," or "meaningful life." And allegiance to such a fact has kept many American Christians from recognizing that theologically it is just as appropriate to speak of Christ as offering "real" or "meaningful" life as to speak of the quantitative aspects of this life. Yet the Greek word used for "life" in the New Testament (*zoe*) focused on *quality* of life. It contrasted within the language with *bios* (animal life) (Bultmann 1964). So the New Testament focuses on a "real, meaningful life" that extends forever. It does not exclude the quantitative dimension, of course, for it makes that dimension explicit by adding the word "everlasting." English, however, since we have only a single word for life, loses the qualitative dimension implicit in the Greek *zoe*, unless the translator makes this dimension explicit in English.

In previous days it has seemed appropriate for Christian communicators (and theologians) in America to present God as providing life that "extends forever and that, incidentally, is very meaningful in the here and now." Due to culture change, however, many English-speaking groups today best hear God's message, which includes both emphases, when it is presented (and theologized) as "God offers life that is very meaningful in the here and now and that, incidentally, extends forever." It is incumbent upon theologies that they be etic in their perspective so that they may be flexible and adaptive to the emic realities of the frame of reference in which they are developed and to which they seek to communicate. We do not do justice to the revelation if we cling to theological expressions appropriate in other cultures or at other times in our own culture in preference to an equally valid and much more relevant expression of the glimpse of absolute Truth involved.

Christian theologies are, like all other Christian understandings, tethered to the Word (model 9c). Though they are to be emically, ethnically valid, they must fall within a biblically acceptable range of variation (model 9b) as measured by the Bible as "yardstick" (model 9a). This range of variation will, of course, include both what the author intended to say and what God intended to say with and through the author. At the receptor's end, due to cultural and temporal distance, the author's intent is only approximately discernable at best. Discerning that emic intent is one of the major reasons for doing biblical exegesis. The doing of good exegesis depends on the ability of exegetes to transcend their own emic perspectives to, as best they can, identify psychologically with the author and to "think the author's thoughts" as if they, the exegetes, were a part of the original context. Of great assistance in this task is for contemporary exegetes to experience life in contemporary cultures similar to those of biblical times. There is not ordinarily enough livingness to library-based exegesis to enable one to achieve the kind of personal identification with the scriptural authors in their cultures that such exegesis demands.

Discerning authorial intent is, however, but one part of the exegetes' task. For *God* is also speaking. And God's speaking is to us and to those to whom he has called us in contemporary emic contexts. The Christian theologian is, therefore, to discover and apply God's meanings (as best they can be determined) in each contemporary cultural context as well. Just as the author's intent, if it could be discovered, and God's intent for the original situation were specific to that situation, so the theological transculturation of God's message through the Word to today's contexts should be specific to those contexts. Even when we feel that we have satisfactorily determined what the author and God intended for the original hearers, we still need to be open to what he seeks to say to contemporary hearers in contemporary cultural contexts. *These messages will be within the range of allowable interpretation of the original utterances but may differ from our emic understandings.*

Absolute supracultural Truth is not synonymous with the theology that John Calvin developed by interpreting Scripture to speak to the needs (as he perceived them) of sixteenth-century Geneva. Nor is it the same as that developed by John Wesley to speak to the needs (as he perceived them) of eighteenth-century England. Nor does it correspond with that of any of the prominent twentieth-century theologians as they struggle to understand the revelation in relation to twentieth-century Switzerland, Germany, England, or America. These are all culture-bound theologies—valuable as expressions of particular perceptions of God's Truth but not synonymous with it. These are all (at least insofar as they are true both to the inspired revelation and to the surrounding cultural context) attempts to translate and transculturate the Truth of God into the linguistic and cultural frames of reference of the people for whom these theologies were developed. They have, however, no inherent claim to perpetuity except and unless people of other times and other cultures discover them (or parts of them) to be of value in their contexts as well.

Theologies, then, become an important part of the necessary repackaging of the Christian message as it moves from culture to culture and from subculture to subculture. If theologies are properly in tune with the surrounding cultures, they will manifest differences of focus, differences of understanding, and differences of expression proportionate to the differences between the cultures and subcultures in which they are involved. This is true even though there are two strong pulls toward uniformity: (1) the fact that theologies in order to be Christian are based upon the biblical revelation, and (2) the fact that beyond cultural differences human beings share an extensive common humanity. But such differences of focus, understanding, and expression are necessary if the theologies are to be meaningful to the consumers of these theologies.

It is tragic, therefore, when a given theological system (or creed based thereon) is adopted by or imposed upon those of another culture or subculture. This error often results when a given approach to theology is regarded as highly prestigious, and/or proponents of that theological system assume that the system is absolutely correct and relevant for all times, places, and peoples, and/or the proponents have the power to impose their system on others. The result is frequently that the receptors are so turned against the given theological system that both the recommended theology and the quest for relevant understandings are abandoned—often with all other commitment to Christianity as well. Such is too often the case in America today, for there is an increasing divergence between the concerns and expressions of academic metaphysical philosophical modes of thought in which much theology (even much "biblical theology") is still couched and the concerns of contemporary Americans. Or, as with many Christian churches in nonwestern cultures, the only approaches to theology offered are often preoccupied with certain theological concerns of a former stage of western culture. These churches are then forced to choose between theological domination by western approaches to theology and rebellion against the proponents of these theologies. The latter choice involves as a concomitant the loss of all the other valuable assistance that these churches have available to them by continuing their friendly association with western missions.

If we could both understand the pressing need for the development of home-grown, culturally relevant theologies which freely borrow from, but are not dominated by, foreign theological models and encourage Christians everywhere in dependence upon the Holy Spirit to theologize freely, the Christian church would be much richer. To date, though, the attitude has often been more one of repression of theological diversity, especially outside western culture. And we of the west, as well as those of other cultures, are being denied theological insight because of this lack of positive regard and respect for the perspectives of those other cultures.

By cutting ourselves off from the insights of people immersed in other cultures, we of the West are in danger of developing and perpetuating certain culturally conditioned kinds of heresies. Without the criticisms of Christians influenced by Islamic understandings, for example, who would point out to us that western theological presentations of the doctrine of the Trinity sound more like tritheism than like monotheism (see Nida 1959). The use of the word "person," which in contemporary English signals that the "persons" of the Trinity are separate individuals, is a major problem in this regard. The use of *persona* (=actor's mask) in Latin to label the three parts that the one God plays seems within the scripturally allowed range. But belief in three Gods which, as Nida points out, is probably the folk belief of large numbers of western Christians, seems clearly outside the allowable range and, therefore, heretical.

Other, perhaps lesser, candidates for accepted substandard doctrinal perspectives perpetuated within western culture relate to the concepts Son of God and Son of Man. Westerners who have not had experience in cultures similar to patrilineal Hebrew culture are likely to automatically interpret the God as Father and God as Son analogies as indicating a hierarchical Father superior/Son subordinate relationship between God and Jesus. In cultures like the Hebrew, however, it may be contended that the firstborn son is at least as important as the father in the household. When Jesus called himself Son of God, his original hearers understood him to be claiming equality with, not subservience to, God (see Lk. 22:70–71; Jn. 10:33–36). The term for Son of Man, on the other hand, meant what the equivalent expression usually means today in languages related to Hebrew—man or human being (see LaSor 1961:42).[4] Monocultural westerners, unable to understand this term as a part of normal language (since European languages do not ordinarily employ such an idiom), have tended to see it as a technical term whereby Jesus claimed messiahship.

Theologizing by those of nonwestern cultures (if within scriptural limits) can both enrich the rest of us and alert us to deficiencies in our commonly held interpretations. Through the study of such theologizing we can better see just how contextualized and culture-bound our theologies are (see Brown 1977:170–74, quoted above). Monica Wilson, in attempting to assess what "special insights" there may be in traditional African religion that could make a contribution both to African Christianity and to the universal church, points to four key ideas. The first area is *in the relationship of human beings to human beings.* Africa can teach the rest of the world much about the closeness of community. The responsibility of one for another and the effects of the actions of each on the other are well known to Africans and could be taught to others to deepen their Christian experience. Second, *Africans are constantly conscious of the reality of evil.*

In Africa evil was seen as anger, hate, envy, and greed festering within men, unconfessed, bottled up, and in one area after another we find a stress on *speaking out,* on confession of anger and hate, for it is thought that reconciliation can only follow the admission of evil thoughts (Wilson 1971:139).

Third, *Africans "bridle" competition.* Competition has gotten out of hand in the West in just about every area of life. Africans know how to be still, how to

---

4. This is true, for example, even in a language as distantly related to Hebrew as Hausa of West Africa.

cooperate, how to get along with each other. And, fourth, *the African "apprehension of reality through ritual rather than dogma"* provides "a balance to the intellectual emphasis of the West" (1971:141). With respect to death, Africans accept it and work out their grief in ritual. This is radically different (and more satisfying) than "trying to pretend it does not exist," as westerners often do (Wilson 1971:137–42).

Western monocultural theological interpretations often appear to be less biblical than such African emphases. *Yet they have been allowed to stand because the interpreters, as members of the same cultural traditions, have shared and failed to question many of the same presuppositions.* It may be helpful, therefore, to cite a few examples of nonwestern theologizing.

NONWESTERN THEOLOGIZING: A CASE STUDY

In seeking to overcome the effects of extractionist theological teaching, a growing number of non-Euro-American thinkers are attempting to imitate in their own cultural contexts the process that the apostle Paul went through in the Greek-speaking world. The following is an attempt to highlight the efforts of several such thinkers, especially in Africa.

John V. Taylor states concerning Africa:

Christ has been presented as the answer to the questions a white man would ask, the solution to the needs that Western man would feel, *the Saviour of the world of the European world-view*, the object of the adoration and prayer of historic Christendom. But *if Christ were to appear as the answer to the questions that Africans are asking, what would he look like?* If he came into the world of African cosmology to redeem Man as Africans understand him, would he be recognizable to the rest of the Church Universal? And if Africa offered him the praises and petitions of her total, uninhibited humanity, would they be acceptable? (1963:24). [Emphasis added.]

To an African, for example, a Christian theology that can offer no more than an impersonal western medical approach to disease is not only culturally unacceptable but scripturally inaccurate. Africans, unlike theologians bound by a western cultural worldview, *know* that illness is not usually caused by mere germs. And when they study the Scriptures they find abundant confirmation of their point of view and abundant disconfirmation of the theological understandings of the West. Illness, by the way, is a matter of *theological* (not simply medical) understanding in virtually all cultures except those characterized by western secularism.

The African expects that anyone speaking for God will automatically be concerned with healing and exorcism. If, then, the person of God attempting to communicate Christ in traditional Africa will not or cannot address the illness problem effectively, the person can expect to make little if any real impact on African worldviews with an *inadequate proclamation of Christian truth*. For that person has failed to follow the example of Christ who, dealing with a people with similar expectations in this regard, combined in himself what we of the overspecialized West regard as two different tasks—the ministry of proclamation and that of healing. In this and other matters of Christian proclamation in nonwestern cultures, all with important theological ramifications, it is

an ironical thing that the West, which is most concerned with the spread of Christianity in the world today, and which is financially best able to undertake the task of worldwide evangelism, is *culturally the least suited for its task* because of the way in which it has specialized itself to a point where it is *very difficult for it to have an adequate understanding of other peoples* (Smalley 1958:64). [Emphasis added.]

So we continue to send out doctors who by customary training and interest are ill-prepared to employ their skills in such a way as to reap maximum benefit. They do not realize that, from African points of view, they alone among the missionaries effectively demonstrate their close contact with God by healing physical illness. Yet these doctors, in keeping with their home-culture perspective, frequently disclaim the spiritual ministry that the receptor culture expects of them. And we compound the error by continuing to train and send missionary and national pastors and evangelists with no knowledge of medicine. These, from African points of view, can "talk a good game" but give no convincing demonstration of their close relationship to God. High on the list of reasons why five thousand or more African independent movements have broken away from missionary Christianity is the fact that the mission churches, preoccupied with the concerns of western theologies, did not pay adequate attention to matters of health and illness—matters which are to the African highly theological (Barrett 1968).

Thus the Christ that we present is only the *partial* Christ we have perceived from studying the Scriptures from within our cultural frame of reference. We tend to present only the part of God's revelation focused upon by our culturally and disciplinarily bound theologians and other expositors as providing answers to the questions in their (and our) minds. Other questions, often of prime concern to the members of another culture, have either not been posed by us at all, or have been posed but seldom taken seriously. Pentecostalism is the exception. It deals positively with the faith/healing issue and is being mightily used of God in Africa, Latin America, and elsewhere.

To Africans and multitudes of others throughout the world there may be nothing clearer in all of God's Word than the fact that *God* (not merely medicine) heals physical as well as spiritual illness—unless it be the fact that God deals effectively with evil spirits. But again western theology, at least as practiced, is virtually silent or even negative toward the existence and constant activity of such spirits. Likewise, the theological treatments of western Christianity regarding people in their group relationships, the spirits of the departed, the significance of ritual—including traditional naming and initiation ceremonies as well as baptism and the Lord's Supper, the place of celebration (including dance) in Christian life and worship, etc.—are less than satisfying to Africans. Westerners have specialized many of these concerns into the realm known as "secular" and, therefore, regard them as beyond the purview of theological consideration. But to the Africans who, in spite of the onslaughts of westernization, are still in possession of a more integrated perspective on life, these are theological issues.

Thus it is refreshing to note the recent emergence of several sincere attempts to apply African insight and perspective to the interpretation of the Bible and of theologically generalized Christian truth based on the Bible. It is not without significance that this growing freedom on the part of Africans comes hand in hand with the very rapid development of African independent churches and other movements toward indigenization of Christianity in Africa. But it is matter for rejoicing nonetheless, for at least two reasons: (1) at last there is hope that African Christianity will begin to hear Christ addressing himself to a larger number of "the questions that Africans are asking," and (2) at last we of the western world will be able to have our own theological horizons broadened by being exposed to the insight of African perceptions of Christian truth.

In *New Testament Eschatology in an African Background* (1971), John S. Mbiti, regarded by many as black Africa's leading contemporary theologian, struggles with the meaning of Christian eschatology to a people (his people—the Akamba of Kenya) with a virtually two-dimensional concept of time. This concept has no distant future. It is, therefore, virtually limited to perceiving reality as either present or past. This kind of conceptualization and other features of the Akamba worldview strongly affect their perception of Christian teaching, and so have important implications for the development of Akamba theological understanding.

Mbiti is no mean theologian even by western standards, and thus is anything but limited to African perspectives in his treatment. Nor does he completely reject western understandings, though he finds them partial and incomplete —providing little more than "the solution to the needs that Western man would feel" (Taylor 1963:24). Rather, on the basis of a deep study of the Scriptures and of western interpretations, plus the assumption of the potential validity of perspectives on time other than the western past-present-future lineal concept, he works toward an African understanding. He concludes that the New Testament—especially those portions directed primarily to Jewish readers—can very well be interpreted from within an African culture. And this can be done without the prior necessity (often naively required by traditional approaches) of the African adopting a non-African concept of time.

Specifically, he sees the Hebrew two-dimensional division of time into "This Age" and "The Age to Come" united in the Incarnation into a single time-transcending, present kingdom of God. This kingdom, though looking forward to the Parousia, does not require a three-dimensional concept of time as prerequisite to understanding it. An understanding of Christian eschatology may, therefore, be legitimately approached from an African two-dimensional background, even though these two dimensions do not correspond exactly with the two Hebrew dimensions.

If such an approach is attempted, the African worldview will not remain unchanged. One result of building Christian eschatology upon an African conception of time will be the invasion of the African worldview by the Christian eschaton, producing perhaps for the first time an African teleology. An approach to such an African-based Christian eschatology and the consequent development of an African teleology have been hindered to date, Mbiti contends, by an excessive overlay of western cultural interpretations of the Scriptures to which Africans have been required to subscribe. Now, after more than a hundred years of missionary effort in Africa, theologians like Mbiti are beginning to emerge who take seriously both Christ and African culture. Mbiti and others making similar attempts may from time to time err as they sail such uncharted seas—making mistakes that will be as African as the insights—but at least certain Africans now know that they can and must look directly to the Holy Spirit for their leading, and this bodes well for the future of theology in Africa.

In another volume, *Biblical Revelation and African Beliefs* (Dickson and El-lingworth 1969), Mbiti joins seven other Africans in dealing with theological issues of special relevance to Africa. The volume is the result of a consultation of African theologians that became

an expression of a deep longing that the churches of Africa might have an opportunity of thinking together of the Christian faith which had come to them . . . through missionaries of a different cultural background who . . . could not fully appreciate the reactions of their converts to their faith in the light of their own traditional beliefs and practices (1969:vii).

In the belief that "the urgent predicament of the Church in Africa today is that of the apparent foreignness of Christianity" (ibid.:13), these African scholars set themselves the task of discovering

in what way the Christian faith could best be presented, interpreted and inculcated in Africa so that Africans will hear God in Jesus Christ addressing himself immediately to them in their own native situation and particular circumstances (1969:16).

Dr. Raimo Harjula, formerly of Lutheran Theological College, Tanzania, defined Christian theology as "the critical reflection on, articulation and translation of God's self-disclosure, especially in Jesus Christ, in and for a given historical and cultural context" (1972:1:18). From this point of view, theology is a functional, dynamic, relevant thing whose purpose is "to interpret . . . Christ in terms that are relevant and essential to African existence" (Sundkler 1960:211). Just as Acts 2 records that the Christian witness went forth in the various languages of the hearers, so must Christian theology be heard by Africans (and others) embodied in their own conceptual categories. For though "the Gospel is absolute, . . . its framework and embodiment . . . are something relative which vary according to the historical and cultural context" (Harjula 1972:2:4–5).

A European theologian like Barth, for example, can perhaps be excused for being pessimistic concerning the value of "natural religion," if one understands his theologizing as at best designed to handle issues of interest to western theologians at a particular point in time. African Christians, however, cannot afford the luxury of such pessimism. They must provide intelligible yet Christian answers concerning what, in the old ways, is compatible and what is incompatible with Christianity. They must develop what Henri Maurier calls "A Theology of Paganism"—an understanding of "the meaning of paganism in the history of salvation" (1968:xi). In what sense (if any) can it be maintained that "the grace of God has never deserted mankind and that, even among the pagans, some men have responded to it?" (Maurier 1968:xii). Perhaps Maurier has the answer in the distinction he makes between (1) the fact that pagans continually search for God and (2) the various non-Christian religious *systems* that imperfect human beings have created as an expression of this search. These expressions inevitably consist of complexes of truth and error and constitute, at best, imperfect means and, at worst, obstacles to people in their search (1968:xii). But whether or not this approach be deemed helpful to Africans (and others), there is no doubt that it attempts to deal with an issue of critical importance to Theologia Africana.

Critical also are a host of related issues of but academic importance to western theologians, such as the question of the identity or nonidentity of a given tribal deity with the Christian God—or even of the son of a tribal deity and the Son of God (as among the Yala of southeastern Nigeria—Buckman 1978). Further, "how is the Christian understanding of Creation and the 'Fall' related to the hundreds of African myths of Creation and the Supreme Being's 'departing' or 'going far away' due to man's misdeed or misbehavior?" (Harjula 1972:5:19). And what about ancestor veneration? Are those who honor their ancestors breaking the first commandment ("no other gods before me"), or obeying the fifth ("honor your father and your mother")? And does Jesus' preaching "to the spirits in prison" (1 Pet. 3:19) hold out any hope for the salvation of Africa's ancestors? Such issues as these, as well as those related to health and spirits, can be virtually ignored by western theologians, but they are live and pressing issues in the minds and hearts of Africans. Many continue to turn sadly from Christ because they hear only solutions to the needs felt by certain western people. African theologians cannot ignore African issues.

Nor can Indian theologians ignore the equivalent issues in Indian culture as they press themselves upon the consciousness of Indian Christians. For to India, as to Africa, Latin America, Oceania, and other areas missionized from the West, Christianity "has been *like a pot-plant transplanted into a garden*" (Boyd

1969:259). In the early days the imported soil in the foreign pot sufficed to sustain its growth. But, as time passed, the roots grew large and shattered the pot from within, often to the dismay of the foreign "gardeners," so that now the gardeners no longer have

to bring the water of the Word from a distant source, for the plant has struck its own deep tap-root to the perennial springs. It grows larger and more luxuriant than it ever did in its bleak northern home. . . . *The western confessions* have indeed been *channels* for bringing the Water of Life, but *they are not the only ones* and *the Indian Church must . . . develop its own confessions* [which will provide for the Indian churches an] understanding of the deepest Christian insights into the very nature and being of God, Christ, man and the world, and their expression in Indian language which can be understood and so accepted (Boyd 1969:259–60). [Emphasis added.]

But the Indian, African, American, and other developers of an indigenous theology must feel free of the obligation to conform to the theological maxims of another culture or subculture. They may or may not have studied western theology. Their guidelines, however, do not lie there but, rather, in their own Spirit-led understanding of Scripture and its applicability to their own cultural world. If a theology is to be a culturally relevant expression of supracultural Truth the theologian

must not keep looking over his shoulder to see if he is in step with Aquinas or Calvin or Barth; rather he must "look unto Jesus," the hope of glory who is present in his Church.
As he does so, basing himself firmly in the Christian Scriptures and using all the resources of thought and terminology which are available to him, the inner, underlying Truth, of the Christian faith will make itself plain (Boyd 1969:261). [Emphasis added.]

So, likewise, should the western theologian demand and make use of such freedom from theological expressions bound to the history and culture of past times and circumstances within western societies. For, if Sundkler is right that theology is meant to be "an ever-renewed re-interpretation to . . . new generations and peoples of the given Gospel . . . in a dialogue with new thought-forms and culture patterns" (1960:211), this necessity for constant renewal applies just as much to the movement from generation to generation within a single society as it does to movement from culture to culture. That is, we need *intra*cultural transculturations of theology as well as *inter*cultural transculturations.

Contemporary western theologizing must not hide its head in the sand of traditional theological models that are becoming increasingly irrelevant in contemporary western frames of reference. We cannot conscientiously ignore pressing theological problems raised by new currents such as the rise of the behavioral sciences. The apathy of contemporary Christians toward what western society knows as Christian theology and toward preaching based thereon provides in our context the same kind of protest as that prominent in

Africa, India, and other missionized areas of the world. This protest against a message that promises so much but is expressed so irrelevantly has, fortunately, led in both areas (the West and the Third World) to a lively surge toward independence that must be regarded as promising. For this independence will result in theological experimentation, with its promise of new and renewed theological insight.

Where such a surge toward independence and theological experimentation has not occurred, only apathy toward Christianity remains. This, unfortunately, is the popular response of much European Christendom where nominal church membership is accompanied by an almost total unconcern for the Christian message and the institutions responsible for proclaiming it. Academicians still study Christianity but seldom transculturate its meanings into vital, life-related, worldview-changing concepts. In Denmark, for example, amid linguistic and architectural symbols betokening considerable past commitment to Christianity, plus 97 percent nominal church membership, estimates of active church involvement are less than 5 percent of the population. The preference of Danish and other European churchmen for preserving, studying, and debating academically the theological products of the past rather than engaging in the transculturating process has had much to do with the deadness of European Christianity at the popular level. This deadness could be the lot of Africa and India as well if the example of men like Mbiti and Boyd is not followed.

What we have termed absolute, supracultural Truth exists—outside culture and beyond the grasp of finite, sinful human beings. But God provides revelation of himself *within* the human cultural context. Much of this, including detailed records of his supreme revelation in Jesus Christ, has been recorded and preserved in the Christian Scriptures. To the understanding of this revelation a variety of Spirit-led human beings apply a variety of culturally, psychologically, disciplinarily, and otherwise-conditioned perceptions. On this basis they develop theologies appropriate to their own insights and experiences, and instructive to others of similar and dissimilar backgrounds.

If, as certain absolutist theologies seem to assume, God simply "did theology" *through* humans, all Spirit-led theologies and theologians would come out with the same answers on all issues. Differences in theologies would have to be explained wholly in terms of the presence of the sin factor. More is involved, however, than simply the sin factor (though I would not want to be interpreted as denying the pervasiveness of sin in human experience). There are sincere culturally and otherwise-conditioned differences in perception that have to be regarded as the primary factors influencing differences in theological understanding. For the sin factor is more or less constant for everyone, whatever the culture and, therefore, affects all (not just certain) perceptions.

But in spite of both sin and culture, God apparently chooses to work in partnership *with* (not simply *through*) humans in theologizing (as in all other areas of life). He seems not to be very concerned with conformity, or even with the absolute correctness of the conclusions reached. He seems to be more concerned with the *process* of theologizing and its *appropriateness* to a given individual or group at the particular stage of Christian development at which the individual or the group find themselves. If this be true we may assume that God is in favor of the development of theologies that not only derive from his revelation of himself in the Scriptures but show a maximum of relevance to the emic-ethnic situation out of which and for which they are developed—as long as they fall within the allowable range of acceptable variation set by Scripture.

In the following part we turn to a consideration of several aspects of the influence of dynamic-equivalence Christianity on the cultural matrix in which it is operated.

PART VI
THE MESSAGE AFFECTS
THE FORMS

16. Dynamic-Equivalence Churchness[1]

The organism that we call "church" should also be dynamically equivalent to biblical models. As with theologizing, however, we have often been content merely to transmit the church *product* developed in one generation to those of another generation or that produced in one culture to those of another culture. As with theologizing, translation, revelation, and all other products of Christianity, however, *it is crucial that each new generation and culture experience the process of producing in its own cultural forms an appropriate church vehicle for the transmission of God's meanings.* We may thus speak of and recommend "dynamically equivalent churchness." Such a new use of previously existing cultural forms plus the necessary borrowing and internal development of new forms brings about change in the culture. This and the following four chapters focus on such Holy Spirit-stimulated change.

In this chapter we treat the people of God within culture, the concept of dynamic-equivalence (D.E.) churchness, and the matter of equivalence to biblical models. The final section of the chapter is a case study in D.E. church leadership.

THE PEOPLE OF GOD WITHIN CULTURE

What does it mean to be the people of God, a fellowship of the committed, within culture? For Israel it first meant the moving of a fair-sized family group (Gen. 12:5) from one part of the Middle East (Haran) to another (Canaan). This family lived according to its familiar Semitic and nomadic customs. But under Abraham, its patriarch who had come out of idolatry into a faith relationship with the true God (Heb. 11:8–9), the family began to modify certain aspects of its culture because of its allegiance to God. Because it had separated itself from its larger culture and become an entity unto itself, Abraham's developing tribe was more free to modify its culture than heretofore. In the cultural history of Abraham's (and God's) tribe as recorded for us in the Bible, we are informed concerning a large number of the cultural concomitants of the divine-human interaction that started when Abraham met and pledged allegiance to God.

We see that Abraham's tribe grew and changed until it became twelve tribes under Jacob's sons, a nomadic people (again) under Moses, a conquering people under Joshua, a rather unsettled but sedentary conglomeration of

---

1. Kraft 1973b is a previous version of parts of this chapter.

related peoples under the judges, a unified theocracy under Samuel, a king-dom under Saul. In each case we see God and his people working together in terms of the changing Semitic culture that Abraham and his family took with them from Haran. At various points in its history Israel needed (or wanted) to revise its governmental patterns. Factors such as changes in lifestyle (from nomadic to sedentary), size, and diversity, with frequent disorganization (as under the judges), required such changes. Changes were also required (and for similar reasons) in the religious patterns. The patriarchal system where the head of each family served as its religious leader worked fine for a small tribe. But a grouping of growing tribes was better served by the specialization of one of the tribes, Levi (see Exod. 32:29), to function as priests. Later there was developed (in several stages) a highly elaborate ritual. Then preachers (called prophets) sprang up whose function differed from that of the Levitical priest-hood and a prophetic tradition became established. By New Testament times we become aware of a number of additional adaptations such as the synagogue, the Pharisees, the Sadducees, the monastic Essenes, and the politically activist Zealots.

All of these developments (with the exception of those listed in the last sentence) are described for us by Old Testament writers in terms of the part God played in establishing each new approach. And well they might be, since he was leading at every point. But there is a human side to the divine-human interaction as well. And even when the change is agreed to grudgingly by God (as when Israel wanted a king—1 Sam. 8:1–9) it is *in response to a cultural felt need on the part of the people of God.* We observe, therefore, throughout the Old Testament, familiar types of human cultural dynamics always co-occurring with the acts of God.

Such adaptation to and of culture has continued in God's workings, as recorded in the New Testament and in subsequent church history. The New Testament records a series of experiments engaged in by the people of God. These, in the cultures of that day, served functions such as government, worship, and ritual equivalent to those served by the parallel cultural forms in Hebrew culture. God had not given up on Israel or changed his mind concern-ing the appropriateness of their forms in former days, as certain interpretations of the Scriptures would contend. He simply continued to do as he had always done—to interact with humans in terms of the appropriate cultural forms.

There was, of course, in Christ a mammoth infusion of new information and new stimulus into the human scene. And this infusion made obsolete ("ful-filled") certain aspects of the previous system (e.g., blood sacrifice) for the Jews. But this infusion, though differing in degree and kind from previous infusions, was in many respects similar in its impact to previous infusions that had come through, for instance, Moses, Elijah, Amos, and many others. The method of operation (i.e., working in terms of the culture as it is) was confirmed rather than discarded.

But the cultural setting in which Jesus and his followers operated had become different in many ways from those depicted in the Old Testament. The Jews were a politically demoralized segment of a large empire and, perhaps because of this, more than ever before aware of the world outside the confines of their nation. Furthermore, their failure to continue to update their religious system had left them religiously demoralized. Some though (e.g., the Essenes and the Zealots), were apparently stimulated to experiment with new approaches to religion or politics (they may not have distinguished between them as thoroughly as we attempt to).

Meanwhile the gods of the Greeks had all but died for them as well. Throughout the Old Testament we are largely left unaware of what God was doing in the rest of the world, except as it impinged upon Israel (as in the captivities and Jonah's trip to Nineveh). This is undoubtedly because the authors and compilers of Old Testament Scripture were neither informed about nor interested in the rest of the world, not because God was inactive there (see Rom. 10:18). But in the more internationally aware context of the New Testament we are not only given glimpses of the Greco-Roman world outside of Israel but see the Hebrew Messiah and his Hebrew disciples vitally concerned for it.

The changes in perspective at every point are primarily *cultural, not theological*. God has always been concerned for the whole world. And he has always entered into interaction with those of any group who have responded in faith to him (Heb. 11:6; Acts 10:35–37). In Hebrew culture, then, there developed a people of God with whom God interacted in terms of the successive stages of that culture (model 4a). They perceived him in terms of their cultural involvement, entered into a culturally required covenant with him, and established and maintained themselves as a tribe and then a nation with a common ancestor (Abraham) and a single God. God confirmed for them with little or no change large portions of their Semitic culture (including, apparently, the majority of the law and the dietary and other cultural regulations) to such an extent that Hebrew culture (including the law) is completely recognizable as Semitic in comparison with other Semitic cultures. There were, however, a great number of changes that occurred in Hebrew culture (as they do in every culture) over the passage of time. And many of these (e.g., movement from henotheism to monotheism, movement from polygamy to monogamy) were, I believe, specific results of the interaction with God that was taking place within Hebrew culture.

In New Testament times we see this interactional process continuing in the more culturally heterogeneous setting of the Greco-Roman world. There is still a people of God interacting with God in terms of first-century Hebrew culture. We may assume that the Jerusalem church, for example, still required circumcision and that its members would not eat pork. But, unlike in the Old Testament, we are also made aware of God's interaction with other than Hebrew groupings of his people. These groupings called themselves "the Way" (Acts 19:9,23) or "Christian" (Acts 11:26) or simply "the Gathering" or "the Group" (the contemporary meaning of *ekklesia*, which has been translated "church") rather than Israel. And they worshiped and ritualized and organized themselves according to a *variety* of culturally appropriate ways rather than simply in a Hebrew way (though Hebrew Christians followed the contemporary Hebrew synagogue pattern).

But the differences between the forms in terms of which the New Testament peoples of God interacted with God and those of the Old Testament Israelites were again primarily cultural rather than theological. The Old Testament operation of God was not, as some evolutionary theological positions contend, merely "a type of the church"—as if God were only practicing at that time for the real game to be played later! It was a full-fledged involvement of God with human beings in the same very serious "game" that is still going on. And they played by the same rules in that day. God's method of operation throughout has been to adapt his approach to human cultures. The fact that today in western cultures we organize the people of God into churches rather than into tribes and nations (like Israel) shows a *cultural* change rather than some drastic alteration in God's method of dealing with humans.

Such cultural changes recorded in the Bible and the large number of subsequent examples of the "*in*culturating" of "people of God-ness" in a variety of cultures help us to better understand God's method of dealing with humans in terms of human culture. And such understanding leads us to relate the topics of the previous section to our understanding of what God intends for the church today. We can see, thus, that (1) the whole of the casebook (including the Old Testament) is useful in instructing us concerning God's operation with his people today, and (2) God desires that today's organizations of his people function in ways dynamically equivalent to those of the best scriptural examples.

DYNAMIC-EQUIVALENCE TRANSCULTURATION OF THE CHURCH (Model 11d)

Contemporary churches should bear the same resemblance to the scriptural models (both Old Testament and New Testament) of God's interaction with humans in culture that a faithful dynamic-equivalence translation of the Scriptures bears to his interaction with humans in language. Such churches should not appear to be cultural "translationese." They should not be filled with cultural forms distorting the true interactional intent of God, such as the "thees and thous," the technical jargon (e.g., justification, sanctification, etc.), and the overliteral idioms (e.g., "bowels of mercies") of the King James Version. *A contemporary church, like a contemporary translation, should impress the uninitiated observer as an original production in the contemporary culture, not as a badly fitted import from somewhere else.*

Those planting and/or operating churches should work in accord with the seven basic propositions for Bible translators outlined in chapter 13. They should (1) recognize, (2) respect and work in terms of the unique genius of the receptor culture, knowing that (3) anything (such as the church) expressible in one culture is expressible in another. However, they should not hesitate (4) to alter the (Hebrew and Greco-Roman) forms in terms of which the original churches were expressed, for they should realize that *the content expressed, not the forms in terms of which that content was originally expressed, is sacred.* They should understand (5) that the biblical cultures were fully human cultures, dignified by the fact that God worked within them but not sanctified thereby; the Bible demonstrates God's willingness to work in terms of *any* culture rather than his desire to perfect and impose a single culture. They should further understand (6) that the church is meant to be intelligible to the world around it; that God expects to be made intelligible to humanity by means of the church. And faithful church people are (7) to work toward this end by consciously attempting to produce church structures within the receptor culture that are dynamically equivalent to those portrayed (though partially) in the pages of Scripture.

Applying this model to church planting would mean eschewing attempts to produce mere formal correspondence between churches in one culture and those in another. A church that is merely a "literal" rendering of the forms of one church—be it an American church or a first-century Greco-Roman church—is not according to the dynamic-equivalence model, for it is not structured in such a way that it can appropriately perform the functions and convey the meanings that should characterize a Christian church. It will always smack of foreignness, of insensitivity to the surrounding culture, of inappropriateness to the real needs of the people and the real message of God to them. For its forms have not been exchanged, via transculturation, for those appropriate in the new setting.

A "formal-correspondence church" usually models itself slavishly after the foreign church that founded it (whether that founding church be a Euro-American missionary body working outside Euro-America or a denominational heritage taken from one part of Euro-America to another). If that church has bishops or presbyters or elders, the younger church will have them too. If that church operates according to a written constitution, the younger church will as well. If that church conducts business meetings according to *Roberts' Rules of Order*, the younger church will likewise. And so it will be with regard to educational requirements for leaders, times of worship, style of worship, type of music, structure of church buildings, behavioral requirements for good standing (e.g., refraining from smoking and/or alcoholic beverages), types of educational, medical, and benevolent activity entered into, even expression of missionary concern (if any) on the part of the younger church.

And all of this may be imposed or, in the case of long-established churches such as those in Europe and America, continued in utter disregard for the culturally appropriate functional equivalents and the indigenously understood meanings of all these things in the culture in which the younger church is supposedly witnessing. The impression such churches give to the people of their cultural world is one of foreignness and outside domination, even though the leadership of these churches may well be "their own people." This "indigeneity" of leadership, however, is only in a formal sense, since these leaders have been carefully indoctrinated into the foreign system in order to attain the positions that they have within the system. By no stretch of the imagination can such a church (whether in Africa or in America) be appropriately labeled "indigenous" or dynamically equivalent to biblical models. It may be "self-supporting, self-governing and self-extending" (see Stock 1899 and Tippett 1973:154–59 for discussions of this three-self formula) and still be "slavishly foreign" (Smalley 1958:52), for the patterns employed are those of another culture or subculture from a foreign geographical area or a previous generation.

Though an indigenous or dynamically equivalent church will ordinarily be characterized by the kind of self-functioning embodied in the three-self formula, not every church that governs, supports, and propagates itself can be properly labeled "indigenous" except in a very superficial, formal sense. For "although these three 'self' elements may be present in such a movement, they are essentially independent variables" (Smalley 1958: 51–52), rather than diagnostic criteria of indigeneity. The mere fact of self-government, self-support, and self-propagation does not ensure that the church in question is "indigenous." *The indigeneity (if present at all) lies in the manner in which such selfhood is expressed.* That is, a simple evaluation of the structured cultural forms of government, propagation, and support is not sufficient. One has to look also at the ways in which these cultural structures are operated and the meanings attached to them both by the church itself and by the surrounding community.

There is, for example, a church which is advertised by its founding mission as a great indigenous church, where its pastors are completely supported by the local church members, yet the mission behind the scenes pulls the strings and the church does its bidding like the puppets of the "independent" iron curtain countries (Smalley 1958:54).

There are many churches where the real power is no longer directly or indirectly in the hands of foreigners. Indigenous people are now in charge, maintaining the foreign forms and imposing them on new generations with little regard for the fact that the forms they impose convey very different meanings to the new generations.

The true aim in this as well as in every other aspect of the propagation of Christianity, however, is not formal correspondence but dynamic or functional equivalence, of the type discussed in chapter 13 for Bible translation. For, as Nida points out, Christianity is not like Islam which through the Koran "attempts to fix for all time the behavior of Muslims" by setting up an absolutely unbending set of forms to be adopted, never adapted. "The Christian position is not one of static conformance to dead rules, but of dynamic obedience to a living God" (1954:52).

A dynamic-equivalence church produces an impact on the people of the society of which it is a part equivalent to that which the scripturally described peoples of God produced upon the original hearers. In that equivalence the church will need leadership, organization, education, worship, buildings, behavioral standards, and means of expressing Christian love and concern to the people of its own culture who have not yet responded to Christ. But a dynamically equivalent church will employ culturally appropriate forms in meeting these needs—familiar, meaningful forms that it will possess, adapt, and fill with Christian meanings.

At the beginning of their employment by the church, these forms may be only minimally adequate to the tasks at hand. But in the course of their employment by the Holy Spirit with the church (see Allen 1956), they will begin the process of transformation so well exemplified in the history of some word forms that the early church "possessed for Christ." Such a word was the Greek *agapao* which, according to Quell (1964:21–35), was a weak word, often meaning no more than "to be satisfied with something." It was, however, transformed by the church into the distinctively Christian word for "love" (see chapter 18 and Kraft 1973a for more detailed discussions).

What is desired, then, is the kind of church that will take indigenous forms, possess them for Christ, adapt and employ them to serve Christian ends by fulfilling indigenous functions, and convey through them Christian meanings to the surrounding society. When the term "indigenous church" means this kind of church, well and good. But such a designation has too readily been assigned on the basis of mere formal correspondence to the sending church rather than on the basis of true dynamic equivalence to a biblical model for the church. And such formal correspondence, carrying with it the pervasive impression of foreignness and irrelevance to real life, is disturbingly counter-productive in terms of the powerful, relevant impact on human beings that Christianity is intended to have.

When, however,

the indigenous people of a community think of the Lord as their own, not a foreign Christ: when they do things as unto the Lord meeting the cultural needs around them, worshipping in patterns they understand; when their congregations function in participation in a body, which is structurally indigenous; then you have an indigenous Church (Tippett 1973:158).

That is, Christians should feel that their church is an original work within their own culture. A dynamically equivalent church, then, is

a group of believers who live out their life, including their socialized Christian activity, in the patterns of the local society, and for whom any transformation of that society comes out of their felt needs under the guidance of the Holy Spirit and the Scriptures (Smalley 1958:55).

DYNAMIC EQUIVALENCE TO BIBLICAL MODELS

According to the foregoing conception, a dynamic-equivalence church would (1) convey to its members truly Christian meanings, (2) function within its society in such a way that it plugs into the felt needs of that society and produces within it an impact for Christ equivalent to that which the first-century church produced in its society, and (3) be couched in cultural forms as nearly indigenous as possible.

This necessitates ascertaining the biblical forms, functions, and meanings to which the church in the receptor culture is expected to develop dynamic equivalence. For this information we look primarily to the New Testament (though for many situations the Old Testament offers more easily transculturated models). The book of Acts and the pastoral epistles provide many insights into matters of organization, leadership, fellowship, witness, and worship. Insights into behavioral matters are likewise found in these books and also in the Corinthian epistles. Certain other epistles focus more on doctrinal matters. To these models contemporary churches, whether in Euro-America or overseas, are to develop dynamically equivalent forms within and relevant to their contemporary cultural matrix.

Techniques of exegesis have been developed to enable us to discover these New Testament meanings for application in western life. Our emphasis now must be on dynamically equivalent exegesis for other cultures. In attempting to discover a dynamically equivalent form of preaching I once asked a group of Nigerian church leaders what would be the appropriate way to present a message such as the Christian one to the village council. They replied:

We would choose the oldest, most respected man in the group and ask him a question. He would discourse, perhaps at length, on the topic and then become silent, whereupon we would ask another question. As the old man talked, other old men would comment as well. But eventually he and the others would do less and less of the talking and the leader would do more and more. In this way we would develop our message and it would become the topic for discussion of the whole village.

I asked them why they didn't employ this approach in church. "Why, we've been taught that monologue is the Christian way," they replied. "Can this be why no old men come to church?" I asked. "Of course! " they said. "We have alienated them all by not showing them due respect in public meetings." Thus it is that a preaching form that may be appropriate enough in Euro-American culture—dynamically equivalent in that culture to New Testament models —loses its equivalence when exported to another culture. It becomes counterproductive.

The same occurs with respect to leadership. Because New Testament churches appointed bishops, elders, and deacons does not mean that churches today must label their leaders by these terms or expect them to lead in the same (rather dictatorial) ways that were appropriate for those leaders in their society. These were simply some of the types of leadership appropriate to the various cultures and subcultures of the areas spoken of in the New Testament.

We see, in fact, not a single, once-for-all leadership pattern (of forms) set down in the pages of the New Testament. We see, rather, a series of experiments with cultural appropriateness ranging from a communal approach (Acts 2:42–47) to, apparently, leadership by a council of "apostles and elders" (Acts 15:4,6,22), to the more highly structured patterns in the pastoral epistles. In each case the pattern developed in response to the felt needs of the members of the culture and subculture in which the particular local church operated. Thus we observe certain organizational differences between the Jewish Jerusalem church and the Greek churches with which Timothy and Titus were concerned. Likewise we observe, in the Acts account of the appointment of deacons (Acts 6:1–6), the development in a culturally apppropriate way of a new form to meet a need not anticipated at an earlier stage in the life of the Jerusalem church.

DYNAMICALLY EQUIVALENT CHURCH LEADERSHIP: A CASE STUDY

The pastoral epistles list in detail attributes felt to be culturally apppropriate to church leaders in the Greco-Roman part of the first-century church.[2] But, as is the case with the various types of leaders referred to above, the focus is constantly on appropriateness of function rather than on standardization of form. The lists of characteristics catalogued for the original hearers illustrate some of the things implicit to church leadership in that society at that time. According to the author of 1 Timothy, such a leader should be of unimpeachable character, which in that culture meant being "faithful to one wife, sober, temperate, courteous, hospitable," etc. (1 Tim. 3:2 NEB). A leader possessing these attributes would attain and maintain the proper reputation within and outside the Christian community.

Assuming that in such a list the Scriptures both designate culturally appropriate forms and point to supraculturally valid meanings, we may ask how such a list ought to be transculturated into other cultures. We suggest that this passage designates (and illustrates for that culture) at least irreproachability, self-control, and good will to others as requirements. In a dynamic-equivalence church the leaders are therefore to manifest such characteristics as will communicate these meanings to the people of their culture. It will thus be possible to generate equivalently appropriate listings of the forms through which these meanings will best be expressed in today's receptor cultures. The

2. The making of such "ethical lists" to state the required qualifications of various types of leaders was, apparently, a common practice in Greek culture. See Easton (1948:197–202) for a useful discussion of this custom and examples of lists of such leaders as King, General, Ruler, and Midwife.

forms in such a list will be functionally equivalent to those in 1 Timothy 3 and Titus 1, but not necessarily the same. For different cultures, while showing a considerable degree of similarity in such matters (due, I believe, to human commonality), focus on slightly differing aspects according to their differing value systems.

In contemporary American culture the criteria would include such scripturally listed items as serious, self-controlled, courteous, a good teacher (or preacher), not a drunkard, not quarrelsome, upright, doctrinally sound. Such items as hospitable, dignified, no lover of money might or might not be specified in such a list but would probably also be expected by Americans. Americans would not, however, necessarily be so insistent that their leaders demonstrate their ability to manage a home and family well, since they tend to choose younger leaders than seem to be in focus here. Such a factor would probably be a consideration with an older person and, Americans might contend, ought to be in any culture if things are to run smoothly. Nor would Americans say, as it was necessary to say in Greco-Roman culture, that irreproachability demands that the person never have more than one marriage,[3] since they allow and even encourage a person to remarry after the death of a first spouse. Many American churches, though, would disallow (that is, not regard as beyond reproach) a pastor, at least, who had remarried after a divorce.

An American list, then, would include most of the items on the Greek list, though some of those specifically mentioned by Paul would probably be left implicit rather than made explicit by us. Americans, though, would probably want to add a few things such as administrative ability and perhaps even youth. Owing to similarities between Greco-Roman and American culture, the lists will be fairly similar.

If, though, Americans develop an equivalent list for a radically different culture such as many in Africa (e.g., Higi of northeastern Nigeria), we will find some additions to and subtractions from the list. And there will be at least one major reinterpretation of a criterion, though the criterion is basically the same. Greed, being the cardinal sin of Higiland, would be one of the major proscribed items, and conformity to culturally expected patterns of politeness one of the more important prescribed items. Hospitality and its concomitant, generosity, would be highlighted to a much greater degree than for either Greco-Roman or American culture. Soberness, temperance, patience, and the like would appear on the Higi list, and more highly valued than on the American list. Higis would, in addition, focus on age and membership in the royalty social class. They would, furthermore, strongly emphasize family management—certainly much more strongly than would Americans and probably even more strongly than did Greco-Romans.

---

3. See such commentaries as *The International Critical Commentary*, *The Moffatt Commentary*, and others on the interpretation of the "one wife" verses (1 Tim. 3:2,12; Tit. 1:6) as referring to "digamy"—the marriage of a man to another wife after the death or divorce of his first wife.

Herein would lie the most significant formal difference between the Higi ideal and either of the others. For, in order for such a leader to function effectively in a way equivalent to that intended for the first-century leaders, he would not only have to manage his household well but would have to have at least two wives in that household! "How," the Higi person would ask, "can one properly lead if he has not demonstrated his ability by managing well a household with more than one wife in it?" The Kru of Liberia, with a similar ideal, state, "You cannot trust a man with only one wife."

If, then, we place the lists side by side and arrange each in approximate order of priority, we can compare the similarities and differences between the culturally prescribed formal characteristics deemed requisite for Christian leadership in the three cultures:

Greco-Roman	American	Higi
1. Irreproachable: One wife (forever) Serious Self-Controlled Courteous Not Quarrelsome	1. Irreproachable: Faithful to Spouse Self-Controlled Serious Courteous	1. Royal Social Class
2. Hospitable	2. Doctrinally sound	2. Hospitable
3. A Good Teacher	3. Vigorous	3. Mature
4. Not a Money Lover	4. A Good Preacher	4. Irreproachable: Generous Patient Self-Controlled Serious Courteous
5. Manage Household Well	5. Personable	5. Manage Polygamous Household Well
6. Mature in Faith	6. Mature in Faith	6. A Good Teacher
7. Good Reputation Outside	7. Manage Household Well	

Fig. 16.1. Leadership lists for Greco-Roman, American, and Higi cultures.

If we added columns listing the formal characteristics of ideal leaders in the various cultural varieties portrayed in the Old Testament it would become even more clear that God chooses to work in terms of the forms of each culture in order to attain his purposes. We deduce, therefore, that the principle of dynamic equivalence in leadership patterns is the ideal recommended by the Scriptures.

It must be made clear, however, that *we are here speaking only of God's starting point*. Once God begins to work within the people of a culture his interaction with these people inevitably results in the transformation of at least certain of their customs. To maintain, as I have above, that a dynamically equivalent Higi church would have polygamous leadership is not to say either that God's ultimate standard is polygamy or that this particular criterion for dynamically equivalent leadership will never be changed. It is, in fact, likely that it will be changed, just as through God's interaction with the Hebrews, polygamy died out in Hebrew culture— over the course of a few thousand years. When, however, a missionary or other leader steps in and attempts to impose foreign criteria on the Higi church, a kind of formal correspondence to foreign model, rather than dynamic equivalence to the New Testament models, is produced. In this way the dynamism so apparent in the early churches is severely compromised.

And so it is with each of the elements in the life, doctrine, and worship of churches. The New Testament needs to be interpreted in its cultural context with respect to the functions served by the forms employed (as illustrated above). Then the various characteristics of the receptor church should be evaluated to ascertain the appropriateness of the forms employed in conveying meanings and meeting needs in ways equivalent to the New Testament models. *The priority must be for conveying in the receptor culture a content that is equivalent to that conveyed in the original culture.* This may require that the cultural forms in terms of which that content is expressed differ widely in the receptor culture from those of either the New Testament or of the source culture. *As with translation, so with the transculturating of the church—the extent of the divergence of forms should depend upon the distance between the cultures in question.*

Evaluating the appropriateness of present and future approaches to church-ness may be done by following an analytic procedure parallel to that described in chapter 13 (Fig. 13.6) as necessary to dynamic-equivalence translation (note the numbering of the steps in Fig. 16.2).

On the basis of such an analysis it is possible to arrive at more ideal bases for what church planters and builders—both indigenous and expatriate—are really commissioned to be involved in with God. For integral to sound theology at this point (and at most points) is sound anthropology. Dynamic equivalence is the model for churches that we should practice and teach. Formal-correspondence models of the church result in the same kind of foreign, stilted product as the Bible translations produced according to that model.

Having considered the dynamic-equivalence model as applied to "church-ness," we now turn to an application of the model to Christian conversion.

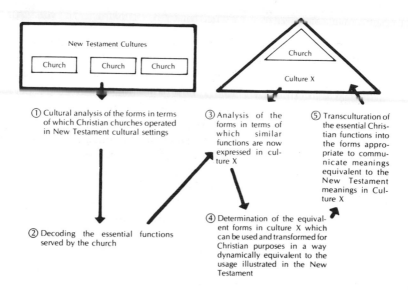

Fig. 16.2 Analytic procedure for arriving at the forms to be employed by a dynamically equivalent church.

17. Christian Conversion as a Dynamic Process

If churches are to be dynamically equivalent to those of the Bible they must be made up of members who have become a part of them in a dynamically equivalent way. But what is this way? To attempt to answer this question we will seek to examine the dynamics of Christian conversion from the perspective being developed here. Our aim is to probe the implications of dynamic-equivalence conversion (model 11e). We will look first at certain inadequate models, then at the biblical concept, constants in the conversion process, and the contrast between conversion to Christ and conversion to another culture.

INADEQUATE MODELS

Because of a lack of awareness of God's desire to adapt his approach to human beings to the cultural matrix in which they are immersed, positions have been developed that advocate but a single method of entrance into the community of God. Such positions are usually defended in terms of the proper time for baptizing converts. Certain denominations (e.g., Baptist, Mennonite) hold strongly to the concept of "believers' baptism." That is, they contend, no persons are properly admissible into the community of God until they have consciously decided for Christ on the basis of their own free choice. Other denominations (e.g., Roman Catholic, Lutheran, Reformed), however, contend that children born into Christian families may validly be initiated into the family of God as children on the basis of a commitment by their parents to raise them in the Christian way. This practice is intended to imply that, at an appropriate point in their lives, those who have already been baptized on the basis of their parents' confession and commitment will themselves consciously opt for Christianity.

Out of recognition of the fact that some initiatory ceremony is appropriate soon after the birth of a child into a Christian home, "believers' baptism" churches have developed dedication ceremonies. Churches practicing infant baptism, on the other hand, have typically developed for their youth a program of catechetical instruction designed to lead them to conscious decision for Christ and his church. At the end of such instruction the fact that these youth have now made such a decision is made public by means of a confirmation ceremony. Thus the advocates of each position have come to recognize the need on the part of their youth for both kinds of ceremony.

What is being recognized, though unwittingly, is the fact of cultural difference between "first-generation Christians"—those converted "out of the world," having consciously chosen to align themselves with the people of God—and "second-generation Christians," who have been raised in Christian homes. In the case of the former, conversion may involve a radical departure from their former lifestyle. In the case of the latter, however, there may be little or no behavioral change evident as a result of the conscious decision to personally affirm one's commitment to the Christian community in which one has been participating since birth.

And Christians, conditioned by the western cultural dictum maintaining that whenever there are competing views on an issue only one of them can be correct, have argued this matter hotly. But, as in so many theological debates, the real issues are not theological but cultural. The cultural situation of a person who has lived for twenty years or more according to habits that disregard Christ and then converted is vastly different from that of a person who, having been brought up in the church, has never really known any other way of life. The behavior of the latter is already largely conformed, at least externally, to what the church regards as Christian standards. If, as is often the case, those who grow up in the church are given the impression that conversion to Christ can only mean a dramatic, Pauline about-face, they are likely to become quite confused.

Delbert Wiens (1965) has come to grips with just such a situation in the Mennonite Brethren Church. He describes how the conversion experience that was, for the "great-grandfathers" of the present generation of Mennonite Brethren, "a violent struggle to 'give in' to God, followed by a shattering experience and then peace" (1965:4), has become for a contemporary six-year-old simply an affirmation "that he has placed himself in the only way of life that he has ever really known" (p. 5). Yet (at the time of Wiens's article (1965), the denomination continued to *require that the youths validate their own experience by recreating something quite similar to the experience of the great-grandfathers* (and of the apostle Paul).[1]

For the young person, even after consciously affirming allegiance to Christ (at a very early age), is taught that conversion is "a radical changing of the way" (p. 6). How, then, are young people to be assured that they are truly saved if they have never lived in such a way that their turning to Christ was a radical departure from that lifestyle? Thus the instruction that the young people of Mennonite Brethren background (and of many other conservative Christian backgrounds) receive in their church concerning conversion

helps to create the necessity of *doubt* and the *rebellion* which *leads to that sinful position* from which the young person can meaningfully turn in a "conversion" that will *match the experience of his great-grandfathers* (1965:6). [Emphasis added.]

1. I understand that there has been a good deal of improvement in this situation among Mennonite Brethren since the early 1960s. Many other denominations are, however, experiencing a similar situation, often without understanding why.

Many, therefore, embark (at least symbolically) upon an excursion, or "detour," into the world in order to experience at least some of those things that the denomination has defined as the kind of "worldly" things on which Christians are to turn their backs. These sins are labeled rather specifically in testimonies by those who, now sure of their salvation, had first committed them and then turned from them. They include such things as smoking, drinking, movie-going (though this is "losing its symbolic power, except for the very protected" (ibid.:11), sexual sins, and the like. Some form of identifying with hippy subculture was for a while a fashionable detour into the world "from which one can be reformed when settling back in the safe patterns of a normal Mennonite Brethren church" (p. 11).

Wiens is struck by the "joylessness of their performance."

It is almost as if they are fulfilling a duty, a duty that builds up a heavy charge of guilt which then is discharged in the "rededication" that follows (1965:11).

The immediate effect of this conversion experience may be very much like that of the great-grandfathers. But the long-term results are too often to produce

a satisfying staid "pillar" of the church who is deeply suspicious of anyone who wants to change any aspect of the status quo. Too often such a person seems to make no further attempt to grow in Christian grace, to grapple with the Scriptures, to deepen his Christian commitment. He remains satisfied with certain symbolic gestures which identify the in-group. He may even tithe (Weins 1965:11).

But churches like the Mennonite Brethren at least require conversion. The extreme to which many of the denominations have gone that induct their members via infant baptism is often much worse. They may give the impression that all those whose names on the church rolls (via infant baptism) are automatically Christians, whether or not they subsequently act upon that membership.

A model of conversion that is equivalent in its dynamics to the examples set forth for us in our divine casebook, however, will focus on more than simply the initiation ceremonies (such as baptism, confirmation, or rededication) or a single act such as a "conversion experience." It will, rather, focus, as the biblical records focus, on the total dynamic relational process that a living, lifetime relationship with God is intended to be. Such a relationship involves many "peak experiences" (Maslow 1964) of which the first may or may not be the most significant. For many, that first real encounter with God was a great one. For many others, however, it was so undistinguished that it has gone unremembered.

It is very important for most people to be clear as to just where they stand in relation to the group (in this case the church) that they are seeking to enter. For this reason, as Van Gennep points out (1908; see Keesing and Keesing

1971:214–17 for a summary), most cultures provide recognition ceremonies or "rites of passage" for their members by means of which cultures inform both the individual and the group at large concerning the stage of development in their relationship. Two kinds of such ceremonies are termed "rites of incorporation" and "rites of consolidation." Any viable group needs both types—the one to induct new members, the other to reinforce regularly the feeling of group solidarity (as Sunday worship services reinforce solidarity in churches). And in general it is good to have more than one incorporation rite and a considerable number of consolidation rites.

According to this terminology, ceremonies that accompany such important times in life as birth, puberty, marriage, and graduation are rites of incorporation for the person(s) entering a new status, for they signal and symbolize the induction of a person into the next stage of his life. They often also serve a consolidational function for those who celebrate with the initiate(s). Such recognitions let the person and the group know where the person stands at a given stage of life. Child dedication, infant baptism, confirmation-class graduation, adult baptism, joining the church—these are all incorporation rites and play an important part in the incorporation of a person into the life of a church. Their importance should not be minimized. More attention should, however, be given to two aspects of this matter: (1) the cultural or subcultural appropriateness of the form employed to symbolize the transition, and (2) the need for additional incorporation rites (with accompanying additional statuses) after the transition into church membership.

1. The early church chose water baptism as the preferred form for symbolizing the passage of a person into church membership. The selection of that particular form was quite appropriate culturally, both for Jews and for many Greeks, because water baptism was employed as the initiation ceremony both for proselytes to Judaism and for entrance into the Greek mystery religions (Oepke 1964:529–46, on *baptizo*). Males were, of course, circumcised as well if they became Jews.

The meaning to be symbolized is, however, *initiation into the people of God.* The choice of form should therefore be based upon its cultural appropriateness for dynamic equivalence to the New Testament in signaling that meaning to those involved. When a traditional form symbolizes something different from its intended meaning (e.g., oppression by a foreign religion, as in India, or pressing one into the old people's mold, as in contemporary America) serious attention needs to be given to revising the form. *Holding to religious forms that have lost their intended meanings, as the Pharisees did, is superstition.*

R. D. Winter has suggested (informally) that a coffin might be a more meaningful initiation form than water in contemporary America. The person being initiated would lie in the coffin with the lid down and be described as "dead in trespasses and sins" (Eph. 2:1). Then the pastor would lift the lid of the coffin, free the person, and announce that he or she is now "raised to new life in Christ" (Eph. 2:4). Many nonwestern societies have indigenous initiatory rites that would in their cultural contexts more adequately convey scriptural meanings to them than either water or coffins. Such forms should be experimented with if contemporary incorporation into the people of God is to have an impact on today's people equivalent to that of baptism on New Testament peoples. The possibility also exists of developing ceremonies according to traditional patterns to which the historical rite of water baptism is added. This would allow both dynamic equivalence in meaning and identification with a worldwide transcultural community that employs the historical form.

2. We need to give more attention to the development of statuses with accompanying incorporation rites beyond induction into church membership. How frequently the impression is given that joining the church signals the *end* of one's Christian training rather than the beginning! For many churches there are no more stages beyond church membership for a person to be incorporated into (except for those few who go on to become church leaders). A. R. Tippett points out that those denominations believing in a "second blessing" or a later "filling" by the Holy Spirit seem to do a better job than other Christian groups in bringing their members to Christian maturity. This is because they designate one or more statuses to be aimed at beyond church membership. There are, then, further stages of incorporation symbolized by rites of incorporation beyond the church-joining ceremony.

Some churches effectively (though often subconsciously) challenge their members to greater maturity by either formally or informally designating involvement in giving (e.g., tithing), missions, Sunday school teaching, visitation, a search for spiritual gifts, and the like as spiritual status-raisers. For other churches, all such attempts are largely ineffective. Many church leaders scorn such efforts to induce and mark spiritual progress toward maturity on the basis of the belief that it is improper to depend on such "unspiritual" means to bring about spiritual ends. I believe that such people fail to understand that God's way is to work with, rather than against, psychologically and culturally appropriate mechanisms to bring about spiritual ends.

One basic problem here is that Euro-American churches are patterned closely after the school system. They fail, however, by providing neither the examinations and grades that push people to new statuses in school nor any functionally equivalent mechanisms. Schools without examinations and grades would stimulate as little learning and growth as churches do. Churches peopled by those who have learned in school to depend on the push toward achievement of exams and grades should not be surprised when school methods minus effective status-raisers produce little growth.

Consolidation ceremonies such as the Lord's Supper, festivals, corporate worship services, retreats, conferences, and the like, though important to the life of the church, will not be treated in detail here. Suffice it to say that these too should be frequent and culturally appropriate. The lack of cultural appropriateness (even to the in-group) of such rituals as worship services (both at home and abroad) is a major cause of the lack of solidarity of many segments of the contemporary church.

THE BIBLICAL CONCEPT OF CONVERSION

Our attention (as westerners), when we turn to the Bible, is most often attracted by such dramatic examples of conversion as those of Paul (Acts 9), the Philippian jailer (Acts 16), the Ethiopian eunuch (Acts 8), the Samaritan woman (Jn. 4), etc. But what about the disciples? When were they converted? And the majority of the major characters of the Old Testament? There is no doubt that these people were consciously committed to God. But how did their commitment come about? Must we postulate for every one of them a dramatic "bolt-out-of-the-blue" type of experience that somehow escaped the notice of those who recorded their other experiences? Certainly not.

Nor can we support a single prescribed pattern for conversion from an informed study of the words employed in the Bible to designate the conversion experience. The key concept signaled by the primary biblical words (Heb. *shuv*; Gr. *epistrepho*) is "turning," or "returning" (Bertram 1971:722–29). In the pages of the Old Testament we see the concept developed with primary reference to those who were, or thought they were, once close to God but needed to return and to reassert their loyalty to the God who had entered into a covenant relationship with them (see Holladay 1958 for a detailed discussion). The New Testament builds upon this same concept in its use of the Greek words for "turning." *The central focus remains that of turning, changing direction, reversing the direction in which one is headed* so that it is *toward* rather than away from God (see Barclay 1964). In the Old Testament prophets and throughout the New Testament this concept of turning is coupled with the need for repentance (Gr. *metanoia*) from the error and willfulness that led one astray.

It is notable, however, that no single set of specific forms for such a radical reorientation is prescribed—in spite of the fact that this turning is to be complete and total. It is to involve repentance and a turning from the previous direction of life. It is to lead to a transformation of all life and relationships. For Israelites such a return to God often involved sackcloth and ashes, since this was the culturally appropriate form for showing contrition. To the disciples Jesus simply said, "Follow me" (meaning, of course, "Commit yourselves to me"). John the Baptist, on the other hand, employed the well-known initiation rite for proselytes to Judaism but with a new meaning. For he was applying it to people who were already Jews. As throughout Scripture, so with respect to conversion, *the requirement is specified as a function*, a dynamic response to an invitation by God. The form that that response takes is not determined once and for all by God or by some statement of Scripture or tradition. It is, rather, to be appropriate as an expression of that meaning to the culture of those to whom the appeal is made.

The fact of the matter is that *the biblical focus is upon a relational interaction that*

may be entered into via a number of culturally and psychologically appropriate ways.
Each of these relationships is both entered into and continued on the basis of a
human faith-response (allegiance) to the divine invitation. But only some are
the result of a crisis-type about-face. Much more frequently we may assume
from scriptural silence on the matter that the human participant in the interaction more or less grew or was trained into relationship with God. Conscious
commitment was there and not infrequently we are treated to descriptions of
peak experiences in the individual and/or corporate lives of these people of
God. But neither the start of the commitment nor any spectacular concomitants of it are very often in focus.

This is especially true throughout the Old Testament where most of the
record deals with those whose home conditioning was such that they were (like
the Mennonite Brethren youth) to all outward appearances already behaviorally more similar to than different from the people of God with whom they
lived. When, however, as in Jonah or in the New Testament (especially Acts),
an appeal for conversion is made to some person or group (either outside or
within Israel) who have neither grown into nor dramatically converted to God,
the response is more likely to be spectacular, since the amount of behavioral
change required is great. But it is the distance between where people are
behaviorally and where they need to be in order to demonstrate their new
heart allegiance that properly determines the spectacularness or lack of it that
should accompany the reorientation. Dramatic concomitants of a turning to
Christ are not ordinarily to be expected of those whose behavior already
largely conforms to standards labeled "Christian" by the community that
they join.

For Paul, who persecuted Christians, the change had to be dramatic in this
one respect at least. Since he was a Pharisee, we may assume that the major
part of the highly commendable habitual behavior of the Pharisees was retained by him—but with the kind of change of reference point (see below) that
Jesus proclaimed as necessary if the Pharisees were to get straightened out. For
the disciples, however, the change was much less spectacular, though no less
real.

CONSTANTS IN THE CONVERSION PROCESS

Though the cultural and psychological forms related to conversion are
variable, we may point to several important *constants* implicit in the biblical
descriptions of God's interactions with his people. These form the grid for our
attempt to understand the biblical concept of conversion.

1. The first of these constants is *a conscious allegiance (faith commitment) to God.*
Throughout the Old Testament it is plain that not all of those biologically
descended from Abraham were the people of God except in a potential sense.
Jesus makes this fact very clear in his denunciations of the scribes and the
Pharisees. And Paul states it plainly when he says that

not all the people of Israel are the chosen people of God. Neither are all Abraham's descendants the children of God. . . . Instead, the children born as a result of God's promise are regarded as the true descendants (Rom. 9:6–8 TEV).

For it is by faithfulness to God (Hab. 2:4; Rom. 1:17; Heb. 11; etc.) that a relationship with God is established and maintained. And faithfulness implies conscious allegiance. In the New Testament, when the Gospel is presented primarily to Gentiles, the need for such conscious faith allegiance is made even more explicit (e.g., Acts 16:31, and throughout Acts).

The Scriptures (Old Testament and New Testament) do not often focus on either the fact or the nature of the initiation of this allegiance. In dealing with Gentiles there is reference to the newness and consequent *discontinuity* of such an allegiance with their previous religious commitment (e.g., Acts 17:30). For Jews, though, the focus is more often on the *continuity* between the Jewish commitment to God and that advocated by Christianity (e.g., Lk. 24:25–27; Acts 2; etc.). The necessity for a conscious pledge of allegiance on the part of the members of each of these groups is emphasized, but whether such a pledge involved radical discontinuity with the past or simply a renewed affirmation of one's commitment to the same God on the basis of new information (concerning Christ) does not seem important to the authors of Scripture.

2. Their focus seems, rather, to be on the second of these constants—the fact of *a dynamic interaction between God and human beings* that issues from a person's conscious allegiance to God. The authors of Scripture usually show sublime unconcern for the satisfaction of our curiosity over just how Noah or Abraham or Joseph or David or Peter or John or Cornelius or Lydia came to their allegiance to God. Did some of them have spectacular conversion experiences? We aren't told. What we are informed about is the continuing series of divine-human interactions that issued from allegiance to God on the part of the biblical personages.

Here I want to digress a bit from this main point to attempt to outline a dynamic view of the decision-making process that human beings employ and God works with in his interaction with people. A. R. Tippett (1973:123) has developed a similar model (from which the following has been developed) but with a slightly different emphasis. The following model (unlike his) focuses in on the fact that the process of conversion is made up of a multitude of (often very small) decisions by human beings in interaction with God. Each of these decisions may be conceived of as the result of a process involving points of stimulus, realization, decision, and "new-habit," interspersed with periods of developing awareness, consideration, and incorporation. This scheme may be diagramed as in Figure 17.1 on p. 336.

The process that leads to decision starts with a *stimulus*. This stimulus may be a matter of communicated information, observation, a new thought that seems to spring into one's mind spontaneously, or any other set of factors. Such a stimulus may then be pondered by the individual or group, increasing

Decision I

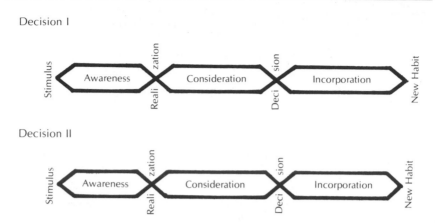

Decision II

Fig. 17.1. Model of the decision-making process.

awareness of its implications, requirements, and above all the need to make a decision with regard to the stimulus. This awareness leads to a point of *realization* of the potential relevance of such a decision to the person or group. This realization in turn issues in a process of *consideration* (the decision-making process) and a point of encounter or *decision*. When the decision is made, then, the process of *incorporating* the new orientation into the life of the person or group begins. This culminates in the development of a *new habit* of behavior, attitude, relationship, etc.

Certain decisions are much more important than others in the sense that they occasion a greater number of other changes in the life of the person or group. There is an enormous difference in this respect between a decision to change the type of toothpaste one uses and a decision to change the point of reference around which one orients one's life from self-interest to Christ. But the process of making each decision is the same.

Likewise, the emotional concomitants will differ greatly from decision to decision and from person to person. One person may without fanfare receive a stimulus to alter hair style, quietly consider it and unemotionally incorporate the idea into habitual behavior. Another, however, might react quite emotionally at every point. With respect to "falling in love," though, I suspect that a very high proportion of Americans are stimulated, come to realization, decision, and habituation in this matter with a considerably greater degree of emotion involved. It may be observed that *the emotionality of the response is directly affected by such things as (a) the newness or unexpectedness of the experience, (b) the psychological makeup of the person(s), and (c) the release of tension (if any) that the decision provides* from what the person or group considered to be pressing problems. Thus various points in many decision-making processes might be "peak experiences" (see Maslow 1964) for certain persons or groups, particularly if their culture encourages a high level of emotion in this area of life. For others, almost no "peaking" will occur. For many, though, the presence or absence of peaking in the decision-making process will depend to a considerable extent upon the degree of release afforded by the decision from the tension of having to live with an unresolved problem.

Returning from our diversion to focus on the dynamics of God's interaction with people in the conversion process, we are now prepared to incorporate the foregoing understanding of decision-making into our discussion. For, when a person or group decides (in the manner above) for God, God becomes a participant with that person or group in the operation of this decision-making process. And even before the decision for Christ is made we are led by the Scriptures to understand that God is active in influencing human beings to decide for him (e.g., Acts 14:17).

What we are dealing with is *a process* that starts prior to the specific decision that one might label the *point* of conversion and that normally continues well after that point. That process consists of *a large number of discrete decisions*, many of which precede the point of conversion and lead up to it. Many of these decisions, however, follow that point and build upon it. And one decision may be identifiable as the one that initiated the turning that we call the conversion point. Many, some, or none of these decisions may be accompanied by high emotion—depending on factors such as those listed above. Furthermore, the level of awareness of the person or group will vary with respect to these decisions. Certain of them may (often due to the emotion involved) remain very vividly in the memory of the participant(s). Others will be noticed at the time but quickly forgotten. Still others will not be noticed at all.

Meanwhile, God is working with us (Rom. 8:28), performing the process of "wooing" while our decision-making leads us to greater awareness, regenerating us as we are converting and sanctifying us while we are maturing. A composite diagram attempting to label God's activity, human activity, and the interactional decision-making process (D) described above follows. Note that each D in Figure 17.2 stands for the whole process (including stimulus, awareness, realization, consideration, decision, incorporation, and new habituation).

3. In addition to the conscious-allegiance and dynamic-interaction constants in the conversion process, there is that of *growth* or *maturation*. The decision-making process described above is not aimless. It has a goal. We are to "continue to grow in the grace and knowledge of our Lord and Savior Jesus Christ" (2 Pet. 3:18). And positively regarded biblical characters like Abraham, Joseph, David, Elijah, the disciples, and Paul demonstrate a process of maturing as a result of their interactions with God. None of these is or becomes perfect, but the direction in which their decisions move them is toward that goal. Thus Joseph, after several years in a dungeon, could see God's hand in the evil actions of his brothers (Gen. 45), David repented of his great sin (2 Sam. 12:13; Ps. 51), Peter and the other disciples grew from fleeing

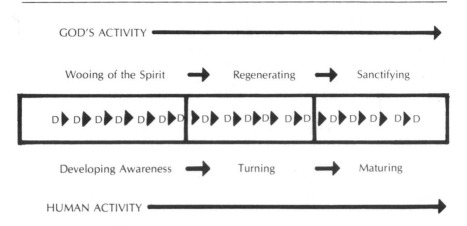

Fig. 17.2. Composite diagram labeling God's activity and human activity in the conversion process.

cowards at the crucifixion into firebrands for God at and after Pentecost, etc. But the growing, maturing aspect of the conversion process is in *continuum* with the turning aspect of the process. It is characterized by the same progression of decisions that run through each of the previous stages of the process.

4. A fourth constant is *the need for the conversion-maturation process to take place in community.* People are made for relationships with other people. The direction in which human beings develop is strongly affected by the type and quality of interpersonal relationships that they enter into. The people of God need other people of God to whom to relate to assure the direction and nature of their growth. This need constitutes one of the major reasons for the institution of God's groups that we call churches.

It is in the context of relationships with other people of God that the initial allegiance is to be fed until it becomes the central point of reference in terms of which believers make all decisions and around which they reorient all living. In this context one's relationship with God becomes vital, habits of Christian behavior are developed, spiritual gifts discovered, and spiritual maturity developed. Woe to the Christian who is not part of a vital, tightly knit, sociologically healthy group of God's people, for they are one's spiritual family. Without them one cannot expect much spiritual growth.

5. The fifth constant (or, perhaps, "desirable," since it often is prevented) is that the human beings' part of the conversion process is to be *in keeping with the culture in which they are immersed.* The forms taken by their developing awareness, their maturing in their relationship to God, and their interrelationships with other people of God are to be those appropriate to their own culture, not to that of some other group. The following section of this chapter treats this constant in greater detail.

CULTURAL CONVERSION VERSUS CHRISTIAN CONVERSION

What the Mennonite Brethren "establishment" is described as expecting of its young people is what I refer to here as "cultural conversion" or "conversion to a culture or subculture that is not that natural to the convert." This expectation is similar to that of the Pharisees who sought to convert everyone to their subculture as a prerequisite to knowing God (see Mt. 23:4,15). It is also the sin of the Judaizers who followed Paul from place to place telling his Gentile converts that conversion to Hebrew culture (the meaning of "circum cision") was pre- or co-requisite with conversion to Christ. The Roman Catholic church (in, e.g., the time of the Reformation), the Anglican church (at, e.g., the time when Wesley broke from it), and virtually every other denomination has fallen into this same error in due time. It is the error of imposing upon one subculture the forms of Christianity appropriate to another subculture (the one in power) but not to that of the group in question. Missionary bodies have frequently erred in this way, requiring the members of other cultures to convert to Christ by first converting to Euro-American culture.

Each of these groups is advocating an indirect conversion to Christ, the primary focus of which is the exchange of the convert's culture (insofar as possible) for that of the witness. This can and frequently does happen with respect to the "vertical" progression of generations within a single culture, as in the case of the Mennonite Brethren. Diagramatically we may represent this situation thus:

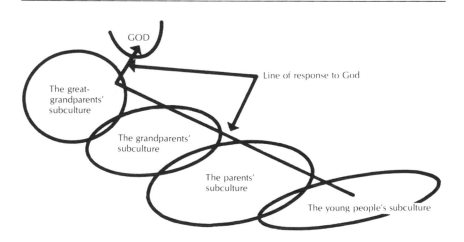

Fig. 17.3. Intergenerational cultural conversion.

Note that the youth are not free to understand or respond to God *directly* in terms of their own subculture. They are expected to convert (at least symbolically) to a previous form of their culture—that which their great-grandparents were comfortable in. That subcultural approach to following Christ had become the norm since the great-grandparents were the ones who developed the denominational distinctives.

When, as with the Judaizers and much modern missionary work, it is prescribed that people respond to Christ via a culture totally different from their own, a kind of "horizontal" conversion takes place—from one culture to another. This differs only in degree, not in kind, from the "vertical" conversion from youth subculture to a variety of adult subculture (that of the great-grandparents) prescribed for Mennonite Brethren youth. This requirement of a "horizontal" indirect response to God may be diagramed thus:

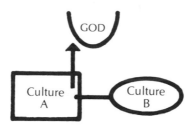

Fig. 17.4. "Horizontal" cultural conversion required in response to God.

This approach to conversion requires that the person from culture B respond to God in terms of cultural forms appropriate to culture A. In order to do so, of course, one must learn a good bit of culture A. When those of culture A present the Gospel with this in mind, they are employing the *extractionist* approach described earlier (chapter 8). Conversion in response to such an approach *may result in a genuine relationship with God* on the part of the convert(s). Or *they may simply convert to the culture of the witness without developing a saving relationship with God.* The tragedy of this latter result cannot be overestimated. Many have perceived Christianity to be simply advocating a new cultural allegiance. The result is widespread nominalism with little real understanding of essential Christianity on the part of young churches.

The early churches struggled with this problem (see Kraft 1963). Peter, for example, was a Hebrew Christian. Though he was a Christian, the message had come to him in the cultural forms of first-century Hebrew (Aramaic) culture and he had responded to it in a Hebrew fashion. He thus continued to live according to Hebrew patterns (Acts 10:15), though at times making certain adaptations (Gal. 2:11–14). In Acts 10, however, God approached Peter in a typically Hebrew way (through a vision) and asked him to carry the message that he had received and responded to in Hebrew culture to Cornelius, a Roman.

Peter could have assumed (and probably did) that only Hebrew culture was a suitable vehicle for God's communication and only a Hebrew type of response acceptable to God. It would have been very natural for him to feel that way. Nevertheless he, like Jonah, agreed to take God's message to an outsider—probably expecting either that nothing would happen, or that if Cornelius responded to God it would be via conversion to Hebrew culture.

Through the vision and the subsequent response of Cornelius and his household, however, God communicated to Peter that at least one group of "unclean" Roman persons was acceptable to God. Peter testifies to his new-found discovery, saying,

> I now realize that it is true that God treats all men on the same basis. Whoever fears him and does what is right is acceptable to him, no matter what [culture] he belongs to (Acts 10:34–35 TEV).

Because of Peter's experience and the much wider experience of Paul, the early church leaders were forced to call a gathering of the apostles and elders (Acts 15) to make a decision with regard to Gentile converts and Hebrew culture. The Judaizing Christians were insistent that Hebrew culture pre-scribed the only proper forms for human response to God. To them there was no coming to Christ without being circumcised and converting to Hebrew culture. But in the Acts 15 council these early church leaders were able to work it out so that it became official policy to not require Gentiles to become Jews as the means of becoming Christians. Thereafter, Gentiles were at least theoreti-cally free to respond on the basis of faith according to Gentile, rather than Jewish, cultural forms.

As mentioned above, church history provides many illustrations of rever-sion to a demand for "cultural conversion." To many contemporary denomi-national and nondenominational groups it is obligatory that one be converted to a particular philosophy, theology, or worldview if one is to be considered Christian by them. *Faith alone is not enough for them. It has to be faith as understood by and expressed in terms of their particular subculture.* Such groups tend to identify *their* understanding of and approach to God with "that of the first century," as if the early churches were unified and contemporary cultural and subcultural diversity were irrelevant.

Unfortunately, many persons possessing such inadequate views concerning culture find their way into pastoral and missionary work, where they advocate a conversion to Christianity which, like that of the Judaizers, is concerned primarily with purely cultural issues. The big thing is to get those who convert to conform to the moral ideals of their variety of western culture (on the assumption that this is nearly synonymous with "Christian culture"). One major focus of certain Christian publications in Africa is even aimed at converting Africans to western dating and courtship patterns! The organizational and worship patterns (including music) of the home denomination are also pressed. And on and on, including theological formulations, anti-polygamy and anti-common-law-marriage rules, etc.

In the matter of conversion, our extreme western cultural individualism has led many of the more open-minded to advocate only conversions that occur "one by one against the social tide" (McGavran 1970:299). And this in disregard often of (1) the fact that the receiving culture allows *no* decisions of such magnitude to be made except as the result of intensive group discussions culminating in a "multi-individual" agreement (see Tippett 1970:31–33) on the part of the group, and (2) the fact that such "people movements" (McGavran 1955) are recorded rather frequently in Scripture (e.g., Jonah; Acts 2:41; 4:4; 10:44; 16:31–34).

Conversion, however, and all its concomitants such as organization and government, moral standards and worship patterns, if they are to be dynamically equivalent to their counterparts in the Scriptures, must be as much a part of the receiving culture as the Hebrew sacrificial system was a part of ancient Hebrew culture and Paul's theologizing was a part of Hellenistic Hebrew culture. We continue to advocate formal correspondence to forms of Christianity appropriate to other cultures or subcultures (see chapter 13) at the expense of serious distortion to the vital here-and-now, right-where-the-hearer-is nature of the Gospel. Conversion, like Bible translation and every other aspect of God's contemporary interaction with humans, is to be dynamically equivalent to its biblical precedents.

The basic question is whether or not the advocates of Christianity recommend that a person or group be free to understand and respond to the Christian message in a manner appropriate to their own culture or subculture. Are they to be "allowed" to interact with God directly, as it were? Or must they come to and grow in Christ via conversion to the cultural forms of the culture or subculture of those from whom the message came to them? Is the proper response to Christ and the process of conversion that accompanies it via Pattern I or Pattern II in Figure 17.5?

If converts respond according to Pattern I, their conversional and maturational interaction with God will be in terms of the culture of the *witness*. They have been "extracted" from their own culture and taught that understandings of Christianity as formulated in terms of the foreign culture are to be their points of reference as they seek to "grow in grace" (1 Pet. 3:18). The quality of their whole subsequent relationship to God will be influenced in major ways by their ability to learn fully the foreign culture.

If converts respond to and learn to interact with God in terms of their own culture, however (Pattern II conversion), the normal problems of growing in

Pattern I

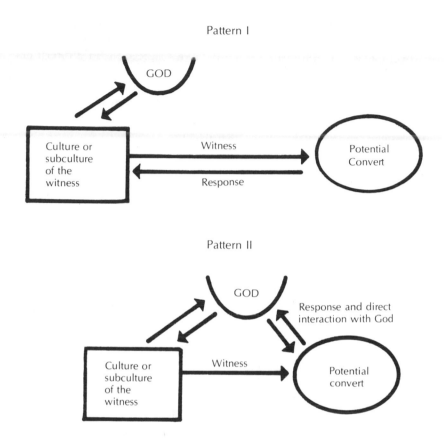

Pattern II

Fig. 17.5 Two patterns of conversion to Christianity.

Christ will not be complicated by the necessity to also learn another culture. The process of conversion after their faith-allegiance decision will be of a radically different nature. The transformation of their life (and that of the group of Christians of which they are a part) will be more freely *from within*, in accord with the principles dealt with in the next two chapters. This kind of freedom to interact directly with God may (ideally) be encouraged by the witness from whom the converts have heard the message. Or it may result from the converts' breaking away from the cultural forms recommended by the witness at some point after they have learned to respond to God in terms of them.

We may usefully summarize several principles concerning the dynamic relationship of Christian conversion to the culture in which it occurs:[2] (a) Christian conversion is not tied to a single culture any more than the Gospel itself is. Conversion can and should take place within and in terms appropriate to the culture of the receptors. God's offer of salvation and the "wooing of the Holy Spirit" are constants. So is the need for a right relationship with God and neighbor on the part of human beings. The divine-human interactions (if any) that take place in response to these constants occur within the cultural frame of reference of the human participants. (b) When people are converted they begin to change their worldview. They go through a paradigm shift (Kuhn 1970:202,204). Within their culture

"Conversion" means a "turning" away from old ways toward new ways, a basic re-orientation in premises and goals, a wholehearted acceptance of a new set of values affecting the "convert" as well as his social group, day in and day out, twenty-four hours of the day and in practically every sphere of activity—economic, social, and religious (Luzbetak 1963:6).

This changing of worldview, while radical, often takes a long time. The accompanying revision of habitual behavior that results from such worldview change is likely to be an especially slow process.

(c) The change accompanying Christian conversion is a three-step process. The first step is a change of allegiance from the old primary allegiance to an allegiance commitment to God. This change of allegiance issues in a new principle of evaluation/interpretation. Seeing things in this new way, then, results in changes in behavior. This process results in change ("transformation") of the culture of the receptors. The process may be interfered with if the converts simply change their culture in the direction of that of the witness, rather than under the direct guidance of the Holy Spirit *within* their culture. (See chapter 18 for a detailed discussion of these steps.)

(d) Christian conversion should be in accord with the decision-making patterns of the converts' culture. The advocates of Christianity need to become familiar with those patterns and to work in terms of them rather than to impose the patterns of their own culture as if those alone were Christian. (e) Openness to Christian conversion on the part of the receptors is usually conditioned by the receptors' ability to relate the Gospel message to their felt needs. A perceptive advocate will be able to discover these felt needs and to present the Gospel in relation to them. An effective witness may also be able to help receptors discover needs of which they were previously unaware. By and large, though,

the willingness to change religion will often depend on how well the present religion meets the daily needs. Because religion is so thoroughly integrated into the total fabric of life, there will be motivation for change only when a system frustrates an individual or a whole society at some rather crucial point (Loewen 1967:53).

2. I am indebted to Thomas Frillman (1977) for stimulating much of this summarization.

18. Transforming Culture with God

In much of the preceding discussion our attention has been focused on the fact that God desires to start where people are in his interaction with them. At various points, however, mention has been made of two additional important facts: (1) culture is always in the process of change, and (2) God desires to participate with human beings in guiding culture change. In alluding to these aspects of our subject I here introduce the concept of "Christian transformational change" (model 13).

In this chapter the concept of transformational culture change is introduced and certain of its aspects elaborated. The places of re-evaluation/reinterpretation and rehabituation in the transformation process are developed. We deal next with the centrality of conceptual (worldview) transformation in the process, proceed to the principle of "working with" culture to bring about transformation, then present a case study dealing with conceptual transformation as exemplified in linguistic change. In the following chapter, we develop certain principles for bringing about Christian transformational change in cultures.

TRANSFORMATIONAL CULTURE CHANGE (Model 13)

A change or series of changes in a culture may be labeled "transformational" if it/they involve a radical (though usually slow) revision of the meaning conveyed via the cultural form(s) involved. This label refers to the nature and intensity of change rather than to any distinctly different kind of change. Many such changes take place quite naturally within culture. Several such transformations are illustrated below. But when the process of cultural transformation is engaged in by the people of God in partnership with God there is an aim, a direction to the change that is different from that of a transformational change motivated by some other set of factors. This aim is to increase the suitability of the culture to serve as a vehicle for divine-human interaction.

The Dutch missiologist J. H. Bavinck labels this concept with the Latin word *possessio*, stating in explanation of his choice of the term that

the Christian life does not accommodate or adapt itself to heathen forms of life, but it takes the latter in possession and thereby makes them new. Whoever is in Christ is a new creature (1960: 178–79).

345

While I agree with Bavinck that Christianity seeks to take possession of cultural forms and to employ them with new meanings, the label he chooses is, to my way of thinking, misleading. It seems to betoken the kind of God-against-culture position dealt with in chapter 6. The picture that *possessio* brings to my mind is of God and his people approaching the forms of culture as outsiders and attempting to capture them by force. While recognizing that there is some truth in this, my preference is for a term like "transformation," which focuses on the fact that Christians, like yeast (Mt. 13:33), are to work with God from *within* culture. We are to use the forms (i.e., the dough) already there in such a way that they are gradually transformed (though occasionally replaced) into more adequate vehicles of the meanings that God seeks to convey through them. This is "possession" of cultural forms but *it is from the inside rather than from the outside*—like spirit possession, rather than like capture. And it will never be complete possession (or transformation), though the impact may be considerable.

This is the kind of change that eventually did away with polygamy in Hebrew culture, so that by New Testament times the custom was disapproved and very seldom practiced within Hebrew culture. Over a period of several centuries the Hebrew people had developed culturally appropriate alternative forms to fulfill the functions decreasingly served by polygamy. A new way of looking after the rights and needs of widows was one thing that had to be developed (see Acts 6:1 and Jas. 1:27 for New Testament Jewish concern over this matter). A system of hiring rather than marrying additional members of a family's labor force was another necessary innovation. An alternative way of handling barrenness (quite frequently, unfortunately, involving divorce) involved the revision of another set of cultural factors. And so on.

The transformational process is not easy. Habits of long standing are not ordinarily replaced rapidly or without some trauma. In general, though, the slower the transformation takes place, the fewer and less drastic the changes that have to be made at any given point in time. And the fewer and less drastic any given set of changes, the less traumatic the transformational process.[1]

Doing away with the practice of slavery in western society is another example. We are near enough to this change to appreciate a bit more both the extent to which the custom was interwoven into the fabric of the lives of at least certain segments of western culture and how extremely difficult it is to work out all the changes that have to be made. The fact that in the United States the slower transformational process was interfered with by the desire of the nonslaveholding segments of the population to impose their will on the slaveholding segments has made many aspects of the process considerably

1. This is the faith position of anthropological orthodoxy. It has, however, been questioned by Margaret Mead (1956), who hypothesizes that the rapid, rather total cultural transformation that took place within a single generation among the Manus islanders was a more humane type of change than a more gradual process would have been.

more traumatic. The pressure exerted by that interference undoubtedly speeded the process somewhat, but it also increased the trauma.

The necessity for the former slaveholders to develop new habits with respect to getting the work on their plantations done is the most obvious of a long series of required changes. The former slaves themselves, however, have undoubtedly suffered most from the fact that the transformation was speeded up, for they found themselves suddenly cast out into a society from which they had always been protected. They often had learned very little of what they needed to know to function successfully as free persons in that society; so many failed. Whites, further, even those who had pressed for emancipation, had not prepared themselves to regard blacks as *people* rather than as "slave things." Thus the rapidity of the change caught both groups by surprise, as it were, and the problems of sorting out the results will, unfortunately, probably take generations yet.

Had the changes taken place more slowly—transformationally rather than revolutionarily—things *might* have been better. It is doubtful that the totality of the trauma experienced by all involved could, in a slower process, have come anywhere near equaling what we have gone and are going through the way it is. For even yet large numbers of blacks have not found it possible to develop the habits, attitudes, and skills that will enable them to function well in contemporary American society. Nor have whites in general learned to accept blacks as human beings. For the conceptual cores of both black and white worldviews have been only slightly altered. We have succeeded in the easy part—we have changed a peripheral custom or two. But, probably because of the rapidity of the peripheral changes, many of us have "holed up" in our traditional worldview (including the strong feelings of what the "place" of blacks and whites should be) rather than seeking to change it in such a way that it supports the changes in the more peripheral areas of our culture.

True transformational change, as opposed to more superficial external alteration is (as pointed out earlier) a matter of change in the central conceptualizations (worldview) of a culture. It is this worldview of a culture or subculture that governs the way the members of that culture/subculture perceive of reality. It also governs the "output" or response of its people to that reality. When change occurs in the worldview, its effects "ripple" throughout the rest of the culture. Changes in any of the other aspects of culture also produce ripples. But such ripples result in pervasive change in the total culture only to the extent that change is effected in the worldview. From there, change is generated throughout the culture.

With respect to attempts to bring about change at the worldview level (such as the emancipation of blacks), *a basic problem of the transformational approach is how to keep the pressure on for change while at the same time assuring that such change will be minimally traumatic.* Many who claim to advocate slow change in areas such as race relations are in reality not pressing for change at all. They are simply ignoring the need for transformation. I do not side with them. A useful discussion of a number of aspects of this problem from a somewhat different point of view is found in Verkuyl and Nordholt 1974.

My aim is to discover (1) how desired change can be brought about *constructively* rather than destructively at the worldview level and (2) how to press for such change in *Christian* rather than unchristian ways. Such problems have faced God and his people through the ages. There is, therefore, a considerable amount of insight to be gained from the Scriptures on these matters. Furthermore, this volume is itself an attempt to assist in the effecting of what I believe to be desirable worldview change in a minimally traumatic way. The discovery of how to do it well is also crucial to the purpose of this book.

We started by suggesting the need of and possibility for conceptual transformation, or "paradigm shift," and have sought to press for such change throughout the volume. This process is paralleled by the processes of Christian witness and conversion that have formed the subject matter of the book. In both transformational processes the same steps need to be followed: (1) a change of allegiance that issues in (2) a concomitant change in the evaluational principles within the person's/group's worldview and (3) a resultant series of new habits of behavior.

1. *The basic change upon which transformational processes are built is the change in allegiance* (model 13a). With respect to Christian conversion, this change is from allegiance to such things as self, tribe, or occupational or material allegiances to faith allegiance (commitment) to God through Christ. With respect to lesser changes, such as that encouraged by this volume, the change of allegiance is from one paradigm or set of assumptions and models to another.

2. *This basic change produces a major change in the worldview principles in terms of which one evaluates as many of the aspects of life as the new allegiance is applied to* (model 13b). Changes in allegiance are of different magnitudes. A change from allegiance to self to allegiance to God is intended to result in transformation in every area of life. Unfortunately, whenever this change is reduced to a mere change of religion, the extent of the transformation is usually severely reduced. Change of allegiance from one religious system to another often devolves into the kind of cultural conversion dealt with in the previous chapter. Other paradigm shifts and model changes are usually also less pervasive than Christian conversion. Often a change of career, a new friendship, marriage, or a change of perspective involves only partial change in evaluational principles. The change of perspective advocated throughout this volume, for example, is intended to be an adjunct to, rather than in competition with, one's basic allegiance to God. Allegiance to the models presented here is intended, however, to affect in a major way certain of the evaluational mechanisms of the reader's worldview.

A short-circuiting of the evaluational process is a frequent occurrence whenever an allegiance that is intended to be pervasive is applied only to selected aspects of life. Such is the case when people evaluate what they do in church on Sunday according to their commitment to God but refrain from applying such evaluation to their business practices throughout the week. Understandings that focus on Christianity as peripheral religion rather than as worldview-generated behavior often give rise to the short-circuiting of Christian transformation in this way.

3. *The intended result of a new allegiance followed by reinterpretation and re-evaluation on the basis of that allegiance is revision of behavior* (model 13c). Psychological and socio-cultural health demand a high degree of consistency between belief and behavior. A new allegiance, if it is to produce health rather than illness, should result in "rehabituation" (see below) as well as in reinterpretation and re-evaluation. As stated in the previous chapter, the overt manifestations of such new behavior may be greater (as in the case of those converted to Christ from radically unchristian lifestyles) or lesser (as in the case of those brought up in the Christian way). But even in the latter case the new habit of relating one's behavior to a new Christian commitment is a significant, though less visible, type of rehabituation.

RE-EVALUATION/REINTERPRETATION (Model 13b)
AND REHABITUATION (Model 13c)
IN THE TRANSFORMATION PROCESS

The task of Christianity vis-à-vis any given culture or subculture is primarily the transformation of the conceptual system (worldview) of that culture. Such transformation is accomplished by bringing Christian understandings of supracultural truth to bear on the worldview of the culture. As has been pointed out continually in previous sections of this book, these understandings of the supracultural will always be clothed in the perceptions and conceptualizations of a cultural worldview. Thus we may learn much about effecting Christian transformation from a study of how cultures in contact influence each other's worldviews.

I do not contend that the Scriptures present us with a culturally unencumbered Christian worldview to which people are to be converted in total replacement of their own cultural worldview (see McGavran 1974:8–9). The view here presented is that we may study many aspects of the process and results of conceptual transformation as seen in the scripturally recorded working of God with his people within a variety of Hebrew and Greco-Roman cultures. The ideal, supracultural worldview (if there is one) is never observable except as its influence is manifested in terms of a specific culture. As Americans our task is not to convert conceptually to a Greek (or medieval European) Christian worldview. We are, rather, to attempt to transform our contemporary conceptual framework in the direction of the insights we discover into supracultural truth from our exposure to case studies such as those recorded in the Bible. An important part of this transformation is *our own* reinterpretation and rehabituation to a new (more Christian) perspective on reality. That is, the place to start is with ourselves as individuals and in groups of committed Christians (churches).

Paul says in Romans 12:2 that we are not to *conform* to the standards of this world (including its interpretations of events) but, rather, we should allow God to *transform* us inwardly—deep down in our minds and hearts. We are to learn in our experience with God to re-evaluate and reinterpret all events from *his* perspective and to make this our habit of life. Re-evaluation and reinterpretation thus become the first step toward transformation (whether for an individual or for a culture), and rehabituation the second.

The Scriptures are full of references to such re-evaluation, reinterpretation, and rehabituation. Jesus both predicted and admonished us to such when he said,

And what happiness will be yours when people blame you and ill-treat you and say all kinds of slanderous things against you for my sake! Be glad then, yes, be tremendously glad—for your reward in Heaven is magnificent. They persecuted the prophets before your time in exactly the same way (Mt. 5:11 JBP).

Joseph re-evaluated and reinterpreted a whole major portion of his life during and after the events that culminated in his great statement to his brothers: "You meant to do me harm; but God meant to bring good out of it by preserving the lives of many people" (Gen. 50:20 NEB). Paul reinterpreted the handicap that he calls a "thorn" (2 Cor. 12:7–10). In writing to Philemon, Paul reinterpreted the relationship between a slavemaster and a believing slave. Symbols such as baptism and the Lord's Supper were reinterpretations of previously existent rituals as, later, were the Christmas tree and the dates of Christmas and Easter. Death is reinterpreted by Christianity to such an extent that Paul (and thousands of others down through the centuries) could regard death as "gain" (Phil. 1:21). Job reinterpreted his sufferings in spite of all the advice of his friends.

My good friend Len Pennel reinterpreted the fact that he was forced to lie on his back day in and day out, unable to walk or to work. For he had learned, like Paul, "to be content, whatever the circumstances may be" (Phil. 4:11 JBP). And the fact that to Len even his incapacitation was to be interpreted as usable by God not only transformed his own use of his circumstances but had a powerful influence on the spiritual development of many of us younger people who regularly visited him.

A Christian interpretation of life leaves us with no doubt that even in trivial events "God works for good with those who love him" (Rom. 8:28 TEV). We are compelled to see God at work in every one of the thousands of "normal" situations in which we are involved daily. I came to see this graphically on one occasion when the brakes failed in my automobile. My Christian evaluational perspective enabled me to see that even car brakes and my operation of them are not merely governed blindly by cause and effect. The Maker and Sustainer of the universe participates with me in my use of both the brakes and the laws of cause and effect that come into play when I step on the brakes.

This, of course, is the Christian rationale for prayer. God is there, he participates with us, he delights in hearing from us, and he even allows us to change his mind on occasion (see 2 Kings 20:1–6; Lk. 11:5–8). And we Christians are to interpret all of life in terms of our recognition of this fact and then to develop habits of thought and behavior appropriate to this reinterpretation. One of my acquaintances has so habitualized this understanding of God's involvement in all of life that his reflex action when he sees or hears of a problem is to immediately pray to God about it. This habit is, in fact, so much a part of him that he has difficulty maintaining an appropriate degree of detachment from the events depicted in television or movie drama. Often he finds himself so wrapped up in such TV presentations that when someone in the drama is depicted as getting into difficulty, his instinctive reaction is to begin to pray for that person! The humor of that particular expression of the habit notwithstanding, such a habit (applied in real-life situations) is, I believe, a proper expression of a Christ-transformed worldview.

But the American worldview denies the participation of God in day-to-day events. Many of the subcultural varieties of the American worldview, in fact, deny the very existence of God. These attitudes toward God, therefore, are prime candidates within this worldview for Christian transformation. Indeed, the atheistic extreme, like the allegiance-to-another-god extreme, is one of the very few conceptual elements of this or any culture that Christianity requires to be transformed as a *precondition* to faith, rather than simply as a fruit of that faith. Such alternative allegiances demand power encounter and replacement, "For anyone who comes to God must believe that he exists" (Heb. 11:6 NEB).

FACTORS AFFECTING CONCEPTUAL TRANSFORMATION

Any attempt to bring about Christian transformational change in a culture (whether one's own or that of another) must constantly take cognizance of two facts. The first of these is that *Christian transformation of a culture is primarily a matter of transformational change in the worldview of that culture.* It is to the heart of a culture, just as it is to the heart of an individual, that God's appeal is made. Paul speaks of the influence applied to the root of a tree affecting the branches that derive their sustenance from that root. The centrality to culture of worldview and its functions with its concomitant conservatism raises one set of problems with regard to any attempt to transform it.

A second fact, however, raises even more problems. This is the fact that *any disequilibrium at the center of a culture ramifies strongly throughout a culture.* If, therefore, some major aspect of a people's worldview comes under attack from without or suspicion from within the culture, the effects of such calling into question will manifest themselves in many areas of the people's thought and behavior. For many American Indian tribes such disequilibrium was brought about when they came into conflict with white invaders. Previously many of these tribes had conceived of themselves as *the* people. They, like the Jews, saw themselves to be a superior people, blessed and protected by God in their own terrritory. Their conquest and subsequent utter domination by whites, however, forced them to abandon this important understanding of their relationship to reality, leading them into demoralization and psychocultural disaster. White Americans, of course, have a similar belief concerning their own superiority, invincibility, and divine support. And much contemporary psychocultural malaise within American society is rooted in the fact that Americans are being forced to take more and more seriously a variety of indications that they have been misled with respect to this part of their perspective on reality.

Cultural disequilibrium is frequently the result, even if it is the influence of Christianity that provides the impetus leading to the questioning of basic conceptualizations. We have discussed one example above (i.e., slavery in America). John Messenger (1959 and 1960) documents a particularly disturbing instance when he describes the disequilibrium occasioned by the calling into question and partial displacement of the Anang (Nigeria) conception of God's attitude toward sin and forgiveness. The indigenous concept of God's response to sin is vastly different from the Christian concept as it has come to be understood by the Anang. But the indigenous view has been largely discredited, at least among the youth.

Whereas *abassi* [God] is conceived in the indigenous religion as one who is largely unforgiving and will punish all misdemeanors, the Christian God is regarded as a forgiving deity. . . Belief in a divine moral code and the ability of *abassi* to punish any deviations from its strictures are the most potent social control devices in Anang society. The acceptance by youth of the concept of a forgiving deity has greatly reduced the efficacy of supernatural sanctions and has actually fostered immorality. Lacking well-developed internal controls and freed from important external restraints, the Christian can deviate from prescribed ways of behaving with impunity (Messenger 1959:102).

Had the Anang been presented (at least initially) with a more Old Testament understanding of God's attitude toward sin (requiring less drastic reinterpretation), the transformation of the Anang conceptualization might have been less traumatic and disintegrative, for an Old Testament understanding is clearly culturally closer to the Anang than the Euro-Americanized understanding of the New Testament. It is, furthermore, scripturally endorsed as a place where God is willing to start.

Given the radical difference between a Christian perspective and that of cultures uninfluenced by Christianity, is it possible to keep them from "cultural explosion"? For some, perhaps not. Perhaps Satan has so taken control of the operation of some cultures that rather sudden and total disruption of their worldviews is the only workable approach to Christianization. But for most it is my conviction that such is not the case. In these it is the gospel as *yeast* rather than as *dynamite* that God desires.

WORKING *WITH* CULTURE TO BRING ABOUT TRANSFORMATION (Model 13d)

Bringing about Christian transformational change is a particular way of using the cultural patterns and dynamics available to us. We have spoken about using culture and the reference points that may be looked to when culture change is consciously encouraged. Christian transformational culture change seeks to be guided by a supracultural point of reference as understood through the Bible and to involve the Holy Spirit in bringing about the reinterpretations and consequent transformations.

In order to bring about such change (if one is inside the culture) or to stimulate it (if one is an outsider),[2] persons are more likely to be effective if they are aware of the cultural patterns and processes of the culture in which they work and if they work *with* or in terms of these patterns and processes to bring about the changes they seek. It frequently happens, of course, that Christian transformation is brought about by those who employ cultural patterns and processes of which they are unaware. Certainly, few of the great transformations of history have involved the kind of analytical understanding of cultural patterns and processes that is available to us. It would, however, be going much too far to suggest that a lack of this kind of analytical knowledge always meant that those who sought to transform were naive concerning their cultures. On the contrary, Calvin in developing a representative type of church government, Wilberforce in his efforts to abolish slavery, the early Christians in deliberately transforming the meanings of countless Greco-Roman linguistic and cultural forms, and many others were aware that they were employing available social patterns for Christian ends.

Indeed, they succeeded largely because they chose to work to a great extent *with* the culture in order ultimately to work against it. Wilberforce and his co-laborers made their point because they appealed to the already partially awakened sensibilities of their compatriots. The process of reinterpretation of the meaning of slavery was already well underway. Likewise with Calvin, who worked in a country "where there already existed the beginnings of a representative democratic system" (Winter 1962). The transformations they sought were *extensions* of processes that were to some extent already underway rather than the initiation of completely new processes. Thus they were working *with* the culture as well as speeding up and at least partially redirecting the process of culture change. It is unlikely that these changes would have taken place as

2. See Barnett 1953 for a discussion of the fact that only those within a culture can innovate within that culture. Outsiders, in order to influence change in a culture, must communicate the need for change to at least one influential insider so effectively that that person convinces others and the change is brought about by those inside the culture.

rapidly or with such widespread impact throughout the culture had it not been for the Christianity-inspired efforts of such men.

At least with respect to the slavery issue there was already a groundswell of public opinion in England on which Wilberforce and the other leaders of the antislavery movement could capitalize. That is, these advocates of change were speaking to a widely felt need within the culture of their country. A large problem arose in England and even more in America, however, over the fact that those who most strongly felt the need for change were not those who were involved in slave-holding. Thus in America's individualistic, pluralistic society the change, once made, involved the imposition of a change advocated by one segment of the society upon another segment of the society. And most of those most vitally affected neither felt the need for the change nor were prepared to make the major adjustments in lifestyle, occupation, acquisition of assistance in labor, etc. that such a change entailed. Nevertheless, speaking in terms of the culture as a whole (rather than in terms of the subcultural varieties within the culture) the antislavery forces were promoting a change that spoke to a widely felt need.

The development and spread of representative democracy in the Germanic countries after the Reformation was likewise due in large part to the widespread existence of a felt need among at least certain of the Germanic subcultures of Europe. An important part of the felt need was the conviction that whatever political system was practiced in or supported by Rome was to be rejected. But even such negative feelings produce important felt needs.

When desired changes can be attached to felt needs, therefore, the advocacy of these changes is facilitated considerably. Usually the advocates can devote their attention primarily to winning others to their point of view (reinterpretations) concerning the issue(s) and to stimulating them into action in changing the present situation. There are, however, frequent situations where we are seriously hindered in our attempts to bring about transformational change by the existence of one or more of the following conditions:

1. The problem may be completely unrecognized by those affected by it.

2. The problem may be more or less recognized but felt to be "natural" (i.e., biological) rather than learned (i.e., cultural). Since it is "natural," it is felt that nothing can be done about it.

3. The problem and the possibility of doing something about it may both be recognized, but there is not sufficient agreement among those who have the influence to advocate change effectively as to what to do to create enough social pressure to effect the change(s).

At points where any of these factors are at work it is important that Christians learn to employ the analytic techniques, including the reinterpretations, of the behavioral sciences as tools to discover both the existence of social problems and possible approaches to their solution. This is equally true whether the problems be those of our own society or those which outsiders (perhaps missionaries) think we can see in other societies. Analyses and proposed solutions must focus on recognitions such as (1) the centrality of worldview, (2) the necessity that cultural equilibrium be maintained (especially as it pertains to the worldview) if the changes are to be properly constructive rather than destructive, (3) the superiority of slow transformational (yeastlike) change to revolutionary (dynamite-like) change, (4) the place of allegiance and paradigm shifts issuing in reinterpretation and rehabituation within the culture in transformational change, and (5) the desirability of an informed use of all these processes to achieve Christian ends.

A CASE STUDY OF CONCEPTUAL TRANSFORMATION[3]

Culture contact typically stimulates changes in culture and language that issue in expansion, redefinition, and replacement of the conceptual categories of the culture. These are expressed in its language. If the contact is at all prolonged or intense, such changes may be extensive, particularly if the receptor culture regards the source culture as prestigious. English, for example, had prolonged contact with French in a context where French was regarded as more prestigious than English. This prolonged culture contact, accompanied by its concomitant definition of the prestige factor and the predisposition of English-speaking people to borrow readily from languages that they regard as prestigious, resulted in the large-scale borrowing into English of French concepts, vocabulary, and even certain grammatical features.

Such processes of expansion and replacement through borrowing of concepts and the vocabulary that labels them are fairly well understood. What is not always so well understood, but is ultimately of greater importance in the interaction of God with people in culture, is the process of cultural and linguistic transformation. This occurs when, through innovation, words and concepts already present in the society are redefined or otherwise expanded in scope to accommodate the "new wine" of the innovative influences. Typically, the forms of the concepts and their word-labels remain virtually the same, but the meanings attached to them and the uses to which they are put change to a greater or lesser extent in accordance with the requirements of the new concepts and situations introduced into the culture. The words and concepts undergo, as it were, the kind of re-evaluation, reinterpretation, and rehabituation process to accord with a new allegiance that is described above for personal transformation. This process, like that of borrowing, is a normal feature of culture change and adaptation. Thus we find the meanings of words changing, sometimes radically, both in denotation and in connotation, as the cultural reality that they express is changed.

In English, for example, we can point to such words as "manufacture" (originally meaning "make by hand") which has been "transformed" via the

---

3. See Kraft 1973a for a previous treatment of some of this material.

Industrial Revolution and the introduction of mass production. When the cultural allegiance to handwork was greater, this word expressed a key feature of that commitment. As the cultural focus (allegiance) changed from handwork to mass production, this central word was "transformed" into a symbol implying large-scale, at least semiautomated, assembly-line production of consumer goods.

The word "turnpike" originally signified a turnstile-like device employed to obstruct an enemy in a narrow passage. When the culture changed so that such a device was more prominent at the entrance to a toll road than as a means of defense in war, the word became transformed to signify the entrance gate to a toll road (whether or not this gate looked like a turnstile). And then, when the toll roads themselves gained greater focus than the entrance gates, the word underwent further transformations (based on changing cultural commitments) to enable it to be employed (1) to designate toll roads with gates, (2) to apply to many toll roads that lost their gates, until now (3) even roads that no longer require toll may be called turnpikes.

A concept like "education" has been changed from referring to child-rearing to signifying formal schooling. "Intercourse" has been specialized from intimate social or business dealings to sexual relations. "Money," though once referring only to metal coinage, now designates paper forms of exchange and even credit cards. "Cool" used to have purely physical connotations but now has come into widespread use to denote calmness under stress. And many, many other concepts can be pointed to as having undergone processes of greater or lesser conceptual transformation in response to the pressures of particular changes in culture.

Some of the most striking examples of linguistic transformation have come from the introduction of the allegiance to Christianity into a culture. The Greek word *agapao* (and its derivatives), for example, was transformed from a word whose "etymology is uncertain, and its meaning weak and variable," a word which lacked "the power or magic of *erao*" and "the warmth of *philein*" and often meant no more than "to be satisfied with something" (Stauffer 1964:36) into the distinctively Christian word for love. This concept was to Paul "the only vital force which has a future in this aeon of death" (ibid.: 51) and to John "the principle of the world of Christ which is being built up in the cosmic crisis of the present" (ibid.: 52).

Likewise the translators of the Septuagint chose to transform the word *kurios* into the Greek equivalent of the Hebrew *Yahweh*, rather than to employ *despotes*, a term "which was also possible and perhaps more natural in terms of current usage" (Foerster 1965:1082). Apparently *kurios* was not widely employed with reference to God, or even to the Greek gods. It meant "lord" merely with reference to one human being who held legal rights over another. And even when, presumably under the influence of the Septuagint, the process of transformation was underway, "it was in common use only in

certain places where it corresponded to native, non-Greek usage" (ibid.:1051).
In these areas, however (especially in Egypt), the word came to be

particularly used in expression of a personal relationship of man to the deity, whether in
prayer, thanksgiving or vow, and as a correlate of *doulos* (=slave) inasmuch as the man
concerned describes as *kurios* the god under whose orders he stands (ibid.:1052).

Thus the way was paved for the use of the term with reference to God the
Father and to Christ with the implication of "the personal, legitimate and
all-embracing sovereignty of God" (ibid..1088) clearly stamped upon it.

Thus, likewise, was *ekklesia* transformed from meaning simply "the lawful
assembly of a Greek city state, comprised of those with full citizenship rights"
(Tippett 1958:12) customarily "summoned and called together by the herald"
(Schmidt 1965:513), into the distinctive designation for the church of Christ in
its local sense (1 Cor. 1:2), in regard to the Church Universal (1 Cor. 10:32),
and, later, in reference to "one of the household Churches (1 Cor. 16:19) which
were springing up throughout the Greco-Roman world" (Tippett 1958:14).
The same type of transformation took place for term after term, concept after
concept in Greek as a result of the birth and development of Christianity and
the commitment of considerable numbers of Greek-speaking people to it.

But Greek is far from the only language within which this kind of semantic
and conceptual transformation has been stimulated by Christianity. The
introduction of Christianity into culture after culture in our own day (not
infrequently combined with massive westernization) has resulted in strikingly
similar linguistic adaptation in hundreds of the languages of the world.
Wherever, for example, a Christian preacher or Bible translator has chosen to
employ indigenous rather than borrowed terms for God, for forgiveness, for
love, for faith, or for any of the distinctive concepts of Christianity, the process
of Christianity-stimulated conceptual transformation has begun.

Thus, at least for Christians of the Kaka and Bulu tribes of southern
Cameroun, the indigenous term chosen to translate the word "God" is undergoing radical transformation. The term *Ndjambie* referred indigenously to an
impersonal, mythical cosmic spider. It is, however, being invested with
meaning-transforming denotations and connotations because of its adoption
by the Christian church as the designation of the Christian God (see Reyburn
1957). This term was chosen, according to Reyburn, because "there is no
better native term . . . and a foreign word would be lacking entirely in the few
equivalences which do exist" (ibid.:192). Some translators in an attempt to
avoid syncretism, have (according to Nida) employed a borrowed term for
"God" on the assumption "that the native people will automatically come to
understand by the borrowed word . . . exactly what we understand by the
same term" (1947:205). This approach is not usually successful, however,
since "in almost every case the native will immediately try to equate this new

name of God with one of the gods of his own religious system" (ibid.). The result is usually some sort of understanding like that of the Aztecs who equate *Dios* with the sun, the Virgin Mary with the moon, and consider Jesus the offspring of the two. "Before the translator realizes it, instead of being able to fill an empty word with the proper meaning, he has a name which has already been given a content from the pagan religion" (ibid.).

Much better is the approach that employs indigenous terms even though they, like "the Greek word *theos*, the Latin *deus*, and the Gothic *guth*, could hardly be termed exact equivalents to the concept of God as taught in the Bible" (Nida 1947:206). These were, however, generic terms rather than names of particular, specific gods such as Zeus, Jupiter, or Woden, each of which was associated with "a great deal of legend as to the individual peculiarities, excesses, and immoral actions of the particular gods" (ibid.). The generic terms that "designated any important supernatural entity" were taken by the Christians and "by context and teaching made [to] apply to only one such entity" (ibid.). Nida recommends that this "transformational" approach be employed in similar situations in today's languages.

Tippett documents the results of nearly a century and a half of such conceptual transformation in Fijian (1948:27–55). In conclusion he summarizes nine types of choices that the church made in this regard to enable them to better express their Christian commitment. These choices and their results are instructive for the greater understanding of how Christian transformation is brought about.

1. The Church took over the lingustic forms of the native people and found her doctrine and ethic expressible in the constructions and thought-forms of the people, and there followed great semantic development within the indigenous heart of the language.

2. Foreign borrowings were restricted deliberately. . . .

3. Many words from the pre-Christian liturgies and sacrificial ritual were preserved because they contained basic elements of worship, not confined to one religion; but these were charged with new meaning as the indigenous theology was developed in the light of scripture translation and Christian experience. Many new combinations were developed. . . .

4. In some cases these words were re-interpreted in the light of the new religion, but in others they were given completely new meaning.

5. Some significant choices had to be made between old words for use in the new. The choice between [the word meaning "priest"] and [the construction meaning "the one sent forth with an important message" as the designation for minister or missionary], for instance, is seen to involve the nature of the Church and ministry—was it to be priestly or apostolic? The semantic study shows the Fijian Church captured the true apostolic concept, and this had social implications.

6. The Church widened the Fijian lexicography by means of word-combination, and thereby assisted the development of an indigenous ethic and theology. The doctrinal potential of the language was discovered and exploited.

7. Both morphological devices and endemic thought-forms were used for the de-

velopment of this potential, and words were found for concepts like incarnation and transfiguration, but are nevertheless conditioned by the scripture narrative. There is real semantic development here.

8. The Church is found to have developed her own original and unique terminology in three respects—

a. arising from her constitution and organizational power,

b. growing from her ever-widening religious experience,

c. arising from the demand for a terminology of Christian ethics.

9. By the reduction of the spoken language to written form, the translation of the Scriptures, composition of hymns, preparation of a catechism and the writing and printing of other books the Church has standardized the language and expanded its vocabulary so that it is quite adequate for the Christian experience of its members. Secular vocabulary has been charged with spiritual significance and the moral quality of many acts is indicated by the word root and morphology much more obviously than in English (Tippett 1958:53–55).

In conclusion, Tippett points to the similarity between the processes of ethnolinguistic transformation in Fiji and those we can trace in New Testament Greek. He refers to these processes as "a continuity of the forces and factors that operated in the Apostolic Church" (ibid.:57) and suggests that

we have here a method of God's work with man. So much there is to glorify Him, which lies dormant in life, awaiting discovery, awaiting the right mind to discover it and give it to mankind. Nothing brings home this truth better than the study of biblical and ecclesiastical ethnolinguistics . . . (ibid.:56–57).

Tippett goes on to suggest that in these modern continuations of the book of Acts (i.e., the young churches) we are able to observe and participate in something truly exciting and truly different from the experience in our "home" churches.

19. Principles for Transforming Culture with God

In chapter 4, as a part of our discussion of culture change (model 3f), we introduced the concept developed by Barnett (1953) that makes a distinction between the cultural insiders who may "innovate," or make changes within their own culture, and those who advocate changes that must be implemented by others. Advocates of change may be cultural insiders or cultural outsiders. Cultural outsiders, though they may advocate change, may never themselves make the changes they advocate in another culture. Only insiders may make such changes.

At this point it is appropriate to apply the advocate-innovator concept to Christian transformational change of culture. We will call this application model 13e. There are important things that can be done by cultural outsiders (out-culture advocates) but these must not be confused with what may be done by cultural insiders. The latter may function only as innovators and in-culture advocates of change.

We will first discuss principles for the outside advocate, then deal with factors influencing the advocacy of change and the place of movements in cultural transformation. To illustrate and amplify the place of cultural insiders in the process of cultural transformation, then, we present a case study on what to do about the "generation gap."

PRINCIPLES FOR THE OUTSIDE ADVOCATE

According to this model the outsider can never be an innovator, only an advocate of change. Christians are, however, commissioned by God to be witnesses to and persuaders of people concerning Christian transformation at both the individual and the group level. We are commissioned to advocate the allegiance to God that issues in Christian reinterpretation and transformation in the lives and cultures of which we are aware (including but not limited to our own culture).

The cross-cultural communication of the need for allegiance to God, the response to that message, and the consequent reinterpretations that lead to transformational change are dealt with throughout this volume. I will not repeat that material here but simply summarize briefly several of the important factors that every advocate of cross-cultural change ought to keep in mind. Each factor is implicit at one or more points in the preceding chapters.

1. It is of paramount importance that advocates of change seek to *understand*

the cultural element that they suspect ought to be changed *from the point of view of the people*. One need not approve of the custom or attitude, but Christian concern dictates that one respect the point of view of the other culture. For those within that culture were taught the integrated lifeway of which that element is a part in the same way that we were taught our lifeway. And they accepted it as the correct way of life just as uncritically as we accepted our own culture.

Cultural practices should be interpreted in their proper cultural contexts, however, not as a denial of scripturally revealed supracultural ethical standards, but as the first step toward advocating change in that direction. In chapter 12 I have attempted to outline the steps to be taken on the basis of this understanding.

Even such a custom as infanticide must be approached in this way. The worldview of one tribal group of northern Nigeria dictated that each young girl prove her fertility before marriage by bearing one or more children. Since personhood in that tribe is defined in terms of involvement in a family and of having passed a certain age (perhaps one and one-half to two years), children born to such young, unmarried girls were regularly exposed to die, without (apparently) feelings of guilt on the part of the adults. From their point of view this act seems to no more be considered murder than contraception is in the eyes of most Americans. For, from their perspective, these children were not yet persons. Their biological birth simply functioned to prove the girl's marriageability. Having served that function, the biological entities were disposed of, lest they become socially alive. Since the society had no structures to look after children born out of wedlock, permitting such children to live would have been very disruptive for the society.

Most Americans are horrified at the very thought of such a custom. Our culturally inculcated worldview (which we often consider to be Christian) tells us that life—defined by our culture as biological life—is sacred. We are also taught the cultural belief that life starts at least at birth, if not before. We therefore find it well-nigh incomprehensible that there might be any other defensible understanding of what life is and when it begins. To these people, however, life is defined sociologically with less reference to biological events such as birth and death than characterizes our culture. That is, life to them is life in proper relationship to society, which involves being part of a properly constituted family and kin group. Furthermore, even as part of such properly constituted groupings, a child's (sociological) life does not begin until, by attaining a certain age, it proves that it has "come to stay." If, then, the group decides that the potential entering of that child into life (at age one and one-half to two) cannot take place properly, it is necessary for the group to dispose of such a potential threat to its well-being.

Understanding such a custom, though, is not approval of it. Such understanding should, however, enable the advocate of change to better assess the extent to which that society would be upset if such a custom were to be legislated or pressured out of existence. Such disruption, if done in the name of

Christianity, would assuredly result in serious miscommunication of vital parts of the Christian message. Understanding the important place of that custom in the culture should considerably modify and improve the outsider's approach to advocating change in it.[1]

2. Advocates seeking effective transformational change should try to *encourage a minimum number of critical changes in the worldview*, rather than a larger number of peripheral changes. Peripheral changes, such as forcing a society to allow all its babies to live or enforcing monogamy in formerly polygamous societies, are more likely to prove hindrances than helps to true Christian transformation—because of the way the changes are brought about, not because the changes themselves are undesirable. For they tend to "ripple" misleading information into the worldview.

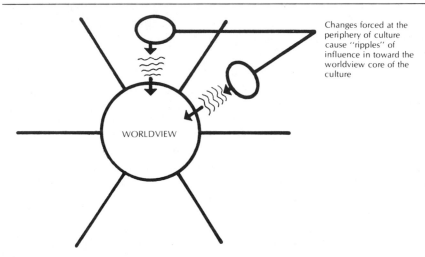

Changes forced at the periphery of culture cause "ripples" of influence in toward the worldview core of the culture

Fig. 19.1. The rippling effect of the interpretations of forced changes on the worldview of a culture.

The typical approach toward polygamy, for example, provides the people with little or no assistance with the basic problems of worldview readjustment. Often, therefore, strange things happen to their concept of God. He may traditionally have been conceived of as endorsing the society's leaders and such values as the society's responsibility to provide marriage (i.e., social security) for every woman. Rippling inward to the worldview, however, move messages concerning God such as: he has turned against traditional leaders (because they have more than one wife) and against traditional customs in general.

1. For the record, the change of this custom has been dictated by governmental forces beyond the control of missionaries. One adaptation is for the group to still require proof of fertility in this way, but for childless Christian couples of other tribes to adopt certain of the babies.

Furthermore, he favors familial irresponsibility on the part of the men (since they are expected to cast out their "extra" wives and children). He no longer wants the women to be socially secure (in the knowledge that the society will provide marriage, home, and fulfillment for each of them) or to be able to get assistance with their work around the home (traditionally provided via polygamy). Nor does God want men any longer to strive to attain prestige (traditionally associated with investment of surplus wealth in larger families involving more than one wife) but, rather, wishes them to be dominated by their wives (who in an enforced monogamous marriage can taunt and disobey their husbands with impunity, since they know that their husbands are not free to resort to traditional disciplinary measures such as marrying another, beating, or divorce).

The God who once was conceived of as supporting them is now seen either as having unreasonably turned against them in favor of the white people and their customs or as having been defeated and displaced by another God—the God of the whites. In either case this single peripheral change in the family structure results in such a high degree of confusion and disequilibrium in the conceptual core (worldview) of the culture that there is little chance for the Gospel message concerning salvation through a faith relationship with God to be heard clearly. If it is heard it will not be attractive to them (since this God appears to be so unreasonable).

The typical result is that thousands of potentially responsive members of traditionally polygamous societies disqualify themselves from becoming Christians, conceive of Christianity as available only to whites and those who convert to Euro-American culture, and equate Christianization with schooling, since only through schools can one learn all the Euro-American conceptualizations concerning God and his rules for Christians.

A more Christian (biblical) approach to the whole polygamy problem would have been to appeal directly to the people at the worldview level for more essential changes first. Outside advocates of Christianity should first study and analyze the key matter of allegiance in the culture in order to discover what the cultural conceptualization of God and his relationship to humans is, and then focus their advocacy of re-evaluation and reinterpretation on the basis of Christian principles at that point. Paul tackles the problem at just this point in his address to the Athenian philosophers on Mars Hill (Acts 17:22ff). If, as happens in many cultures of Africa, God is seen as far away and basically unconcerned with humans, though positive toward them, the transformation of that conceptualization alone would be a fruitful starting point. Indeed, where great turnings to Christ have occurred it is usually because the people have transformed their conceptualization at just this point in the direction of a Christian understanding of God and his relationships with human beings.

If God comes to be seen (and experienced) as near, concerned and active in his relationships with people, ripples from understandings such as the following move out from the worldview to the periphery of the culture: (a) God is basically supportive of our way of life, (b) the power of God is to be utilized to enable us to live up to our own ideals first and then to transcend them if necessary, (c) God favors family and other types of social stability, (d) God wants things done "decently and in order" (1 Cor. 14:40), (e) God seeks to help us with problems that *we* recognize as problems rather than to turn our eyes to matters concerning our way of life that are bothersome to others, (f) if we commit ourselves in faith allegiance to God, he wants us to re-evaluate and reinterpret every aspect of our cultural life in terms of our commitment to him and to revise our cultural behavior accordingly.

By first transforming such a core concept as the people's understanding of and commitment to God, such peripheral matters as polygamy and infanticide will be dealt with in due time, and with a minimum of trauma, under the leading of God—mediated, frequently, through the helpful counsel of aware and understanding outsiders. Meanwhile, though, the people of God will follow him according to their own intelligible customs. In polygamous societies the people of God may not only include but be led by Christian polygamists (just as in the Old Testament) until such a time as changing the custom becomes a Spirit-led priority item of God's people. Without the interference of the static caused by outside pressure to change such a peripheral custom, then, the message of God will be heard as *good news* concerning salvation rather than as bad news concerning polygamy (Nida 1954:131).

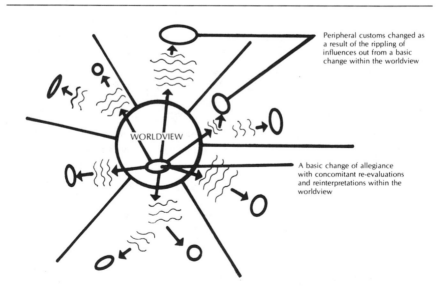

Fig. 19.2. Change in worldview results in the rippling of change out into the periphery of culture.

3. A third important factor in advocating change relates to *those to whom the appeal is initially made*. We must assume that God is interested in seeing whole groupings of people turn to him rather than simply a minimum number of relatively easily reachable fringe people. Through study of the society, then, outside advocates need to discover who the *opinion leaders* are in the society. These are not necessarily those who appear to the outsider to be in political or religious power in a society. The latter are often largely *preservers* of the status quo and/or implementers of decisions made at other levels. Preservers and implementers often lose their followings if they change their views. An opinion leader, on the other hand, is one whose opinions are sought and followed whether or not the person is in an official position of leadership and whether or not the person suggests change in the status quo. An outside advocate needs to discover who these people are and to appeal to them to alter their views and to influence the rest of the society to alter its views.

Advocates of Christianity have tended to ignore, to steer clear of, or to give up on such opinion leaders. But if such persons are not won over as friends, they will inevitably become enemies and lead the resistance against Christianity. We would do well, therefore, to approach them directly. It is of great importance that they be won over, both for the sake of the initial communication of Christianity and for the sake of the leadership they will provide in the often massive reinterpretation process issuing on such conceptual change. (See Gerlach and Hine 1970 and the writings of McGavran and Tippett for further treatment of this and the following factor.)

4. Closely related to the previous factor is the recognition that transformational change is accomplished more efficiently and effectively if *advocated by groups* than if advocated simply by individuals. "Social change of any magnitude at all cannot be made by individuals" (Gerlach and Hine 1970:xxii). This is why *movements* are of such great importance in cultural transformation. Undoubtedly this recognition lies behind the fact that God seeks to establish in every culture one or more communities called by his name.

In 1955 McGavran began to bring to our attention the fact that history is full of "people movements" to Christ. From the great turnings recorded in Acts (2:41 and 4:4) to a number of significant turnings in India, Africa, New Guinea, and elsewhere in our day this kind of "multi-individual" Christward movement has been mightily used of God to expand his kingdom. When people come in groups, the process of cultural transformation is typically both facilitated and speeded up. For, on the one hand, there are more people working at it and, on the other, there is greater cross-fertilization of ideas, producing greater stimulus to change. Appeals for both conversion and cultural transformation should, for maximum effectiveness, be directed primarily to socially homogeneous groupings of people and to leaders who will influence such groups (see below on the place of movements in cultural transformation).

5. The final factor to be dealt with here is the *time factor*. If transformation is to be effective it needs to take place both at the level of thought and at the level

of behavior. And developing the habitual behavior (rehabituation) appropriate to new conceptualizations ordinarily takes a considerable amount of time. All too frequently, those of us accustomed to the relatively rapid rate of change occurring in many sectors of western culture tend to underestimate the time required for most societies to habituate transformational changes adequately. Our tendency is to want them to move much more rapidly than is consonant with the depth of the changes required. Consequently, a second and a third and a fourth major change is often recommended before the first one has been fully assimilated. Under such pressure for rapid change the kind of cultural disequilibrium discussed above is a foregone conclusion. People need time to reformulate their lives (see Loewen 1968b:198–99; Loewen 1968a, 1968b, and 1969 provide an excellent treatment of this whole area).

It is better to encourage change in such a way that (a) only a bare minimum of basic changes in worldview are recommended, (b) the appeal for such changes is made to opinion leaders who, when convinced, will influence large numbers of their compatriots, (c) attention is devoted, on the one hand, to providing the Scriptures in their language and, on the other, to providing instruction in how to use the Scriptures in direct dependence upon the Holy Spirit as their point of reference for Christian transformational change.

FACTORS INFLUENCING THE ADVOCACY OF CHANGE[2]

The worldview of the receptor pervasively influences any attempt to advocate change. This is true whether the advocate is regarded as an outsider or an insider, for it is the worldview of a culture, subculture, or individual that will specify which, if any, areas are closed to change (transformation) and which are open. And for those areas specified as open, the worldview determines just how open and on what conditions.

We may usefully summarize a representative number of these factors in the following figure. The stance taken by the worldview with respect to each of these factors and to groupings of them greatly influences the attitudes and behavior of one group with respect to ideas that come to it from the members of another social group. A discussion of the factors follows.

If (no. 1 in Fig. 19.3) the basic premises on which the worldview of the receptor is based are similar to those of the advocate, the potential for acceptance, or at least of understanding, is increased. Understanding and acceptance are not, of course, the same thing. But, other things being equal, an increase in the ability of the receptors to understand will increase the possibility that they will be favorably disposed toward the idea. If, for example, one's worldview regards the addition of fertilizer to the soil as impermissible tampering with an area of life that lies wholly within the province of God, it is unlikely that a simple recommendation that fertilizer be used will be either understood

2. This section is a revision of part of Kraft 1974.

Factors	Hindering Acceptance	Facilitating Acceptance
1. Basic Premises of Source and Receptor Worldviews	Very Different	Very Similar
2. Attitude of Receptor(s) toward Their Own Culture	Highly Positive	Very Negative
3. Attitude of Receptor(s) toward Source Culture	Despised	Respected
4. Openness to New Ideas	Closed	Open
5. Pace of Present Change	Slow	Rapid
6. Borrowing Tradition	Rejection	Borrow Freely
7. Morale	Proud	Demoralized
8. Self-Sufficiency	Self-Sufficient	Doubting Self-Sufficiency
9. Security	Threatened	Secure
10. Flexibility	Resistant	Adaptive
11. Advocate	Nonprestigious	Prestigious
12. Relation of Idea to Felt Needs	Perceived as Unrelated to Felt Needs	Perceived as Filling a Felt Need
13. Fit of Idea	Discontinuous with Present Worldview	Congruent with Present Worldview

Fig. 19.3. Factors influencing acceptance or rejection of worldview change.

or accepted. If, however, both the recommender's worldview and that of the potential receptor accept the premise that such tampering is legitimate, the arguments of the recommender are likely to be understood and regarded as convincing.

If, even in spite of similar worldviews, such a recommendation were to come to the members of a social group whose (2) attitude toward their own culture was so positive that they believed they had no need of suggestions from outside, the likelihood is that even good ideas would be rejected. Such was the case when attempts were first made to innovate western (Christian) schools into Hausa (Muslim) society. The Hausas, who believed in and operated Koranic schools, saw no need for what they regarded as inferior western schools promulgating an inferior western value system. Today, however, they find themselves competing at a disadvantage with their more thoroughly westernized compatriots of other tribes because their cultural pride led them to reject, while certain other tribes, manifesting perhaps a less positive attitude toward their own educational techniques, accepted educational innovation.

Likewise, (3) the attitude of a group toward the source of a would-be innovation affects the likelihood of acceptance. If a group despises the source, the likelihood of acceptance of ideas from that source is diminished—no matter how persuasively such ideas may be communicated.

Because of their worldviews, certain groups are (4) more open to cross-culturally communicated ideas than others. Western culture in general has manifested a remarkable openness to such innovation. We believe in and expect to find good ideas coming to us from cultures and subcultures other than our own—especially if we respect the source. Many cultures have, however, traditionally taken the opposite posture and have been virtually closed to innovations advocated by outsiders.

In cultural dynamics (5) change tends to beget change. A culture that is changing rapidly tends to believe in change, and therefore to readily accept recommendations for further change, even if the recommenders are outsiders. If, further (6), there is a tradition of borrowing in the society, the potential for acceptance is increased. If, however, the tradition is one of rejection, the potential for acceptance is decreased.

In our day when the intensive impact of westernization is producing widespread cultural disruption, the effect is frequently greater or lesser (7) demoralization on the part of the receptor culture. Such demoralization constitutes a serious morale problem resulting frequently in both the questioning of the (8) self-sufficiency of the ideological underpinnings of the culture and a predisposition to experiment with innovative approaches to a restructuring of the ideology. People cannot live without values and when the old values are called into question they will bend every effort to discover new values and to integrate them into a new, more satisfying worldview.

A. L. Kroeber documents such a happening among the Kota of the Nilgiri plateau in South India (Kroeber 1948:503–8), while Anthony Wallace points to such occurrences in literally thousands of cultures throughout the course of history (Wallace 1956; see also Ramseyer 1970). In each case cultural breakdown issuing in psychological demoralization and doubt of the sufficiency of the traditional answers to life problems has issued in a conscious attempt on the part of certain members of the culture to reformulate or accept from an outside source a more satisfying worldview around which to reconstruct their culture. The roots of most of the world's religious movements—from Christianity to nativistic religious, political, and economic movements—are usually to be found in such revitalization of societies that were in some advanced state of self-doubt and demoralization. Societies in such a condition are peculiarly susceptible to the communication of Christian concepts.

Before this stage of cultural demoralization is reached, however, there may be an almost opposite attitude toward ideological change. If a group feels (9) threatened rather than secure in the face of intensive outside influences toward change, it may be less, rather than more, receptive to the advocacy of change. Such is the case with many Latin American Indian tribal groupings who, due to their lack of socio-psychological security, are prone to react to even very worthy suggestions by rejecting them without serious consideration.

Such cultures tend to develop (10) a highly resistant rather than an adaptive attitude toward new ideas. American fundamentalists (and other closed conservatives) have been characterized by a similar approach to issues such as evolution, biblical criticism, and cultural relativity. Rather than considering the possibility of revising their worldview to incorporate any truth in the new ideas, fundamentalists have characteristically built their walls higher and thicker to keep themselves and their children insulated from concepts that they define as "anti-Christian." The result is frequently the opposite of their hopes. For, one way or another, many children of fundamentalists become exposed to such ideas and end up adopting them all uncritically in more or less total reaction against their fundamentalist ideology. A more adaptive worldview will characteristically examine even initially threatening concepts and accept at least those parts of the new concepts that can be easily integrated into their value system.

With regard to (11) persons who advocate a given idea, much depends upon the prestige assigned to them by the potential receptor group. The worldview of a group will lead it to expect worthy ideas from certain types of persons and not from others. If a culture believes that the privilege of innovation belongs only to those of royal lineage, it may well require that even an outsider demonstrate royal connections before the new ideas will be taken seriously. Or, if a group expects to accept innovative ideas only from those who have demonstrated their abilities from within their cultural context, it is unlikely that a person who has not acquired such credentials will be taken seriously. For this reason certain Nigerian cultures have been very resistant to agricultural innovations even from Euro-Americans (whose prestige is generally high otherwise), since they have never observed these "agricultural experts" to have actually grown a superior crop (or any crop) of guinea corn.

The (12) relationship of the proposed idea to an area of felt need in the culture is clearly an important factor in its potential acceptance. All worldviews have within them areas of inconsistency and/or inadequacy that are to a greater or lesser degree a part of the consciousness of the society. Wise Christian advocates seek to discover the questions concerning reality that the people of the society regard as beyond their ability to answer. They then attempt to communicate in such a way that the hearers perceive a relationship between that communication and questions that they feel to be left unanswered or poorly answered by their present perspectives.

Similarly, an idea is more likely to gain acceptance if it (13) is congruent with the receptor culture's present frame of reference than if it is discontinuous with it. If the new can be built upon or grafted into the old rather than being introduced as unconnected or even in competition with it, the likelihood of acceptance is increased. In recognition of this fact perceptive doctors working among peoples whose concept of disease is that it is always caused by personal forces have learned to discuss germs as if they were personal rather than impersonal forces. Likewise, with respect to the acceptance or rejection of a "world religion" such as Christianity or Islam. The crucial issue is not the dedication of the advocate but whether or not the recommended changes in worldview can be fitted into the receptor's conceptual framework without completely remaking it.

These factors are not mutually exclusive. They frequently overlap or occur in association with each other. It is clear that a culture with a highly positive self-image (2) may also be characterized by such things as lack of respect for other cultures (3), pride (7), and self-sufficiency (8). Or it might feel itself so secure (9) that it adopts a very adaptive posture toward new ideas (10). And the list is by no means exhaustive.

It should be clear by now that such worldview-based factors as these pervasively affect both the process and the results of Christian advocacy. No communication takes place in a vacuum. There are always presuppositions, beliefs, understandings, concepts in the minds of the participants that pervade the presentation and the reception of the communication. Furthermore, the personal worldviews of two persons within the same social group will differ slightly, affecting the communication process in a variety of ways. The worldview differences between members of the same social group will, however, be very small compared to the differences between persons of different groups. The greater the difference in worldview between groups, the smaller the number of mutually accepted presuppositions and the greater the difficulty in adequately and effectively advocating Christian change.

MOVEMENTS AND CULTURAL TRANSFORMATION

A significant study of two "movements of social transformation" within American society appeared in 1970 (Gerlach and Hine 1970). The findings of that study are largely compatible with this approach. The authors deal explicitly with a topic that has remained largely implicit in this volume—the relationship between "movements" (including Christian movements) and social transformation. It is important, therefore, that we survey their findings in our attempt to come to better understandings of the principles for transforming culture.

To this point we have allowed the assumption that transformational change is primarily a slow, gradual process. Such an assumption is largely true, but it is not the whole story. Much transformational change is gradual from start to finish, but much deep and lasting cultural transformation has involved what we might term a cultural "peak experience" or paradigm shift. This is not unlike (on the cultural level) the point of conversion that we described on the individual level (chapter 17).

Typically, transformational culture change that involves such peaking will involve (as with individual conversion) a series of preparatory developments that take place over a period of time. Such developments often produce what Tippett calls a "reservoir of tension" (1964:81–82) that eventually becomes intolerable and issues in a kind of "flash point" for change (Barrett 1968). This is followed by a bringing together of the various cultural factors into a new conceptual configuration (a paradigm shift). Such a shift in turn sparks a series of rapid socio-cultural readjustments, most of which start within a short period of time. Less rapid changes of many kinds develop from such peaks over an extended period of time.

Culture, however, does not have an existence independent of the people who operate it. Thus, when we speak of cultural transformation, whether gradual or rapid, we must assume that we are speaking also of the people who bring about that change. When we speak of a culture's being prepared for rapid transformational change, we mean that the people within that culture (or at least sizable groupings of them) have felt a need and prepared themselves to bring about the changes necessary to meet that need. Such recognition and preparation typically issues in the mobilization of the concerned and the mounting of a "movement" with the specific aim of bringing about the changes recommended. To do this the participants in a movement set about implementing such changes in the lives of the concerned group(s) and converting others to their cause.

Gerlach and Hine define the phenomenon of "movement" as

a group of people who are organized for, ideologically motivated by, and committed to a purpose which implements some form of personal or social change; who are actively engaged in the recruitment of others; and whose influence is spreading in opposition to the established order within which it originated (1970:xvi).

Christianity at its start became such a movement, as did Islam, communism, the Protestant Reformation, the Industrial Revolution, the evangelical awakening, black power, women's liberation, Pentecostalism, and countless other developments. These phenomena are often of the same nature as the "scientific revolutions" described by Kuhn (1970). Some movements have been culturally revitalizational (Wallace 1956), providing the necessary reintegration to give a dying culture a new lease on life. But many, though dramatic, have merely redirected the course of part or all of a fairly healthy culture. People movements to Christ may fit into either category. It is of great concern to those who seek to extend the kingdom of God on earth to learn how to advocate such Christward movements effectively.

According to Gerlach and Hine, a movement is characterized by at least five key, "operationally significant" factors:

1. *A segmented, usually polycephalous, cellular organization* composed of units reticulated by various personal, structural, and ideological ties.

2. *Face-to-face recruitment* by committed individuals using their own pre-existing, significant social relationships.

3. *Personal commitment* generated by an act or an experience which separates a convert in some significant way from the established order (or his previous place in it), identifies him with a new set of values, and commits him to changed patterns of behavior.

4. *An ideology* which codifies values and goals, provides a conceptual framework by which all experiences or events relative to these goals may be interpreted, motivates and provides rationale for envisioned changes, defines the opposition, and forms the basis for conceptual unification of a segmented network of groups.

5. *Real or perceived opposition* from the society at large or from that segment of the established order within which the movement has risen (1970:xvii; see also p. 199).

The presence and interaction of such factors result in "an autonomous social institution" that "lifts off" and becomes capable of social life and growth even beyond the limits of the conditions that originally gave birth to it (ibid.:199). Such an institution, then, continues its transformational activity among the originating group and spreads to "groups where the generating conditions do not and never did exist" (ibid.:xxiii). Gerlach and Hine study Pentecostalism and black power as examples of movements that are, from their point of view, both "revolutionary" and "religious" (ibid.:xviii).[3] Though both movements are studied within American society, and are therefore in many respects suspect as bases for cross-cultural generalizations, there are a number of principles that should at least be tested cross-culturally. Furthermore, Gerlach as an anthropologist is sensitive to the cross-cultural dimensions of their study.

In spite of the tendency for Pentecostals to be politically conservative and negative toward social action,

the social change associated with Pentecostalism, especially in non-Western societies moving toward industrialization, is largely an inadvertant consequence of personal change, but is nonetheless real (1970:xix).

The Pentecostal movement, though overtly seeking to be only religious, is revolutionary whether it seeks to be or not. Black power, on the other hand, seeking to be revolutionary may be seen as religious, if that term is used to designate *any* rather all-encompassing allegiance rather than simply an allegiance to a supernatural being.

Pentecostalism, we suggest, is conceptually revolutionary. It encourages an experience

---

3. The more comprehensive approach being developed in this volume obviates the necessity of postulating what I believe to be a false dichotomy between "religious" and "revolutionary." As I see it, both groups are actively pursuing worldview change via advocacy of the three-pronged process described above. Each seeks to bring about change in allegiance, evaluational perspective, and consequent behavior. It is unhelpful to employ the term "religious" change to designate what is a much more widely occurring phenomenon—a basic change in primary allegiance from which flows radical, often revolutionary, change of belief and behavior. Gerlach and Hine, in order to make this point, find it necessary to apply the terms "revolutionary" and "religious" (which, though complementary, they see as contrasting) to both groups.

through which an individual believes himself to be radically changed; many converts behave accordingly in social situations.

Black Power, on the other hand, is clearly a movement which seeks to accomplish social change with entirely human means. But it is religious in the sense that it requires the commitment of the individual to something greater than self. . . . If we view as religious a commitment of oneself to something not only greater than oneself, but transcending even the body of believers, then the Black Power Movement can be viewed as religious (1970:xix).

The kind of movement for socio-cultural transformation that Gerlach and Hine describe is both conceptually revolutionary and characterized by a religious type of commitment. This is the kind of mechanism for transformation of greatest interest to us. The authors, furthermore, identify these movements as parts of and contributions to greater social changes that are occurring. They suggest that major cultural "advances" are accompanied by radical allegiance changes of this kind. This they see as presently occurring worldwide. It is thus possible to see Pentecostalism and black power, along with other contemporary movements, "as parts of a cultural revolution that is broader in scope than a mere social revolution within one society" (1970:204).

In studying movements,

the first question to ask . . . is, are the five basic factors present and interacting? The second concerns its relationship to the particular society in which it has risen: is it an isolated phenomenon or does it seem to be one strand in a multilinear change? The third question is, what is its relevance beyond that society (Gerlach and Hine 1970:203)?

Several helpful points concerning the place of movements in cultural transformation can be usefully summarized as follows:

1. A movement does not require that a majority of the people in a group favor it before it can be initiated. A movement is, in fact, a good example of "the type of social change that can be caused by a dedicated minority willing to call out the repressive force of the majority" (ibid.:204).

2. Once a movement has achieved a life of its own "the only type of crackdown which can stop it decisively is complete and crushing force" (ibid.:205). Gerlach and Hine are interested in the place of social opposition in the development of movements. In the characteristics of movements cited above they see "real or perceived opposition from the society at large" as necessary. Whether or not this is universally true, we can point to early Christianity and many other movements for illustrations of the importance that social opposition can have. The authors frankly state that for any number of past and present movements,

opposition to the movements, no matter how justified or on what grounds, simply strengthens movement adherents and propels them in the direction they are already going (1970:207).

3. With respect to attempts to reform churches without the presence of a movement, the authors suggest that

contemporary efforts to revitalize, either from the top of the religious bureaucracy down or from the bottom of the local church up, have resulted in remarkably little lasting change in the overall picture (ibid.:207).

Concern for the lack of vitality and even the initiation of programs to change the situation have little effect, for, "without the enthusiasms of a true movement, the inertia of tradition is too strong" (ibid.:207). Probably the advocacy of any paradigm shift (including the one advocated in this volume), without the accompaniment of a movement is doomed to substantial failure. For example, throughout the bureaucracies of America's government, churches, and educational institutions,

individuals and groups are generating ideas about how to solve problems of education, jobs, housing, and community relations. But it appears that changes are being successfully implemented only if they are on a small enough scale so that a group of dedicated people in one department or organization can actually initiate and carry them out (Gerlach and Hine 1970:208).

4. In facing the problems of a society or an institution there is a basic difference between the way participants in a movement seek solutions and the way the "establishment" seeks solutions.

Movement participants seek ways to resolve or remedy the generating conditions . . . which can lead to revolutionary change, . . . while members of the established order seek solutions as a means of avoiding revolutionary social change (Gerlach and Hine 1970:209).

Often when the power structure attempts to attack "the problem," they attack also any movement-type operations that are seeking to remedy the problem.

5. Most revolutions are not generated with the idea of fomenting revolution. They begin as protests of one kind or another with

demands for changes in the existing system, not specific blueprints for social institutions of the future. Positive goals are only vaguely defined in terms of large-scale ideals (Gerlach and Hine 1970:210).

To some extent those who advocate Christian transformation may become exceptions to this rule if they add to their "vaguely defined . . . large-scale ideals" some more "specific blueprints." We hope that this volume will help us to do this more effectively than heretofore.

6. Movements involve major changes in the self-image of the participants. In the black power movement Gerlach and Hine see a major contribution to a "new image of the male role and of family structure in black society"

(1970:211). Conversion and commitment to a cause can, in this respect, accomplish "what social workers and integrated blacks have been trying unsuccessfully to accomplish for years by persuasion and moralistic preachment" (ibid.:211), for "a movement taps a source of human energy which is unavailable to those using conventional means" (ibid.).

7. Long-term social changes often result from the fact that movements, whether or not they succeed, initiate experimental new approaches to the solution of needs that are more widely recognized throughout the society. For example, recent youth movements within American society have begun experimenting with new approaches to problems considered as at best "necessary evils" by much of the rest of society. Among these are "rigid scheduling of time, depersonalization of work, escalating material demands, non-democratic corporate structures" (Gerlach and Hine 1970:213). By refusing "to train for 'successful' participation in the existing order," stressing "cooperation rather than competition," rejecting "the traditional American bases for division of labor," and innovating in "marriage patterns, child rearing practices, and methods of group decision making," it is possible that these youth are initiating changes that will survive even if their movement fails. It is even possible, if their movement succeeds, that it "might constitute a better 'survival group' in the event of large-scale disaster than any that exists in conventional society" (Gerlach and Hine 1970:213-14).

Whatever happens to the movement itself, the models that it pioneers often diffuse into the rest of the society. Such diffusion frequently brings about a shift in value orientations (worldviews) from which the rippling of changes throughout the culture is generated. As such changes "in grass roots activities" are instituted,

the more adaptive of the small innovations diffuse and crystallize until an ex post facto recognition of the new social structure is possible (ibid.:216).

The "interactions between the movement and the established order" create "selective pressures" in the direction of the changes being advocated by the movement. Such factors as the degree of commitment of the participants, the movement's viability as a continuing operation, and the response of the members of the established order affect the ability of the movement to effectively bring pressure for change to bear on the rest of the society.

Those who are neither committed to a movement nor definitely opposed to it, who have escaped the so-called polarization, occupy what might be called the interface between the movement and the established order. As one student of the dynamics of social change has suggested, accelerated change occurs at the interfaces of the human world—just as geological shifts occur along fault lines. It is not the mere aggregation or acquisition of disparate ideas from which the great advances of mankind have come, but from a "certain type of mental activity which is set up by the opposition of different idea systems" (Gerlach and Hine 1970:216 quoting from Fabun 1967).

Those cultural insiders (innovators) who seek to participate in the advocacy throughout a society of the changes pioneered by a movement need, according to Gerlach and Hine, to orient themselves in several ways if they are to be effective. Those who, either by chance or by choice,

find themselves along the interface between a movement and the established order must: first, understand the nature of the movement and the five basic factors crucial to its growth; second, allow movement participants, demagogues, and preachers to identify the areas of social, economic, political or religious life that require change; third, accept the necessity for fundamental rather than developmental change and be able to tell the difference; fourth, either in relation to or independently of the movement, embark on the Vision Quest for the shape of things to come (Gerlach and Hine 1970:216–17).

Movements, in addition to their power to bring about change directly, are powerful indirect forces for change. They serve to heighten the consciousness of many of those outside the movement itself, to identify aspects of the cultural system that require change, and to experiment with models for new structures. Movements also frequently win converts to the possibility of using "the dynamics of a movement" to bring about whatever changes they deem important. Conscious understanding of movement dynamics "makes possible the intentional utilization of the vitalizing energy produced by the process" (ibid.:217). For those who seek to participate in a movement, the authors point out that it will involve five things:

1. Personal commitment on the part of individuals who believe they have the power to initiate changes within their own sphere of influence;
2. enthusiastic persuasion of friends, relatives, and neighbors to join in the small-scale effort;
3. articulation of beliefs and ideals appropriate to this particular period in national and world history and to this particular stage of technological development;
4. flexible, non-bureaucratic cell-group organizations which can be created, altered, or dissolved at the desire of participants; and
5. expectation of and willingness to face opposition from those dedicated to the maintenance of the status quo in spite of its present deficiencies, weaknesses, and flaws. Opposition may come in the form of physical force, or various types of pressure exerted through institutional channels. Or it may come in the form of ridicule from those who are still secure in the notion that power is based only on position within and ability to manipulate the existing power structure (Gerlach and Hine 1970:217).

Such a consideration of movements is very helpful to us in our attempts to understand the factors that can be important in Christian transformation of culture. Apparently God already knows that

the most obvious fact about social, religious, or political movements is the amount of power that can be mobilized *outside* the power structure of a society, and the surprising pressure this power can exert upon that structure (Gerlach and Hine 1970:218).

The whole Bible demonstrates the power of a few who are deeply committed to God in bringing about impressive culture change. So does postbiblical church history. So do contemporary Christian movements such as Pentecostalism in Latin America (Wagner 1973) and African independent churches (Barrett 1968).

PRINCIPLES FOR INSIDERS:
WHAT TO DO ABOUT THE "GENERATION GAP"

Cultural insiders may innovate (i.e., make changes) in their own cultures. They may also become "inside advocates" who attempt to persuade others within their cultures to make changes. Christians are called to do both. On the basis of our Christian allegiance to God through Christ we are to evaluate every aspect of our lives within our culture and to change our usage of our culture in keeping with this allegiance. (The matter of re-evaluation and rehabituation has been dealt with in chapter 18.) Those principles apply to all Christians who innovate Christianity within their culture. Principles of witness presented throughout this volume and the principles of advocacy above apply to the cultural insider seeking to persuasively advocate change for others. What follows illustrates the application of many of the principles dealt with throughout this book to the problem of how a Christian may innovate Christian transformational change in response to the American "generation gap" problem.

Many useful examples might be cited to illustrate the value of reinterpretive understandings that come to us via the analyses of the behavioral sciences in our attempts to transform at least our own use of culture. One of these is the recognition stemming from the anthropological fieldwork of Margaret Mead in Samoa (Mead 1928) that not biology but culture makes the adolescent years turbulent for American youth. Starting from her research we now realize that American youth rebel because they have been carefully (though unconsciously) taught that they must achieve beyond the level of their parents' generation. In order to do this they must set themselves against that generation in theory and in practice, thus establishing their own position in life. Samoan youth (and those of many other cultures) were not taught such things concerning their relationship to their elders and therefore did not rebel (see Mead 1970 for her analysis of the American generation gap).

As Christian Americans we may decide that youthful rebellion against parents is not appropriate to Christianity. Yet we and our children find ourselves so conditioned by our culture that not only they (who perhaps don't know any better) but we ourselves (who ought to know better) automatically

come to relate to each other in terms of the expected intergenerational hostil-
ity. What do we do about this?

The approach here advocated would be (1) to recognize the problem, (2) to
recognize our ability to transform at least our own approach to the matter,
(3) to deepen our analytic understanding at least to the point where we
understand the major cultural components that produce the situation, and
(4) to develop a strategy for dealing with it in a more Christian manner than
would be possible if we simply allow ourselves to be driven along blindly by
our culture. We should come to realize, for example, that our school system
plays a major role in producing the problem, for our children are carefully
taught in school that their parents cannot be trusted for expert knowledge
about very much. Flowing from this is the categorization of two important
groups of adults into antithetical groups of experts (e.g., most teachers,
scientists, authors, etc.) and parents (together with a variety of other adults,
including certain teachers who seem to be behind the times). A frustrated
pastor once came face to face with the effects of this cultural conditioning when
he asked his youth leader, "How come you can say the same things to my
daughter that I say, but she takes them from you?" For that daughter, the
youth leader fit into the "expert" category.

There are at least four levels on which Christian parents may work to
transform their own (and others') use of American culture to counteract such
intergenerational antipathy and the part the schools play in producing it:

1. They would do well to help their children to change their conceptualization (their model) regarding education to recognize that *the term "education" is
not synonymous with schooling*. Rather, education is a much broader and deeper
process in which we are all engaged at all times. What we learn in school is but
a small part of the totality of our educational experience. And the information
we obtain in the classroom or from books is only a part of the overall educational experience in which we are engaged. Furthermore, the significant factor
in education is the ability of the learner to learn a wide variety of things by
transforming every event into a learning experience. Thus the myriad of
nonacademic things that go on inside and outside school (including at home)
are at least as important to one's education as the academic things. The large
number of people other than teachers (even parents) whom one encounters are
at least as important to learn from as teachers are. But learners must see to it
that they use every opportunity educationally and look to every adult as a
potential teacher.

2. Parents should recognize the child's conditioning with respect to the
source of expertise and *work with* (or in terms of) *this conditioning* in order to
make it work in the desired direction rather than in an undesirable direction.
They should see to it that their children are put in constant contact with people
in the expert category (e.g., school and church teachers, pastors, etc.) who will
endorse and reinforce the kinds of things the parents wish to have their

children learn. For most, this should mean the choosing of church, community, and friends with careful attention to the needs of the children. For some it will mean the placing of their children in parochial schools. There is, however, a tendency for many teachers and administrators of parochial schools to regard such schools as escapes from cultural reality rather than as more effective means of facing and transforming reality. This fact should cause those who adopt my point of view to study the school carefully before going that route.

3. Another constructive approach to this problem is for parents to realize that *both the parent and the teacher categories are basically depersonalized "thing" categories (stereotypes)* to the young person. This fact is also due to the child's American cultural conditioning. That is, the young person has simply learned to categorize people as the rest of American society does into landscape (or scenery[4]), machinery, and people (Iwanska 1957). To the young person both teachers and parents fit, to some extent, into the second of the impersonal categories—they are machines. Machines are those upon whom one depends to perform vital functions but whom one doesn't get to know as real human beings. Aware parents, seeking to use but transcend the ordinary impact of this characteristic of American culture, will do what they can to become *persons* to their children. This would, of course, involve the (probably gradual) sharing of themselves with their children—as human beings, not as stereotyped parents. It should cover the wide spectrum of their experience, not in a preachy way but in a person-to-person, friend-to-friend way. This kind of relationship typically allows even the sharing of personal hangups, kidding over parental mistakes, treatment of the youngsters as *persons* (they are often in the parents' "thing" category) who are listened to and granted respect, trust, and responsibility. Such a use of culture not only transforms the performance (use) of the culture by parents and their children, but transforms their relationship as well.

4. Another approach to this problem of intergenerational antipathy is for *parents to win their way into the teacher (expert) category* by proving to the children their expertise in some area of importance to the children. This approach is not as available to all parents as the previous three, since the child, by school experience, is conditioned to respect primarily academic-type activities. A father who, for example, sought to win his way into the expert category by proving his excellence at auto-mechanics might not succeed with his children, since their schooling has labeled auto-mechanics as a second- or third-class specialty. A combination of this approach with the expansion of the young people's awareness of what education is may, however, bring about success. A mother who is a teacher, however, may so win her youngsters' respect that they seek to learn more by choosing to do research projects on topics like "what my mother teaches."

---

4. The scenery category includes the mass of fellow students and any similar group that the child doesn't get to know or become involved with.

Practicing and communicating to others such ways of *working in terms of one's culture in order to transform it for Christ* can provide significant input for others who are struggling with the same kinds of problems. Felt needs may combine with demonstrably effective approaches to produce a broader cultural transformation. This is especially true when groups of people (like churches) band together to bring about such cultural transformation, first in their own usage and then rippling out to the usage of others.

This could be the case if we would study and learn from Christian communities such as the Hutterites. The Hutterites have taken control of their use of Euro-American cultural patterns and made modifications that "mainline" Christians could well emulate in at least four important areas (Kraft 1972a; see also Beals and Spindler 1973:207–61; Hostetler and Huntington 1967; Hostetler 1967):

1. The Hutterites *emphasize community.* Human beings are social creatures and need interinvolvement to a much greater extent than the American brand of western culture encourages. The process of individuation by means of which culture prevents such close personal interinvolvement between people is consciously resisted by the Hutterite communities and their example should be seriously considered by any who seek Christian transformation of American culture.

2. Within their communities, the Hutterites

educate more for living (not simply for thinking) in schools that provide an extension of the family and a continuation of the family's teachings rather than becoming competitors for the children's allegiance and contradictors of the values endorsed by the home (Kraft 1972a:15).

3. The Hutterites *provide for their young people well-defined transition points* at which each youth first becomes an apprentice adult (age fifteen) and then a full adult (age twenty). In this way both the youth and the adults know the stage at which anyone is at any given time and what the expectations are. There is, apparently, very little of the teenage insecurity so evident in other American subcultures, occasioned by the fact that neither teenagers nor adults know at any given time whether the former are to be regarded as children or as grownups.

4. The Hutterites seem to have *learned the lesson of smallness.* They organize their communities into groups of about 125 in order to preserve and encourage the kind of face-to-face interaction among their members that will enhance their interdependence, mutual concern, and mutual involvement. In these ways they produce and maintain community and effectively work in terms of the majority of western cultural patterns in order to transcend them.

From the perspective of "standard" American culture, the Hutterite adaptations seem ideal. There is, however, at least one major problem. They train their children to live only in a "closed" society. If for some reason the Hutterite youth leave the community, they discover that they have been poorly prepared to handle the bewildering array of choices, decisions, lifestyles, and people with differing opinions with which they are faced in the "open" society. They have been taught the validity of only one way of life and often cannot effectively cope with the diversity outside (see Beals and Spindler 1973).

Certain Christians may feel that they should imitate aspects of the Hutterite pattern, such as taking control of the children's schooling. If so, the problem of whether to train for an open or a closed society needs to be faced squarely. Many Christian schools train for a closed society, but no such society is provided for the young people to enter. They are expected to enter the open society effectively but with the kind of training that often cripples them for maturely facing and choosing between a wide variety of options. The alternative is Christian schooling that teaches how to live responsibly in an open society, including how to evaluate and choose among a number of available alternatives on the basis of Christian principles. Though I believe this could be done, it would take a greater degree of openness than ordinarily exists on the part of those who run Christian schools.

20. An Apostolic Faith?

Can contemporary Christianity regain the dynamic of the Christianity that turned the first-century world upside-down? Throughout the preceding chapters we have attempted to suggest that it *can* be done and to show how to go about it. Here we summarize by recommending a return to an apostolic faith. A personal postscript concludes the book.

AN APOSTOLIC FAITH?

Those possessed of dynamic, apostolic faith dared to work with God at the transformation of Hellenistic culture. And this same dynamic, daring, experimenting attitude has been adopted by Fijian Christians (see chapter 18), African independent churches, Latin American (and North American) Pentecostals, "Jesus People," and countless other Christians in a variety of cultures—working with God at the transformation of their cultures. However, whenever and wherever the church has turned from venturesomeness and retreated into static forms of expression it has lost its dynamic. In the institutional church today most people would probably point to such areas as theology, organization, and worship as dead areas. The reason is not hard to find—"establishment" Christianity (the party in power) has tended to content itself with indoctrinating new generations and new cultures into forms of Christianity that are no longer culturally appropriate. Established Christianity has feared to alter the forms lest in so doing the content should be lost. By so doing, however, it has unwittingly *assured* that the content would be largely lost.

The dynamic of Christianity, however, is not in the sacredness of cultural forms—even those that God once used. The Christian dynamic is in the venturesomeness of participating with God in the transformation of contemporary cultural forms to serve more adequately as vehicles for God's interactions with human beings. What we seek is a Christianity equivalent in its dynamics to that displayed in the pages of the New Testament. But we often fear to let loose from the old familiar forms. We may recognize the need for a new dynamic but our cultural conditioning often mitigates against our engaging in the kind of experimentation that might lead us to discover it.

For American culture, like all others, has designated certain areas of culture for experimentation, while others remain "as they always have been." We are encouraged to doubt previous solutions, to seek new answers, to experiment, to innovate in technology, foods, travel, clothing and, even, lately, sex. We are continually beseiged with the latest "discoveries" in styles in soap, toothpaste, automobiles, appliances, etc. We are encouraged to develop new wants to stimulate us to purchase more and more of these items. It may escape our notice, however, that in certain areas of life, American culture takes a very different attitude. Innovation is neither valued nor, often, even allowed in many areas of the American legal system, where "precedent" is the major criterion in coming to a decision. Likewise in government, athletics, and religion. In such areas American culture is quite conservative.

Thus our cultural conditioning is in the direction of static conformance to religious tradition rather than motivating us to experiment and innovate in this area. And such conservatism in religion seems to be the rule rather than the exception in cultures, especially in areas (often labeled "religious") that actually are basic to the whole worldview of the culture. Far more cultures manifest conservatism than an experimenting attitude in this area—that is, until it becomes obvious to the members of a culture that their religion (or worldview) isn't doing its job. Then sometimes their attitude changes, for, as we have pointed out (chapter 3), worldview forms the core of culture. It bridges the gap between the "objective" reality outside people's heads and the culturally agreed-upon perception of that reality inside their heads.

Worldview and religion in a "healthy" culture are integrated with and supportive of each other. When a worldview and its religion get out of step, things fall apart. No longer do American Christians, for example, look to Christianity to validate large segments of their culture. More often they see their culture as in conflict with Christianity. For a static religion poorly serves a dynamic culture (even if the culture designates religion as a conservative area).

But this Christianity that is proving inadequate is not essential Christianity. The religion that Americans (and the victims of western secularism around the world) are turning their backs on is not the dynamic equivalent of the faith that turned the first-century world upside-down. The Christianity they know is culture-bound. It is simply the religious aspect of a culture that seeks, almost superstitiously, to preserve the "sacred" forms of worship, organization, and theology, that have been passed on by former generations. This Christianity has been found wanting because it is static. Its doctrines seem eternal because, as James points out, they deal with an unreal conceptual world where nothing moves (James 1968:88). Miracles and other visible forms of God's manifestation of himself are often understood as something that once happened but will not again. God, after briefly breaking into the human scene to do some very unreal things, seems to have died or departed into a far country never to work in that way again. The church is seen by many as a mechanism for preserving the static memory of such events by regularly transporting its adherents back to first-century Palestine. Sermons have become mere history lessons.

Life is not like that, however. And there is another perception possible of the

God who *inter*acted and continues to interact with human beings, of the case histories of real life events that are recorded in the divine casebook, of the church that can result from this divine-human interaction. A re-examination of the data from the point of view developed here can alert us to and instruct us in that living perception. From this point of view, the lifeless biblical characters begin to live again—and, surprisingly, look and act just like people we meet every day. Furthermore, biblical English, Greek, and even Hebrew begin to look like workable languages, operated by real human beings, rather than like carefully constructed philosophical systems that trip up all but the most expert. Jesus becomes believable and God comes back to life.

We badly need such a dynamic understanding of Christianity, for our culture is headed for hard times. Things have already fallen apart for millions of our contemporaries because they have turned from the faith commitment to God that could provide a vital core to their culture. As the anthropologist Kluckhohn has said:

A system of beliefs, profoundly felt, is unquestionably necessary to the survival of any society, but an increasing number of Americans debate the extent to which the dogmas of any organized Christian Church are compatible with contemporary secular knowledge (1949:190).

Addressing himself to a similar cultural situation ages ago, God asked Jeremiah:

If you have raced with men and the runners have worn you down, how then can you hope to vie with horses? If you fall headlong in easy country, how will you fare in Jordan's dense thickets? (12:5 NEB).

How indeed will we fare when life tumbles in on us if we haven't learned to participate with God daringly in a Christianity that is dynamically equivalent to that of New Testament times? Such Christianity not only transforms individuals, but can transform cultural forms such as American individuality into organic groupness (which is what the church is meant to be). It can transform an unimaginative, impersonal, propositional, "sacred" but dead preaching form into something genuinely communicative (e.g., drama, dialogue, etc.). It can transform static theological formulations into understandings of the creative divine-human use of culture that dynamic interaction between human beings and God demands. It can, in fact, provide the spark around which our rapidly disintegrating culture revitalizes.

For cross-cultural studies demonstrate that, in order to survive,

every culture must define its ends as well as perfect its means. The logical and symbolic expressions of the ultimate values of a civilization cannot arise directly from scientific investigation . . . . A mechanistic, materialistic "science" hardly provides the orientations to the deeper problems of life that are essential for happy individuals and a healthy social order. Nor does a political philosophy such as "democracy." Men need tenets that . . . are meaningful to the viscera and the aesthetic sensibilities. They must be symbolized in rites that gratify the heart, please the ear and eye, fulfill the hunger for drama (Kluckhohn 1949:248–49).

The ideological impoverishment of American society seriously cripples it, and this kind of crippling is a contemporary fact in all societies that, under the influence of western culture (often mediated by Christian missions), have had their indigenous wordviews irreparably damaged. And

this process of deterioration can, if not checked, lead to the death of the society. Population may fall even to the point of extinction as a result of increasing death rates and decreasing birth rates; the society may be defeated in war, invaded, its population dispersed and its customs suppressed; factional disputes may nibble away areas and segments of the population (Wallace 1956:270).

Or there may be communicated to the disheartened society a new ideology, usually supernaturalistic in focus, around which the society rallies and re-builds. Such "deliberate, conscious, organized efforts by members of a society to create a more satisfying culture" (Wallace 1956:279) are termed by Wallace "revitalization movements." Wallace holds that literally thousands of such occurrences have taken place in history, including a wide variety of nativistic, revivalistic, vitalistic, millennarian, and messianic movements both outside and within western cultures. The origins of Christianity, Islam, and possibly Buddhism as well as many other religious phenomena are theorized to have been in revitalization movements (Wallace 1956:267,279).

Social breakdown, therefore, provides a fertile setting for the return of Christians to a more dynamic understanding and expression of their faith and for the communication of this faith to others. May all Christians return to a vital, apostolic faith. May we then fearlessly venture out with God from the staticness of our culture-bound religion to participate actively with him in the transforming power of dynamically equivalent Christianity.

A PERSONAL POSTSCRIPT

We have now come to the end of this presentation. I have attempted to develop at least certain aspects of a cross-cultural approach to Christian theologizing. To do this I have suggested a series of thirteen models as grids in terms of which to view the realities we seek to understand. I have attempted to apply certain of the perspectives of anthropology, linguistics, communication science, and translation theory to the task of theologizing.

Has the effort been worthwhile? For me it has, even though I am not entirely satisfied that I have always said what I intend to say in the best way. As a part of my becoming whatever God is making me, though, the attempt to formulate these thoughts has been a valuable exercise. I can point to measura-ble growth in myself as a result. Whether or not this particular product is of value to anyone else, the process of producing it has for me been an exciting learning experience.

Has the effort been worthwhile for you, the reader? Only you can answer that. Certain readers of previous versions of this volume have told me that they have been considerably helped. This, of course, is greatly encouraging to me. Others, however, have been disturbed—at least by portions of the book. They feel that I have been too daring, perhaps unwise or even heretical. I am sorry for that kind of reaction but pray that those of you who find yourselves in this category will do two things: (1) be patient, God is not finished with me yet, and (2) choose those things here presented that you regard as helpful to you in your present circumstances, use them, and ignore the rest. I have tried in the early chapters to make you feel free to reject those parts of this presentation not congenial to you. This is but one perspective on a reality that is bigger than all of us. It is a sincere groping after the truth, but it is not itself that truth. It has been helpful to me, but you are different from me. Perhaps this approach can be of maximum help only to those most like me. The point is, you are free to disagree and/or to pick and to choose what seems most valuable to you and present those insights to others like yourself.

Some of you may not see much of value here because you feel it has all been said before. My discovery of Ramm, *Special Revelation and the Word of God* (1961), was in response to the comment of one who heard me present a portion of this material. He simply said, "Bernard Ramm has already said all that!" I have tried in several chapters to respond to the truth of that comment by quoting Ramm extensively. I am grateful to the person who made the remark, though I have forgotten his name. If you are in that position, I apologize to you for being unable to challenge you more.

Will this effort be judged worthwhile as a stimulus to more effective Christian witness "to the regions beyond"? I pray so. I am hard on missionaries. I *am* a missionary and my standards are high for myself and for my colleagues. We dare not handle a first-class message in a second- or third-class way. My prayer is that God will use this effort to lead at least some to first-classness in their transmission of a more clearly understood message.

Will this effort enable any who have found Christianity wanting to retain or to return to their faith? I pray so. This approach has helped me to face more confidently many of the issues that have turned others from God and Christ. Not all problems have neat answers even yet, but I feel that I am not now forced to live with as great an amount of ambiguity as formerly. My prayer is that some of those for whom the old models have failed will find it possible via these models to retain and develop their Christian commitment.

Will this effort help to release some evangelicals from the hold of reactionary, fear-based theological positions (e.g., Lindsell 1976) into the "dynamic obedience to a living God" (Nida 1954:52) that is, I believe, the birthright of those committed to Christ? I pray so. The God who has accepted and worked with such cultural and personal diversity as we see in the Scriptures just doesn't seem as concerned as closed evangelicals and fundamentalists are over which *theory* of inspiration or of the atonement, or of matters of biblical criticism his people adhere to. Whether or not one adheres to a particular metaphysical philosophy in developing such theories seems secondary in God's eyes to whether or not one demonstrates allegiance to God via love toward sisters and brothers (see 1 Jn. 3:10–11; 4:7–8,11). No set of fallible theories or models for interpreting God and his workings is worth advocating in unchristian, unloving ways.

Is this effort to do theology differently a partial fulfillment of Rosemary Ruether's prophecy In answer to the question, "Whatever Happened to Theology?" I don't know. She says:

For the foreseeable future the pioneering edge of thought will come . . . from places on the edge with little prestige, from the meetings and communities of those who can recognize this crisis, not as the "end" but as the only avenue to new hope (1975:110).

Ruether claims that "the entire paradigm of consciousness that has governed the line of Western culture and its reflection in theology has lost its credibility" (ibid.). Míguez Bonino feels that contemporary theology "has tried to prolong its existence when the conditions that gave it birth and made it possible have entered their decline and demise" (1975:112). In a similar vein, John Cobb sees the decline of theology as "a result of the widening gap between the beliefs nurtured in the Church and the dominant culture of our time" (1975:117). If these contentions are even partly true, perhaps experimenting with different models such as these will help. Perhaps such experimentation can point the way toward something to replace the kind of closed conservatism that the fear of relativism has driven many to (see the prediction of Dayton 1976:979). I don't know.

I hope this exercise is at least an example of the "deprovincialization" of theology that Harvey Cox calls for (1973:169–71). In another place Cox states:

Theology is being done today—in curious places, under unusual sponsorship, by unauthorized persons, unnoticed by those who read only the right journals (1975:115).

Perhaps I can at least claim that distinction for this volume. I invite you to join me in this experiment.

Appendix
An Overview of the Models and Submodels[1]

A. PERSPECTIVE MODELS (Chapters 2–5)

As basic perspective models we list the concept of model itself, the concept "biblical Christian," and the application of anthropological insights. These concepts are basic to all that follows.

Model 1 is the concept of *models* itself. This is a conceptual perspective and subject to the limitations discussed in chapter 2 for all models. A model is a tool that we use in our attempts to understand portions of reality. If we are correct in identifying the concept of model with the "dim image in a mirror" (1 Cor. 13:12) concept, we may be able to claim an important correspondence between this understanding and the way things really are. If not, we are still searching. For better or worse, though, this presentation assumes the validity and usefulness of the model concept.

Model 2 is an attempt to conceptualize a *biblical Christian*. This model (developed in chapter 2) is both a basic perspective model and a revised theological model. Much of the support for it comes from the building up of the argument of this book. If the initial presentation of it in chapter 2 is not convincing, please read on. The model may be more credible by the end of the book than it is at the beginning. It seems important, though, to present at least these basic assumptions at the start, since everything that follows depends on them in a major way.

a. Model 2 postulates a *difference between the inspired scriptural documents and all human interpretations of that data*. It is biblical to refuse to venerate traditions of interpretation. All such theological systems are fallible, no matter how helpful they may have been to other people in other times and places. Each such interpretive system is developed from a given perspective that was at least potentially valid for those who developed it. The needs of today's peoples, however, are not best served by simply adopting the *product* of valid past efforts at interpretation (as if that too were inspired). Rather, today's peoples themselves must engage in the *process* of developing scriptural interpretations as valid for them in their contexts as past interpretations were for those who developed them in their contexts.

b. Biblical Christianity, whether in theological or other areas, is *dynamic, not*

---

1. See the Outline on pp. xvi–xviii.

static. It recommends that we engage in a process equivalent to that portrayed in the Bible. We are not simply to preserve the past as the Pharisees and Judaizers attempted to do, for the God of the Bible is alive and we are to be alive in and with him. Life demands growth and dynamic change. Conservatism for its own sake is contrary to biblical Christianity.

c. Biblical Christians are to be *open to innovation and diversity* as God's Spirit leads them individually and in groups in growth. Growth is risky and venturesome, and is not characteristic of closed-minded persons. Our biblical examples are, therefore, venturesome, open to the Spirit's leading and growing. The closed-minded Pharisees and Judaizers who, like the unprofitable servant in the parable of the Talents, sought to preserve rather than to risk and grow, are not to be imitated by biblical Christians. Biblical Christians are to be open rather than closed conservatives.

Model 3 (chapters 3–5) is the *application of anthropological insights* to topics that have been considered "theological." This model involves the application of several models (seven are here specified) developed within anthropology. The most basic of these deal with anthropological views of culture and basic humanity. Though there is a good bit of discussion within the discipline concerning these understandings, I have attempted to hold close to anthropological orthodoxy, except where Christian assumptions are injected.

a. The *culture concept* is (within anthropology) complex and pervasive enough to be regarded as a full-fledged theory, or paradigm, rather than simply as one or more models. It is so basic to the perspective of this book that two chapters (3 and 4) are devoted to developing the understanding of culture here assumed. In those chapters I postulate both a view of reality that sees certain phenomena as best explained in terms of a mental construct called *culture*, and a particular (one hopes, orthodox) understanding of that mental construct. That is, I here attempt both to look at reality via the culture model and to develop a model of culture itself. In the conceptualization of culture here assumed, there are certain closely related submodels that are crucial to the understandings toward which I seek to lead the reader. Many or all of these could be subsumed under the culture model but it seems best to make them explicit by giving them a more independent status as anthropological concepts whose importance for our purposes is in many ways parallel to that of the culture concept itself.

b. The *cultural* (including linguistic) *validity submodel* is more frequently known as "cultural relativism." It postulates, on the one hand, the nonabsoluteness of any cultural or linguistic forms and, on the other, the essential equal validity of the way in which different cultures structure the lives of those immersed within them. This anthropological model forms the basis for model 4e (chapter 6).

c. A *worldview* is seen as lying at the heart of every cultural entity (whether a culture, subculture, academic discipline, social class, religious, political, or economic organization, or any similar grouping with a distinct value system).

The worldview of a cultural entity is seen as both the repository and the generator of the conceptual models in terms of which the adherents of that entity, the subscribers to that value system, perceive of and interact with reality. I suggest that the basic appeal for Christian conversion and for whatever conceptual transformation this book can bring about is to be made at the worldview level. I use interchangeably the terms "paradigm shift," "worldview change" (or "transformation"), and "conceptual change" (or "transformation").

d. Another important submodel from anthropology is the *form, function, meaning, usage model* (developed in chapter 4). A cultural form is any cultural element, whether material or nonmaterial. Any custom, any word or other linguistic pattern, any material or nonmaterial product of human activity is a cultural form. These forms are developed and perpetuated within a cultural system because they serve *functions* regarded by their *users* as important. As they are used, they become vehicles of *meaning* from and to their users.

I contend, in applying this model to the relationships of Christianity to culture, that it is the intent of God to see Christian meanings communicated through human cultural (including linguistic) forms. Meanings, according to this model, are conveyable to human beings only via cultural forms (often called "symbols"). The forms employed in any given communication are therefore crucial to the success or failure of the communication. It is thus incumbent upon the communicator to use those cultural forms that will best convey the intended meaning to the receiver of the communication. For, it is observed, within a variety of cultural contexts a variety of cultural forms must be employed if essentially the same meaning is to be conveyed. There do not seem to be any cultural forms that convey exactly the same meanings in every culture (Nida 1960:62–93). We observe, furthermore, that if the same form is retained from culture to culture, the perceived meaning gets changed. Apparently, constancy of meaning from context to context is maintained by altering or replacing the forms employed in such a way that they signal the intended meaning within that specific context.

e. Another important submodel of the culture concept (as here developed) is *the distinction between the patterns or structuring of culture and the uses to which that structuring is put (the cultural performance).* It distinguishes between the essentially neutral forms and functions of culture and the non-neutral, subjective use that human beings make of their cultural patterns. This usage stems from subjectively held meanings and results in subjectively perceived meanings. In building our approach to Christianity on this model, it is postulated that sinfulness lies primarily, though not exclusively, in these subjective usages and meanings rather than in the cultural structures themselves (see Rom. 14:13–23 for what I understand to be a scriptural recognition of this principle). It is also postulated that divine-human encounter takes place within cultural structures at the usage and meaning level rather than as a result of a negative stance that God takes toward the structures themselves (see chapter 6).

f. Spinning off from these understandings of culture is a model of *culture change.* This model recognizes that cultures are constantly changing as a result of the choices made by the people within them. Stimulus for change may come from within or outside of a culture and is closely related to the evaluations that people make concerning their cultural behavior. Negative evaluations of cultural behavior frequently lead to changes in cultural performance. These, in turn, lead to alterations in the patterning of the culture. Understandings of culture change and of reference points for change lay the groundwork for the discussion (in chapters 18 and 19) of cultural transformation on the basis of Christian input.

g. Though cultures differ markedly from each other, the superstructure of *human commonality* (chapter 5) on which they all are built demands that they provide satisfying answers to essentially the same sets of questions. The approaches to answering such questions and the conclusions arrived at show remarkable human creativity and understanding as well as limitations of various kinds. But underlying the cultural diversity "people are more alike than cultures" (Goldschmidt 1966:134).

B. ETHNOTHEOLOGICAL MODELS I (Chapters 6–7)

The first of two series of revised theological (ethnotheological) models is developed in chapters 6 and 7. This series is the result of the application of the preceding anthropological models and submodels to theologizing.

Model 4, the *God, humanity, and culture* model, postulates a particular relationship between God, human beings, and the cultural matrix within which they interact. Five aspects of this model are detailed.

a. The first aspect of this model (chapter 6) suggests that the Christian God should not be perceived either as *against,* merely *in,* or simply *above* culture. It sees *God* as outside culture but *working in terms of or through culture* to accomplish his purposes. Since human beings exist in total cultural immersion, God chooses to relate to us in terms of our cultural matrices. His attitude, therefore, is not to be seen as either negative or positive to human culture as such. Culture is, rather, a vehicle that, though often used by humans contrary to God's will, may be used by him for his purposes.

b. Within this model, *theology is seen as culture-bound perception* (chapter 7) with, as pointed out under model 2a, no inherent claim to sacredness simply because it deals with sacred subject matter. Theological insight is culture-bound even though the meanings (truth) into which theologians probe originate outside of culture with God.

c. The *primacy of* such *supracultural meanings over* the *cultural forms* that God employs to convey them must, therefore, be recognized. As model 3d shows, the cultural forms that are used for God are extremely important. For they can either accurately convey or utterly confuse the transmission of God's truth. But the forms are important as *means,* not as ends. It is the *meanings* of God that are crucial.

d. The concept of *the supracultural and the cultural* is detailed as part *d* of this model. Under this heading we seek to make explicit the culture-boundness of human beings, on the one hand, and the freedom from culture-boundness of God (except when and as he chooses to work in and through culture), on the other. Note that it specifically does not postulate any kind of God-endorsed culture. It employs the term "supracultural" only adjectivally to mean "non-culture-bound." "Supracultural" can apply only to beings and meanings that originate outside of culture. These meanings may also be called "Christian" if they are from God. The cultural forms through which they are channeled to culture-bound human beings can be called neither supracultural nor Christian.

e. *Biblical cultural relativism* postulates that God recognizes and employs the cultural validity principle (model 3b). He is seen to take into account (1) the endowment and opportunities of people, (2) the extent of revelation available to them, and (3) their cultural patterns. His interactions with people are therefore relative to these factors. This is not an absolute relativity, of course, but a recognition on God's part of the reality of human immersion in culture.

Imitating God in this respect means that we are to apply the Golden Rule (Mt. 7:12) at the cultural level as well as at the individual level, since God is no more partial to one culture over another than he is to one individual over another (Acts 10:34). Nor does he seek to impose the forms of one culture upon another as the Pharisees (Mt. 23 and elsewhere) and the Judaizers (Acts 15:1–2 and elsewhere) did.

Model 5 is labeled *ethnotheological hermeneutics.* In many ways the implications of the present study have their greatest significance within theological study for the way biblical hermeneutics is done. This model attempts to outline four important features of an ethnotheological approach to interpretation in culture. The remainder of this book elaborates on these and suggests additional features.

a. As an important part of this model we postulate that *human perception of God's truth may be adequate, though never absolute.* God's communication of himself is purposeful. Human understanding can discern and respond to what God has revealed in such a way that his purpose is accomplished even though we see dimly rather than absolutely (1 Cor. 13:12).

b. A second aspect of this model is the importance of going beyond the "grammatico-historical" method to a *"culturo-linguistic"* or *"ethnolinguistic" method of interpretation.* We are in strong agreement with the conviction of biblical scholars that the biblical writings need to be interpreted in their cultural contexts. The input of the perspectives of contemporary anthropology and linguistics, however, enables us to probe more carefully and more surely into those contexts than did the perspectives of history and philology upon which grammatico-historical methodology is based.

c. Attempting to understand supracultural meanings as presented in their cultural contexts involves the necessity to discern *differing levels of abstraction.* Certain of these meanings are presented in Scripture via specific applications in the original cultural contexts. Other meanings are stated in more general "propositions." It is postulated that there are three levels of abstraction: the culture-specific level, the general-principle level, and the basic-ideal level.

d. The total process of biblical interpretation involves attention both to the original biblical cultural contexts and to the cultural context within which the interpreter lives. Thus biblical interpretation becomes a "dialogic" process between the interpreter in his or her cultural context and the message of God presented in and through the biblical cultures. We therefore discuss the sense in which *biblical interpretation is a "two-culture dialogic" process.*

C. COMMUNICATION MODELS (Chapter 8)

Model 6, the first of the models from communication science, is that of *receptor-oriented communication* developed in chapter 8. Ten basic principles of communication are outlined in relation to this and the next model. Model 6 holds that the evaluation of any communicational event must be made at the receptor's end. It is not enough for the initiator of the communication to speak or behave accurately. What the communicator says and does must be perceived by the receptor as the communicator intends if the communication is to serve its proper purpose. Three important aspects of this model are:

a. The aim of each communicational interaction must be to bring about a substantial *correspondence between the intent of the communicator and the understanding of the receptor.* There are, however, slippage and interference in communicational interactions that assure that what is understood is never identical with what is intended. Communicators aim at bringing about as great an identity as possible between their meanings and those of their receptors. They settle, however, for an understanding of their intent within a range of variation that is acceptable to them (see model 9b below).

b. For the *receptor is the final formulator of the message.* The meanings that result from the communication are formulated in the receptor's head in response to the stimulus of the communicator's message. These meanings depend at least as much on how the receptor perceives the message (plus paramessages) as they do on how the communicator formulates it. Communicators may, however, present new information in their messages that the receptors add to their store of building materials for new meanings.

c. But the *meanings* that ultimately result from the communicational process are *made largely from materials already resident in the receptors* (Berlo 1960). This the receptors combine with any new information in response to the stimulus of the communicational interaction. The symbols used to communicate messages are, therefore, stimulators of meaning within the receptors rather than conveyors of meaning from the communicators. What the receptors respond to is (according to this model) the result of the impact of the symbols (cultural forms) employed on the concepts that already exist in the receptors' heads.

Model 7, communication with impact (chapter 8) is the next model. If impact is crucial to effective communication, it is of great significance that communicators know how to bring it about. A message that is simply intended to convey information does not have to relate closely to the felt needs of the receptor. Messages intended to influence the behavior of the receptor, though, if they are to be effective, need to be presented in such a way that the symbols employed stimulate the desired response. The impact of the message is judged by the kind of response it stimulates. We detail five features of this model.

a. For a message to have high impact it needs to be understood as personally as possible by the receptor. *Person-to-person* communication maximizes the possibility that the impact will be high, especially if there is high identification between the participants. When impersonal communication techniques are employed and/or when people relate to each other not as human beings but in terms of their stereotypes of each other, communicational impact is decreased.

b. The potential for high-impact communication is increased the more completely the communicator, the message, and the receptor participate in the *same frame of reference*. Either the frame of reference of the communicator or that of the receptor may be chosen. The impact on the receptor, is, however, likely to be considerably greater if the receptor's frame of reference is employed. Though much Christian communication seeks to "extract" the receptors from their context into that of the communicator, God's communication seems to be "identificational"—i.e., involving the communicator in adapting to the frame of reference of the hearers.

c. Within the same frame of reference, the *credibility of the communicator* is crucial to the kind of impact that the message conveys. Communicators who earn high credibility with their audiences will be able to convey high-impact messages. Communicators isolated from their receptors by stereotype barriers tend to find the impact of their messages low. To overcome the barrier created by a stereotype, communicators need to act in a way that identifies them not with the stereotype but with the human being to whom they seek to communicate. Such "unpredictability" in terms of the stereotype increases the communicational impact. God employs this principle also.

d. When the *message is credible by relating specifically rather than generally to the receptor's real life*, the impact is increased. General messages elicit general, low-impact responses. Messages specifically related to the receptors' felt needs, on the other hand, have high impact. God's communications (both past and present) are specific to the lives of his receptors, and therefore have high impact.

e. Meanings that the *receptor discovers* have higher impact than the mere presentation of predigested informationalized messages. Communicators who seek high impact should try to present themselves and their messages in such a way that the receptors are led to discover a life-changing relationship to both. The ultimate impact of communicational events is signaled when the receptors identify with the communicator and the message by committing themselves to the communicator's cause. This is the kind of impact that God seeks and he conducts his communicational activity accordingly.

D. ETHNOTHEOLOGICAL MODELS II

Model 8 (developed in chapter 9) deals with the *nature and components of God's revelation in culture.* It applies communication-science insight to an analysis of what God has done in the process of revealing himself to human beings. This model has eleven subparts.

a. The first assertion made under model 8 is that *God is receptor-oriented* in his revelational activity. His concern is not simply to make an impression on humanity but to be understood accurately and forcefully in order to elicit the response he seeks from his human receptors. The receptor-oriented communicational model is here applied to understand better how God goes about revealing himself.

b. Such receptor-oriented revelation involves God in *communicating across the gap between his supracultural realm and that of culture-bound humanity.* To do this he is seen as employing the communicational principles detailed in chapter 8 (models 6 and 7). In seeking to be understood by human receptors, God interacts with them within their frames of reference via credible human communicators to present a life-specific and life-transforming message in such a way that humans can discover its validity for their lives and commit themselves to God and to his cause. In this God seeks to stimulate the development of impact-laden meanings in the receptors. The ultimate example of impactful receptor-oriented revelation is the incarnation of God in Jesus.

c. Whenever God communicates, he reveals something new concerning himself. The basic message (the meanings) remains quite similar but its *encasement in new specific vehicles (cultural forms) results in partial newness of meaning.* Such revelation ranges within the acceptable (to God) limits of variation set forth in Scripture (see model 9).

d. Revelation from this point of view is *a dynamic, continuing communicational process,* rather than something that started and stopped in the past and has now become static. The livingness of God, the livingness of his receptors, and the dynamic nature of communicational interaction seem to demand a dynamic concept of revelation.

e. The *information* that is an important part of the revelational process must, therefore, be *distinguished from the dynamic process itself.* Information from God is important both as an input to God's revealing activity and as a product of it (Ramm 1961) but it must not be equated with revelation itself. There is general and special revelational information, but each needs activation to become revelation in a contemporary context.

f. The process of revelation results from the application of *revelational (divine) stimulus* to the information available (whether general or special) in such a way that it has God's intended impact on the receptor(s). The revelational process, like certain glues, requires a base (information) plus an activator (the personal stimulus of God, usually in partnership with a human being) to come into being. Neither the base nor the activator is effective all by itself even if, as in the case of the Scriptures, the information therein presented is the "deposit" (Ramm 1961) of certain of God's previous revelational activities. Even that base needs activation via "repersonalization" (see chapter 11 for further elaboration).

g. Revelation, like redemption (Vos 1948:6), *is both objective (or objectified) and subjective*. Some prefer to label the objectified (enscripturated) component "revelation" and the subjective (contemporary) component "illumination" or "enlightenment" (Vos). The model here presented labels what appears to be the same process by the single term "revelation." We distinguish, though, the objectified and subjective components employed in the process.

h. We postulate that the revealing activity of God today is equivalent in its dynamics within today's cultural contexts to that which we read about in the Bible. We label this *dynamically equivalent revelation* and thus seek to make manifest the similarities between this process and a series of other processes within Christianity that are also to be dynamically equivalent to the processes recorded in the Bible (see model 11).

i. In an attempt to combat the western cultural error of equating revelation with information (see model 8e, above), we suggest that the traditional distinction between "general and special revelation" should be seen as a distinction between two kinds (or sources) of information, not as a distinction between two kinds of revelation. We thus develop the concept of *general and special revelational information* in chapter 11.

j. The full-orbed process of revelation requires, then, both *an informational base and a Spirit-led personal activator*. The repersonalization of revelational information functions with respect to that information much like the activator functions with respect to the base in the application of substances such as epoxy glue.

k. The recognition that we have greater understanding of God by the end of the Scriptures than was available to those at the beginning needs to be registered. In recognition of the constancy of the message (model 10b), though, it needs to be pointed out that what is often termed "progressive revelation" consists of the *increase of revelational information* from beginning to end of the Bible, not the evolutionary superseding of one of God's approaches by another, as if he couldn't quite make up his mind. This understanding is closely related to model 9h, and they are treated together in chapter 11.

Model 9 conceptualizes the *nature and functions of the Bible in culture*. Eight features of this model are treated.

a. Among the important functions that *the Bible* can serve is *as a yardstick* by means of which to measure God's contemporary revelations of himself and his will. The adequacy of the biblical repository of previous revelation is such that contemporary messages from God will not fall outside the range there allowed. Making such evaluations with preciseness is still a problem but it is helpful to recognize that:

b. The Bible allows *a range of acceptable variation* rather than contending for one single right ideal with everything else labeled unacceptable. A latitude must be allowed in the correspondence between the perception of the receptor and the intent of the communicator. God takes this factor into account and works with people whose understandings and behavior, though subideal, fall within an allowed range of variation. Communicationally, latitude must be allowed at two points: (1) where the divine intent is encoded in inadequate human language, and (2) where the receptor perceives and responds to the message. This concept anticipates the starting-point-plus-process aspect of model 10.

c. In addition to providing measurement (model 9a, above), we see *the Bible as a tether.* As the confirmed inspired record of the way God works, the Bible provides the "set radius" within which contemporary revelational encounters may occur. Events that occur outside that range are by definition not revelational. Within this tether the contemporary repersonalization of the Scriptures is also to occur. Parts *a, b,* and *c* of model 9 combine to conceptualize the fact that the Scriptures show us both the range within which God works and the borders at either extreme of that range. We recognize that God often presents ideal understandings (e.g., Mt. 5:28 on adultery and 5:21–22 on murder), exhibiting one extreme of the range. But he also shows where he is willing to start at the other end of that range. The biblical range, then, provides the tether within which contemporary interaction with God can move and the yardstick by means of which it is possible to evaluate whether or not contemporary practices can be considered biblical.

d. The Bible, then, is seen as an *inspired collection of classic cases* from history (chapter 10) exemplifying certain of God's past interactions with human beings for the instruction and guidance of those who now seek to follow in their footsteps. This understanding contrasts with those models that either explicitly or implicitly represent the Bible as if it were simply a kind of technically worded textbook on history and/or theology. The casebook model does not deny either the existence or the importance of the historical and theological material in the Bible. Nor does it deny the right, even the obligation, of students of the Bible to develop theological generalizations (conceptual formulations) on the basis of scriptural data. This model simply speaks to the fact that the Scriptures are a collection of "classic" materials (i.e., time-tested and found to be of enduring value) that were produced for particular people at particular times and places. When there is in the Bible historical and theological systematization (as there frequently is) it is done with the particular target audience and situation in mind. Each document is a specific presentation (a case study) dealing with the problems and participants in a specific context. The Bible is not a generalized, highly coordinated, textbook presentation.

e. The Bible is a joint product of *human and divine* activity. It is both God's Word and human words (Berkouwer 1975:22–23). It is a product of the interactions between God and human beings in culture, as well as an inspired record of certain of them. It records God's communicational (revelational) activity and enhances the continuation of that activity in other places and times. It records God's message and method as perceived (under inspiration) by human beings and spoken/written by them in terms comprehensible to other humans.

   f. The *inspiring* activity of God is understood to be *dynamic*—an example of the continual leading activity of God—rather than static—an example of a method God once used but has since abandoned. Static views are postulated as arising from fallacies endemic in western culture such as the overvaluing of printed material, the search for an authority beyond the taint of human fallibility, and the tendency to overestimate the differences between what happened in history and what is happening now.

   g. Such dynamic inspiring/leading of God results in a Bible that presents *truth with impact.* The Bible, like all of God's communicational activity, is receptor-oriented for maximum impact. It does not merely present information as a textbook might but, in casebook fashion, records the kind of "alive and active" (Heb. 4:12) events that it seeks to stimulate. It seeks to bring about true relationships, not simply to record true information. It is truth presented with impact.

   h. God's constant message and method is presented in the Scriptures in a *variety of cultural forms.* This fact is instructive to us in a historical sense and as an exemplification of the variety of cultural understandings and expressions of the message that lie validly within the biblical "tether" today. The divine-human interactions recorded in the Scriptures occurred in various cultural contexts, even though several of them may be labeled "Hebrew." This fact makes explicit for us a variety of acceptable expressions of such interactions based on differences of culture, extent of knowledge available, and, consequently, human perception.

   Such insight into the breadth of the culture, knowledge, and range of perception within which God is willing to work today is extremely useful for those attempting to witness faithfully in a multicultural world. The Bible provides "zoom-lens" views of God at work in each of the varieties of culture therein represented. This increases our understanding of how he desires to work in present-day cultures that are similar to those represented in Scripture.

   The cultural contexts in which God is scripturally recorded as working are, therefore, to be seen "horizontally" rather than "vertically." Each cultural variety is as valid as each other (model 3b). There is no essential superiority to the presentation of the Gospel message to Hellenistic audiences in terms of a focus on their core values (e.g., grace, *logos*) over the presentation to Hebrew audiences in terms of their core values (e.g., tradition, law, sacrifice). The accumulation of revelational information (model 8k) should, of course, make a difference for those who know that information. But how to relate to this fact is also shown in a "horizontal" view of biblical revelation—people are accountable for what they know (model 10g). Knowledge, then, is increased within the context of Christian commitment (model 10c).

Model 10 deals with the way in which *God interacts with human beings.* This model has at least the following seven aspects to it.

a. In chapter 10 we introduce the *constancy of method* concept. The point made is that the Bible reveals the constant method by means of which the unchanging God (Mal. 3:6) seeks to communicate his constant message (model 10b, below). This method, well articulated by Paul in 1 Corinthians 9:20–22, involves extensive adaptation by the communicator (God) to the cultural context of the receptors in order by all means to win those within that context. God, like Paul, is seen as approaching Jews in Jewish ways, Greeks in Greek ways, Euro-Americans in Euro-American ways. God is seen as always working in partnership with human beings in terms of the communicational principles developed in chapter 8 to lead people revelationally (i.e., in and into his will). The majority of differences between one portion of the Scriptures and another (including those called "dispensations") are here seen as applicational, cultural differences rather than differences in the basic method or message. All of these, plus the large number of other scriptural additions to our knowledge concerning how God works, are seen as revelational in that they all add to our understandings of things that we could or would not have discovered otherwise.

b. The unchangingness of God (Mal. 3:6) demands a recognition of the *constancy of his message* (chapter 11). This concept holds that the basic meanings (i.e., the message) that God seeks to communicate remain constant throughout the Bible and history. There are differences of application and expression of this message in a variety of cultural and personal contexts, a selection of which have been recorded in the Scriptures. There is, furthermore, a significant cumulative increase of information concerning God and his works from beginning to end of the Bible (model 8k). But the basic message is just as available to the peoples reported on in the early portions of the Old Testament as to those of the New Testament (Heb. 11 documents this). That basic message has not undergone change from the beginning of time.

This is a different view of God's revelational activity than that of models postulating changes in the message at points in history when God involves himself in some major new manifestation (e.g., the fall, the giving of the law, the coming of Christ, Pentecost). Such models tend to give the impression that increases in information concerning the workings of God (often termed "progressive revelation") add to that which must be known as a precondition to salvation. We here distinguish between valuable knowledge *about* God's message (the total revelation) and that essential message itself (the core of the revelation).

c. All of this demands a *starting-point-plus-process* concept (chapter 12). It can be observed from scriptural data that, though allegiance to God is central to the message (model 13a), God allowed for a range of understanding of himself (model 9b). There are two additional dimensions of this range: (1) a variety of potential starting points, and (2) a revelational progression from a subideal starting point toward the ideal. With respect to the former, we know that God would not accept as valid (i.e., saving) a faith allegiance to another god (e.g., 1 Kings 18:17–40). He did, however, accept, on the basis of their faith commitment to him, those who believed in the existence of other gods (e.g., Jonah). He also accepted as valid starting points Old Testament understandings of himself that appear to us overbalanced in the direction of seeing him to be excessively distant (Deut. 10:17; Job 33:13), judgmental (Deut. 32:39–43), and even capricious (1 Sam. 2:6–8; Job 9:12). Such distance between God and human beings is understood as being bridged by mercy, like that of an exalted, powerful king toward his subjects (Exod. 20:6; 33:19). From such perceptions of God, we see in Scripture the people of God moving over time to models of understanding him as close (Mt. 1:23), like a father (Mal. 2:10; Rom. 8:15), and relating to human beings in love (1 Jn. 4:8; Rom. 8:39).

This understanding can be applied (as in chapter 12) to understanding any doctrine of Scripture (e.g., sin, salvation, doctrine of humanity, etc.) and any scriptural treatment of behavioral patterns (e.g., marriage customs, the Ten Commandments, love of neighbor, etc.). It can, furthermore, be applied to contemporary witnessing situations where the question is, "Will God accept such a subideal belief or custom as a starting point in his working with the group? Or must that belief or custom be immediately rejected if these people are to be called by God's name?" Scriptural evidence suggests that God allows, but seeks to transform, *most* subideal beliefs and practices except those that require faith allegiance to another god (see model 13).

God *starts where people are*, rather than demanding that they immediately conform to his ideals. All people seem, however, to live according to a dual standard. They have cultural ideals, but ordinarily live somewhat below them at what anthropologists call the level of "actual" (also misleadingly called "real") culture. This is, we believe, where God starts—if that behavior lies within his allowable range.

d. Contrary to much culture-bound western theologizing, we postulate that God has a *"directional" rather than a "positional" basis* for accepting or rejecting humans. Though many groups, such as the Pharisees and the Judaizers, maintained doctrinal and behavioral positions that would seem to be acceptable to God, they were rejected. It is postulated here that the reason lay in the fact that they were moving (or had moved) *away* from their allegiance to God. The thief on the cross, on the other hand, though behaviorally and doctrinally outside any humanly defined acceptable position vis-à-vis God, cast himself *in the direction* of a saving faith allegiance to God and was saved.

e. In leading people from their initial faith response toward maturity, God adopts a two-step process (chapter 12). He first seeks to lead and (by the Holy Spirit) empower people to live closer to *their own ideals* than they have ever before been able to. His first standard in the process that issues on conversion is the cultural ideals already known by the convert—providing, of course, that these lie within God's allowable range. And his first step is to lead people to live closer to those ideals.

f. As the second step in this process, then, comes the *raising of the ideals* in the direction of God's ideals as made explicit in Scripture. In spite of much contemporary western Christian practice that seems to assume that God is less patient today than in biblical times in leading people toward his ideals, we maintain that his method remains the same in this regard.

g. In view of these aspects of God's interaction with human beings, we postulate that God's method and message are today the same as they always have been with respect to those who may be *chronologically* A.D. *but information-ally* B.C. That is, since God's method and message have not changed, he must interact with those who are today informationally like Old Testament peoples on the same basis as that which he employed with those peoples. The Scriptures give us ample insight into these matters. This insight, then, is contemporarily applicable, not merely of historical interest.

Model 11 is the *dynamic-equivalence* model (developed in chapter 13 and applied in chapters 13–17). Much of what is presented in chapters 6–12 both contributes to and presupposes this model. It is closely related to anthropological and communicational concepts (see especially models 3d, 4c, 6–10, and particularly 8h) but is most clearly developed within (Bible) translation theory (see Nida and Taber 1969). It maintains that the aim of translation is to bring about an equivalence between the response of the contemporary hearers/readers of the translation and that of the original hearers/readers of the communication recorded in the document being translated. This model sees the translated Word acting as a communicational stimulus toward the re-creation of an impact on today's receptors that is (roughly) equivalent to that recorded in the Word.

This theory of translation contrasts with the form-oriented literal-translation ideal. That ideal, based on what today appear to be inadequate understandings of language and culture, seeks simply to move from the language forms of the source language directly to the corresponding forms of the receptor language. It fails to see the often radical differences between the worldviews underlying the structuring of languages and cultures and the consequent need for interpretation and paraphrase in translation to make the intent of the original intelligible to the new receptors. Dynamic (functional) equivalence theory seeks to go more deeply both into an understanding of the dynamics of the original situations and into the receptor language and culture to create there a communicational stimulus that will function in an equivalent way today.

a. This model, since it has been developed by Bible translation theorists, is applied to and exemplified with relationship to *Bible translation* while it is being explained (chapter 13).

b. The *transculturating*, or contemporary communication, of the message in word and life should be dynamically equivalent to (i.e., should serve the same function today as) the examples of such communication that we see in the Scriptures (chapter 14).

c. Theologizing (doing theology) is to be dynamically equivalent today to biblical examples (chapter 15). We are to re-create the scripturally endorsed theologizing *process*, not simply to transmit the theological *products* of yesteryear.

d. The *church*, too, is to function in a manner equivalent to that of the early churches, not simply to reproduce their forms (chapter 16). The purpose of the church is seen to lie in the transmission of Christian meanings to and in today's world, not in the preservation of traditional cultural forms. The latter may have served well in past times and other places but need to be replaced by appropriate receptor-culture forms that convey equivalent meanings today.

e. Christian conversion should also be dynamically equivalent today to its scriptural antecedents (chapter 17). It should not be changed, as it was by the Pharisees and Judaizers, into mere conversion from one culture to another. Conversion is a lifetime process, consisting of continuous divine-human interaction and a continuing series of human decisions.

Model 12 (developed in chapter 15,) elaborates on the concept of *cross-culturally valid theologizing* that is at the heart of this book. Much of that material has been anticipated in previous sections of the book, but at this point three useful contrasts, implicit in the model, are introduced.

a. It is possible to distinguish between narrow culture-specific theologies (such as western theologizing) and the more broadly based theological perspective developed in this book by labeling the former *ethnic theologies* and the latter *ethnotheology*. Ethnic Christian theologies attempt to develop and apply theological insights within a single culture or, as with western cultures, within a single set of closely interacting cultures. *Christian ethnotheology* seeks to study as wide a variety as possible of such ethnic theologies and to develop cross-culturally valid understandings of God and his workings.

b. The descriptions of ethnic theologies may be called *theographies* just as, within anthropology, descriptions of individual cultures are called "ethnographies." The term "theology" then, would be reserved for use as the label for the cross-culturally valid understandings labeled "ethnotheology" above.

c. Looking at God and his works from *inside* a given culture gives one what may be termed an *emic* understanding of theology. An *outside* analyst who seeks to understand theology cross-culturally, on the other hand, attempts to develop an *etic* understanding of theology.

Model 13 is the *Christian transformational change* model (chapters 18 and 19). I see both Scripture and anthropology advocating effective cultural change from the inside out. Changes in worldview (paradigm shifts) are the most pervasive and effective kinds of cultural change, though usually the most difficult to initiate. Such changes need to be initiated by those inside a culture (Barnett

1953; see model 13e, below). They then work like yeast (Mt. 13:33), to transform the culture from within (see model 13d, below) in such a way that first the meanings and then at least some of the structures of that culture (the forms) are altered to serve God's purposes better. The changes in meaning and usage are the most important part of this process, since most of the structures (forms) are essentially neutral and, therefore, just as usable for Christian purposes as for other purposes.

a. The use of this transformation process by Christianity is seen as initiated by a *change of allegiance* to God from whatever previous allegiance(s) were in vogue. This change of allegiance involves one or more "power encounters" (Tippett 1973).

b. The second step is at least a start on the reformulation of worldview in such a way that *evaluations and interpretations* of each aspect of life are made in terms of the claims of the new allegiance. "What does God desire in this area of life?" is a primary worldview-transforming question.

c. The re-evaluation and reinterpretation lead to *rehabituation*—changes in habitual behavior issuing from the new allegiance and the consequent re-evaluational process.

d. The whole process of working to bring about transformational change in that within which one is immersed necessitates some such model as *working within in order to change.* We need to learn to employ cultural mechanisms for change, not to destroy the culture and those processes along with it.

e. The place of advocates and innovators (Barnett 1953) is crucial to the transformation process. Principles are developed in chapter 19 to assist us in understanding the place in this process of those who actually effect changes (innovators) and those who seek to persuade others to make changes (advocates).

This completes the summary of the models here employed. There are additional concepts to be found throughout the book that could probably be elevated to model or submodel status. But this listing should suffice to highlight at least the major models and their constituent features. Note that one presupposition of the use of model theory is that models (and even constituent features of models) can stand or fall by themselves. These models and constituents do not necessarily all stand or fall together. If you, the reader, find one or more of these concepts unacceptable, you are free to reject it/them without rejecting the remainder of the presentation.

Bibliography of References Cited

Allen, Roland
    1956   *The Spontaneous Expansion of the Church* (original ed. 1927). London: World Dominion Press.

American Bible Society
    1975   *Record* vol. 120, no. 5, May.

Anderson, J. N. D.
    1970   *Christianity and Comparative Religion*. London: Tyndale Press.

Anderson, Rufus
    1838   "Missionary Schools," *The Biblical Repository* 11:87–113 (reprinted in Beaver 1967:147–67).

Arensberg, C. M., and A. H. Niehoff (eds.)
    1971   *Introducing Social Change*. Chicago: Aldine Publishing Co.

Armerding, Carl E. (ed.)
    1977   *Evangelicals and Liberation*. Nutley, N. J.: Presbyterian and Reformed Publishing Co.

Aronoff, Joel
    1967   *Psychological Needs and Cultural Systems*. Princeton, N.J.: D. Van Nostrand Company.

Barbour, Ian G.
    1974   *Myths, Models and Paradigms*. New York: Harper & Row.

Barclay, William
    1964   *Turning to God*. Philadelphia: Westminster Press.

Barker, Glenn, William Lane, and J. Ramsey Michaels
    1969   *The New Testament Speaks*. New York: Harper & Row.

Barnett, Homer G.
    1953   *Innovation: Basis of Cultural Change*. New York: McGraw-Hill.

Barney, G. Linwood
    1957   "The Meo—An Incipient Church," *Practical Anthropology* 4:31–50.

Barr, James
1961   *The Semantics of Biblical Language.* London: Oxford University Press.

Barrett, David B.
1968   *Schism and Renewal.* London: Oxford University Press.

Bavinck, Herman
1928   *Gereformeerde Dogmatiek*, vol. 1. Kampen: J. H. Kok.

Bavinck, J. H.
1960   *An Introduction to the Science of Missions* (trans. from 1954 Dutch ed. by D. H. Freeman). Philadelphia: Presbyterian and Reformed Publishing Co.

Beals, Alan R.
1962   *Gopalpur, a South Indian Village.* New York: Holt, Rinehart and Winston.

Beals, A., and H. Hoijer
1959   *An Introduction to Anthropology*, 2nd ed. New York: Macmillan.

Beals, Alan, and George and Louise Spindler
1973   *Culture in Process*, 2nd ed. New York: Holt, Rinehart and Winston.

Beaver, R. Pierce (ed.)
1967   *To Advance the Gospel: Selections from the Writings of Rufus Anderson.* Grand Rapids: Eerdmans.

Beekman, John
1957   "A Culturally Relevant Witness," *Practical Anthropology* 4:83–88. Reprinted in Smalley (ed.) 1967:132–35.

Bennett, John C. (ed.)
1975   "Whatever Happened to Theology?" a symposium in *Christianity and Crisis* 35:106–20.

Berkouwer, G. C.
1955   *General Revelation* (trans. from Dutch by Alegemene Openbaring). Grand Rapids: Eerdmans.
1975   *Holy Scripture* (trans. and ed. by Jack B. Rogers). Grand Rapids: Eerdmans.

Berlo, David R.
1960   *The Process of Communication*. New York: Holt, Rinehart and Winston.

Bernard, J. H.
1928   *Gospel according to St. John*, 2 vols (in International Critical Commentary series). Edinburgh: T. & T. Clark.

Bertram, George
1971   *Epistrepho* in Friedrich (ed.), Bromiley (trans. and ed.) 1954–1974, vol. VII, pp. 714–29.

Black, Max
1962   *Models and Metaphors*. Ithaca, N.Y.: Cornell University Press.

Blair, Edward P. (ed.)
1975   *Abingdon Bible Handbook*. Nashville: Abingdon Press.

Bock, Phillip H.
1969   *Modern Cultural Anthropology*. New York: Knopf.

Boyd, R. H. S.
1969   *An Introduction to Indian Theology*. Madras: The Christian Literature Society.

Brauer, Jerald C.
1971   *The Westminster Dictionary of Church History*. Philadelphia: Westminster Press.

Bright, John
1953   *The Kingdom of God*. Nashville: Abingdon Press.

Bromiley, Geoffrey
1968   "The Limits of Theological Relativism," *Christianity Today*, May 24, p. 6–7.

Brown, Robert McAfee
1977   "The Rootedness of All Theology," *Christianity and Crisis*, July 18, pp. 170–74.

Brunner, Emil
1943   *The Divine-Human Encounter*. Philadelphia: Westminster Press.

Buckman, Allan R.
    1978   "The Introduction of Christianity among the Yala People."
                    Unpublished D. Missiology dissertation. Pasadena, Calif.:
                    School of World Mission, Fuller Theological Seminary.

Bultmann, Rudolf
    1958   *Jesus Christ and Mythology*. New York: Scribners.
    1964   *Zao* in Kittel (ed.), Bromiley (trans. and ed.) 1932–1976 vol. II,
                    pp. 832–75.

Calvin, John
    1953   *Institutes of the Christian Religion*, 2 vols. (trans. by Henry
                    Beveridge). Grand Rapids: Eerdmans.
    1961   *Epistle to the Romans and Thessalonians*. New Testament Com-
                    mentaries, vol. 3 (ed. by David W. and Thomas F. Torr-
                    ance, trans. by R. Mackenzie). Grand Rapids: Eerdmans.
    1963   *Epistle to the Hebrews*. New Testament Commentaries, vol. 12
                    (ed. by David W. and Thomas F. Torrance, trans. by R.
                    Mackenzie). Grand Rapids: Eerdmans.

Carnell, Edward J.
    1959   *The Case for Orthodox Theology*. Philadelphia: Westminster
                    Press.

Carroll, J. B. (ed.)
    1956   *Language, Thought and Reality: Selected Writings of B. L. Whorf*.
                    Cambridge, Mass.: MIT Press.

Childs, Brevard S.
    1962   *Memory and Tradition in Israel*. Naperville, Ill.: Allenson.

Cobb, John
    1975   "Whatever Happened to Theology?" *Christianity and Crisis*
                    35:117–18.

Coleman, R. J.
    1972   *Issues of Theological Warfare: Evangelicals and Liberals*. Grand
                    Rapids: Eerdmans.

Conant, J.
    1951   *Science and Common Sense*. New Haven: Yale University Press.

Conn, Harvie M.

1977   "Contextualization: Where Do We Begin?" in C. Armerding
        (ed.) 1977:90–119.

1978   "Contextualization: A New Dimension for Cross-Cultural
        Hermeneutic." *Evangelical Missions Quarterly* 14:39–46.

Cox, Harvey

1973   *The Seduction of the Spirit.* New York: Simon and Schuster.

1975   "Whatever Happened to Theology?" *Christianity and Crisis*
        35:114–15.

Cullmann, Oscar

1967   *Salvation in History* (trans. by S. G. Sowers). London: SCM
        Press.

Dayton, Donald W.

1976   "The Battle for the Bible: Renewing the Inerrancy Debate,"
        The Christian Century 93:976–80.

Dewart, Leslie

1966   "Have We Loved the Past Too Long?" *America* 15:798–802.

Dickson, K. A., and P. Ellingworth

1969   *Biblical Revelation and African Beliefs.* London: Lutterworth.

Downs, James F.

1975   *Cultures in Crisis*, 2nd. ed. Beverly Hills, Calif.: Glencoe Press.

Dye, T. Wayne

1976   "Toward a Cross-Cultural Definition of Sin," *Missiology*
        4:26–29.

Easton, B. S.

1948   *The Pastoral Epistles.* London: SCM Press.

Eitzen, Daniel

1977   "God and Culture." Unpublished term paper. La Mirada,
        California: Biola College.

Engel, James, and H. Wilbert Norton

1975   *What's Gone Wrong with the Harvest?* Grand Rapids: Zonder-
        van.

Eusebius, Pamphili
1955   *Ecclesiastical History*, Book 9 (trans. by R. J. Deferrari), vol. 29
            in The Fathers of the Church. New York: Fathers of the
            Church, Inc.

Fabun, Don
1967   *The Dynamics of Change*. Englewood Cliffs, N.J.: Prentice-
            Hall.

Fast, Julius
1971   *Body Language*. New York: Simon and Schuster.

Foerster, Werner
1965   *Kurios* in Kittel (ed.), Bromiley (trans. and ed.) 1932–1967, vol.
            III, pp. 1039–58, 1081–98.

Friedrich, Gerhard (ed.)
1954–73   *Theological Dictionary of the New Testament*, vol. V–IX (trans.
            and ed. by G. W. Bromiley, 1967–74). Grand Rapids:
            Eerdmans.
1965   *Kerusso* in Kittel (ed.), Bromiley (trans. and ed.) 1932–1967,
            vol. III, pp. 683–718.

Frillman, Thomas
1977   "Conversion and Culture." Unpublished term paper. La
            Mirada, Calif.: Biola College.

Fueter, Paul D.
1971   "Communicating the Bible," *International Review of Mission*
            60:437–51.

Fuller, Daniel P.
1969   "Hermeneutics." Unpublished syllabus in use at Fuller
            Theological Seminary. Pasadena, Calif.

Gartner, Bertil
1955   *The Areopagus Speech and Natural Revelation* (trans. by C. H.
            King). Uppsala: Almquist and Wiksells.

Gearing, Frederick O.
1970   *The Face of the Fox*. Chicago: Aldine.

Geertz, Clifford
1966   "Religion as a Cultural System," in Banton, M. (ed.),
            Anthropological Approaches to the Study of Religion. London:
            Tavistock.

Gerlach, L. P., and V. H. Hine
  1970   *People, Power, Change: Movements of Social Transformation.* New
              York: Bobbs-Merrill Co.

Gillin, John
  1948   *The Ways of Men.* New York: Appleton-Century-Crofts.

Goldschmidt, Walter
  1966   *Comparative Functionalism.* Berkeley: University of California
              Press.

Goodman, George
  n.d.   *The Heathen. Their Present State and Future Destiny.* London:
              Pickering and Inglis.

Goodman, Mary E.
  1967   *The Individual and Culture.* Homewood, Ill.: Dorsey Press.

Greenberg, Joseph
  1966   *The Languages of Africa.* Bloomington, Ind.: Indiana Univer-
              sity, and The Hague: Mouton.

Haley, John W.
  1874   *Alleged Discrepancies of the Bible* (reprinted 1953). Grand Rapids:
              Baker Book House.

Hall, Edward T.
  1959   *The Silent Language.* New York: Doubleday.
  1966   *The Hidden Dimension.* New York: Doubleday.
  1974   *Handbook for Proxemic Analysis.* Washington, D. C.: Society for
              the Anthropology of Visual Communication.

Harjula, Raimo
  1972   "Theology as Service in Africa," *Pro Veritate*: part 1, June, pp.
              17–20; part 2, July, pp. 4–5; part 3, August, pp. 16–18; part
              4, September, pp. 16–17; part 5, October, p. 10,
              November, pp. 19–20; part 6, December, p. 20.

Harris, Marvin
  1968   *The Rise of Anthropological Theory.* New York: Crowell.

Henle, Paul (ed.)
  1958   *Language, Thought and Culture.* Ann Arbor: University of
              Michigan Press.

Henry, Carl F. H.
  1976   *God, Revelation and Authority*, vols. I and II. Waco: Word
              Books.

Henry, Jules
1963   *Culture against Man.* New York: Random House.

Hercus, John
1962   *Pages from God's Casebook.* Chicago: Inter-Varsity Press.

Herendeen, Dale S.
1975   "Conversion and Indigeneity in the Evangelical Church of Vietnam." Unpublished D. Missiology dissertation, School of World Mission, Fuller Theological Seminary.

Herskovits, Melville J.
1948   *Man and His Works.* New York: Knopf.
1965   "Foreword" in F. Boas, *The Mind of Primitive Man,* rev. ed. New York: The Free Press.

Hesselgrave, David
1973   "Identification—Key to Effective Communication," *Evangelical Missions Quarterly* 9:216–22.

Hiebert, Paul G.
1976   *Cultural Anthropology.* Philadelphia: J. B. Lippincott.

Hodge, Charles
1871–73   *Systematic Theology,* 3 vols. reprinted 1975. Grand Rapids: Eerdmans.

Hoebel, E. Adamson
1972   *Anthropology: The Study of Man,* 4th ed. New York: McGraw-Hill.

Hoijer, Harry (ed.)
1954   *Language in Culture.* Chicago: University of Chicago Press.

Holladay, W. L.
1958   *The Root subh in the Old Testament.* Leiden: Brill

Holtrop, Philip C.
1977   " A Strange Language," *The Reformed Journal* 27:9–13.

Hooke, S. H.
1938   *The Origins of Early Semitic Ritual.* London: Oxford University Press.

Hostetler, John A.
1967   "Total Socialization: Modern Hutterite Educational Practices," *Mennonite Quarterly Review* 44:72–84.

Hostetler, John A., and Gertrude E. Huntington
 1967   *The Hutterites in North America.* New York: Holt, Rinehart and
             Winston.

Hunter, David, and Mary Ann Foley
 1976   *Doing Anthropology.* New York: Harper & Row.

Irwin, Barry
 1972   "The Liability Complex among the Chimbu Peoples of New
             Guinea," *Practical Anthropology* 19:280–85.

Iwanska, Alicja
 1957   "Some American Values." Paper read to the American An-
             thropological Association annual meeting, Chicago (dis-
             cussed in Smalley 1958b).

James, William
 1956   *The Will to Believe.* New York: Dover Publications (republica-
             tion of volume first published in 1897).
 1968   *Some Problems of Philosophy.* New York: Greenwood Press (text
             c. 1911, prepared for publication after author's death by H.
             M. Kallen.)

Jeremias, Joachim
 1969   *Jerusalem in the Time of Jesus.* Philadelphia: Fortress Press.

Jordan, Clarence
 1968   *The Cotton Patch Version of Paul's Epistles.* New York: Associa-
             tion Press.
 1970   *The Cotton Patch Version of Matthew and John.* New York: As-
             sociation Press.
 1973   *The Cotton Patch Version of Hebrews and the General Epistles.* New
             York: Association Press.

Kallen, H. M.
 1925   *The Philosophy of William James.* New York: The Modern Li-
             brary.

Kautzsch, E.
 1904   "Religion of Israel," *Hastings' Dictionary of the Bible*, 5 vols.,
             James Hastings (ed.). New York: Charles Scribner's Sons.
             Vol. 5, pp. 612–734.

Keesing, Felix M.
 1958   *Cultural Anthropology.* New York: Rinehart and Company.

Keesing, R. M. and F. M.
  1971   *New Perspectives in Cultural Anthropology*. New York: Holt,
            Rinehart and Winston.

Kittel, Gerhard
  1967   "Word and Speech in the New Testament" *(lego/logos)*, in
            Kittel (ed.), Bromiley (trans. and ed.) 1932–1967, vol. IV,
            pp. 100–36.

Kittel, Gerhard (ed.)
  1932–1967 *Theological Dictionary of the New Testament*, vols. I–IV (trans.
            and ed. by G. W. Bromiley, 1964–1967). Grand Rapids:
            Eerdmans.

Kluckhohn, Clyde
  1949   *Mirror for Man*. New York: McGraw-Hill. Fawcett edition
            1957.
  1953   "Universal Categories of Culture," in Kroeber (ed.) 1953, pp.
            507–23.
  1959   "Common Humanity and Diverse Cultures," in Lerner (ed.)
            1959, pp. 245–84.

Kluckhohn, Clyde, and Dorothea Leighton
  1962   *The Navaho*, rev. ed. Garden City, N.Y.: Doubleday.

Kluckhohn, Clyde, and William Morgan
  1951   "Some Notes on Navaho Dreams," in G. B. Wilbur and W.
            Muensterberger (eds.), *Psychoanalysis and Culture*, pp.
            120–31. New York: International Universities Press.

Kraft, Charles H.
  1963   "Christian Conversion or Cultural Conversion," *Practical An-
            thropology* 10:179–87.
  1969   "I Know You Believe You Understand What You Think I
            Said . . ." *World Vision Magazine*, April, pp. 10–12.
  1972a   "The Hutterites and Today's Church," *Theology, News and
            Notes*, October, pp. 15–16.
  1972b   "Theology and Theologies I," *Theology, News and Notes*, June,
            pp. 4–6, 9.
  1972c   "Theology and Theologies II," *Theology, News and Notes*,
            October, pp. 17–20.
  1973a   "Church Planters and Ethnolinguistics," in Tippett 1973, pp.
            226–49.
  1973b   "Dynamic Equivalence Churches," *Missiology* 1:39–57.

1973c   "God's Model for Cross-Cultural Communication—The Incarnation," *Evangelical Missions Quarterly* 9:205–16.

1973d   "North America's Cultural Heritage," *Christianity Today*, January 19, pp. 6–8.

1973e   "The Incarnation, Cross-Cultural Communication and Communication Theory," *Evangelical Missions Quarterly* 9:277–84.

1973f   "Toward a Christian Ethnotheology," in Tippett 1973, pp. 109–26.

1974   "Ideological Factors in Intercultural Communication," *Missiology* 2:295–312.

1977   "Can Anthropological Insight Assist Evangelical Theology?" *Christian Scholar's Review* 7:165–202.

1978   "The Contextualization of Theology," *Evangelical Missions Quarterly* 14:31–36.

Kraft, Robert A.
1975   "The Development of the Concept of 'Orthodoxy' in Early Christianity," in G. F., Hawthorne ed., *Current Issues in Biblical and Patristic Interpretation*. Grand Rapids: Eerdmans.

Kroeber, Alfred
1948   *Anthropology*. New York: Harcourt, Brace and World.
1950   "Anthropology," *Scientific American* 183:87–94.

Kroeber, Alfred (ed.)
1953   *Anthropology Today*. Chicago: University of Chicago Press.

Kroeber, Alfred, and C. Kluckhohn
1952   *Culture: A Critical Review of Concepts and Definitions*. New York: Vintage Books.

Kuhn, Thomas S.
1970   *The Structure of Scientific Revolutions*, 2nd ed. enlarged. International Encyclopedia of Unified Science, vol. 2, no. 2. Chicago: University of Chicago Press.

Kümmel, W. G.
1958   *Das Neue Testament*. Munich: Karl Alber.

Kuyper, Abraham
1954   *Principles of Sacred Theology*. Grand Rapids: Eerdmans.

LaSor, William S.
 1961   *Great Personalities of the New Testament.* Westwood, N.J.: Re-
                vell.

Lerner, Daniel (ed.)
 1959   *The Human Meaning of the Social Sciences.* New York: Meridian
                Books.

Levy-Bruhl, Lucien
 1923   *Primitive Mentality* (trans. from French by L. A. Clare). New
                York: Macmillan.

Lewis, C. S.
 1956   *The Last Battle.* New York: Macmillan.
 1970   *God in the Dock.* Grand Rapids: Eerdmans.

Lindsell, Harold
 1976   *Battle for the Bible.* Grand Rapids: Zondervan.

Linton, Ralph
 1936   *The Study of Man.* New York: Appleton-Century-Crofts.

Linton, Ralph (ed.)
 1945   *The Science of Man in the World Crisis.* New York: Columbia
                University Press.

Livingstone, Frank B.
 1964   "On the Nonexistence of Human Races," in *The Concept of
                Race*, Montagu (ed.), 1964.

Loewen, Jacob
 1965   "Self-Exposure: Bridge to Fellowship," *Practical Anthropology*
                12:49–62. Reprinted in J. Loewen 1975:54–67.
 1967   "Religion, Drives and the Place Where it Itches," *Practical
                Anthropology* 14:49–72. Reprinted in J. Loewen 1975:3–26.
 1968a   "Socialization and Social Control," *Practical Anthropology*
                16:145–56. Reprinted in J. Loewen 1975:211–22.
 1968b   "The Indigenous Church and Resocialization," *Practical An-
                thropology* 15:193–204. Reprinted in J. Loewen 1975:
                223–34.
 1969   "Socialization and Conversion in the Ongoing Church,"
                Practical Anthropology 16:1–17. Reprinted in J. Loewen
                1975:235–51.

1974   "The Inspiration of Translation," in R. G. Bratcher, et al.,
            Understanding and Translating the Bible. New York: Ameri-
            can Bible Society, pp. 86–99.
1975   *Culture and Human Values*. South Pasadena, Calif.: William
            Carey Library.

Luzbetak, Louis J.
1963   *The Church and Cultures*. Techny, Ill.: Divine Word Publica-
            tions. Reprinted, South Pasadena, Calif.: William Carey
            Library, 1975.

Madvig, Donald H.
1977   "The Missionary Preaching of Paul: A Problem in New Tes-
            tament Theology," *Journal of the Evangelical Theological Soci-
            ety* 20:147–55.

Malinowski, Bronislaw
1925   "Magic, Science and Religion," in J. Needham (ed.), *Science,
            Religion and Reality*. London. (Reissued 1948 as *Magic, Sci-
            ence and Religion*. Boston: Beacon Press.)

Maslow, Abraham
1954   *Motivation and Personality*, 2nd ed., 1970. New York: Harper
            & Row.
1964   *Religions, Values, and Peak-Experiences*. Kappa Delta Pi (Viking
            Press ed., 1970).
1971   *The Farther Reaches of Human Nature*. New York: Viking Press.

Maurier, Henri
1968   *The Other Covenant: A Theology of Paganism*. New York: New-
            man Press.

Mayers, Marvin K.
1974   *Christianity Confronts Culture*. Grand Rapids: Zondervan.

Mbiti, John S.
1971   *New Testament Eschatology in an African Background*. London:
            Oxford University Press.

McBane, George W.
1976   "Does God Allow for Belief in Other Gods?" Unpublished
            paper. Pasadena, Calif.: School of World Mission, Fuller
            Theological Seminary.

McGavran, Donald A.
1955   *The Bridges of God.* New York: Friendship Press.
1970   *Understanding Church Growth.* Grand Rapids: Eerdmans.
1974   *The Clash Between Christianity and Cultures.* Washington: Canon
         Press.

Mead, Margaret
1928   *Coming of Age in Samoa.* New York: William Morrow.
1956   *New Lives for Old.* New York: William Morrow.
1964   *Anthropology: A Human Science.* Princeton: Van Nostrand.
1970   *Culture and Commitment.* Garden City, N.Y.: Natural History
         Press/Doubleday.

Messenger, John C.
1959   "The Christian Concept of Forgiveness and Anang Morality,"
         Practical Anthropology 6:97–103.
1960   "Reinterpretations of Christian and Indigenous Belief in a
         Nigerian Nativist Church," *American Anthropologist* 62:
         268–78.

Mickelsen, A. Berkeley
1963   *Interpreting the Bible.* Grand Rapids: Eerdmans.

Míguez Bonino, José
1975   "Whatever Happened to Theology?" *Christianity and Crisis*
         35:111–12.

Montagu, Ashley (ed.)
1964   *The Concept of Race.* New York: Collier Books.

Montgomery, John Warwick (ed.)
1974   *God's Inerrant Word.* Minneapolis: Bethany Fellowship.

Morgan, G. Campbell
1945   *The Acts of the Apostles.* London: Pickering and Inglis.

Murdock, George P.
1945   "The Common Denominator of Cultures," in Linton 1945:
         123–42.

Nash, Leonard
1963   *The Nature of Natural Science.* Boston: Little, Brown.

Nash, Ronald H.
1977   "Truth by Any Other Name," *Christianity Today* 22:15–17,
         19.

Neill, S., G. H. Anderson, and J. Goodwin
    1971   *Concise Dictionary of the Christian Mission.* Nashville: Abingdon
             Press.

Nida, Eugene A.
    1945   "Linguistics and Ethnology in Translation Problems," *Word*
             1:194–208.
    1947   *Bible Translating.* New York: American Bible Society.
    1954   *Customs and Cultures.* New York: Harper & Row (reprinted
             1975 by Wm. Carey Library, South Pasadena, Calif.)
    1959   "Are We Really Monotheists?" *Practical Anthropology* 6:49–54
             (reprinted in Smalley 1967:223–28).
    1960   *Message and Mission.* New York: Harper & Row (reprinted 1972
             by Wm. Carey Library, South Pasadena, Calif.).
    1964   *Toward a Science of Translating.* Leiden: Brill.
    1971   "Implications of Contemporary Linguistics for Biblical Scho-
             larship," *Journal of Biblical Literature* 91:73–89.

Nida, Eugene A. (ed.)
    1972   *The Book of a Thousand Tongues.* London: United Bible Society.

Nida, Eugene A., and C. R. Taber
    1969   *The Theory and Practice of Translation.* Leiden: Brill.

Niebuhr, H. Richard
    1951   *Christ and Culture.* New York: Harper & Row.

Oden, Thomas R.
    1974   *After Therapy What?* Springfield, Ill.: C. C. Thomas.

Oepke, Albrecht
    1964   *Baptizo* in Kittel (ed.), Bromiley (trans. and ed.) 1932–1967,
             vol. 1, pp. 529–46.

Olsen, Walther A.
    1976   "The Man Who Has Never Heard." Unpublished Paper.
             Pasadena, Calif.: School of World Mission, Fuller Theolog-
             ical Seminary.

Packer, James I.
    1958   *"Fundamentalism" and the Word of God.* Grand Rapids: Eerd-
             mans.

Padilla, René
    1978   "Hermeneutics and Culture." Prepublication draft of paper
             presented at the Willowbank Consultation on the Gospel
             and Culture, January 1978.

Pelto, Perti
    1970   *Anthropological Research.* New York: Harper & Row.

Phillips, J. B.
    1952   *Your God Is Too Small.* London: Macmillan.
    1954   *Plain Christianity.* London: Macmillan.
    1958a   *The New Testament in Modern English.* London: Geoffrey Bles.
    1958b   "Translator's Foreword," in *The New Testament in Modern English.* London: Geoffrey Bles.

Piddington, Ralph
    1950   *An Introduction to Social Anthropology*, vol. I. Edinburgh: Oliver and Boyd.

Pike, Kenneth
    1962   *With Heart and Mind.* Grand Rapids: Eerdmans.
    1967   *Language in Relation to a Unified Theory of the Structure of Human Behavior*, 2nd ed. The Hague: Mouton.

Pinnock, Clark
    1967   *A Defense of Biblical Infallibility.* Philadelphia: Presbyterian and Reformed Publishing Co.
    1976a   "Inspiration and Authority: A Truce Proposal," *The Other Side*, May/June 1976, pp. 61–65.
    1976b   "The Inerrancy Debate among the Evangelicals," *Theology, News and Notes* (special issue), pp. 11–13.

Quebedeaux, Richard
    1974   *The Young Evangelicals.* New York: Harper & Row.

Quell, Gottfried
    1964   *Agapao* in Kittel (ed.), Bromiley (trans. and ed.) 1932–1967, vol. I, pp. 21–35.
    1965   *Kurios* in Kittel (ed.), Bromiley (trans. and ed.) 1932–1967, vol. III, pp. 1058–81.

Ramm, Bernard
    1961   *Special Revelation and the Word of God.* Grand Rapids: Eerdmans.
    1970   *Protestant Biblical Interpretation*, 3rd rev. ed. Grand Rapids: Baker Book House.
    1971   "Evangelical Theology and Technological Shock," *American Scientific Affiliation Journal* 23:52–56.

Ramseyer, Robert L.
1970   "The Revitalization Theory Applied to Anabaptists," *The Mennonite Quarterly Review* 44:159–80.

Redfield, Robert
1953   *The Primitive World and Its Transformations.* Ithaca, N.Y.: Cornell University Press.

Reuss, Edward
1891   *History of the Canon of the Holy Scriptures in the Christian Church* (trans. by D. Hunger). Edinburgh: R. W. Hunter.

Reyburn, William D.
1957   "The Transformation of God and the Conversion of Man," *Practical Anthropology* 4:185–94.

Richardson, Don
1974   *The Peace Child.* Glendale, Calif.: Regal Books.

Rogers, Jack
1974   *Confessions of a Conservative Evangelical.* Philadelphia: Westminster Press.
1976   "Is God a Man?" Unpublished paper. Pasadena, Calif.: Fuller Theological Seminary.
1977   "The Church Doctrine of Biblical Authority," in Jack Rogers (ed.), *Biblical Authority.* Waco, Texas: Word.

Rogers, Jack, Ross MacKenzie, and Louis Weeks
1977   *Case Studies in Christ and Salvation.* Philadelphia: Westminster Press.

Ruether, Rosemary
1975   "Whatever Happened to Theology?" *Christianity and Crisis* 35:109–10.

Samovar, L. A., and R. E. Porter
1972   *Intercultural Communication: A Reader.* Belmont, Calif.: Wadsworth.

Sapir, Edward
1929   "The Status of Linguistics as a Science," *Language* 5:207–14.
1931   "Conceptual Categories of Primitive Languages," *Science* 74:578.

Schaeffer, Francis
1968   *The God Who Is There*. Chicago: Inter-Varsity Press.
1969   *Death in the City*. Chicago: Inter-Varsity Press.
1976   *How Should We Then Live*. Old Tappan, N.J.: Revell.

Schmidt, Karl Ludwig
1965   *Ekklesia* in Kittel (ed.), Bromiley (trans. and ed.) 1932–1967, vol. III, pp. 501–36.

Skinner, B. F.
1971   *Beyond Freedom and Dignity*. New York: Knopf. References from Bantam edition, 1972.

Smalley, William A.
1955   "Culture and Superculture," *Practical Anthropology* 2: 58–71.
1958a   "Cultural Implications of an Indigenous Church," *Practical Anthropology* 5:61–65.
1958b   "The World Is Too Much with Us," *Practical Anthropology* 5:234–36.
1959   "What Are Indigenous Churches Like?" *Practical Anthropology* 6:135–39.

Smalley, William A. (ed.)
1967   *Readings in Missionary Anthropology*. Reprinted 1974 by William Carey Library, South Pasadena, Calif.

Smalley, W. A., and M. Fetzer
1948   "A Christian View of Anthropology," in F. A. Everest (ed.), *Modern Science and Christian Faith*. Wheaton, Ill.: Van Kampen Press.

Smith, Paul
1975   Editorial in *Communiqué* (fall issue). Cedar Hill, Texas: Bible Translations on Tape.

Snaith, Norman H.
1964   *The Distinctive Ideas of the Old Testament*. New York: Schocken Books.

Spradley, James M.
1972   "Foundations of Cultural Knowledge," in J. M. Spradley, *Culture and Cognition*. New York: Chandler Publishing Company, 1972, pp. 3–38.

Sproul, Robert C.
1976   "Controversy at Culture Gap," *Eternity* 27:13–15, 40.

Stauffer, Ethelbert
1964   *Agapao* in Kittel (ed.), Bromiley (trans. and ed.) 1932–1967, vol. I, pp. 35–55.

Stendahl, Krister
1976   *Paul Among Jews and Gentiles and Other Essays.* Philadelphia: Fortress Press.

Stock, Eugene
1899   *History of the Church Missionary Society.* London: Church Missionary Society.

Sundkler, Bengt
1960   *The Christian Ministry in Africa.* London: SCM Press.

Taber, Charles R.
1978a   "Hermeneutics and Culture." Prepublication draft of paper presented at the Willowbank Consultation on the Gospel and Culture, Jan. 1978.
1978b   "The Limits of Indigenization in Theology," *Missiology* 6:53–79.

Taylor, John V.
1963   *The Primal Vision.* London: SCM Press.

Tennant, F. R.
1962   "Theology," in *Encyclopaedia Britannica*, vol. 22, pp. 61B–66.

Tertullian, Quintus
1953   *Apology* (trans. by T. R. Glover). Cambridge: Harvard University Press.

Thornton, L. S.
1950   *Revelation and the Modern World.* Westminster, Md.: The Dacre Press.

Tillich, Paul
1959   *Theology of Culture.* New York: Oxford University Press.

Tippett, Alan R.
1958   "The Integrating Gospel." Unpublished manuscript. Pasadena, Calif.: School of World Mission, Fuller Theological Seminary.

1964   "The Acceptance and Rejection of Christianity." Unpub-
                lished manuscript. Pasadena, Calif.: School of World Mis-
                sion, Fuller Theological Seminary.
1970   *Church Growth and the Word of God*. Grand Rapids: Eerdmans.
1973   *Verdict Theology in Missionary Theory*, 2nd ed. South Pasadena,
                Calif.: William Carey (1969 ed. Lincoln, Ill.: Lincoln
                Christian College).
1974   "The Church Which Is His Body," *Missiology* 2:147–59.

Tippett, Alan R. (ed.)
1973   *God, Man and Church Growth*. Grand Rapids: Eerdmans.

Toynbee, Arnold
1948   *Civilization on Trial*. New York: Oxford.

Trench, Richard C.
1874   *Notes on the Parables of Our Lord*. London: Macmillan.

Turnbull, Colin
1972   *The Mountain People*. New York: Simon and Schuster.

Two Brothers from Berkeley
1971   *Letters to Street Christians*. Grand Rapids: Zondervan.

Tylor, Edward B.
1871   *Primitive Culture*. London: John Murray.

United Bible Societies
1975   "World Annual Report 1974." *Bulletin of the United Bible
                Societies* 98.

Van Gennep, A.
1908   *The Rites of Passage* (trans. by M. Vizedom and G. Caffee)
                Chicago: University of Chicago Press, 1960.

Vawter, Bruce
1972   *Biblical Inspiration*. Philadelphia: Westminster Press.

Verkuyl, Johannes, and H. G. Schulte Nordholt
1974   *Responsible Revolution* (trans. and ed. by Lewis Smedes). Grand
                Rapids: Eerdmans.

von Allmen, Daniel
1975   "The Birth of Theology," *International Review of Mission*
                44:37–55.

Vos, Geerhardus
   1948   *Biblical Theology*. Grand Rapids: Eerdmans.

Wagner, C. Peter
   1973   *Look Out! The Pentecostals Are Coming*. Carol Stream, Ill.: Creation House.

Wallace, Anthony F. C.
   1956   "Revitalization Movements," *American Anthropologist* 58: 264–81.
   1966   *Religion: An Anthropological View*. New York: Random House.

Warfield, Benjamin
   1881   *In The Presbyterian Review* 6:245.
   1948   *The Inspiration and Authority of Scripture*. Philadelphia: Presbyterian and Reformed.

Watson-Franke, Maria-Barbara, and Lawrence C. Watson
   1975   "Understanding in Anthropology: A Philosophical Reminder," *Current Anthropology* 16:247–54.

Webster's *Collegiate Dictionary*
   1947   5th edition. Springfield, Mass.: G. and C. Merriam.

Webster's *Seventh New Collegiate Dictionary*
   1967   Springfield, Mass.: G. and C. Merriam.

Weigle, Luther
   1946   "The English of the Revised Standard Version of the New Testament," in *An Introduction to the Revised Standard Version of the New Testament* by Members of the Revision Committee, The International Council of Religious Education.

Welbourn, F. B., and B. A. Ogot
   1966   *A Place to Feel at Home*. London: Oxford University Press.

White, Leslie A.
   1949   *The Science of Culture*. New York: Grove Press.

White, W. L.
   1969   *The Image of Man in C. S. Lewis*. Nashville: Abingdon Press.

Whorf, Benjamin L.
   1940   "Science and Linguistics," *Technological Review* 42:229–41, 247–48.

1941   "The Relation of Habitual Thought and Behavior to Language," in L. Spier, A. I. Hallowell, and S. S. Newman, *Language, Culture and Personality*, pp. 75–93.

Wiens, Delbert

1965   *New Wineskins for Old Wine*. Hillsboro, Kans.: Mennonite Brethren Publishing House.

Wilson, Monica

1971   *Religion and the Transformation of Society*. Cambridge: Cambridge University Press.

Winter, Ralph D.

1962   "The Great Revolution." Unpublished English translation of *La gran revolución*. San Juan Ostuncalco, Guatemala.

1976   "Who Are the Evangelicals?" *Christianity Today* 20:731–34.

Wittgenstein, Ludwig

1953   *Philosophical Investigations*. New York: Macmillan

Wright, G. Ernest

1950   *The Old Testament against Its Environment*. London: SCM Press.

1952   *God Who Acts*. London: SCM Press.

Zadeh, L. A.

1965   "Fuzzy Sets," *Information and Control* 8:338–53.

Index of Biblical References

Index of Persons

Subject Index

Abraham, 230, 254, 315
Abstraction
    basic ideal level of, 140, 141, 142
    general principle level of, 139, 140, 141, 142
    specific cultural level of, 142
    surface level of, 140
Abstractness, 176, 180
Academicians, 145, 378
Acceptance, 366
Accountability, 126, 127
Activators, 216-225
Actualization, Actualizers, 223-225
    external, 223
    internal, 224
Adaptation, 38, 57, 355
Adequate human perception of supracultural truth (Model 5a), 116, 122, 129-134, 393
Adolescence, 85; *see also* Generation gap
Adultery, 6, 7, 126
Advocate/innovator, 75, 360, 366, 369, 376, 404
    Christian, 365, 369, 370
    "in culture", 191, 192
    outside, 75, 360-366
    place of, 360-370, 404
    principle for, 377-381
Africa, 9, 14, 108, 109, 130, 151, 153, 163, 165, 298, 305, 342, 365
    Independent churches of, 307, 377
    myths of, 309
    religion of, 304, 305
    view of Christ in, 111
    view of God in, 109, 110
Africans
    attraction to Gospels of, 234
    attraction to Old Testament of, 234
    conversion of, 342
    perception of, 109, 110, 130, 304, 305
Agapao, 274, 275, 321, 355
Agreements, cultural, 117, 132
Agriculture, 360
Akamba, 307
Allegiance, 28, 39, 41, 93, 94, 231, 239, 242, 243, 244, 351, 355, 356, 363
    change of (Model 13a), 344, 345, 349, 372, 404
    to children, 380
    conscious, 334, 335, 337

cultural, 340, 355
    to God, 38, 41, 93, 94, 105, 242, 254, 255, 329, 334, 360, 364, 377, 401
Alma, 274
Ambassador, 277, 278, 279
Ambiguities, 273
America, 352, 354
Americans, 361, 384
    and characteristics requisite for Christian leadership, 324, 325
    Christian, 377, 383
    courtship of, 47, 48
    efficiency principle of, 91
    evaluative tendencies of, 39
    generation gap of, 377
    ideology of, 55
    society of, 347, 372, 374, 379, 385
    view of God of, 107
    white, 352
    worldview of, 349, 351
American Standard Version, 265, 266, 269
Analogy, Analogizing, 32, 199, 289
Analytical knowledge, 353
Analytical procedure, 326, 327
Analytical technique, 354
Analytical understanding, 378
Anang, 352
Ancestor veneration, 309
Angels, 120
Anthropology, 16, 25, 33, 34, 41, 116, 118, 124, 144, 385, 390, 391, 392
    and culture concept (Model 3a), 35, 45-48, 390
    insights of (Model 3), 45ff.
    and linguistics, 144
    models from, 82, 293
    perspective of, 8, 33, 34, 35, 82, 117
    and theology, 18, 116-120, 124
    understanding of, 34, 35
Anthropologists, 18, 28, 117, 267, 272, 299, 377
    Christian, 28, 299
Antithetical groups, 378
Appropriateness, cultural, 156, 177, 318, 320, 323, 331-334, 346, 382
Aramaic, 292
Assumptions, 57-60, 81, 132
Athenian philosophers, 363
Athens, 289
Attitudes, 366